Adolescent Pregnancy in an Urban Environment

Adolescent Pregnancy in an Urban Environment

Issues, Programs, and Evaluation

Janet B. Hardy, M.D.C.M.
Professor Emeritus of Pediatrics
Department of Pediatrics
Johns Hopkins University
School of Medicine
Baltimore

Laurie Schwab Zabin, Ph.D.
Associate Professor
Department of Population Dynamics
Johns Hopkins University
School of Hygiene and Public Health
Baltimore

with 10 contributors

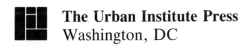
The Urban Institute Press
Washington, DC

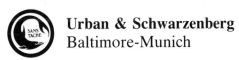
Urban & Schwarzenberg
Baltimore-Munich

Published jointly by

Urban & Schwarzenberg
428 East Preston Street
Baltimore, MD 21202

The Urban Institute Press
2100 M Street, NW
Washington, DC 20037

Distributed by
University Press of America
4720 Boston Way
Lanham, MD 20706

Library of Congress Cataloging-in-Publication Data

Hardy, Janet B.
  Adolescent pregnancy in an urban environment: issues, programs, and evaluation / by Janet B. Hardy and Laurie Schwab Zabin; with contributions by Babette R. Bierman . . . [et al.].
    p.   cm.
  Includes bibliographical references and index.
  ISBN 0-87766-519-2 Hardcover
  ISBN 0-87766-520-6 Paperback
  1. Teenage mothers—Maryland—Baltimore—Case studies. 2. Teenage pregnancy—Maryland—Baltimore—Case studies. 3. Maternal health services—Maryland—Baltimore—Case studies. 4. Teenage pregnancy—Maryland—Baltimore—Prevention—Case studies. 5. Birth control—Study and teaching—Maryland—Baltimore—Case studies. I. Zabin, Laurie Schwab. II. Title.
  HQ759.4.H37   1991
  362.83'92—dc20   90-12908
                                                                       CIP

Sponsoring editor: Charles W. Mitchell
Managing editor: Kathleen C. Millet
Manuscript editor: Andrea Clemente
Design and Production: Stony Run Publishing Services, Baltimore, Maryland
Compositor: EPS Group Inc., Baltimore, Maryland

5 4 3 2 1
95 94 93 92 91

Contents

Contributors

The Authors

Janet B. Hardy, M.D.C.M.
Professor Emeritus of Pediatrics
Past Director of the Johns Hopkins Adolescent Pregnancy and Parenting
    Programs, 1976–1985 and of the Pregnancy Prevention Program, 1980–
    1985
Director of the Children and Youth Program, 1982–1985
Principal Investigator of the Resource Use by Pregnant and Parenting Ado-
    lescents, 1982–1986
Principal Investigator and Program Director of the Johns Hopkins Collabo-
    rative Perinatal Study, 1959–1978
Johns Hopkins University School of Medicine, Baltimore, Maryland 21205

Laurie Schwab Zabin, Ph.D.
Associate Professor, Department of Population Dynamics
Director of Evaluation for the Johns Hopkins Adolescent Pregnancy Pre-
    vention Program
Johns Hopkins University School of Hygiene and Public Health, Baltimore,
    Maryland 21205

Contributing Authors

Babette R. Bierman, M.S.W., L.C.S.W.
    Friends of the Family
    Baltimore, Maryland 21218
    Formerly: Social Worker in the Johns Hopkins Pregnancy and Parenting
        Program (Teenage Clinic and Parenting Program, TAC)

Ronald T. Burkman, M.D.
    Professor and Chairman
    Department of Gynecology-Obstetrics
    Henry Ford Hospital
    Detroit, Michigan 48202
    Formerly: Professor of Gynecology and Obstetrics, Johns Hopkins Univer-
        sity and Director of the Johns Hopkins Fertility Control Center

Catherine DeAngelis, M.D.
    Professor of Pediatrics

Associate Dean for Academic Affairs
Johns Hopkins University School of Medicine
Baltimore, Maryland 21205

Anne Kaszuba Duggan, Sc.D.
Assistant Professor
Department of Pediatrics
Johns Hopkins University School of Medicine
Baltimore, Maryland 21205

Marcia P. Gratton, C.N.M., M.P.H.
Planned Parenthood Federation of America
Baltimore, Maryland 21201
Formerly: Nurse Midwife in the Adolescent Pregnancy Prevention Program
    (Self Center) and the Adolescent Pregnancy and Parenting Program,
    Johns Hopkins University School of Medicine

Timothy R. B. Johnson, M.D.
Associate Professor
Department of Gynecology-Obstetrics
Director, Division of Maternal and Fetal Medicine
Johns Hopkins University School of Medicine
Baltimore, Maryland 21205

Theodore M. King, M.D., Ph.D.
Professor
Department of Gynecology-Obstetrics
Johns Hopkins University School of Medicine
Vice President for Medical Affairs
Johns Hopkins Health System
Baltimore, Maryland 21218

John T. Repke, M.D.
Associate Professor
Department of Gynecology-Obstetrics
Medical Director, Johns Hopkins Adolescent Pregnancy Program
Johns Hopkins University School of Medicine
Baltimore, Maryland 21205

Rosalie Streett, M.S.
Executive Director
Friends of the Family
Baltimore, Maryland 21218
Formerly: Director of Health and Parenting Education for Adolescent Preg-
    nancy and Parenting Program and Children and Youth Program, and
    Administrator of the Self Center, Johns Hopkins University School of
    Medicine

Linda Carr Watkinson, M.S.
Health Educator in the Johns Hopkins
Adolescent Pregnancy Program
Department of Gynecology-Obstetrics
Johns Hopkins University School of Medicine
Baltimore, Maryland 21205

Foreword

Every 31 seconds an adolescent becomes pregnant in the United States and every 2 minutes a teen gives birth. The United States has one of the highest pregnancy rates among adolescents in the western world, with approximately one million teenagers becoming pregnant each year. What are the underlying reasons and what are the characteristics of those who become pregnant and those who bear children? What are the consequences of these events for the young mothers, their partners, and their infants, and how can we change these statistics? These are the questions that Drs. Hardy and Zabin have addressed so completely in their significant work on adolescent pregnancy.

The authors set the stage by providing an in-depth discussion of national and local statistics regarding teenage and adolescent pregnancy and the developmental issues involved in understanding and influencing adolescent behavior. From there, using a city-wide, random sample of adolescent births, the problems and adverse consequences of adolescent pregnancy in an urban setting are explored, including those of the young mothers, the fathers, and the babies. A model pregnancy and parenting program and its evaluation are described in detail, within a practical framework. Chapters have been written by experts in the various disciplines needed to establish such a program. These include the medical management, nutrition, social service, educational, nursing, and ethical aspects of program implementation. The issues of contraception and abortion are then discussed and, importantly, successful interventions in pregnancy prevention are explored. Lastly, the authors give us practical, scholarly, and wise suggestions for future policies. Appropriate, clear, and detailed national and local urban statistics highlight the issues in all sections and point to the greater concentration of problems in poor, inner-city areas.

Several approaches are unique to this text on adolescent pregnancy. All too often little attention is given to the developmental status of adolescents who become pregnant, a pervasive theme throughout this volume. The authors demonstrate that pregnant adolescents are not one homogeneous group. In particular, adolescents below 18 and particularly below 15 can have very different outcomes than teenagers over 18. The relationship of race to outcome is also explored in depth. Frequently, it is assumed that inner-city black or Hispanic pregnant adolescents have the worst outcome. Drs. Hardy and Zabin demonstrate that young white mothers and their children had similarly poor, if not worse, outcomes. The authors also explore relationships that often are only addressed globally or not addressed at all. For example, the relationship between poverty and the risks of pregnancy and childbirth is explored in depth.

Unique to this text is the combination of clinical and research aspects of adolescent pregnancy. Often programs or textbooks address only one aspect. Similarly, even within the sections on clinical management, the medical and social aspects of patient care complement one another. The authors, while focusing on clinical practice and clinical, epidemiological, behavioral, and evaluation research, have combined their knowledge and expertise for the advancement of both. The reader gains from this synthesis of knowledge and experience, just as the programs profited from insights provided by the research sector.

Successful interventions are critical to making an impact on this national problem. The authors give examples of effective, caring interventions that stress the development of personal responsibility. Not only are programs needed to intervene with pregnant teens, but effective modalities are necessary to reach teens before they become pregnant. The Johns Hopkins Pregnancy Prevention Program, described in this book, accomplishes this in perhaps the most difficult of groups: inner-city, poverty-stricken adolescents. The authors not only describe the Johns Hopkins programs in detail but emphasize the practical applications of available knowledge. Emphasis is placed on the importance of objective and rigorous evaluation of such programs by investigators who have no direct service responsibility.

If the problems resulting from premature sexual activity are to be resolved, then the results of such programs need to mold regional and national policies. The final section of this book translates the lessons derived from the many years of Hopkins experience into serious, specific recommendations for policy formulation and program planning. Drs. Hardy and Zabin have produced a complete, original, and significant contribution to the literature on adolescent pregnancy. This book will be useful not only to those concerned with policy formulation and the allocation of resources, but also to the physicians, social workers, educators, and psychologists who work with adolescents on a day-to-day basis.

Lawrence S. Neinstein, M.D.
Associate Professor of Pediatrics and Medicine
University of Southern California
School of Medicine
Los Angeles

Foreword

Our collective future is in jeopardy. Heartbreaking stories of disintegrating families, neglected children, and homelessness fill the daily papers. States are spending more on building prisons than on building schools. Our most basic arrangements for caring for our young, and for assuring that they will grow up to lead productive and responsible lives, seem to have unraveled. High rates of childbearing among unmarried teenagers—higher by far than in any other industrialized nation—add to our sense that things are spinning out of control. Worst of all, the belief that nothing can be done pervades the public discourse.

Every American, therefore, has reason to be grateful for the good news in this book. Parents, legislators, policy analysts, and health professionals will be informed and inspired by the stories of programs that have changed the life odds among disadvantaged urban youngsters. The precise content and the philosophical undergirdings of the services that have been so successful are vividly described and the improvements in long-term outcomes are rigorously documented. The dramatic process by which rates of pregnancy, abortion, and early childbearing were reduced, birth outcomes improved, and the average age of first coitus raised, is presented here in careful and nuanced detail. The complexities raised by adolescent sexuality and childbearing in the U.S. society are sensitively and intelligently explained.

Adolescent Pregnancy in an Urban Environment draws on the experiences of gifted clinicians in several disciplines, who collaborated with gifted researchers—not only in designing effective interventions, but in continuing efforts to shape their programs in response to new needs and new findings. It chronicles the life of programs that scaled the Mount Everest of social dislocation—the sexual and child-rearing behavior of the population group at highest risk of long-term damage because they are poor, urban, and adolescent. And it shows, beyond the shadow of a doubt, that when high-risk populations receive the best of services, life outcomes improve.

The programs that are the centerpieces of this splendid work were made possible by the vision, competence, and perseverance of a group of individuals who cared more about changing outcomes among high-risk youngsters than about achieving more conventional and comfortable professional goals.

Pediatrician Janet Hardy had been overseeing Johns Hopkins' participation in a large-scale, multi-city, perinatal study, when she became appalled at the number of very young mothers who were bearing babies that were too small or otherwise damaged. Along with several colleagues, Dr. Hardy established a clinic to provide more accessible and more appropriate prenatal care to adolescents. She found that it was indeed possible to improve significantly the outcomes for their babies at birth, but that the future still looked dismal for both mothers and babies. Dr. Hardy thereupon initiated a second program—to provide health care for the babies, and parenting education and family planning services for the young mothers. These programs produced significantly improved results for both mothers and babies. Yet it was clear that even the most successful young mothers and their babies would have been better off if the girls had postponed childbearing. In exploring the possibilities of establishing a program aimed at preventing first pregnancies among school-age girls, Dr. Hardy invited health and parenting educator Rosalie Streett, and researcher Dr. Laurie Zabin to collaborate.

Dr. Zabin's earlier work had focused on what could be done about the high proportion of unintended pregnancies that occur as soon after youngsters first become sexually active. She had established that the risk of pregnancy is highest during the first months of intercourse, and the younger the girl, the higher the risk. Building on these findings, Dr. Zabin had gone to thirty-two family planning clinics in eight cities to find out why young teenagers waited so long to use contraception, and why so many stayed away until they feared they were already pregnant. Dr. Zabin found that while some teenagers lacked the motivation to avoid pregnancy, many more lacked accurate information and appropriate services. The programs here described incorporate her research conclusions, that childbearing among school-age girls could be reduced if they had access to information and services that were close, cost-free, confidential, and provided in an atmosphere that teenagers perceive as caring about them.

The results of the pregnancy prevention program exceeded even the optimistic expectations of those responsible for the program. Not only was the rate of child-bearing among junior high and high school students reduced, but so was the rate of pregnancy and of abortion. The outcomes constitute dramatic reassurance for those who fear that the provision of contraceptives in schools causes promiscuity. Students in the program schools postponed the onset of sexual activity, showing that the promotion of abstinence and the provision of contraceptive information and services can succeed side by side.

The programs that proved effective in improving birth outcomes among pregnant adolescents were comprehensive, and included psychosocial support, education about health and parenting, and excellent medical care—all provided in an accessible, warm and caring environment. The services that reduced the incidence of school-age childbearing, and raised the average age at which sexual intercourse began, had similar characteristics. They took into account the developmental imperatives of adolescence, the importance of caring and respect, and the wide range of complex needs of most inner-city junior high and high school students. They linked school and clinic components, personal counseling, and classroom instruction, with the provision of contraceptive services. Comparisons with more narrow medical programs made clear that the nonmedical ingredients of the effective programs were crucial to improving not alone social, but also medical outcomes, and that the programs providing a broader range of services actually produced greater long-term savings. Their beneficial effects are likely to be strong not only in this generation, but also in the next.

These findings confirm the experience being amassed in communities throughout the nation, though few had the expertise and funding to incorporate the rigorous evaluation that has characterized the Johns Hopkins programs. The evaluation process described in this volume should be emulated widely, for its rigorousness as well as for its focus on real-world outcomes that are important to policymakers and the public.

The evidence presented here shows clearly that youngsters growing up at risk need ready access to high-quality reproductive health services with strong social supports. The authors conclude by pointing out the equally strong need among disadvantaged youngsters for a decent education, and for reasons to develop a stake in their own futures, so that more attractive alternatives to early parenthood are clear and credible.

If any taxpayer, policymaker, program administrator, or parent needed more evidence to be persuaded that while there are no quick fixes, there are programs that work to improve outcomes among high-risk youngsters, this volume provides it.

But the pages that follow also confirm that this nation is not yet ready to act on what is known. As the authors point out in their concluding chapter, the program that succeeded so splendidly in reducing the rate of childbearing among school-age youngsters in Baltimore no longer exists.

Programs can succeed in achieving widely sought-after objectives, and document their success, and still be abandoned. That has been the history of the vast majority of successful social programs of the last two decades. We continue to be reluctant to invest in better outcomes for youngsters at risk because the returns on the investment are not immediate, and they don't always show up on the budget that bears the original cost. In making decisions about how programs are financed and held accountable, and in how professionals are trained, we continue to deny the implications of new understandings about what works—especially for disadvantaged youngsters. For, if services must be comprehensive to be effective, if social supports and education can be as important as medical technology, and if services rendered in the context of respectful, caring relationships are the ones most likely to lead to positive outcomes, then changes in financing, accountability, and training arrangements are essential preconditions for the large-scale spread of successful programs.

Everyone who cares about the future of America, and is in a position to affect decisions about the allocation of public and private energies, talents, and resources, owes a deep debt of gratitude to all who contributed to this volume, and to the noble efforts it describes and analyzes.

Lisbeth B. Schorr, Ph.D.
Lecturer in Social Medicine
Harvard University
Cambridge

Acknowledgments

The number of people to whom we are indebted for ideas, encouragement, and assistance is legion; would that it were possible to acknowledge our thanks to each individually.

Special gratitude is extended to Eunice and Sargent Shriver, whose dedication to improving the life chances of pregnant and parenting adolescents set us on our way.

We wish to express deep appreciation to our colleagues in each of our endeavors: Dr. Theodore M. King, M.D., Ph.D., whose support as Professor and Chairman of the Department of Obstetrics and Gynecology made much of the work possible; Denise A. Shipp, M.Ed., who played an important role in the early development of the Hopkins Adolescent Pregnancy Clinic (HAC); Rosalie Streett, M.S., for her role in the development of the organization and educational programs for the Teenage Clinic (TAC), for her inspired leadership in the Self-Center project, and for educating us about the importance of caring; Anne K. Duggan, Sc.D., for her role as evaluator of HAC and TAC and, as Project Director of the Resource Use Study, for the analysis of the epidemiological data on Baltimore adolescents and their families; Marilyn B. Hirsch, Ph.D., who had major responsibility for the analysis of data in the Pregnancy Prevention Program; Edward A. Smith, Dr. PH., and Mark Emerson for their work with those data; Catherine DeAngelis, M.D., for her role in the development of primary adolescent and pediatric primary care for the young mothers and their children in TAC; Charles D. Flagle, Dr. Eng., for helpful advice on evaluation and systems management over many years; John Repke, M.D., the obstetrician in charge of HAC; and to the service staff in each of those clinics whose dedication and concern for their young clients made the programs work.

We wish to acknowledge generous programmatic and/or research support from the following sources: The Joseph P. Kennedy, Jr. Foundation; The Educational Foundation of America; the Health Care Financing Agency; the Office of Adolescent Pregnancy Programs; the Ford Foundation and the William T. Grant Foundation; the Maryland State Departments of Health and Human Resources and the Baltimore City Department of Health.

We gratefully acknowledge the programmatic and administrative assistance of: Drs. Annelies Zachary and Eric Fine of the Maryland State Department of Health; Dr. Juanito Lopez, Mr. John Sweitzer, and Mr. Joseph Saladini of the Baltimore City Health Department; and Baltimore City School Superintendents Dr. John Crewe and Mrs. Alice Pinderhughes. We would like to acknowledge our debt to the students, principals, faculty, and staff of the four Baltimore City schools who made the Pregnancy Prevention Program possible; because of our desire to preserve their privacy, they must remain anonymous—but they know who they are and how much we owe them.

We wish to express our gratitude to staff members of the Urban Institute Press and to their anonymous reviewer for constructive criticism and helpful suggestions. We would also like to thank the Educational Foundation of America and the Ford Foundation for underwriting the production of this volume. We appreciate the contribution of Shelby J. Roth, whose assistance in the preparation of the manuscript was invaluable, and of our editors, Charles Mitchell and Katey Millet, for their help and patience.

Finally, but of greatest importance in making our work possible over the years, has been the encouragement, support, and forebearance of our husbands, Paul H. Hardy, Jr., M.D., and the late James Barton Zabin.

This book is dedicated with respect and affection to those from whom we have learned so much: The young people of Baltimore and the colleagues who have cared enough to serve them well.

Part I

The Philosophical Context

1

The Odyssey
The Development of Programs at the Johns Hopkins Hospital

Premature sexual activity and adolescent pregnancy, childbearing, parenting, and abortion are frequent occurrences in the United States (Hayes, 1987). They are conditions that are often associated with high medical and social risks for both the adolescents and any children they may bear. The societal costs are large, both in human and financial terms. These consequences have been carefully researched, and studies over the past decades have documented educational, economic, and social deprivation among many who become mothers too soon. These often tragic sequelae and their financial costs are prohibitive. Public costs for the medical care and social support of families in which the mother had her first birth as a teenager were estimated to be $16.6 billion in 1985 (Burt, 1986), increasing to $19.8 billion in 1988 (Center for Population Options, 1989). These are cumulative estimates that, therefore, increase with each year. Additional costs are associated with the high frequencies of elective abortion and sexually transmitted disease among young people. None of these financial costs would be excessive if they really alleviated the human costs or prevented their repetition. However, for interventions that are palliative at best, they *are* excessive.

The varied experiences reported in this volume by an interdisciplinary group of clinicians and researchers working together or in parallel in one university setting, describe many aspects of these related problems as identified in an urban setting, problems which were addressed through direct service programs and research. Our objective is to allow these clinical and research experiences, which have informed and strengthened one another, to suggest fruitful directions for public policy and program design. Lessons learned from each source and from their interaction emerge in each chapter; they are addressed directly in Part VI.

The experiences are unusual in a number of aspects.

1. They are based on almost 20 years of work with urban adolescents and their families, living in one of the largest and most poverty-stricken of American cities. Baltimore has among the highest rates of teenage pregnancy and childbearing and the largest proportion of all births to teenage mothers of any American city with a population in excess of 500,000 (Children's Defense Fund, 1985). Most published statistics describing teenagers who give birth are derived

from small, nonrepresentative samples from clinics or schools or from national or regional data sets. Because of the inclusion of lower risk, more affluent, suburban and rural teenagers in these latter population bases, the experience of those living in high-risk urban areas tends to be diluted and, thus, understated. As a result, the complexity and extent of the problems having their origin in the premature onset of sexual activity among the urban poor may not be fully recognized and, thus, not adequately addressed.

2. The major descriptions of the young mothers, their infants, families, and the fathers of their babies provided in this volume are based on city-wide, randomly selected samples drawn from all birth certificates within given time periods. Such a selection process obviates biases that may be inherent in samples drawn from one or more clinics or schools.

3. Rigorous evaluation, both process and outcome, was included from the outset of each of the programs described to help guide its development and to measure its possible effectiveness.

Program Evolution

The confluence of two separate streams of activity formed the primary roots from which the programs described in the volume evolved. One root was grounded in clinical practice and the other in clinical, epidemiological, and behavioral research. The two became inextricably entwined as they nourished and enriched one another.

The activities of the clinical root were initiated late in 1973 by Dr. T. M. King, Professor and Chairman of the Department of Obstetrics and Gynecology, in response to the special needs of the increasing number of pregnant adolescents seeking care at the Johns Hopkins Hospital. In collaboration with Dr. Annelies Zachary, then Director of Maternal Health in the Baltimore City Health Department, a special program for the prenatal care and delivery of pregnant adolescents, below age 18 years, was established. The program was initially directed by Dr. David Youngs, who had been trained both in obstetrics and psychiatry. The program administrator (and major-domo) was Denise Shipp, an experienced health educator. The program, which became known as the Johns Hopkins Adolescent Clinic, or HAC, was similar in concept to the young mothers' program that had been established at the Grace New Haven Hospital some years earlier (Sarrel and Klerman, 1969; Klerman and Jekel, 1973).

The Johns Hopkins Program expressed a deep commitment to a comprehensive approach to the pregnant adolescent that included psychosocial support and health, nutrition, pregnancy, and early parenting education as well as excellent medical and obstetrical care. It was unusual in the extent of its community linkages to obtain services for its young patients and in the warm and caring environment provided by staff. In keeping with other obstetrical programs, its services ended with the postpartum visit four weeks after delivery. The results of the initial period of approximately two years have been described elsewhere by Youngs et al. (1977).

While the immediate pregnancy outcome for these young mothers, at high obstetrical risk, was distinctly improved, problems remained. By 1975, it was apparent that a substantial number of infants were being admitted to the hospital during the early weeks of life with conditions that reflected ignorance and/or neglect on the part of the young mothers. Some children died. In addition, young mothers were returning to HAC within a few months, pregnant again.

At about this point in time, the research roots began to take hold. They grew from the results of the 8- to 12-year follow-up of women delivering their children in the prospective, multidisciplinary Johns Hopkins Collaborative Perinatal Study (JHCPS), carried out in the 1960s and 1970s. The study, which has been described by Hardy (1971), was part of the National Collaborative Perinatal Study (Broman et al., 1975; Hardy, Drage, et al., 1979; Niswander and Gordon, 1972). A study of factors influencing pregnancy outcome and the development of children, it provided an opportunity to document the adverse consequences of pregnancy among adolescents delivering a baby at age 17 years or below. The immediate and longer term pregnancy outcomes for both adolescent mothers and their children were compared with those of mothers aged 20 through 24 years and their children. The adolescents and their children were overrepresented in virtually every negative outcome category examined. Furthermore, as described in Chapter 9, the children of adolescents had higher risks of low birth weight, perinatal mortality, cognitive impairment, and school failure than those of older mothers (Hardy et al., 1978). The young mothers had less education, more unstable families, greater welfare dependency, and greater fertility than the mothers who were older when their first child was born.

It was during these years that the importance of possible interactions between health and socioenvironmental factors as determinants of the development of children and adolescents became apparent, and the formulation of a life course, interactive model to facilitate understanding of the forces at work began to take shape. The model we have used is described in the next chapter of this volume.

Let us turn now to a brief description of the evolution of the programs that arose from these roots and are the major focus of this book. Their designations, names, and dates of initiation are shown in Table 1-1.

The Johns Hopkins Adolescent Pregnancy and Parenting Program (APP)

In 1975, the two streams of activity described above converged to focus on how best to intervene to improve the immediate and longer term outcomes for adolescent mothers and their children.

With the active encouragement of Eunice and Sargent Shriver and support from the Joseph P. Kennedy, Jr. Foundation, the services being provided in the Adolescent Pregnancy Program or Hopkins Adolescent Clinic (HAC) were extended and offered to larger numbers of pregnant girls. Some services were made available to the putative fathers as well. A follow-up teenage program for adolescent mothers and their infants, the Johns Hopkins Teenage Clinic and Parenting Program, which came to be known by the acronym TAC, was established in 1976. The routine collection of data for ongoing program analysis was begun.

The follow-up program was designed to meet multiple needs of adolescent mothers and their infants with comprehensive services, medical, psychosocial, and health education, in a setting designed to emphasize caring and concern for adolescents as special people with individual needs. Services that could not be provided in-house were made available by referral through liaison with a network of community agencies.

Table 1-1 Major Clinical Service Programs that Form the Basis for This Report

Designation	Description
APP	The Johns Hopkins Adolescent Pregnancy and Parenting Program, which was initiated in 1976 as a service demonstration project and institutionalized in 1982 as part of the Hospital's C&Y Program, had two components, HAC and TAC.
HAC	The Johns Hopkins Adolescent Pregnancy Program or Hopkins Adolescent Clinic, a comprehensive adolescent pregnancy program, begun in late 1973, provides prenatal care and labor and delivery services for high-risk adolescents below 18 years of age (Chapter 11).
TAC	The Teenage Clinic and Parenting Program was begun in 1976 for the follow-up care of young HAC mothers and their infants. Comprehensive services for mother-child pairs continued for 3 years after delivery (Chapter 16).
C&Y	The Johns Hopkins Children and Youth Program, initiated in 1974 with Maternal and Child Health Demonstration funds, became a Title V Maternal Infant Care (MIC) program, providing primary medical care for 17,000 East Baltimore residents, 0 to 18 years of age (Chapter 19). Until 1982, its services included prenatal care for pregnant enrollees. In 1982 this service was replaced by the incorporation of HAC and TAC as separate components within C&Y. Half of the subjects reported in Chapter 22 were recruited in this program.
Self Center	The Johns Hopkins Adolescent Pregnancy Prevention Program was a self-limited research and service demonstration project. It was initiated in 1981 in a junior and a senior high school; the adjacent clinic was known to the students as the Self Center. Two similar schools, without special services, served as controls. It was a cooperative effort between the Johns Hopkins Departments of Obstetrics and Pediatrics and the Baltimore City Departments of Education and Health. The research ended in 1984 and the clinical services in 1985.

Initially, follow-up services in TAC were provided as a joint effort of the Department of Pediatrics and the Baltimore City Health Department. Preventive health services for the baby and psychosocial support and parenting educational services for the young mothers were provided by program staff. Health Department staff provided family planning services, including education, reproductive health services, and contraceptives. Mothers and children were seen at the same visit in a nearby Health Department Clinic. This plan had obvious limitations in that preventive and acute health care were fragmented in a population found to have needs for acute care well above average levels for age and race.

With funding from the Health Care Financing Agency and the assistance of Dr. Catherine DeAngelis, a plan providing complete pediatric and adolescent primary health care was implemented. As may be seen from chapters later in this book describing the program evaluation (Chapters 11, 16, and 19), these services also met their objectives.

In mid-1982, both HAC and TAC were institutionalized as regular hospital services by inclusion as separate entities within the Johns Hopkins Children and Youth Program (C&Y), and this program, which provided ongoing preventive and acute pediatric and adolescent care for some 17,000 East Baltimore children, was redesigned to emphasize pregnancy prevention among its adolescent clients.

The evaluation efforts that guided the development of these programs and demonstrated their success have been of great importance in several ways.

1. Data from the preliminary evaluation of HAC were used with good effect in Congressional hearings in support of the Adolescent Pregnancy Care and Family Life Act of 1978. Passage of this legislation led to the creation of the Office of Adolescent Pregnancy Programs, in the Office of the Secretary of the Department of Health and Human Services.
2. In 1979, the Johns Hopkins Pregnancy and Parenting Programs (HAC and TAC) served as models for a national symposium, helping in the initiation of similar interventions around the country.
3. As mentioned above, at Johns Hopkins, the demonstration of improved outcomes for program adolescents, as compared with similar adolescents receiving care elsewhere, led to the transfer of these programs from time-limited grant support to institutionalization as part of the hospital's ongoing services.

The demonstrated effectiveness of the programs notwithstanding, the predominant lesson learned was that most of these young women had not planned to become pregnant; most had not wanted to have a child at this time in their lives. As a result, our efforts turned toward preventing the *initial* adolescent pregnancy.

The Pregnancy Prevention Program (Self Center Program)

Much of the experience described above, and independent research findings, guided the next phase in the evolutionary process, an attempt at the primary prevention of pregnancy among adolescents. A study completed in 1979 at the School of Public Health (Zabin et al., 1979) had shown that 50% of all first premarital pregnancies of adolescents occurred in the first 6 months of their sexual exposure, 20% in the first month alone (see Part V). Throughout the 1970s, there had been documented increases in the clinical services available to teens, and reports of high utilization of these facilities; nonetheless, rates of unintended pregnancy remained intransigent. These research findings helped to explain this apparent paradox, by suggesting that a large part of adolescent clinic utilization *followed* rather than *preceded* first conception. In fact, a study carried out in 1980, based on 32 clinics in eight cities nationwide, showed that the mean delay to first clinic attendance was over 16 months, and the median almost a year (Zabin and Clark, 1981). It also showed that 36% of the first clinic attendance was motivated by the perceived need for a pregnancy test; it was crisis care, not prevention. The 1979 study highlighted the importance of reducing that interval to first attendance. It also documented the fact that young girls whose first coitus occurred at 15 years and below experienced a higher proportional risk in the first months of intercourse than those who delayed sexual contact until their later years (Zabin et al., 1979). The lower rates of contraceptive use observed in the younger group resulted in their increased risk, which was not offset by the irregularity of their youthful ovulatory cycles.

It was apparent from the research results that, if pregnancy was to be prevented in the inner-city population served by the Johns Hopkins Hospital, large proportions of adolescents had to be reached at an early age. The only effective way to accomplish this was through the schools, even if medical services were provided elsewhere. It was also clear that young people of middle school age should be involved. A pregnancy prevention research and service demonstration program was, therefore, initiated in collaboration with the Baltimore City Departments of Health and Education. The service demonstration was funded by private funds generously made available by The Educational Foundation of America; the service component was administered by Rosalie Streett. Marilyn B. Hirsch was a coinvestigator in the evaluation effort that was funded primarily by the Ford and William T. Grant Foundations. Some 8 months were consumed in securing the necessary agreements, laying the groundwork in the community, and in the design of educational and evaluation materials and procedures. Four schools were selected. A junior and a senior high school, in close proximity to the hospital, were to collaborate in the program. Two similar schools were selected by the Superintendent of Schools to serve as comparision schools; data were collected in these two schools but no special services provided.

With the onset of the school year, in September 1981, the work in the program schools began. Parents were informed by letter of the program intent, the services that would be offered, and the data that would be collected. Baseline data for the evaluation were collected, and the educational and counseling components began. In January 1982, the Self Center, the *school-linked* reproductive health clinic, and its related educational and psychosocial services began operation (Zabin et al., 1984; Zabin and Hirsch, 1987). In all, during the ensuing 2½ years, some 33,000 student-staff contacts were recorded (Zabin, Hirsch, et al., 1986; Zabin, Hirsch, Smith, et al., 1988; Zabin, Hirsch, Streett, et al., 1988).

This program, like those which preceded it, met its objectives. The average age at onset of coitus was substantially delayed, the use of contraceptives among those students who chose to be sexually active was significantly improved, and the frequency of pregnancy decreased in those schools where the program was in operation, both in absolute number and especially as compared with the control schools where no special services were available (Zabin, Hirsch, et al., 1986) (see Chapters 23 and 25).

Effects of Abortion

Even with the best of preventive efforts, some young women will conceive, and the vast majority of young Americans do not have access to such creative interventions. Once conception has occurred, the consequences of childbearing have been well-described in the literature; the sequelae of abortion, however, have largely been unexplored among this age group. Although it is widely recognized that abortion is a medically safe procedure for adolescents (Cates et al., 1983; Grimes and Cates, 1979; Ory, 1983; Stack, 1980; Stubblefield et al., 1984), there has been some suggestion by those who oppose these services that terminating a pregnancy might have adverse effects on psychological well-being. Therefore, the next research effort focused on the consequences of pregnancy loss to teenage women, exploring outcomes in seven areas: schooling; jobs and economic well-being; household status and living arrangements; health; growth; sexual behavior, including coitus, contraception, and fertility; and several psychological measures. Young women receiving pregnancy tests in the Johns Hopkins Children and Youth Program or Planned Parenthood of Maryland were followed for 2 years. The study sample consisted of adolescents with positive tests who terminated their pregnancies. Control populations were selected from those most similar to the study sample and included: 1) those whose tests were also positive but who continued their pregnancies and, 2) those whose tests were negative (see Chapter 22).

Characteristics of Urban Adolescents and Their Use of Resources

While premature sexual activity, pregnancy, and childbearing were everyday events in the inner-city areas where we worked, they appeared, on the basis of our clinical experience, to be relatively rare events among adolescents living in less disadvantaged areas of the city. This observation combined with the desire for a more objective, population-based evaluation of the effectiveness of "comprehensive" services for pregnant adolescents and for young mothers and their children led to the final phase in our odyssey. In collaboration with Dr. Anne K. Duggan, a series of epidemiological studies (Hardy et al., 1986) was undertaken to describe teenage and adolescent pregnancy and childbearing in Baltimore. City-wide data derived from Certificates of Live Birth and reports of elective abortions, within specific time periods, have been used to describe the characteristics of the adolescents who became pregnant and of the communities in which they lived, as well as to assess the effect of resources used in their care.

These data, reported in early chapters in this volume, provide an ecological framework for interventions described in later chapters. They emphasize the serious extent, pervasiveness, and cost of the problems that may arise from premature sexual intercourse. The remainder of the book suggests intervention efforts to minimize the consequences (secondary prevention) and, of even more importance, to prevent the occurrence (primary prevention) of adolescent pregnancy.

Lessons Learned

Those of us who have been intimately involved in the various aspects of care of many of Baltimore's urban adolescents, boys and girls, white and black, have learned some lessons that have been important to our success. These lessons are applicable to both intervention and research. They have become integral to the philosophy that has guided our efforts. Of overriding importance to working successfully with adolescents is an understanding of adolescent maturation and the factors that determine outcome along the life course from conception to adulthood. An overview of development issues, and their interaction with sexual and parenting behavior, is presented in Chapter 2. Development and the behavioral effects of the stages of adolescent development are described and are recurring themes in this volume. The implications of normal adolescent development for the design of effective intervention are addressed throughout.

Another fundamental lesson pertains to the importance of caring about urban adolescents as individual people, deserving of consideration and respect. Caring about them and being sensitive to their needs are essential to success with adolescents. Caring about self is a basic requirement for the development of the positive self-esteem and self-identity that lend direction to one's life. Many of these young people have not been exposed to good parenting and have had little opportunity to acquire the skills and information needed for making sound decisions, clarifying personal values, and setting objectives. They need help in developing the responsibility and discipline required to care about themselves, to implement their decisions, to bring some order to their lives, and to become adequate parents. The staff members who work with them, therefore, must be selected on the basis of both their understanding of adolescent development and their ability to be caring and effective role models. They often become surrogate parents.

An interdisciplinary team approach to the provision of pregnancy care and the follow-up care of adolescent mothers and their children is essential in meeting the multiplicity of needs of urban adolescents. An individual case management system, which involves input from *all* staff members on a regular basis, is mandatory for the effective functioning of such a team.

Finally, we have found most of the adolescents with whom we have worked to be extraordinarily honest and forthright. In answering anonymous survey instruments, they have made important contributions because they appear to have recognized the importance of their candor to the improvement of services for others. Once personal rapport is established in a service or research setting, they give information freely. They are avid for information on all sorts of topics, sometimes topics of a very personal nature. They deserve equal honesty and forthrightness in return. Defensiveness and critical judgment are counterproductive. It is to these vulnerable young people, whose responsiveness and trust have taught us so much, that this book is ultimately dedicated.

2

Developmental Issues
The Context
of Adolescent Pregnancy

As the popular press has focused attention on the phenomenon of adolescent pregnancy, the terminology has tended to imply that "teenage" refers to a fixed time of life—that "teen parenthood" is a monolithic problem to which young women (and only young women) are exposed from puberty until their passage into the maturity of the twenties. Indeed, the semantics may have stood in the way of society's response to this intransient social dilemma. We see the issue not as monolithic but as a complex developmental issue related both to intergenerational factors of social condition and to the nature of adolescence itself.

The process of individual development from conception throughout the life course is infinitely complex, with many adjustments along the way. That process, and the factors that determine the developmental course, are best understood in terms of a life course, intergenerational model. Furthermore, the recognition that age is a complex variable suggests that the effects of age in its many manifestations— chronological, gynecological, developmental—are crucial to our understanding of the etiology, consequences, and management of premature conception. An appreciation of the nature of adolescence and adolescent behavior is essential to an understanding of the phenomena of premature sexual activity and other risk-taking behaviors prevalent among present day adolescents and older teenagers. It is also the key to the successful design and effective implementation of interventions to prevent pregnancy in these age groups and to mitigate the adverse effects should pregnancy, childbearing, and parenting occur.

There has been considerable recognition of the differential effects of age on the *consequences* of adolescent childbearing, but little study of the differential effects of developmental level on the nature of the behavior itself or on its etiology. This book brings a developmental perspective to these problems. The objectives for this chapter are to: 1) provide definitions and rationale for use of the terms *adolescent pregnancy* and *teenage pregnancy*; 2) present a theoretical structure to facilitate understanding of the many biological/health and family/environmental factors that determine development along the life course; and 3) describe some of the physical and psychosocial aspects of adolescent sexual development and their effects on sexual onset, sexual decision making and contraceptive use, and on the various risk-taking behaviors with which fertility behavior is related. Such models facilitate our attempt to understand *who* the at-risk adolescents are, *why* they behave as they do, and *what* may be effective in preventing undesirable behavior and in mitigating its adverse effects.

The broad definition of adolescence as a period in the life course that extends through the teens to adulthood is supported by the longstanding tradition that groups ages 15 through 19 years for the statistical reporting of pregnancies and birth. However, this broad definition can be counterproductive, because it omits the pubertal years and groups together young females with markedly different developmental characteristics as if they were members of a homogeneous group. The characteristics of a 13-year-old child who becomes a mother are vastly different from those of an 18- or 19-year-old teenager who has graduated from high school and may be in the work force. A strong case can be made for subdividing the teenage group into older teenagers of 18 or 19 years and true adolescents. The latter group includes those between puberty, which may have its onset as early as 9 or 10 or as late as 15 or 16 years of age, through age 17. The older teenagers will, in general, have ceased growing. They will also be more mature in cognitive and socioemotional development. Many will have finished high school; some will be working, and some will be married. Their obstetrical risks will, on the average, be less than those of younger teenagers, unless they have already borne a child during their early adolescence (in which case risks will be increased). Their social risks will, in general, be higher than those of women who delay first birth until 20 years of age, especially if the teenager is a single parent, living in a disadvantaged environment.

Pregnant adolescents, on the other hand, are generally at high risk both medically and socially. In general, they are still growing and may, therefore, be in competition with their fetus for nutrients. The likelihood of anemia, which is common during the normal adolescent growth spurt, is enhanced by the pregnancy, and other complications of pregnancy are frequent. As a result, in the absence of comprehensive prenatal care, preterm delivery and low infant birth weight (LBW) occur with higher frequency in this age group than in women who delay childbearing until they have reached maturity (see Chapters 3 and 4). School dropout, single parenthood, the early repetition of pregnancy, and employment difficulties are commonplace among mothers who started childbearing as adolescents. Furthermore, personal characteristics that are normal during adolescent development are the antithesis of those attributes required for good parenting.

There are legal as well as developmental reasons for subgrouping adolescents and older teenagers separately. In most states, the age at which majority is attained is 18 years; adolescents are minors, in most instances still dependent upon parents for physical, psychosocial, and financial support. Older teenagers are, at least in legal terms, independent and able to make legal decisions on their own. Laws in many states allow minors to make their own confidential reproductive health decisions. Despite the importance of those legal assurances, the distinction between minors and older teenagers is a common one.

But even these distinctions may not be sufficiently detailed to catch important differences. Early and late adolescence have characteristics of their own, although precise age limits are difficult to apply. Adolescence is preeminently a period of flux, of change, and of growth; there is no period, with the possible exception of infancy, in which age plays so important and complex a part. The role of age is further complicated because the stages of adolescent development are differently timed for different individuals; although the sequencing of physical, emotional, moral, and mental maturation are similar from one individual to another, they may proceed on different tracks; their timetables can be very different. The various areas of development over these crucial years are rarely in synchrony. Cognitive development, for example, can lag behind physical or emotional development or can charge ahead of them; pubertal development, however consistent its sequence may be, proceeds with little regard for any other phase of maturation. The consequences of these uneven patterns of development, as they are reflected in adolescent sexual, contraceptive, and fertility behaviors, make even more difficult a sensible societal response in a field permeated with ambivalence and contradiction.

Determinants of Child and Adolescent Development

Many determinants of child and adolescent development are intergenerational. A model, such as that shown in Figure 2-1, can take account of sequential interactions between the individual and biological and environmental factors influencing the subsequent development course. In this model, specific biological/health influences and the life stage from conception through adolescence during which they may exert an effect, are shown down the left-hand side. Family and environmental influences are listed on the right. The mediating effects of potential interactions, risk factors that lead to vulnerability to developmental failure, stressful life events that may exacerbate social risk, and protective factors that offset risk are indicated down the center of the diagram. The outcome of this complex process for each individual will determine adult status and, in turn, influence the health, cognitive, and social development of his or her children.

Intergenerational Influences

An intergenerational perspective is important for several reasons, both environmental and biological.

1. The *culture* to which parents, particularly mothers, are exposed will have a strong influence on their behavior with respect to such parameters as pregnancy and health care, education, employment, religion, family resources, and parenting. Parental behavior is a strong determinant of the behavior of the child.
2. *Genetic* influences may have a profound effect on development. The genetic material that is passed from each parent to the fetus at conception will determine such basic characteristics as race and sex. Genetic factors may, in addition, result in the expression of profound physical and/or biochemical abnormalities, for example, Down syndrome or phenylketonuria. The potential effect of other genes, such as those that determine height or intellectual ability, may be limited by interaction with unfavorable environmental factors. For example, the potential for physical growth may be reduced by severe illness or restriction in available nutrients. Similarly, the potential for cognitive development may be reduced by health factors, such as severe injury, communication disorders, such as impaired hearing, illness, and malnutrition, or by environmental factors that result in stress, lack of cognitive stimulation, and/or opportunities to learn needed skills. On the other hand, a favorable environment will enhance the likelihood that individual potential will be more nearly reached.
3. *Maternal health* and developmental status prior to and during pregnancy may affect the quality of intrauterine development and outcome for the fetus. For

DETERMINANTS OF HUMAN DEVELOPMENT
SELECTED INFLUENCES ALONG THE LIFE COURSE

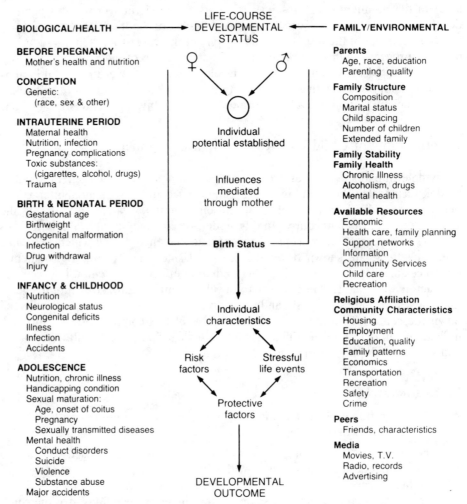

Figure 2-1 A life course model depicting the continuing interactions between biological/health and family/environmental influences that determine developmental outcomes at different stages from preconception through adolescence.

example, chronically undernourished women are at risk for fetal growth retardation and/or low birth weight (LBW). Similarly, substance abuse and chronic illness may impair reproductive capacity, and maternal infection with a sexually transmitted disease may result in fetal and infant morbidity and mortality (Strobino, 1987).

Biological/Health Influences

Biological influences associated with both favorable and adverse effects on fetal development and on the later physical, cognitive, and socioemotional development of children have been well-documented by many investigators. Those factors, operative during pregnancy, that are associated with LBW, intrauterine growth retardation (IUGR), and perinatal mortality have been well-summarized in a report from the Committee on Low Birthweight of the Institute of Medicine (1985) and by Hofferth (1987a).

Many conditions mediated through the mother, such as socioeconomic deprivation, cigarette smoking, substance abuse, and inadequate prenatal care, have adverse fetal effects, manifested by LBW and IUGR, that may, in turn, directly compromise later physical and cognitive development during childhood (Hardy and Mellits, 1977; Starfield et al., 1982) or establish a state of vulnerability that, in concert with an unfavorable environment, may reduce developmental potential (Drillien, 1964; Werner, 1986).

The effects of childhood illness on development are less clear. Children in disadvantaged environments are, in general, at greater risk for health problems than those living under more favorable conditions (Haggerty, 1983; Miller et al., 1974; Starfield et al., 1982). Repeated or chronic infections, such as otitis media, may result in hearing deficits that impede learning. Cognitive and socioemotional development may also be impaired by noninfectious problems, such as hearing and other communication deficits, visual impairment, learning disabilities, and attentional deficits, some of which may be sequelae of perinatal problems. Major illness, severe accidents, and mental health problems, such as conduct disorders, adjustment difficulties, and substance abuse may also be disruptive of personal function.

Interaction of Biology and Environment

Drillien (1964), in her classic study of the development of LBW infants followed to early school age in Scotland, demonstrated the importance of interactions between LBW, a biological risk factor, and environmental influences on developmental status. She reported that if LBW infants escaped profound neurological injury, those reared in middle-class homes had average school achievement which was not different from their normal birth weight siblings. However, similar LBW infants reared by lower-class parents had an average school achievement substantially lower than that of their normal birth weight siblings reared in the same environment. Vulnerability associated with LBW interacted with risk factors present in the less favorable, lower-class environment, resulting in a less favorable developmental outcome for LBW children than their normal siblings.

Werner and Smith (1982) and Werner (1985, 1986), in a longitudinal study of children born on the Island of Kauai in 1955, have shown that: 1) perinatal stress and social stress, independently or acting in concert, may establish a state of vulnerability with respect to risk of developmental failure; and 2) innate characteristics of the child and protective factors in the environment, singly or together, may offset the adverse effects of stress and the expression of vulnerability permitting normal development despite otherwise adverse circumstances. The relative impact of risk factors and stressful life events and the effectiveness of protective factors were found to differ with sex of child, his or her developmental stage, and the characteristics of the social and economic environment in which she or he lived. In Werner's studies, as the number of risk factors increased so did the number and strength of protective factors required to balance their negative influences and ensure a positive developmental outcome. Werner (1985, p. 353) stresses the importance of early assessment and intervention in preventing the lasting effects of perinatal, i.e., biological risk factors.

Family/Environmental Influences

The development of children and adolescents is strongly influenced by the family and environmental circumstances in which they live. The diagrams in Figure 2-2,A to D, suggest the relative levels of influence of major components (i.e., family, school, and community) at different stages along the life course between infancy and adolescence.

The infant is, in general, isolated from outside (i.e., community) influences within the family on whose members he or she is dependent for survival and nurturance (Fig. 2-2A). Such influences are indirect, mediated through the family. (A relatively recent exception to this rule results from the placement of infants in day care settings while their mothers work or continue their education.) As the

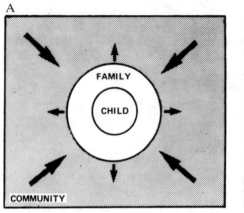

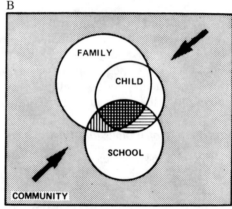

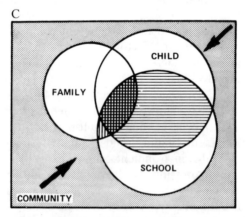

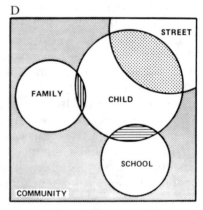

Figure 2-2,A-D   Diagram depicting the influence of family/environmental influences on child/adolescent development at several points along the life course. **A** shows the situation during infancy when the child is largely isolated within the family from outside community influences. **B** shows interrelationships between family, child, and school within the larger community during elementary school. Family influences still predominate. **C** shows these relationships at the high school level, when the child and school each have a larger role. **D** depicts a socially pathological model in which family and school have little influence, while the influence of peers and the "street" culture predominate.

infant grows into toddlerhood and beyond, his or her horizons are extended, and contacts with the outside world increase. As age increases, school and community have more direct and increasingly strong influences on the development of children, sometimes overlapping and sometimes separate (Fig. 2-2,B and C). Family influences normally remain substantial throughout adolescence.

Figure 2-2D suggests a different situation, one that occurs all too frequently in areas of urban poverty. In these areas, there may be relatively few intact families. Single mothers with limited resources may be subject to multiple stresses in trying to provide such basic necessities as food or shelter, and, thus, have little energy or time for their children. If they are working at low paying jobs, their children may be "latch-key kids" left for long hours without supervision. In these situations, the child may be exposed to influences that lack coherence, and the family's influence is diminished. There may be little or no parental-school communication, in turn diminishing the influence of the school. The role of the school may be further eroded by the child's lack of academic success and reinforcement and by frequent absences or even premature termination of schooling. In these situations the child may, at an early age and certainly by puberty, become more dependent on community influences for stimulation and learning. The influence of his or her peers and young adults "on the street," who are not in school and not employed, may be conducive to socially undesirable behaviors, which frequently cluster (Jessor and Jessor, 1977; Zabin, Hardy, et al., 1986) such as drug and/or alcohol abuse, premature sexual activity, and delinquent or criminal activity to produce income.

Involvement in community activities that promote personal responsibility and growth, such as participation in sports, scouting, recreational and library programs, volunteer work, and church-oriented activities, can be "protective" and encourage growth in positive directions. To be effective such activities must be available, accessible, and acceptable to the child/adolescent. Parental encouragement and/or outreach may be required to facilitate participation. Sadly, in those areas of the city and those communities that need positive reinforcement the most, "street" influences are generally most dangerous and alternative activities least available.

Family Characteristics

Family variables, as listed in Figure 2-1, include those pertaining to characteristics of parents, family structure, stability, health, religious affiliation, and the resources available for caring for family members. For optimal development, children require a close and stable affectional relationship with a parent, preferably two parents, or a parent and grandmother, and other caring adults (Kellam et al., 1977, 1982; McLanahan, 1983, 1985). Werner (1985, 1986) suggests that such a relationship "protects" and facilitates the development of children living in socially disadvantageous circumstances. An environment that provides harmony and order within the family and sufficient resources—material and informational—to promote good parenting and child care and to prevent chronic stress will facilitate the health and learning of children. However, such favorable family environments are difficult to provide for children living in socioeconomically deprived areas, where single parenthood and poverty abound. Furstenberg (1976), Furstenberg et al. (1987), and Boyce et al., (1985) have documented the importance of family supports in enhancing the development of adolescent mothers. Among the important findings of the longitudinal follow-up of Furstenberg et al. (1987), spanning almost 20 years in the lives of adolescents giving birth to a first child at age 17 or below, are: 1) the great diversity in long-term outcomes; 2) the importance of family supports to the continued development of the young mother; and 3) the enduring capacity for upward mobility, even after many years of public dependency, as the result of a favorable change in environmental circumstances, for example, acquisition of further education, job training, employment, or a good marriage. However, a fourth important finding, of negative effects among the children of these mothers, suggests that the stress they were under as teenage parents passed on deficits to their offspring, which even the parent's eventual success could not ameliorate. This can be seen as reinforcing the importance of the immediate environment in the early years of childhood.

Community Characteristics

The characteristics of the community in which the child lives will, as indicated above, influence his or her development both indirectly and directly. Figure 2-1 lists the more important community variables. Characteristics such as housing quality and density, lack of privacy, opportunities for employment, day care, transportation, and human services are important in determining the standard of living of the family and its available resources. The quality of education, recreation, and medical care and the characteristics of peers and friends have a more direct influence on the adolescent's motivation and expectations for future employment and family formation. The ability of the family and community to interact with the adolescent, to reward socially acceptable behavior, and to censure that which is undesirable, will help determine the opportunity structure available to the adolescent and establish the limits the young person may perceive.

When family stability and cohesion break down and parental control is lost, maladaptive or deviant behavior may occur among the children. As shown in Figure 2-2D and discussed above, family and school may fail to exert a positive influence during a period in which it is normal that the influence of peers becomes more compelling. Under such circumstances, community characteristics that are conducive to maladaptive behavior, such as drug abuse, delinquency, and crime, can have a devastating effect.

Transition to Adulthood

The life course model of development provides a useful perspective from which to consider the sequence of events that usually occur during the transition from one stage in the life cycle to the next. The transition from adolescence to adulthood is accomplished over a period of several years. We suggested above that a distinction between adolescents and older (18- to 19-year-old) teenagers, although useful, was probably not sufficient to amplify our understanding of premature pregnancy and childbearing because of the magnitude of the change that takes place each year during the pubertal and postpubertal period. The younger the age at physical maturity, the greater may be the discrepancy between cognitive, emotional, and social development, on the one hand, and physical development on the other. Although these phases of human development may have coincided in the past and may still overlap in some parts of the developing world, they rarely do so in the industrial West.

Physical Maturation

Mean age of menarche in the western world has gone through a long period of decline; for about 100 years, ending more than a generation ago, the age of young Americans at puberty decreased by about 3 to 4 months each decade (Marshall and Tanner, 1974). There has been extensive literature on the reasons for this decline, but it is, most probably, a result of changes in body mass based on nutrition. There is also a documented genetic inheritance, and health and environment may also play roles. Whatever the interplay of cause and effect, a discontinuity in various areas of contemporary human development occurs because "psychological development is tied to calendar age, but psychosexual development is ultimately determined by nutritional events which control the time of onset of puberty" (Short, 1976).

Age of menarche is important for several reasons, including the obvious fact that, having reached that benchmark, a young woman is exposed to the risk of conception. Puberty is also important because, through several mechanisms we discuss below, there is an association between age of puberty and age of first intercourse among males and females alike. Figure 2-3, based on the self-report of an inner city black student population, juxtaposes age of menarche or first wet dream with age of first coitus; the two curves are remarkably similar in shape for each sex, while differing between the sexes (Zabin, Smith, et al., 1986). The sharply peaked distribution of menarcheal age for young women, with over 75% reaching menarche between 11.0 and 13.9 years of age, is echoed by a similar distribution of first intercourse approximately 2 years later. For young men, the distribution is wider and the two curves peak at the same age, 13.5. Their means are a year apart, with first intercourse averaging only 12.0 years of age (among those who have started sex), reflecting the considerable amount of prepubertal sex these young men report. Even without the information they give on their first wet dream, sex at the ages they describe would have to be considered prepubertal.

Even these interesting relationships between menarche or wet dream and age of first intercourse do not tell the most relevant part of the story. They mask an important differential that becomes clear upon closer examination of the proportion of young girls and boys who start sexual activity at each age. Figure 2-4 illustrates the initiation of intercourse by young women, controlled by menarcheal age, and young men controlled by their age at first wet dream. The solid line at the left reflects, in each case, the cumulative proportion sexually active among those whose pubertal event is early, at 11 or younger. Subsequent cumulative percentages of first coitus indicate that puberty is, indeed, associated with sexual initiation, although the effect attentuates over time. At early ages, age of menarche is associated with wide differentials in sexual activity, with as much as a 30-point difference apparent at 13 years of age. For young men, the association is similar but is neither as consistent nor as longlasting; by 15 it has virtually disappeared. However, in the very early years of exposure, the spread is even more extreme than that observed among women of different pubertal ages, with a 36-point difference in sexual initiation between early and late maturers reflected at the 12-year mark. Thus, there seems to be little doubt that early physical maturation in young men and women alike is associated with the onset of coitus, especially in the early years of adolescence.

These are the very years in which the discrepancies between cognitive, emotional, and physical development are greatest for those whose biological maturation

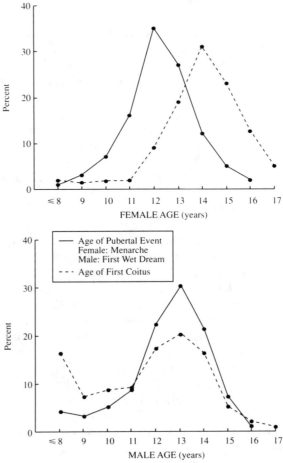

Figure 2-3 Percent distribution of ages of puberty and ages of first coitus among black male and female students, 1981. (Reproduced by permission from Zabin et al. *Demography* 23:595-605, 1986. ©Population Association of America.)

occurs early. It is this discontinuity that makes the exact age of sexual onset so critical. The young woman who is able to bear a child may not yet have completed the developmental tasks of her own childhood. The implications of her level of cognitive and emotional development for her sexual, contraceptive, childbearing, and parenting behaviors are profound.

Development and Sexual Behavior

Researchers differ in the relative weight they attribute to genetic, environmental, and biological roles in maturation; they also differ in the rigidity with which they describe "stages" of development. But the notion that, at different ages, certain developmental tasks are completed in a reasonably predictable sequence is generally accepted. Cognitively, Piaget sees the formal stage, initiated at about 12 years of age, as the beginning of a young person's conception of "possibility," or of abstract thinking not dependent on experience or actual objects. The adolescent learns to utilize present resources to prepare for future contingencies; thus, "the

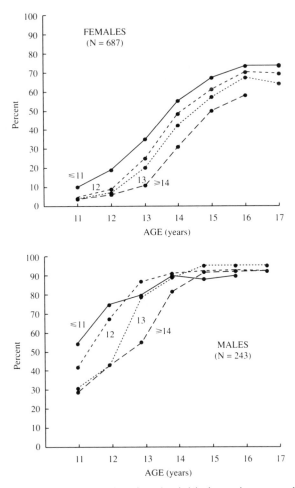

Figure 2-4 Cumulative percent of males, females initiating coitus at each age, by age at first wet dream, menarche.

hallmark of operative thinking is anticipation" (Piaget, 1972). But the learning process is a gradual one, and educational initiatives must be tempered to the capacities of youngsters who may still think in very concrete terms. Elkind (1975) elaborates the formal stage into diversified phases, each of which increases the adolescent's ability to recombine new propositional operations. It seems clear that, for most individuals, developmental status is a limiting factor in the ability to handle some concepts, although the notion that specific ages can be assigned to these cognitive stages has been questioned.

It also seems clear that psychological changes often parallel cognitive development. These changes include what Erikson (1963, 1965) describes as identity formation, the development of a stable self-concept, which enables the young person to make crucial decisions about the future. During the early latency period, social controls are internalized, and the way is prepared for adolescent ego development. In both cognitive and psychological development, the "task" of each stage is seen as an important prerequisite to the structuring of the next. Thus, adolescent role diffusion, or lack of commitment, is intensified if identity has not been developed in a prior phase.

Elkind also describes a construct known as the "personal fable"; with the egocentrism of youth, adolescents believe they are different from others, and assume that they are not liable to the risks that threaten their peers, even risks that, on an intellectual level, they may comprehend. This belief in one's own invincibility may result directly in adolescent risk-taking behavior. With continuing cognitive development and with changes during the teen years in the young person's perception of "self" relative to "others," this egocentrism of early adolescence should be outgrown. The older adolescent becomes capable, both cognitively and emotionally, of understanding the consequences of his or her own behaviors (Elkind, 1967, 1975). Moral reasoning may also be related to the process of identity formation and the young person's evolving cognitive abilities. Not all persons develop moral judgment *equivalent* to their cognitive levels, but Kohlberg (1969) contends that they cannot form moral judgments *beyond* their levels of cognitive understanding.

Even this brief sketch of a few developmental tracks suggests how important the relationship might be between cognitive and emotional development and a young person's ability to handle sexual maturity. It is not difficult to believe that there would be a strong relationship between the growing understanding of future contingencies associated with mature cognitive function and the ability to avoid unintended pregnancy. For example, Elkind suggests that the teenager's assumption that "pregnancy can't happen to me" is a reflection of the egocentric construct of early adolescence; however mature the adolescent's objective knowledge of risk, he or she may feel, subjectively, invincible. Unprotected sex may be only one expression of that sense of invulnerability; substance use, excessive speed behind the wheel, and drinking while driving are others. Elkind describes early relationships as not primarily sexual, but a part of the search for identity; this accords with the explanation young people often give of their sexual contacts: they prove "that I am a man (woman)." Reiss (1967) reports that the young person develops increasingly permissive attitudes through the teen years, while evolving a personal ethic separate from that of the primary family. These changes in permissiveness may be related to the evolving cognitive capacities of young people, as well as to the transfer of their focus from the values of parents to those of their peers.

Whether adolescent development is described in terms of stages or more continuously as a "process," it is clear that these are years of important change. Jessor and Jessor (1977) suggest that there are correlations between transitions to various problem behaviors and the development of attitudinal and personality changes, which differ for those whose transitional behaviors occur outside of the normative sequence. In their longitudinal study of the relationship between personality, the perceived social environment, and behavior in adolescence, they state that "many of the important transitions that mark the course of adolescent development involve . . . age graded behaviors, behaviors that, when engaged in earlier, depart from the regulatory age norms defining what is appropriate at that age or stage in life." Because "much of the behavior is problematic only in relation to age, and problem proneness can often mean no more than developmental precocity," problem behavior must be understood from the perspective of normal development. Adolescent pregnancy, then, can be seen as an interruption of the "normative schedule" by which the usual sequence of education, employment, marriage, and childbearing is more commonly ordered.

The life course is normatively patterned not only by physical development, but by social norms. Although, in our culture, there is not a single, prescribed ritual marking the transition to adulthood, there are events that generally occur in a predictable sequence (Marini, 1984). These events occur quite late in the teen years, commencing with high school graduation, including higher education or work force participation, family formation, and childbearing. Informal social support from family and others, and many of the more formal programs that provide social assistance, are organized around these steps in the normative life cycle. Therefore, major deviations either in the timing or the ordering of these events can have serious social consequences for the individual (Elder, 1975; Teachman and Polonki, 1984). Furstenberg's (1976) review of the literature on disturbances to the normative schedule indicates that although transitions to motherhood frequently can be accomplished prematurely, they often serve to retard progression from one stage to another. Whether the onset of sexual relations, in the absence of pregnancy, represents a similar disruption is not often addressed. However, it is not unreasonable to believe that the "developmental precocity" to which Jessor and Jessor refer might revolve around early physical maturation, particularly when it occurs out of synchrony with other developmental events. Certainly, the consequences of premature sexual contact, at an age when the cognitive and emotional status of the adolescent prevent any kind of reliable preventive behavior, have important implications for the entire life course.

Age at First Coitus

It should be noted that the influence of age at first coitus on pregnancy history can be manifested in many ways: 1) age can affect the risk of conception merely because the period of *exposure* is longer for those whose coital onset is early; 2) interpreted socially, it can affect *related behaviors*, such as frequency of coitus, relationships with partners, and contraceptive use; 3) interpreted biologically, it can have an effect on the *fecundity* of the young woman (or the fertility of her partner) when age is measured in years pre- or postpuberty rather than in chronological years; 4) interpreted developmentally, it can influence the degree to which a young person can be reached by interventions that depend for their success on his or her level of ability to respond, cognitively, psychologically, and educationally. Finally, 5) it can have an effect on the role a pregnancy might play in the life cycle, on the perception of that role by the young person, her partner, and others in her social setting—and thus impinge on the likelihood that she will make a conscious effort to avoid it.

If the age at which coital behavior is initiated is as important as it appears to be, the influences that affect age of onset need to be better understood. That age is influenced, on the one hand, by pressures that are individual and developmental and, on the other hand, by pressures and restraints that are culturally based, and social or normative in nature. We saw, above, that age of maturation and age at first intercourse are associated, and that the association is closest in early adolescence. This may not be surprising, because androgen levels are related to an individual's physiological timetable, and Udry and his colleagues (1985, 1986) have shown their direct influence on both coital and noncoital sexual experience. Zabin, Smith, et al. (1986) confirmed the association of biology and behavior, but demonstrated that the strength of that relationship weakens over time. ". . . age of puberty exerts an influence separate from the normative pattern and, when it is low, applies a downward pressure on the age of sexual onset. As age of puberty increases, the cultural influence of social norms, as opposed to the individual developmental timetable, becomes stronger." If the influence of biological development was equally strong at all ages, one would expect the interval from menarche to sexual onset to remain the same at every chronological age. In fact, the probability of sexual onset within 12 or 24 months following menarche increases dramatically with age. For those who mature later in their teen years, the normative pressures toward sexual socialization are greater and increase the probability that first intercourse will occur close to the age at menarche.

It should not be implied that biological influences and normative influences are necessarily conflicting or even separate. An interdisciplinary or interactive perspective is proposed by Smith (1988) based on the research of Udry and his colleagues. Pubertal development necessarily affects the perception of teenagers by others—peers, potential partners, etc., and family as well. Thus, it has its effects on the teenager's self-perception, as well. Self-perception, in turn, has its effect on the selection of peers, whose independent influence on social behavior is documented below. The interaction of social and biological pressures suggests that an individual's biological time clock actually helps to create the social world in which he or she is acculturated. Where social restraints are strongest, the effects of early physical maturation are weaker, but among more permissive social groups, the effects of libidinal development and of friends' behaviors are more direct and obvious.

Normative Influences

Purely social, or normative, effects can be expressed in many ways. The rapid decrease in age of first intercourse during the 1970s in the United States, apparent in all social and economic groups in the country, gave evidence that a strong downward normative pressure was at work. Simultaneously, sanctions against nonmarital intercourse weakened. Although the largest continuing decrease in age at first intercourse occurs among young white females, the evidence for earlier coital onset among young blacks appears strong. This suggests that cultural influences exert pressure over and above the changing patterns of behavior reflected in the national media and in national statistics. Cultural pressures may work through the behavioral patterns of the ethnic/racial, religious, geographical, and/or economic subgroups in which the child is acculturated. Ambient patterns can affect not only the age at which certain behaviors are considered appropriate, but even the sequencing of these behaviors, and the individual's perception of the significance of various expressions of sexual intimacy. For example, although heterosexual contact may begin at similar ages for a young white girl and a young black girl, a series of sexual behaviors (clothed petting, unclothed petting, etc.) often precedes coitus in the former group, while intercourse is likely to be an earlier form of sexual expression in the latter (Smith, 1988).

Another example of cultural difference is the fact that, among white females who have initiated coitus, there appears a pattern of more partners and more frequent intercourse than among blacks of the same age who have initiated intercourse at approximately the same time. Young blacks, in turn, often report less frequent coitus and fewer different partners (Zabin et al., 1979; Zelnik et al., 1981). Examples such as these indicate how inaccurate it is to describe one group as more "promiscuous" than another in any absolute sense; rather, there are different ways in which sexuality is expressed in different cultural subgroups.

Peers have an hypothesized relationship to sexual behavior, not only as potential partners but as embodiments of the social norms of the group. It is not clear what is cause and what is effect in these relationships, but Udry et al. (1985) report a significant relationship between the probability of initiating sex and the behavior of one's "best friend" (Billy and Udry, 1985a and b; Billy et al., 1984; Morris et al., 1982). The belief that peers are sexually active is a good predictor of sexual behavior among adolescents, and so is the perception that their friends are permissive in their sexual attitudes (Cvetkovitch and Grote, 1980). There is a general finding that young people often overestimate the sexual activity of their peers, which may encourage them to behave in ways consistent more with their assumptions about their friends than with the actual norms of the group. Jessor and Jessor (1977) find that transitions to nonvirginity are related to "a greater decline in value on academic achievement, greater increase in value on independence relative to achievement, and a greater increase in models of non-virginity among friends than characterizes the development of the group that retains its virgin status."

It seems clear that, as they begin to develop a personal standard of permissiveness, young people relate more and more strongly to their peer group, and the influence of the primary family begins to wane (Reiss, 1967). That developmental process is occurring, typically, during the years of early sexual contact. (The nature of those transitions when the primary setting is already permissive in its message is not well explored.) It is possible that very early sexual contact, accelerated by early maturation, short circuits that important task of adolescence: the development of a personal standard of behavior.

Families, nonetheless, exert important pressures, although the ways in which influence is expressed is not well-understood. Studies that find less effect than has been hypothesized have often been unable to address the *quality* of communication, a difficult dimension to capture. Furthermore, even the *quantity* is difficult to assess because parents and their offspring are likely to report different levels of discussion when asked about the same subjects (Smith and Zabin, 1985). It is possible that some of the parental effects that have been observed operate indirectly through example, rather than directly through oral communication. It is also possible that biological inheritance (e.g., appearance and early puberty) has its effect. Furthermore, the level of social control, whether through curfews, limits placed on the independence of the adolescent, or regulation of the quantity or quality of free time, has its effect. Of course, the degree to which the family is present to supervise the minor is not always a matter of choice; unfortunately, the presence or absence of a parent when a child is at home is often an economic imperative.

The strongest influence of family on sexual onset, however, may be on the young man or woman's perception of possibility—of options, opportunities, expectations, and aspirations for the future—and the ability of the individual to understand the role of personal behavior and a personal value system in translating those perceptions into reality. Ultimately, we believe that the individual's perception of self and his or her trust in others and, in turn, in self have a crucial role in the complex decision-making processes that sexual behavior entails. The family, the central world in which each child is formed, must necessarily have a powerful influence on the place each young person sees him- or herself occupying in the larger universe.

Role of Self-Concept in Interactive Model

However self-concept is defined, it is clear that the same cultural setting can produce a wide variety of sexual behaviors and widely disparate ages of sexual onset. In different cultural settings, young people with similar ages of maturation demonstrate different normative patterns of sexual onset, but even within one cultural setting, there is great individual variation. There is clearly an important role for the individual, whatever the nature of the pressures upon her or him. For reasons such as these, there has been considerable emphasis in recent literature on "self-esteem" as an essential ingredient in the decision-making process, despite the lack of clear evidence that lower self-esteem is associated with early sexual onset or childbearing (Hayes, 1987). There has been, perhaps, too little emphasis on cognitive capacity, an essential ingredient of the decision-making process. Given the ability to make choices, however, ego strength also plays a role. To the extent that a strong sense of personal identity increases the ability of an individual to develop a value system and act upon it, it is logical to believe that early onset, before that identity is well-developed, might be more capricious and more exposed to the pressures of biology and environment.

Whatever the pressures and restraints on sexual onset, they must be processed by each individual as he or she writes a personal "sexual script," a process described by Simon and Gagnon (1987) as intrapersonal, but nonetheless social in nature. Others have considered the process in econometric terms: each male or female is seen computing a personal equation of the utilities and costs of sexual relations (Bauman and Udry, 1981). In this conception, the especially early onset of coitus among black males is attributed to the fact that, according to the authors' index, black males' expectations of the positive utility of sexual onset is higher than white

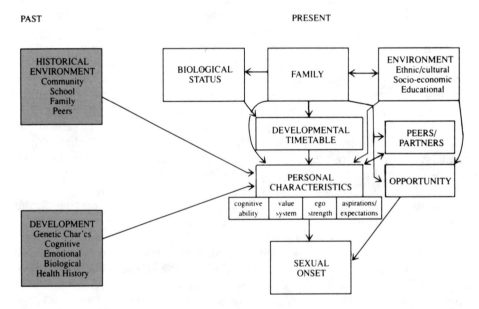

Figure 2-5 Model depicting influences upon the onset of coitus and interactions between them.

males' expectations; earlier sexual onset is then explained as the product of a higher "subjective expected utility."

In an attempt to explain why those who have more motivation to continue their education into the future might be less likely to engage in early coital activity, more likely to contracept, and less likely to elect to carry an unintended pregnancy to term, a role for aspirations and expectations for the future has been proposed (Hayes, 1987; Furstenberg, 1976; Mott and Marsiglio, 1985). The higher value placed on education may, in turn, be related to cognitive ability and to prior achievement, which has a logical effect on self-esteem. Hofferth (1987a) sees the final determinant of sexual activity as a reward structure—"how he or she evaluates the consequences of certain behaviors"—which, given the opportunity to engage (or not engage) in coitus, provides the incentives on which action is predicted.

Such forces are, no doubt, part of the serial decisions some young people make to engage or not engage in coitus, to contracept or not contracept when engaged in coitus, and to bear or not bear a child when faced with an unintended conception. In each case, knowledge and the capacity to utilize knowledge effectively are important preconditions of responsible behavior. And, in each case, the young person must evaluate her own aspirations and expectations for the future and the degree to which her behavior is putting them at risk. That process involves not only a rational appraisal of the real world in which a young person lives but also her subjective perceptions of that world and her place in it. Perhaps a choice is made, whether it is conscious or unconscious; unfortunately, all too often it never takes place on a conscious plane.

In the model proposed here (Fig. 2-5), social or cultural environment, including the immediate setting of the family, the influence of peers, the interaction of biological maturation and environmental setting, and the direct influence of hormonal development all affect sense of the self at puberty. The historic dynamic has been taking place since birth, and even before. Although that self-concept will continue to evolve into the future, at the time that an opportunity for coital contact occurs, ambient pressures are processed by the individual based on calculus of his or her own that is in place at that developmental moment. A past history of achievement or failure, of cognitive and psychological tasks completed or incomplete, and of aspirations and expectations that grow out of that history all affect the crucible in which those influences are translated into action. Thus, individuals are not seen simply as products of biology, family, or culture, but as interactive agents whose ability to resist the pressures of society and of their pubertal development are, and remain, their own, however strongly they are affected by that long, intergenerational history.

Interventions, then, have many potential points of entry; ideally, they would address the larger environment in which young people are acculturated and the local or family setting in which opportunities are presented and choices are made. But they can focus, too, on the self that will make those choices. They can give the young person reason to trust in others, and ultimately to trust him- or herself. And they can focus on changing the young person's real prospects for the future, as well, not merely on the legacy of the past, because a vision of the future can rationally inform the choices that individuals make. That, in turn, entails focusing on the adolescent not only as a sexual being but as a potential parent and on the quality of the future he or she passes on to a child.

The Two Problems of Teenage Pregnancy

Differences between the behaviors of one subgroup in the United States and another should not mask the great changes that have occurred in recent decades in the sexual conduct of young Americans of all walks of life. Little was known of the actual timing of sexual onset until the National Survey of Young Women was conducted in 1971 by two professors, Melvin Zelnik and John F. Kantner, from The Johns Hopkins School of Public Health. Repeating the procedure in 1976 and 1979, they documented not only the extent of coital contact among young women, but the rapidity of change. (The 1979 survey added young men to the equation.) Sexual union, family formation, and childbearing are such fundamental aspects of cultural stability that the evidence of significant changes within 5, or even 3, years' time presented by these researchers was surprising. The magnitude of the changes they reported in basic human behaviors could not but put pressure upon the institutions of our society. However, the fact that the sexual revolution was nationwide should not imply that these problems are monolithic. We proposed at the outset that the semantics of "teenage" sex and "teenage" pregnancy may actually cloud our understanding and contribute to the intransigence of the problem.

We perceive not one but two aspects of the problem of teenage sexuality, pregnancy, and childbearing. One is the problem of sexual involvement in middle and late teen years and the consequent high level of accidental conception. The other is pubertal and even prepubertal sexual contact, and conception and child-bearing in early adolescence. The first is well-described in national data; it is nearly universal in the geography and economic strata it encompasses. It developed during years of great social change in the mores of adult men and women, as well, and is typified by the large numbers of 17-, 18-, and 19-year-olds involved in premarital sexual liaisons. It is quite possible that sex as young as 16, or even 15 in some social settings, is largely a legacy of the sexual revolution. Accidental pregnancies do occur among those who initiate sex at these ages; in fact, in absolute numbers, young women of 16 and over are responsible for the vast majority of the unintended teen births in the country, many more than youthful adolescents. They require comprehensive reproductive health services well beyond those available at present. However, it is our belief that services similar to those available in the past, augmented by more realistic education and better outreach, could probably provide most of the social and medical supports necessary.

That is not true of the aspect of the problem we focus on here, one largely rooted in the underclass. We do not believe that the sexual and pregnancy experience of the adolescent involved in sexual contact at puberty or even before puberty, at risk of conception in the early postpubertal years, can also be seen solely as a legacy of the sexual revolution. Of course, the same influences that affect all young Americans surround her, as well, and make the outcome of early sexual contact more predictable, but we believe that at these ages the etiology of her sexual behavior is much more complex.

Early coital onset may evolve from her economic context. For example, over-crowded housing may be implicated, when the sexual behaviors of adults are visible, to be watched and imitated by children. Because they have not yet developed a stable self-image, and because they are not yet capable of understanding what they see, they are certainly incapable of limiting the ways in which what they see impinges on their own private worlds. The disorganized settings of poverty are breeding grounds for disorganized relationships, including involuntary sexual contacts—whether forced or surprised—that so often are associated with early coitus.

Limited cognitive function, an underdeveloped sense of identity, or an immature perception of personal risk may also underlie her early sexual contact. For some, the added pressure of early maturation compounds the young girl's need for contact and affection and may accelerate sexual experience before she is cognitively or emotionally prepared to understand its implications. That experience, in turn, may short-circuit the completion of the psychological tasks of her latency phase, the process of her individuation, and the development of a strong self-image. Reaching these young women and their children will require a great deal more than traditional sex education and reproductive health services; it is the task of this book to address those special needs.

3
Teenage Pregnancy
The National Scene

Approximately one million American teenagers become pregnant each year. Just under one-half of these young women are adolescents below age 18 years. Of those teenagers who become pregnant, just under 50% give birth and about 400,000 terminate their pregnancies by elective abortion. The remainder experience a spontaneous abortion or later fetal death (Table 3-1). A very large proportion of these pregnancies are unintended (Hardy et al., 1986; Zelnik and Kantner, 1980). Estimates by Forrest (1986), based on 1981 data pertaining to teenage births and abortions, suggest that 40% of white and 63% of black 15 through 19 year olds experience a first pregnancy before their 20th birthday. However, the majority of teenagers do not become pregnant.

Teenage pregnancy and childbearing and their adverse consequences are not new phenomena. In fact, the 469,862 births among 15- through 19-year-olds reported in 1986 is 26% less than the 616,280 reported in 1972 (Table 3-1). It is the changes in the social context in which the pregnancies, births, and abortions occur that have generated many of the problems and costs and thus given greater visibility to the phenomena. The most significant social changes that affect the development of children and adolescents include: the erosion of the nuclear family; changing marriage patterns; the more explicit treatment of sexual material by the media; absent fathers (R.I. Lerman, unpublished data, 1985); and the women's movement, with entry of increasing proportions of women with children into the work force, from 45% in 1960 to 62% in 1985 (Hayes, 1987). Among single mothers with children under 18, 66% were working. Edelman (1987) estimates that by 1990, one in every five white infants and three of every four black will be born to a single parent. Given the high frequency of out-of-wedlock births among teenagers, many of these single mothers will be less than 20. Although the availability of effective contraception and the increased availability of abortion following its legalization in 1973 have been documented to have reduced unwanted child bearing, access to contraception unfortunately has been reduced by cuts in federal funding for family planning services, and abortion has been restricted since 1982 for poor women who are unable to pay for the procedure. As pointed out in Chapter 2, the family and social contexts in which the individual grows are important determinants of developmental outcome. Prevailing sociocultural attitudes, values, beliefs and expectations are influential in the individual's development (Elder, 1980). The changes in attitudes toward adult sexual behavior in the 1960s and 1970s, as part of the sexual revolution, have undoubtedly influenced the behavior of teenagers as well.

Table 3-1 Numbers of 15- Through 19-Year-Old Females, Pregnancy Outcome, United States, 1980 Through 1984

Year	Number in the population	Teenage females 15–19 yr					Birth rate/1000	Total births all ages	% Births 15–19 yr
		Number births	Number abortions	Number fetal deaths	Number pregs.	Pregnancy rate/1000			
1972	9,517,000	616,280	181,908	141,447	919,635	97	0.65	3,258,000	18.9
1976	10,585,000	558,744	326,680	148,071	1,069,441	101	0.53	3,168,000	17.6
1980	10,081,000	549,472	444,785	154,910	1,151,851	114	0.55	3,612,258	15.2
1984	9,219,000	469,682	401,128	134,049	1,004,859	109	0.51	3,669,141	12.8
1986	—	461,905[a]	—	—	—	—	—	3,756,547[a]	12.3

Adapted from Moore, KA, Wenk, D, Hofferth, SL, and Hayes, CD. Statistical Appendix, Table 3-1, pp. 414-415. *In* Hofferth, SL and Hayes, CD (eds.): *Risking The Future, Adolescent Sexuality, Pregnancy and Childbearing*, Vol. 2. National Research Council, National Academy Press, Washington, DC, 1987.

[a]From Monthly Vital Statistics Report, Advance Report of Final Natality Statistics, 1986. National Center for Health Statistics, Vol. 37, No. 3 Supplement, Table 28, July 12, 1988.

As Hayes (1987) points out, the events of the 1960s and 1970s have resulted in major changes in "the social, economic and cultural context of adolescence." Different subgroups in American society have been differentially affected, as reflected by national trends in sexuality and fertility in the 1980s. Within subgroups, individual sexual decision making and behavior also vary. Teenagers are not a monolithic, homogeneous group.

The major objective of this chapter is to provide a brief, national overview of pregnancy and childbearing among American women, aged 20 years or below, to facilitate comparisons aimed at developing an understanding of underlying factors. The first set of comparisons is between the United States and those other developed countries that are culturally most similar to it. These comparisons, based on studies sponsored by the Alan Guttmacher Institute (Jones et al., 1986) are discussed in this chapter. The second and, in the context of this book, the more important set, involves comparisons between data for the United States as a whole and those derived from city-wide studies of urban teenagers and adolescents in Baltimore. The national statistics for teenagers, presented here by specific year of age and race, establish a point of reference for the consideration of data pertaining to the urban adolescents, below age 18, described in succeeding chapters.

Comparisons with Developed Countries

Among westernized countries with reasonably comparable cultural and socioeconomic characteristics, the United States has by far the highest rates of pregnancy, childbirth, and elective abortion among its teenagers (Jones et al., 1986). It is the only country in the group in which the rate of pregnancy per 1,000 teenage women has not been decreasing substantially during recent years. In the five other countries most similar to the United States (Canada, England and Wales, France, Sweden, and the Netherlands) teenage birth rates have declined fairly steadily since 1971. In the United States these rates declined sharply until 1976 and then leveled off with only small declines since that time (Table 3-1).

The data from the Guttmacher study (Jones et al., 1986) indicate that:

- Even though the pregnancy, birth, and abortion rates of white teenagers in the United States are lower than those of black, the rates for whites are substantially higher than overall rates in the other five countries.
- The largest differential between the United States and the other developed countries is between the youngest teenagers, i.e., those below age 15 years, where pregnancy, abortion, and birth rates in the U.S. are relatively high. For example, the birth rate among United States 14-year-old girls, 5/1,000, is four times that of Canada, the country with the next highest rate. As seen in Figure 3-1, birth rates among teens in seven westernized countries increase progressively with age; those in the United States increase more sharply during the early teen years (<17) than in the other countries.
- The rate of elective abortion among teens in the United States is close to, or higher than, the overall teenage pregnancy rate in each of the other countries (see Fig. 21-1, p. 290), and as seen in Figure 3-2, the percentage of American teenagers married and living with their husbands declined markedly between 1968 and 1982 among older teens. The frequency of marriage among

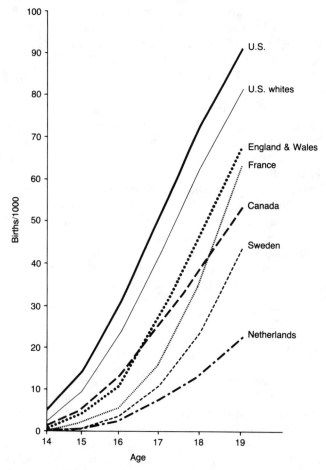

Figure 3-1 Births per 1,000 teenage females, by single year of age, developed countries, 1980. (Reproduced with permission from Jones EF, et al. *Teenage Pregnancy in Industrialized Countries.* Yale University Press, New Haven, CT, 1986, Fig. 2-1, p. 31.)

15- to 17-year-old adolescents, which was much lower initially, declined less markedly.
- Few pregnant and childbearing United States teenagers are married, as compared with those in other developed countries.

The results of the study of Jones et al. indicate little difference in the frequency of sexual experience between American teenagers and those in other westernized countries (Fig. 3-3). They suggest that the differences in the pregnancy and related rates are associated with contraceptive use, particularly the use of oral contraceptives. Contraceptives are more readily available at low cost in the five other countries. Also, in those countries, knowledge about reproduction and contraception is made widely available through the schools and other institutions and by the media. Unintended teenage pregnancy is perceived in these five countries as a problem that can be resolved by practical means rather than as a moral dilemma. This pragmatic approach appears to be more successful in preventing pregnancy than the morally dictated "Just Say No" advocated by many in the United States.

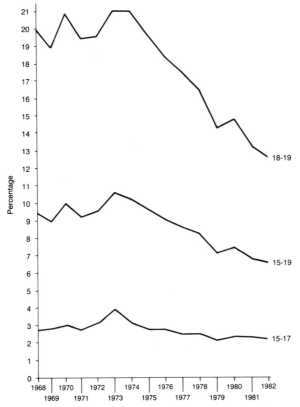

Figure 3-2   Percentage of teenagers, aged 15 to 19 years, married and living with their husbands, 1968 to 1982, United States. (Reproduced with permission from Jones EF, et al. *Teenage Pregnancy in Industrialized Countries*. Yale University Press, New Haven, CT, 1986, Table 3-1, p. 8.)

It is perceived in these other nations that the role of government is more appropriately the prevention of unintended pregnancy and sexually transmitted disease, and the reduction of the need for abortion, than the endorsement of any particular pattern of sexual behavior.

United States: Trends in Teenage Pregnancy

The interpretation of statistical data pertaining to teenage pregnancy and its outcome during the past 15 years is complex, and results can be confusing unless the whole picture is considered. In short, the number of births to teenage women declined by just over 25% between 1972 and 1986 (Table 3-1). However, the likelihood of pregnancy and the number of pregnancies in this age group steadily increased between 1972 and 1982 and was essentially unchanged in 1984 (Hayes, 1987) and in 1986 (National Center for Health Statistics, 1988). These changes were occurring during a period of substantial decline in the number of teenagers in the population, and during a period when adult women were increasing their ability to control unintended conception. Between 1980 and 1984, the number of 15- through 19-year-old persons in the population declined by 11.4% (Bureau of

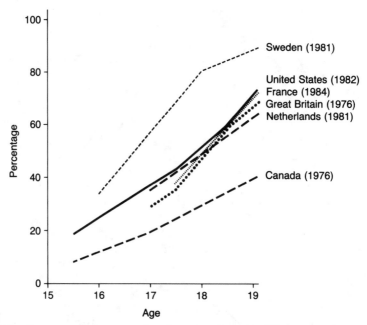

Figure 3-3   Percentage of teenage females reporting sexual intercourse by age, developed countries. (Reproduced with permission from Jones, EF, et al. *Teenage Pregnancy in Industrialized Countries*. Yale University Press, New Haven, CT, 1986, Table 9-4, p. 212.)

the Census, 1988). As a result, the overall pregnancy *rates* in this age group increased from 94/1,000 in 1972 to 110/1,000 in 1982. The rate in 1984 was 109 (Table 3-1). Examination of pregnancy rates among sexually active teenagers, during the period 1972–1984, shows a modest decline, from 272/1,000 in 1972 to 233 in 1984. This decrease, during a period when rates of sexual activity were increasing, is attributed to increased use of contraceptives (Hayes, 1987).

Between 1972 and 1982, the proportion of pregnancies among teenage women that resulted in a live birth decreased from 66.2% to 46.7%. Concomitantly, with the legalization of abortion in 1973, the proportion of pregnancies among teenage women electively terminated by abortion doubled, from 20.1% in 1972 to 40% in 1982. During this same period, the proportion of pregnancies reported to have terminated in a spontaneous abortion or later fetal death decreased slightly from 1.5 to 1.3%. Elective abortion is discussed in Chapter 21.

Births to Teenage Women: Maternal Characterisics

The data presented in this section have been derived from statistical reports prepared by the National Center for Health Statistics. Specific sources are listed for each table.

Proportion of all Births Accounted for by Those to Teenagers

As indicated above, the number of births to teenagers has, in general, declined during the past 15 years. However, those to black 18 and 19 year olds have declined less steeply than those for other ages, and those for the youngest whites have increased slightly.

The proportion of all births accounted for by teenagers has relevance for public health and human service program planning because of the increased need for medical and human services in this age group. This proportion, at any given point in time, reflects an interaction between a number of different factors. It reflects the number of births to young women less than 20 years of age, which has been declining with the decline in numbers of teenagers in the population, even though the number of pregnancies has declined very little. The proportion of all births accounted for by teenagers has declined substantially on a national level since 1972. However, the decline has slowed markedly during the 1980s. The substantial decline in the proportion of all births accounted for by teenagers, from 18.9% in 1972 to 12.6% in 1986, is in large part due to an increase in the total number of births to women of all ages, an increase which to a large extent is accounted for by the increased births among the "baby boom" generation, now in their thirties (Table 3-1). The decline also reflects increased recourse to the option of abortion and the decreasing number of teenagers in the population.

Maternal Age

Table 3-2 shows the distribution of resident births in the United States by age of mother and race or ethnic origin of the child in 1986. It also shows the proportion of babies within each ethnic group whose mothers were below age 20 years. These proportions varied substantially from a low of 1.1% among Asian American babies to 22.8% among African Americans. The proportion among Native Americans was almost as high as that among blacks.

It should also be noted that the numbers and proportions of births to adolescent mothers below age 18 years varied in similar fashion by race. Overall, 38% of births to women below 20 years of age were among adolescent mothers (<18 years).

Differences in the statistics of various subgroups lead one to speculate that the examination of cultural and ethnic differences in the rearing of children and adolescents and/or in the circumstances in which they live might yield insights valuable in preventing premature pregnancy among all American teenagers.

Parity and Repeat Pregnancies

Table 3-3 provides the disturbing information that almost 22% of white and 30% of black teenagers who bore a child in 1986 already had one or more live born children. The data are disturbing because it is difficult for an adolescent with one child to finish high school; the problem is compounded by additional children whether they were born prior to a given birth or followed soon afterward. The likelihood of a rapid recurrence of pregnancy among teenage mothers is well-recognized. Data from the Zelnik and Kantner (1971 through 1979) surveys of metropolitan area teenagers, aged 15 through 19 years, indicated that half of those premaritally pregnant who subsequently married were pregnant again within 24 months. Among white premaritally pregnant teenagers, the likelihood of a subsequent pregnancy increased between 1971 and 1979, whereas among blacks the risk declined. This decline was attributed to contraceptive use (Koenig and Zelnik, 1982).

Table 3-2 Live Births by Age of Mother, Race of Child and Proportion to Young Women 10 to 19 Years of Age, United States, 1986

Age of mother (yr)	All races	White	Black	Native American	Asian or Pacific Islander				
					Chinese	Japanese	Hawaiian	Filipino	Other
All ages	3,756,547	2,970,439	621,221	42,645	18,284	9,654	7,304	22,490	61,540
Under 15	10,176	4,007	5,877	164	—	4	14	20	86
15	25,951	13,505	11,730	419	6	11	43	53	168
16	54,220	32,585	19,884	1,023	18	27	117	114	419
17	88,401	58,830	26,835	1,550	35	52	190	251	607
18	127,794	87,992	35,689	2,207	63	82	336	330	1,008
19	165,539	118,416	41,591	2,836	78	109	424	552	1,429
15–19	461,905	311,328	135,729	8,035	200	281	1,110	1,300	3,631
% 19 yr and below	12.6	10.6	22.8	19.2	1.1	3.0	15.4	5.9	6.0

From Table 28 of the Monthly Vital Statistics Report, Advance Report of Final Natality Statistics, 1986. National Center for Health Statistics, Vol. 37, No. 3 Supplement, July 12, 1988.

Table 3-3   Distribution of Births by Young Mother's Age, Parity, and Race of Child, United States, 1986

Mother's age:	Years		
	<15	*15–19*	*20–24*
White births			
Total	4,007	311,328	853,662
1st Order	3,892	247,384	432,157
2nd order or above	77	62,051	417,254
% 2nd order or above	1.9	19.9	48.9
(Not stated)	0.9	0.6	0.4
Black births			
Total	5,877	135,729	208,882
1st order	5,664	96,696	82,986
2nd order or above	166	38,354	125,076
% 2nd order or above	2.8	28.3	59.9
(Not stated)	0.8	0.5	0.4

From Table 2 of the Monthly Vital Statistics Report, Advance Report of Final Natality Statistics, 1986. National Center for Health Statistics, Vol. 37, No. 3 Supplement, July 12, 1988.

Education

While it must be recognized that some teenagers drop out of school before the onset of pregnancy, or are at greater risk of doing so because of preexisting characteristics, young women who bear a child prior to completing their education are likely to encounter special difficulty. American teenagers who have a child have considerably lower educational attainment at delivery than older women, for example, those 20 through 24 years of age at delivery, as shown in Tables 3-4 and 3-5.

Table 3-4   Live Births by Educational Attainment of Mother, Age of Mother and Race of Child: Total of 47 Reporting States and the District of Columbia, 1986

Age of mother and race of child	Total	*% Distribution of years of school completed by mother*					
		0–8	*9–11*	*12*	*13–15*	*16 or more*	*Not stated*
White							
Under 15	2,696	77.6	18.3	—	—	—	4.0
15	9,405	36.3	60.4	0.7	—	—	2.6
16	23,431	15.9	80.0	2.0	0.1	—	2.1
17	43,012	8.7	74.9	14.4	0.2	—	1.7
18	65,305	6.2	48.9	41.5	1.7	—	1.7
19	88,745	4.6	33.9	52.5	7.4	0.1	1.6
20–24	646,270	3.4	18.4	52.9	19.5	4.4	1.5
Black							
Under 15	5,150	75.2	22.3	—	—	—	2.5
15	10,234	29.9	67.2	0.8	—	—	2.1
16	17,256	10.0	86.1	2.3	—	—	1.6
17	23,199	3.9	77.8	16.6	0.2	—	1.4
18	30,814	2.6	47.1	46.5	2.3	—	1.5
19	35,589	1.9	32.3	55.1	9.1	0.1	1.4
20–24	177,028	1.8	23.2	51.4	19.4	2.6	1.5

From Table 22 of the Monthly Vital Statistics Report, Advance Report of Final Natality Statistics, 1986. National Center for Health Statistics, Vol. 37, No. 3 Supplement, July 12, 1988.

Table 3-5   Proportion of Young Mothers 17 Years and Over, by Age and Race of Child, with Educational Attainment of 12 Years or More at Delivery, 1986

Age of mother	White: 12 or more years			Black: 12 or more years		
	No. with education stated	*number*	*%*	*No. with education stated*	*Number*	*%*
17	43,012	6,272	14.6	23,199	3,899	16.8
18	65,305	28,201	43.2	30,814	15,049	48.8
19	88,745	53,166	59.9	35,589	22,892	64.3
20–24	646,270	496,333	76.8	177,028	130,061	73.5

Calculated from Table 22 of the Monthly Vital Statistics Report, Advance Report of Final Natality Statistics, 1986. National Center for Health Statistics, Vol. 37, No. 3 Supplement, July 12, 1988.

As one would expect, average educational attainment tends to increase with the age of the mother for blacks and whites alike. However, even among white 19-year-old mothers who might be expected to have completed high school (that is, completed 12 or more years of schooling), only 60% had reached that level, and few (7.5%) had progressed beyond; it is similar among blacks. In contrast, among the 20- to 24-year old mothers, 77% of the white and 73% of the black had completed high school or gone beyond. It is of interest that among black teenage mothers at each age, 17 through 19 years, the frequency of high school completion is somewhat higher than for whites, while among mothers aged 20 to 24, whites have a slightly higher frequency of high school completion than blacks (Table 3-5).

Marital Status

Even though, as mentioned above, one in five young American women delivered a baby prior to age 20, relatively few were married, 39% overall in 1986. However, within the teenage group the proportion married decreased sharply as age decreased (Fig. 3-2). There were also marked differences by race. Among white teenage mothers, 52% were married at delivery as compared with only 10% of blacks (National Center for Health Statistics, 1988). The striking reduction in the proportion married at delivery between 1964 to 1966 and 1980 is shown in Table 3-6 and Figure 3-2. This decrease should be of great public concern because of the strong association between single parenthood and living in poverty and the difficulties experienced by women and children living under such adverse conditions (Cherlin, 1989; Edelman, 1987).

Prenatal Care

As indicated in Chapter 2, developmental outcome over the life course depends upon a multiplicity of factors, biological and family/environmental. Biological integrity at birth, as manifested by infant birth weight and Apgar scores, has important implications for the quality of future development. Timely and adequate prenatal care are important in the assessment and management of obstetrical risk to assure optimal outcome (Hobel et al., 1973). A useful index of the adequacy of prenatal

Table 3-6 Numbers of First Births to Teenagers Ages 15 to 19 Years and % Distribution of Marital Status at Conception and Delivery, by Race, for 1980, 1972, and 1964 to 1966 (Averaged), United States

	1980	*1972*	*1964–66*
Number of first births	305,000	294,000	340,000
White			
% Married at:			
Conception	30.5	52.0	50.0
Delivery	63.9	75.5	85.0
Black			
% Married at:			
Conception	4.8	12.1	15.1
Delivery	10.6	20.7	41.9

From Monthly Vital Statistics Report. Trends in marital status of mothers at conception and birth of first child. National Center for Health Statistics, Vol. 36, No. 2 Supplement, May 29, 1987.

care is the trimester of pregnancy during which such care was initiated. The initiation of care during the third trimester of pregnancy or failure to seek care at all are strong indicators of inadequate care. As seen in Table 3-7, the adequacy of care in terms of registration for prenatal care in the first trimester of pregnancy was strongly associated with maternal age and race, increasing in frequency with increasing maternal age for both white and black mothers. The frequency of late or no care decreased quite markedly with increasing age among whites, where 7% of older mothers had inadequate care as compared with 22% of those less than 15 years of age. Among blacks, the frequency of inadequate care also decreased with

Table 3-7 Prenatal Care: Trimester of Onset of Care by Age of Mother and Father and Race of Child, Percent Distribution, United States, 1986

Mother's age (yr)	Total number	Trimester care initiated (% distribution)[a]			
		First	*Second*	*Third*	*None*
White					
<15	4,007	41	43	15	7
15	13,505	47	41	12	5
16	32,585	52	38	10	4
17	58,830	55	36	9	4
18	87,992	58	33	8	3
19	118,416	62	30	7	3
20–24	853,662	75	20	5	2
Black					
<15	5,877	37	48	15	7
15	11,730	42	45	13	6
16	19,884	46	43	11	5
17	26,835	49	41	11	5
18	35,689	51	39	10	5
19	41,591	54	37	10	5
20–24	208,882	62	30	7	4

Calculated from figures in Table 30, Advance Report on Final Natality Statistics, 1986. National Center for Health Statistics, Vol. 37, No.3 Supplement, July 12, 1988.

[a]Percents calculated exclude those not stated and those receiving no care.

increasing age but to a lesser extent. Black women in general had less adequate care than white women.

Low Birth Weight (LBW)

Low birth weight (less than 2,500 g or 5½ pounds), because of its strong association with infant mortality and later developmental problems in surviving children, is an indicator of potentially adverse pregnancy outcome (Butler and Alberman, 1969; Hardy, Drage, et al., 1979; Institute of Medicine, 1985). The frequency of low birth weight among infants of young American women is shown by mothers' age and race of child in Table 3-8. As mothers' age increases, the frequency of low birth weight among infants in all racial groups decreased progressively. White infants at each maternal age had the lowest frequency of low birth weight, while black infants had the highest. The proportion of low birth weight among white infants decreased from 11.2% of those whose mothers were under 15 years to 5.7% of those born to 20 through 24 year olds. Among blacks the proportions were 15.7% and 12.2%, respectively, reflecting the increased risk of low birth weight among black women in general.

Adoption

The option of adoption is one that seems to find little favor among American teenagers who become pregnant, even though adoption agencies have long waiting lists of suitable couples desiring to be adoptive parents. There is, however, little statistical information pertaining to national practices, because no records of adoption have been maintained on a national basis since 1975, when the national adoption reporting system was discontinued. Teenage mothers who place their children for adoption are reported to have more traditional attitudes about family life and adoption and to be more competent students, with higher educational goals, than those who elect to rear their own children (Resnick, 1984).

Table 3-8   Frequency of Low Birth Weight (below 2500 gm) by Age of Mother and Race of Child, United States, 1986

| Age of mother (yr) | Race of child | | | | | |
| | White | | Black | | Other | |
	Number	%	Number	%	Number	%
Under 15	445	11.2	924	15.7	952	15.4
15	1,302	9.7	1,701	14.5	1.766	14.2
16	2,805	8.6	2,709	13.6	2,853	13.2
17	4,837	8.2	3,512	13.1	3,724	12.6
18	6,596	7.5	4,564	12.8	4,883	12.3
19	8,194	6.9	5,344	12.8	5,733	12.2
15–19	23,734	7.6	17,830	13.1	18,959	12.6
20–24	48,993	5.7	25,404	12.2	27,939	11.2

From Monthly Vital Statistics Report, Advance Report on Final Natality Statistics for 1986. National Center for Health Statistics, Vol 37, No. 3 Supplement, Table 15, July 12, 1988.

Fathers of Babies Born to Teenage Mothers

In 1986, 12.6% of all women giving birth were less than 20 years old at delivery. By contrast, only 2.7% of all fathers were teenagers (National Center for Health Statistics, 1988). Sonenstein (1986) reports that according to the National Center for Health Statistics (NCHS) over half of infants born to white teenage mothers and 26% of those born to similar black women had fathers who were aged 20 or above.

In contrast to the abundance of national data available to describe teenage mothers, there is remarkably little pertaining to the fathers of their babies (Elster and Lamb, 1986a; Smollar and Ooms, 1987). Even data compiled from Certificates of Live Birth by NCHS, which provides a relatively large amount of demographic and medical data about the young mothers and newborn infants, are limited in the information provided about the fathers. A further problem reflects missing data. For example, father's age was missing in 32% of birth records from some areas (Sonenstein, 1986). Missing information was particularly common among out-of-wedlock births.

Another source of national data is that collected in the National Longitudinal Surveys of Labor Market Experience of Youth (NLSY) initiated by the United States Department of Labor in 1966 for men aged 14 through 24 and in 1968 for young women of similar age (National Longitudinal Survey of Youth, 1966). Cohorts of approximately 5,200 respondents of each sex, representing a multistage national probability sample, were enrolled. A broad range of demographic and experiential information has been collected on an annual basis through 1988. Data pertaining to the family situation of these young people and to their fertility were also included. In 1982, 2% of 18-year-old males and 4% of those age 19 reported being a father for the first time (Mott, 1983). Birth rates for the teenage women in the sample were much higher; 9.5% of 18 year olds and 15.5% of those age 19 reported a first birth. Mott, in 1982, reports that there are discrepencies between these frequencies of fatherhood and later reports from the same sample, and it is suggested that males report pregnancy history less reliably than the young women involved. The fact that many fathers of babies born to teenage mothers are 20 and above at the birth of their child also plays a role. It should be noted that there is even less information about the male partners of the large proportion of young women terminating their pregnancies by abortion.

Marsiglio (1987) used NLSY data to describe the living arrangements, marital status, and education of teenage fathers in the United States. He found that 50% lived with their first-born child during the first few months after birth. Only one-third of those responsible for a nonmarital conception were married within 12 months of conception. Educational attainment was less than for nonfathers of similar age. Card and Wise (1978), using the very large national data base developed in Project Talent, also showed that young men who became fathers as teenagers were at educational and occupational disadvantage in later life as compared with their peers who delayed childbearing.

The paucity of data pertaining to the fathers of babies born to older teenagers and adolescents reflects the relative inaccessability of these young men. Many of the teenage fathers are school dropouts and/or unemployed. They do not usually come to the attention of those providing medical care for the mothers. From the studies of pregnancy among Baltimore's urban teenagers described in the succeeding chapters, even the older fathers involved in a teenage pregnancy appear to be at considerable disadvantage as compared with those men whose parental partners are women aged 20 and above.

Children Born to Teenage Women

With the exception of information about neonatal status, there are even fewer national data describing the outcome for the children of teenage mothers than there are for the fathers. This aspect of the problem will be discussed when the children of urban adolescents are described in Chapter 7 and in terms of the long-term consequences of adolescent pregnancy in Chapter 9.

Costs

The costs of teenage pregnancy and childbearing are undoubtedly very large; exactly how large is unclear. The estimation of costs is made difficult by the complexities of the antecedents and consequences of these events and the association of teenage childbearing with poverty and social disadvantage.

Overall estimates of cost are further complicated by the need for their definition in both human and financial terms and in terms of opportunity cost related to unrealized human capital formation (i.e., by the development of competent, self-sustaining adults who contribute to the economy and raise competent children). Further complexities result because the adverse effects of teenage childbearing tend to be of long duration, affecting not only the parents and children born during the mother's teenage years but also her subsequent children. The human toll of premature, unintended, and often unwanted childbearing may be compounded by maternal depression, family instability, lack of resources, and the early recurrence of unintended pregnancy and childbearing.

The financial costs can be divided into those incurred as public sector expenditures for services and research and those costs that are underwritten by the private sector. Private sector costs may, in turn, be subdivided into those underwritten by: 1) voluntary agencies such as hospitals, community agencies, and church groups for health and human services; 2) foundations for the provision of service and for research; 3) financial assistance and physical and emotional support provided by family members; 4) opportunity costs to society as mentioned above.

Moore and Burt (1982), in a volume entitled "Private Crisis, Public Costs: Policy Perspectives on Teenage Childbearing," provide insight to the issues involved in estimating costs of childbearing by teenagers. Burt and Levy (1987) provide a comprehensive review of studies concerned with costs. They describe some of the issues involved and the assumptions and methodologies used in estimating costs. They make clear the difference between single year costs and cohort costs. For example, the single year estimate of public costs in 1975 was $8.6 billion for those families assisted by Aid to Families with Dependent Children (AFDC), in which the mother had her first birth as a teenager. These costs included financial support, Medicaid, and food stamps. Such mothers accounted for 56% of all mothers receiving AFDC in 1975, indicating that the welfare caseload is disproportionately made up of teenage mothers. According to Moore (1978), households that had their beginning in a teenage birth have a 1-in-4 probability of being AFDC dependent, whereas those where the first birth occurred at age 20 or beyond have a 1-in-10 likelihood of requiring AFDC support.

Cohort costs are estimated using as a population base all teenagers having a first baby during a given year. The costs incurred are projected over a period of time, usually 20 years, by which time the child is grown and should be independent. Because not all teenage mothers qualify for public support, the costs of those families that do receive it are diluted by being part of the whole cohort. Thus, the costs appear to be somewhat less than those estimated by the single year method. For example, for the estimated 442,000 first births to teenagers in 1979, workers at SRI International estimated an average public cost of $18,710, extending over a 20-year period. The average cost increased somewhat as the age of the mother declined. It cannot be assumed that, when mothers overcome disadvantage in the long term, these costs disappear.

Burt and Levy (1987) offer more current estimates of cost that reflect changes in several dimensions, i.e., a substantial reduction in the number of births to teenagers and inflationary pressures on costs, and more stringent eligibility requirements for AFDC since 1981 (in an effort to curb Welfare expenditures). The change in eligibility requirements is thought to be in large part responsible for the reduction of estimated cost. Three different estimates are provided: 1) the single year public cost attributable to teenage childbearing in 1985; 2) the single birth public cost of a family having its origin in a single first birth to a teenager in 1985, projected over 20 years from 1985 through 2004; and 3) the single cohort public cost of all families begun by first births to teenagers in 1985, projected over 20 years from 1985 through 2004. Estimates are in 1985 dollars, discounted by 4% (the difference between inflation at 3% per year, and the potential for earned interest of 7% per year, if the 1985 cost had been invested).

1. The *single year public cost* of teenage childbearing was estimated to be *$16.65 billion* (including administrative costs) in 1985. These are *minimal* costs as costs were limited to AFDC, Medicaid, and food stamps. Costs that were not generally available, for example, those for other social services, protective services, and foster care, special education, and housing were excluded.
2. The single birth, full average cost for the 371,131 first births to teenagers in 1985 was estimated at $13,902.
3. The 20-year single cohort cost was estimated to be $5.16 billion.

These investigators also estimated that the 14-year-old mother who received welfare continuously for 10 years would represent a public cost of $46,456 over the 10-year period; the 15 through 17-year-old mother receiving welfare over a period of 7.5 years would have an average public cost of $44,201, and an 18- to 19-year-old mother, with an assumed welfare dependency, would have a public cost of $30,955, on average. These costs, while considerably higher than the estimates projected over 20 years by investigators at the Stanford Research Institute (1979), are in the same direction, i.e., lower costs for older teenage mothers. These estimates, like those of Burt and Levy, point to the importance of the cost savings realized with each year during which teenage childbearing is delayed.

Maryland ranks fourth among states with respect to high rates of teenage pregnancy and childbearing, in large part a result of the exceptionally high rates of these events in Baltimore City. In 1985, teenage births in Maryland numbered

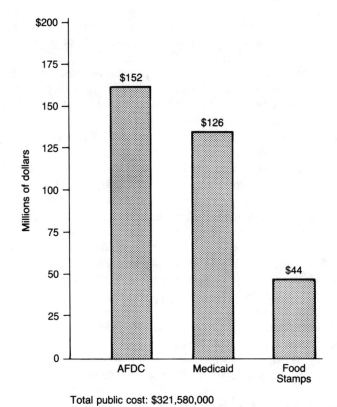

Total public cost: $321,580,000

Figure 3-4   Estimated public costs (in millions of dollars) of teenage childbearing in Maryland, in 1985, for Aid to Families with Dependent Children (AFDC), Medicaid, and food stamps. (Reproduced with permission from Governor's Council on Adolescent Pregnancy: *Fact Sheet*, January/February, 1989.)

8,143; almost one-third (2,921) were among residents of Baltimore. The costs in Maryland for AFDC, Medicaid, and food stamps are shown in Figure 4-4. The total cost of $321.6 million for 1985 is an underestimate because it does not include costs for special education, repeating a grade, subsidized day care, and other human services utilized by the teenage mothers and their children.

Summary

Among teenagers, immediate pregnancy outcome is related to both maternal age and race. In general, the younger the mother the higher is her obstetrical risk and the greater is the likelihood that she will have a later onset of prenatal care or none at all. Black teenagers are at even higher risk than white ones. They have, in general, an earlier onset of sexual intercourse and a greater likelihood of being sexually active at a given age than white girls.

Recourse to the option of abortion has had a major impact in reducing the number of births to teenagers. In fact, should the option of legal abortion be made unavailable, the potential exists for the number of such births to almost double—with a commensurate increase in adverse consequences related to teenage childbirth and its public costs.

Teenage childbearing is enormously costly to society. The costs cited above are minimal, because they do not include those for many social, health, and educational services provided to teen mothers and their children. In considering the estimates provided, it must be remembered that they are based on national figures. Because poverty is associated with higher rates of childbearing among teenagers, particularly among adolescents in families with less ability to provide support, higher adolescent pregnancy rates are associated with a greater need for public services. Costs at the regional and local levels may, therefore, differ considerably, depending on the ability of the individual families in the community to care for their own children and grandchildren.

Part II

The Urban Context

We turn now to an exploration of pregnancy among urban adolescents. We present epidemiological and ecological information that addresses three sets of questions: 1) Does the immediate pregnancy outcome among adolescents differ from that among older teenagers and older women? 2) What are the characteristics of adolescents who become pregnant and bear children? and 3) What are the antecedents, concomitants, and consequences of these events for the young mothers, their partners, and their infants?

Information pertaining to the adverse consequences (Alan Guttmacher Institute, 1976 and 1981; Baldwin and Cain, 1980; Card and Wise, 1978; Furstenberg, 1976; Hardy et al., 1978; Hayes, 1987) and societal costs of pregnancy among teenagers is plentiful (Burt, 1986; Maryland Governor's Council on Adolescent Pregnancy, 1989; Moore and Burt, 1982; Stanford Research Institute, 1979). However, the detailed, age-specific, population-based data required for the planning of effective intervention for both management and preventive purposes are generally not available. National statistics, for the most part, are presented as grouped data, combining 15- through 19-year-old teenagers, even though personal and developmental characteristics differ greatly by age in this group and those under 15 cannot be ignored. Furthermore, as a result of combining high- and low-risk groups, these statistics tend to understate the problems found in populations at high risk for pregnancy.

To understand the dimensions of the problems surrounding adolescent pregnancy and childbearing in a high-risk urban setting it is necessary to view them in the perspective of two separate frames of reference. First, how do the dimensions of the urban problem compare with those revealed by national statistics? Second, how do the problems of pregnancy and childbearing among adolescents ($\leq$17 years) differ from those of older teenagers, age 18 and 19, in the same population? Only when the dimensions of a problem are defined in some detail can effective intervention for management and prevention be devised and implemented.

In Chapter 3 of Part I, a brief overview of teenage pregnancy is presented from a national perspective. In Chapter 4, the frame of reference is narrowed to pregnancy and its resolution among urban teenagers, by specific year of maternal age. Chapters 5 through 9 are concerned with aspects of the problem among adolescents in an urban environment.

In this introduction, a brief description of Baltimore is followed by a description of the methods used in the extensive studies conducted to assess the outcome of teenage pregnancy as compared with that of older women and the characteristics of pregnant and childbearing adolescents, the fathers of their babies, the babies themselves, and the resources used by the adolescent mothers and their children (Chapters 5 through 8). This work was carried out in collaboration with Dr. Anne Duggan and was supported, in part, by a grant from the Office of Adolescent Pregnancy Programs (Hardy et al., 1986). The final chapter in this section, Chapter 9, provides a brief description of the long-range outcomes for adolescent mothers and their children as compared with those of similar mothers, aged 20 through 24 years, and their children, followed in the Johns Hopkins Collaborative Perinatal Study for 12 years after birth (Hardy et al., 1978).

Baltimore: The Ecological Setting

Baltimore, an old, industrial city, with a population of 786,775 (Census, 1980) in 1980, ranked among the 20 largest cities in the United States. It was the poorest of these cities, with the highest rates of single parent families and teenage pregnancy and childbearing and the highest proportion of all births to teenage mothers among U.S. cities with populations in excess of 500,000 (Children's Defense Fund, 1985). Extensive and well established health and human services have existed for many years. Special services for pregnant adolescents have been available since the early 1960s, when Sinai Hospital had one of the first obstetrical programs in the country targeted to adolescents. Comprehensive adolescent pregnancy programs have been evolving at two universities and one community hospital since the mid-1970s. A special school for pregnant girls, the Paquin School (originally The Poe School), has been part of the city school system for 25 years, and other special programs exist in the City Departments of Education, Health and Human Services. Numerous other public and private agency services have provided services for adolescents and older teenagers (Hardy et al., 1986) and the Mayor now has an Advisory Committee on adolescent pregnancy prevention.

Despite this awareness, interest, and concern, the pregnancy rate among Baltimore's 14 through 17-year-olds was 98.8 per 1,000 in 1983, a substantial increase over that of 93/1,000 in 1980. Rates increased for both black and white teenagers: 113/1,000 in 1983 as compared with 107/1,000 in 1980 for blacks, and 63.6 up from 60.9 in 1980 for whites. While birth rates for older teenagers had been declining during the prior 5 years, those for adolescents increased and have continued to increase. In 1987, there were 3,160 births to Baltimore teenagers (Maryland Governor's Council, 1989), the highest number since 4,542 in 1970, despite a continuing decline in the number of teenagers in the population (Vital Statistics, Baltimore, 1985).

Baltimore experienced population growth with immigration from the South and West during World War II, as the need for industrial workers intensified. Since the end of the war, there has been a steady decline in population as many more affluent families took advantage of the amenities of suburban living. To an extent, light industry and service operations have followed, and activity in the heavy industrial sector has steadily declined. As a result of these changes, Baltimore has become poorer and, like many large American cities, has a dense, poor minority population living in the central city. In 1980, the minority population, of which blacks make up 98%, accounted for more than half (56%) of all residents. Most inner city areas are predominantly black. Unemployment rates are very high, particularly among blacks of 15 through 24 years of age, among whom 50% of the males and 58% of the females are without jobs. There is a high proportion of female-headed, single parent families. In 1983, over 60% of all births (Maryland Department of Health and Mental Hygiene) were to single mothers; in 1986, the proportion was 64.4% (Baltimore City Preliminary Vital Statistics Report, 1986).

Housing in the inner city is a mix of large subsidized public housing projects, many of which are high-rise and high crime, and decaying single family houses, apartments, and tenements in close proximity to heavily traveled streets. A high prevalence of lead intoxication among the children results from exposure to lead paint in the old houses and from automobile emissions. As there is little open space, children play on the sidewalks and in the streets. Shopping facilities are limited and relatively expensive, as is public transportation. A substantial proportion of inner city households live below the poverty level, and many are eligible for public assistance.

Educational opportunities in the inner city are generally substandard. Many of the schools are old and dreary with little outdoor play space. Books and educational materials are often in short supply, and security problems necessitate keeping the schools locked. There are a few after school activities; even those that a school would like to offer are hampered because poor transportation makes it necessary for most students to leave with the school buses at the end of the academic day. Many inner city children perform academically well below national norms. Absenteeism and truancy are rife, and only about 50% of those entering high school graduate. As patterns of family structure have changed, many school-aged children of single, working mothers are now "latch key children," on their own, without supervision after school.

Another significant change in the past decade has been the increasing levels of alcoholism and illicit substance abuse in the population and the increasing violence that has accompanied these changes. These have made life even more difficult and dangerous for children and adolescents growing up in the inner city. High rates of sexually transmitted disease, including acquired immune deficiency syndrome (AIDS) and HIV infection, have added to the problems, the misery, and the anxiety of inner city living.

Changes in the characteristics of the city and its population have affected the inner city also. There has been a substantial decline in births among older inner city residents during the past 25 years. Families are smaller, and the extended family group, while still present among blacks, is less prevalent. With the steady decline in births, the number of teenagers in the population is substantially less than it was 15 years ago. Nonetheless, because of the short interval between generations and higher than average death rates among inner city residents, the population of the inner city is still predominantly young. The better educated, more affluent, and generally more self-sufficient members of the population, both white and black, tend to be distributed peripherally in the city, where the ambience and quality of life are better. In these areas, social disadvantage is less, as are rates of teenage pregnancy and childbearing. This impression led to detailed investigations of the geographical distribution of pregnancy, abortion, and childbirth among Baltimore adolescents whose pregnancies terminated prior to age 18 years (A.K. Duggan and J.B. Hardy, unpublished data, 1990).

Geographical Distribution Within
Baltimore of Births and Abortions Among Adolescents

Understanding the geographical distribution of births and abortions among adolescents helps to illuminate the causes of these phenomena and aids in the development and targeting of interventions. Two lines of investigation were pursued.

The first step involved plotting the actual births, separately by race, among
mothers (< 18 years) terminating in 1983, by the census tract of residence of the
mother. As seen in Figure II-1, black adolescent births tended to be concentrated
in the four most poverty-stricken areas in the city, with some dispersion in more
peripheral areas. Although among whites (Fig. II-2) the number of births was much
less, and the concentration, therefore, less intense, a somewhat similar pattern,
with concentration in poor census tracts, is also seen. In the most affluent census
tracts in the northern parts of the city, there were few, if any, births. When, in
the second step, elective abortions among adolescents were examined, the pattern
was different. In Figure II-3, which shows the geographical distribution for blacks
and whites combined, abortions are noted to have been more widely distributed
than births throughout the city. However, as with pregnancies, there were fewer
in the more affluent northern areas. The distribution pattern of adolescent births
is essentially the same as those of infant mortality, homicide, and violent death
among youth, violent crime, and illicit drug use, all problems of high prevalence
in poor and socially disadvantaged areas.

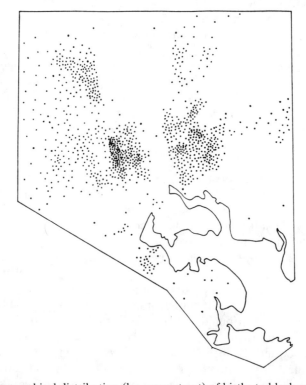

Figure II-1   Geographical distribution (by census tract) of births to black adolescents, aged
17 or below at delivery, in Baltimore in 1983. Each dot represents one birth.

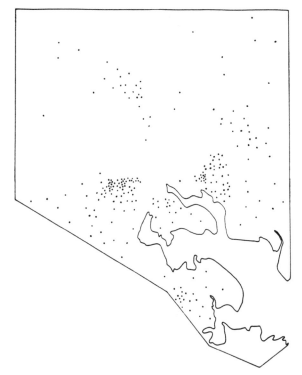

Figure II-2 Geographical distribution (by census tract) of births to white adolescents, aged 17 or below at delivery, in Baltimore in 1983. Each dot represents one birth.

These findings suggested a relationship between poverty and social disadvantage and an increased risk of adolescent pregnancy and childbearing. This hypothesis was explored in a study of pregnancies among Baltimore adolescents (age 15 through 17) terminating in the 5-year period of 1980 through 1984. Work in progress suggests positive relationships between six indices of poverty within the census tract of residence and adolescent pregnancy and childbirth rates among whites. The relationships are less strong for blacks. Abortion rates were not related to indices of poverty, and the likelihood of abortion as a pregnancy option increased as the affluence of the census tract increased. Not only was pregnancy less likely in the more affluent areas, but also when it occurred it was more likely to be terminated by abortion (A.K. Duggan and J.B. Hardy, unpublished data, 1990). Maryland does provide free abortion services for poor women but only under very restricted circumstances (to save the mother's life, in cases of rape and incest promptly reported, and when the fetus is malformed). Abortions under other circumstances must be paid for by the recipient, even if poor, or by her family. This is an impenetrable barrier for some women bearing an unintended and unwanted pregnancy. As seen in the chapters that follow, very large proportions of adolescents were dependent on Medicaid funding to defray the costs of other aspects of their health care.

Population Differences

As described below, most analyses were conducted separately for black and white adolescents as well as for the total group. Similarities as well as some significant

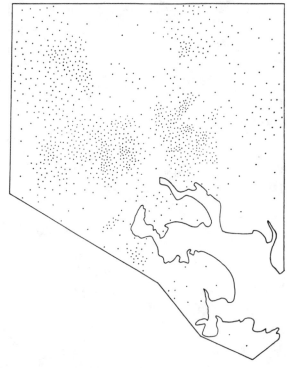

Figure II-3 Geographical distribution of elective abortions among black and white adolescents, aged 17 or below, in Baltimore in 1983. Each dot represents one case.

and surprising differences between racial groups were observed. Childbearing adolescents in each group were generally poor and socially disadvantaged, but, contrary to the generally expected stereotype, the young white mothers were on average at greater disadvantage than those who were black. They had significantly less educational attainment, and their own health status and that of their children were less favorable than those of black adolescent mothers.

Methods

Let us turn now to a brief description of the methods used in the studies reported in Chapters 4 through 8. These investigations were part of the Resource Use Study of which Dr. Anne Duggan was Project Director (Hardy et al., 1986).

Sources of Information

Sources of data included: 1) the Certificates of Live Birth and abortion records for Baltimore residents in 1983 (specific names and addresses were excluded from the abortion data); 2) interview data which is described briefly below; and 3) interviews with adolescents enrolled in the Johns Hopkins Adolescent Pregnancy and Pregnancy Prevention Programs, which provided data pertaining to the number of sexual partners and frequency of intercourse in this age group.

Study Population: The Resource Use Study

The Resource Use Study, as indicated above, made use of 1983 birth certificates for Baltimore adolescents both as a source of data and as the basis for selection of the study population. A stratified random sample of all births to adolescents below 18 years at delivery was selected. The selection process was based on the age/race distributions of births in 1981. A disproportionate, stratified random sampling technique was used in order to have a sufficient number of cases in each age/ race subgroup for valid analytical results. The strata were defined by race (white, black), mother's age at delivery ($\leq$ 14, 15, 16, and 17 years), and parity (i.e., whether or not the adolescent had borne one or more prior living child). In some cells where numbers were small, for example, whites with prior children, all available subjects were included. In others, where numbers were relatively large, for example, blacks aged 17 with no prior children, only one case in five was selected. Selections were made at monthly intervals until all adolescent births in 1983 had been reviewed. Once a subject was selected, a letter was sent to her by restricted delivery, certified mail. This letter described the proposed study and solicited her participation. A card that she could send back indicating her refusal to participate was enclosed with the letter. In the event of refusal, further contact by the study staff was prohibited by the City's Legal Department. Of the 525 subjects selected, 389 (74%) were interviewed at 3 months after delivery and 366 (95%) of these were interviewed again at 15 to 18 months ($\overline{X}17.6$). The major reasons for nonresponse were return of the card indicating refusal to participate (11% of the 525 selected), refusal of informed consent at the time of the interview (5%), inability to locate the adolescent using the address on the birth certificate (5%), and change in residence to beyond the city limits (5%).

Representativeness of the Sample

The representativeness of the study sample was assessed by comparison between respondents and nonrespondents plus those not selected for study, using the following data from 1983 birth certificates: trimester of registration for prenatal care; method of delivery; presence/absence of complications of pregnancy; gestational age of fetus at delivery, over 36 completed weeks versus 36 weeks and below; infant birth weight, 2,500 g and above versus less than 2,500 g; Apgar scores at one and five minutes of 7 and above versus 6 and below; and Medicaid status. Comparisons using Chi-square determinations were made within each age/race/ parity stratum. As no differences significant at $p = .05$ were identified, the sample was considered representative of Baltimore births in this age group.

Sources of Data

As indicated, certain demographic characteristics of both parents, the census tract in which they lived, the mother's obstetrical history, and the infant's neonatal course were available from the birth records. An assessment of the adequacy of information from birth records is provided in Chapter 4, see Appendix Tables 4-1 to 4-3.

The major source of information was the mother, visited at her home, by a trained interviewer at three months after delivery (interview I) and again approximately one year later when the child was 15 to 18 months old (interview II). In all, 389 mothers were interviewed at 3 months and 363 at $\overline{X}17.6$ months after delivery. The data collected pertained to the characteristics of the adolescents and their families, the fathers of the babies, and the infants. In addition, considerable information was collected with respect to the utilization of private and public resources, for health care, social and financial support, and education by the adolescents and their infants. The purpose underlying the collection of these data was to describe the characteristics of adolescents who bore children and to evaluate the effect of utilization of certain resources upon the outcome of adolescent pregnancy. The evaluation of resource use has not yet been completed, and only limited data from this part of the study are reported here. Other important sources of information included review of human service records in the Maryland State and Baltimore City Departments of Human Resources and information available from the 1980 Census and interim estimates available from various sources.

Quality and Completeness of Data

The quality and completeness of the data were examined. Data from birth certificates in Baltimore appear remarkably complete, with little or no missing data pertaining to mother's race, age, and marital status. Father's age was missing for 5% of whites and 3% of blacks, in marked contrast to the high frequency of missing data for this item available in National Statistics (Sonenstein, 1986). However, data pertaining to pregnancy complications seem less reliable, and those for infant congenital malformations are virtually useless because of variability of reporting by hospitals (see Chapter 4, Appendix Tables 4-1 to 4-3) and difficulty of diagnosis in the neonatal period (Hardy, Drage, et al., 1979).

Table II-1 Interviewer Assessment of Selected Respondent Characteristics at First and Second Interview

	Interview I (N = 389) (%)	Interview II (N = 363) (%)
Respondent's level of intelligence:		
Well above average	2	4
Above average	14	20
Average	70	62
Below average	13	13
Well below average	1	1
Respondent's understanding of the interview:		
No difficulty	66	72
Just a little	19	17
A fair amount	13	9
Much difficulty	3	1
Respondent's cooperativeness:		
Very cooperative	87	88
Fairly cooperative	11	8
Not too cooperative	2	3
Openly hostile	0[a]	0[a]

From Hardy, JB, Flagle, CD, and Duggan, AK. Resource Use by Pregnant and Parenting Adolescents. Final Report to the Office of Adolescent Pregnancy Programs, Grant No. APR 000906-03-0, June 1986.

[a]One case = 0.3%.

Data from the interviews were complete except for some items pertaining to the father, when his whereabouts were unknown to the mother. Footnotes to the tables account for missing data. The reliability of the interview data was assessed by a follow-up telephone interview with a 10% random sample of the respondents. The data were found to be reliable. In our experience, inner city adolescents, when treated with kindness and respect, are remarkably frank and forthcoming with information about themselves and their families.

Finally, the interviewer was required to make an assessment of the adolescent mother's level of intelligence, understanding, and cooperativeness during the interviews. The results are shown in the accompanying tables. Cooperation and understanding were generally satisfactory (Table II-1).

Analysis

Descriptive and comparative analytic techniques were used to describe pregnancy outcome, profile the characteristics of the adolescents, and determine the significance of differences between groups; frequency distributions, ranges, means and SDs were employed for descriptive analysis and Chi-square determinations, *t*-tests, and one-way ANOVA for purposes of comparison.

Table II-2 Comparision of Results Using Unweighted and Weighted Values for Key Variables

	Unweighted		Weighted	
	n	*(%)*	*n*	*(%)*
Low birth weight (<2,500 g)	52	(13.4)	58	(14.0)
Cesarean section	56	(14.4)	60	(15.3)
Baby's number hospital day at birth:				
2	111	(28.9)	110	(28.5)
3	149	(38.8)	150	(39.0)
4	29	(7.6)	28	(7.2)
5	24	(6.3)	25	(6.4)
6	15	(3.9)	14	(3.6)
7	20	(5.2)	20	(5.2)
8–13	13	(3.4)	13	(3.3)
14–21	8	(2.1)	10	(2.6)
22–30	6	(1.6)	7	(1.9)
31+	9	(2.3)	11	(2.8)
Mother:				
Hospitalized since 1983 birth	65	(16.2)	65	(18.3)
Repeat pregnancy within 12 months	79	(22.1)	79	(22.1)
Still in school or graduated[a] at Interview II	158	(44.3)	166	(46.5)
On Welfare at Interview I	257	(66.4)	262	(67.5)
Baby:				
Used emergency room	253	(69.7)	252	(69.4)
Trauma requiring OPD care	67	(18.5)	66	(18.1)
Has not had 3 DPT's by Interview II	74	(23.1)	73	(22.7)
Hospitalized	71	(19.6)	66	(18.2)

Adapted from Hardy, JB, Flagle, CD, and Duggan, AK. Resource Use by Pregnancy and Parenting Adolescents. Final Report to the Office of Adolescent Pregnancy Programs, Grant No. APR 000906-03-0, June 1986.

[a]From high school or GED program.

Because disproportionate sampling was used to compensate for small numbers of subjects in some cells, stratum-specific weights were applied to adjust for these manipulations in the analyses, and to achieve a sample distribution that was representative of the original population, in terms of those variables that defined the strata (i.e., maternal race, age at delivery, and presence/absence of prior living children). While these manipulations were necessary to meet the conditions of the study, in fact, the weights made little difference to the distribution of most outcome variables as may be seen in the accompanying table (Table II-2).

4

Teenage Pregnancy
The Baltimore Scene

The data in this chapter and in Chapters 5 through 8 were developed in collaboration with Dr. Anne K. Duggan as part of the study of "Resource Use by Pregnant and Parenting Adolescents" (Hardy et al., 1986). Those presented in this chapter are used to establish a frame of reference for the more detailed discussions of adolescent pregnancy, childbearing, and abortion that follow in succeeding chapters. To this end, immediate pregnancy outcome was examined, by specific age and race, for all teenagers resident in the City of Baltimore whose pregnancies terminated in 1983 and compared with the outcomes of older women, aged 20 years or above, who delivered during the same period.

In 1983, 13,134 births were recorded for women resident in Baltimore City. This was the largest number in any year since 1972. The number has increased from its low point of 10,956 in 1976. The increase has been primarily among births to older women. Births to teenagers have declined in number, reflecting a sharp decline in the number of adolescents in the population. However, the proportion of all births accounted for by teenagers has declined much less, and the likelihood or risk of pregnancy and giving birth has increased among the youngest adolescents, as reflected by increased pregnancy and birth rates per 1,000 adolescent females. By 1987, the number of births to young women (10 to 19) had increased slightly to 3,109 from 2,992 in 1983 (Maryland Governor's Council on Adolescent Pregnancy, 1989). The population of Baltimore City was 44% white, 54% black, and 2% other races. In the analyses that follow, all nonwhites were considered to be black.

Methods

Data were available on computer tape pertaining to all residents, recorded live births, spontaneous fetal deaths, and elective abortions in Baltimore City in 1983, except for specific names and addresses. Data pertaining to births were derived from the Certificates of Live Birth and Fetal Death and were provided by the Baltimore City Health Department. Maternal age was computed using birth date and date of delivery. Data for abortions were from aggregate data from reports to the Maryland Center for Health Statistics. Abortion reports provide little demographic information beyond age, race, and census tract of residence. No information about the male partner is available. The data were examined by age for whites and blacks separately. Because of relatively small numbers of births to younger teenagers, maternal ages 15 years and below have been combined. Because of little difference in maternal characteristics, ages 18 and 19 have been grouped; the comparison group consists of all older women aged 20 years and above.

Validity of Data from Birth Records

The usefulness and validity of national data from birth certificates have been called into question because of large amounts of missing data, particularly where the mother is a teenager or belongs to a minority group (Sonenstein, 1986). Therefore, an assessment was made of missing data for Baltimore City in 1983 by maternal age, race, and hospital of delivery. The results are shown in detail in Appendix Tables 4-1 to 4-3 in the appendix to this chapter and are discussed briefly below.

In Baltimore, birth certificates have been closely monitored for some 40 years, and very little demographic data were found to be missing. For some hospitals, few data of any type were missing. However, for others, there were large proportions of missing values for certain variables, such as complications of pregnancy and fetal malformations. Another source of possible bias is the differences in distribution by race and maternal age between hospitals, with some delivering considerably higher proportions of the black and the young than others. These problems notwithstanding, the data for teenagers, in general, appear reliable, as the majority were delivered in hospitals providing relatively complete data.

Age of mother was available for all births with the exception of one white woman. The age of father was missing on 3% of all black and 5% of all white births. Fathers' education was missing in 14% of black and 10% of white births. Missing data were minimally more frequent among births to teenagers than to older women.

Results

Pregnancy Outcome

The numbers and outcome of pregnancies among white and black women are shown, by age, in Table 4-1. Of the 19,023 pregnancies recorded, 74% were among blacks, reflecting both their larger representation in the population and their greater fertility. A total of 5,234 pregnancies were recorded among teenage women, 27.5% of all pregnancies. Teenage mothers accounted for 26% of all births, as compared with a national average of 14% (National Center For Vital Statistics, 1985). In an additional 2% of Baltimore births, the mother was older but the father was a teenager.

Among teenage pregnancies in Baltimore, the frequency of elective abortion was inversely proportional to age; 38% of older women and 42% of teenagers had abortions. Among teens, 46% of adolescents below 18 years and 61% of black and 78% of whites below age 15 had abortions. Spontaneous fetal deaths, over 20 weeks gestation, accounted for only a small proportion of all pregnancy outcomes.

In considering the overall frequency of teenage pregnancy, the underreporting of elective abortion and spontaneous fetal deaths below 20 weeks gestation must be accounted for. It has been estimated (Tietze and Bongaarts, 1985) that these

Table 4-1 Number of Resident Recorded Live Births, Reported Fetal Deaths, and Reported Induced Abortions by Age and Race, Baltimore, 1983

	Total	20 or over	Under 20	Under 18	Under 15	15	16	17	18/19 yr
All races	19,023								
Total		13,789	5,234	2,438	291	443	716	988	2796
Live births		8,378	2,992	1,312	107	195	400	610	1680
Fetal deaths[a]		90	31	18	2	3	2	11	13
Induced abortions[b]		5,321	2,211	1,108	182	245	314	367	1103
Black	13,997								
Total[b]		9,825	4,172	2,001	268	375	574	784	2171
Live births		5,852	2,402	1,071	102	161	326	482	1331
Fetal deaths[a]		77	29	17	2	3	1	11	12
Induced abortions		3,896	1,741	913	164	211	247	291	828
White	4,913								
Total		3,890	1,023	418	19	69	136	196	605
Live births		2,526	590	241	5	34	74	128	349
Fetal deaths[a]		13	2	1	0	0	1	0	1
Induced abortions		1,351	431	176	14	33	61	68	255

From computer tape of Vital Statistics for Baltimore, Maryland, 1983.

[a]Limited to fetal deaths of 20 weeks or longer gestation.

[b]Includes 113 induced abortions with missing data on race.

early fetal deaths equal 20% of live births and 10% of abortions. Thus, there may have been 6,050 teenage pregnancies rather than 5,234 in Baltimore in 1983.

Tables 4-2 and 4-3 present data pertaining to the prevalence of abortion among Baltimore teenagers by age and race and by age and duration of pregnancy at the time the procedure was carried out. The points that stand out concern the young age of some of the girls and the relatively large numbers of abortions performed after the first trimester of pregnancy, a not surprising observation in view of the well recognized tendency among teenagers to delay seeking pregnancy care. However, less than 10% were carried out after 16 weeks gestation and very few (0.3%) after 20 weeks.

Age and Race of Parents of Liveborn Infants

Certificates of Live Birth were used to examine the age and race of parents having a baby in 1983. As shown in Table 4-4, within each race, parental age was divided

Table 4-2 Reported Induced Abortions among Baltimore Teenagers in 1983 by Age and Race

Age (yr)	Total no.	White	Black	Other or unknown
12	7	0	6	1
13	51	3	46	2
14	124	11	112	1
15	245	33	210	2
16	314	61	243	10
17	367	68	289	10
18	543	123	403	17
19	560	132	416	12
≤ 19	2211	431	1725	55
Percent:	100	19.5	78.0	2.5

Data kindly provided by J. Saladini, Baltimore City Health Department, 1986.

Table 4-3 Reported Induced Abortions, Baltimore Teenagers, 1983, by Age and Duration of Pregnacy at Termination

Age (yr)	Total no.	Gestation (wk)				
		<8	9–12	13–16	17–20	>21
12	7	1	2	1	3	0
13	51	12	22	9	8	0
14	124	37	58	14	15	0
15	245	75	110	29	29	2
16	314	100	147	34	31	2
17	367	114	176	35	40	2
18	543	179	273	44	46	1
19	560	117	301	44	38	0
≤ 19	2211	695	1089	210	210	7
Percent:	100	31.4	49.3	9.6	9.6	0.3

Data kindly provided by J. Saladini, Baltimore City Health Department, 1986.

into four categories. In 12% of all births both parents were teenagers; in 14% the mother was a teenager, but the father was older, and in 2% the father was a teenager but the mother was older. In 72% both parents were 20 years or above (69% of the black and 80% of the white). Thus, 28% of all births involved at least one teenaged parent, usually the mother. Almost 14% of all fathers were teenagers, more than a fourfold increase over the national figure of 3%.

Characteristics of Fathers

In Table 4-5, the percent distribution of fathers' age is shown by age and race of mother. White fathers were, in general, older than black fathers at each maternal age, and the range of fathers' age was wide, with some fathers being much older than the mothers. Among teenagers, white fathers were, on the average, about 4 years older than the mothers; among blacks, the parents were closer in age, with only a 2- to 3-year difference.

Table 4-6 shows the distribution of fathers' education and marital status for first order live births, by the age of the father and the age and race of the mother

Table 4-4 Percent Distribution of Resident Recorded Births by Age and Race of Parents, Baltimore, 1983

Parents less than 20 years of age	Total[a] (n = 11,143)	Race of mother[b]	
		Black (n = 8,112)	White (n = 3,031)
Both	12.0	13.9	6.7
Mother only	14.1	15.0	11.7
Father only	1.7	1.8	1.3
Neither	72.3	69.3	80.3

Reproduced with permission from Hardy, JB, and Duggan, AK. *Am J Public Health* 78:918–922, 1988.

[a]Percentages calculated excluding 228 births with missing data on age of parent(s).

[b]Race of mother of baby.

Table 4-5 First Order Resident Recorded Live Births: Percent Distribution,[a] Mean, Standard Deviation, and Range of Age of Father by Race and Age of Mother, Baltimore, 1983.

Age of father (years)	Age of mother (years)						
	≤14	15	16	17	18/19	20	≥21
Black	(n = 92)	(n = 152)	(n = 275)	(n = 381)	(n = 914)	(n = 367)	(n = 1390)
≤14	3	2	0	0	0	0	0
15	14	7	3	1	0	0	0
16	24	19	11	3	1	0	0
17	18	21	19	12	4	2	0
18/19	26	33	41	46	31	10	2
20	4	7	8	15	16	18	3
≥21	10	10	18	23	47	70	95
Mean	17.7	18.0	18.8	19.6	21.2	22.9	28.0
(SD)	(3.1)	(2.6)	(3.2)	(3.0)	(3.5)	(4.1)	(6.3)
Range	14–33	14–32	15–50	15–44	15–40	17–43	16–64
White	(n = 4)	(n = 29)	(n = 61)	(n = 101)	(n = 245)	(n = 113)	(n = 855)
15	0	10	3	2	0	0	0
16	0	14	10	3	0	1	0
17	25	14	13	15	4	1	0
18/19	50	31	33	29	20	13	0
20	0	7	12	13	18	12	1
≥21	25	24	30	39	57	73	98
Mean	19.0	19.0	20.2	20.5	22.2	23.7	29.3
(SD)	(1.6)	(3.3)	(4.7)	(3.9)	(4.3)	(4.8)	(5.7)
Range	17–21	15–27	15–43	15–39	15–44	16–43	17–60

Reproduced with permission from Hardy, JB, and Duggan, AK: *Am J Public Health* 78:918–922, 1988.

[a]Percentages may not total 100 due to rounding and are calculated excluding 57 black and 47 white births with missing data on father's age.

for all Baltimore births in 1983. The educational status of all fathers involved in a teenage pregnancy, particularly those who were white, was dismal; among white fathers over age 20 years in this category, 28% had not progressed beyond 9th grade. Among black fathers of babies born by teenage mothers, very few were married; among whites the proportions were somewhat larger.

Characteristics of Women Giving Birth

Let us turn now to consideration of certain characteristics of those Baltimore women who had a live birth in 1983. Table 4-7 displays their past pregnancy history, by age of mother and race. The table examines prior pregnancies, births, and fetal deaths, including both spontaneous and induced. The number of women having a first pregnancy terminating in 1983 decreased steadily with age. Among all black teenagers, 62%, and among white, 68% had no history of prior pregnancies; 78% and 80%, respectively, had no prior live births.

Selected characteristics of women having a first live birth are shown in Table 4-8. Striking differences are seen by both age and race in the distributions of several variables. Educational attainment at delivery is of particular interest because of its relationship with long-term outcome. With the exception of education beyond the high school level, where older whites outrank blacks by 44% to 36%, black mothers, at each age, had more education at delivery than whites. Among older women

Table 4-6 Percent Distribution[a] of Selected Paternal Characteristics by Age of Father and Age and Race of Mother: First Order Resident Recorded Live Births

Age of mother:	Under 20 years						20 years and above					
Race of mother:	Black			White			Black			White		
Age of father (yr)	<17	18/19	>20	<17	18/19	>20	<17	18/19	>20	<17	18/19	>20
(Numbers)	(333)	(645)	(836)	(61)	(108)	(271)	(8)	(57)	(1692)	(3)	(17)	(948)
Father's highest grade completed												
<9	34	6	4	66	38	28	0	6	3	67	7	7
10/11	56	41	22	27	38	29	71	31	13	0	43	10
12	10	50	66	7	23	37	29	56	57	33	43	34
>12	0	3	8	0	0	5	0	8	27	0	7	49
Married to child's mother at time of birth	1	1	5	16	24	38	0	7	24	0	35	76
Missing data (N)												
Father's schooling	(23)	(86)	(123)	(6)	(17)	(28)	(1)	(5)	(182)	(0)	(3)	(55)

Reproduced with permission from Hardy, JB, and Duggan, AK: *Am J Public Health* 78:918–922, 1988.

[a] Percentages calculated excluding cases with missing data. No missing data on marital status at time of birth.

Table 4-7 Percent Distribution of Pregnancy History by Race and Age at Delivery: All Resident Recorded Live Births, Baltimore, 1983

First order live births

	Black						White				
	Total *(5,083)*	*≤15* *(255)*	*16* *(288)*	*17* *(384)*	*18/19* *(922)*	*≥20* *(1,779)*	*≤15* *(36)*	*16* *(65)*	*17* *(106)*	*18/19* *(260)*	*≥20* *(988)*
Prior pregnancies (Prior fetal deaths)[a]											
None	73	93	89	75	75	64	100	91	88	80	70
One or more	27	7	11	25	25	37	0	10	12	20	30

Second or higher live births

	Black				White		
	Total *(6,170)*	*≤17* *(141)*	*18/19* *(397)*	*>20* *(4,008)*	*≤17* *(30)*	*18/19* *(88)*	*>20* *(1,506)*
Prior pregnancies							
One	35	77	60	27	80	65	40
Two or more	66	23	40	73	20	35	60
Prior fetal deaths[a]							
One	27	13	19	29	21	21	24
Two or more	14	4	5	17	0	4	10
Prior live births							
One	56	92	82	50	100	83	58
Two or more	44	9	18	50	0	17	42

[a]Includes all prior stillbirths, miscarriages, spontaneous abortions, and therapeutic abortions as reported on birth certificate.

having a first child, 86% of the blacks versus 77% of the whites had graduated from high school. Among teenagers the frequency of high school graduation varied with age, but 69% of the blacks versus 39% of the whites had graduated. The educational attainment of the mothers paralleled that of the fathers.

Only small proportions of black mothers were married when their babies were born: 23% of the older mothers, only 5% of 18/19 year olds, and almost none of the black adolescents. Among older white mothers, 26% were not married at delivery. Among white teenagers, the likelihood of marriage varied with age from a high of 35% for 18/19 year olds to a low of 11% of those aged 15 or below.

The time of onset of prenatal care and the number of prenatal visits bear important relationships to the adequacy of care and the quality of pregnancy out-come. Among older mothers, 86% of the white and 70% of the black registered for prenatal care during the first trimester of pregnancy, and only 3% and 6%, respectively, registered in the third trimester or had no prenatal care at all. Older white mothers made an average of almost 12 prenatal visits and older blacks almost 11 visits. The teenagers fared less well. Among black teenagers, first trimester registration varied from 43% for the youngest to 55% for 18/19 year olds and inadequate or no care from 15% for those 15 or below to 7% for those aged 18/19 years. The average number of prenatal visits varied from 8.7 for the youngest to 9.9 for 17 year olds. Among white teenagers, fewer had inadequate or no prenatal care, and the number of prenatal visits was only slightly below that for older women.

With the exception of white women aged 20 or above, among whom 13% received Medical Assistance to cover the costs of delivery, large proportions of all other age and race groups received such support. For example, 54% of older black women, 77% of black 18/19 year olds, and 68% of whites aged 15 and below received Medical Assistance (MA) (Table 4-8).

Women having second or higher order births, particularly teenagers, were even more disadvantaged with respect to having less education and later onset of prenatal care with fewer visits, as compared with those having a first child. Greater proportions received Medical Assistance (81% of black and 74% of white teens), and somewhat larger proportions were married (5% of black and 40% of white teens).

Selected pregnancy characteristics are shown in Table 4-9, by age and race for women having a first birth in 1983. Complications of pregnancy and reported intercurrent illness appeared to be somewhat more frequent among teenagers than older women and among blacks as compared with whites. Complications of labor and delivery occurred with high frequency, which did not appear to vary much with either age or race. However, as already noted, these variables may not be reliable. Cesarian section was employed to effect delivery less frequently among teens than older women, with little difference by race.

The average duration of pregnancy was shorter for blacks than for whites, as has been described previously (Niswander and Gordon, 1972). The duration steadily increased with age of mother, from 37.6 to 38.8 completed weeks for blacks and 38.7 to 39.7 for whites.

Characteristics of Infants

We come now to infant outcome, also shown in Table 4-6. Not surprisingly, because of the variation in length of gestation with race and age, the frequency of preterm

Table 4-8 Percent Distribution of Selected Maternal Characteristics by Race and Age at Delivery: All Resident Recorded First Order Live Births, Baltimore, 1983

	Total (5,083)	Black					White				
(Numbers)		≤15 (255)	16 (288)	17 (384)	18/19 (922)	≥20 (1,779)	≤15 (36)	16 (65)	17 (106)	18/19 (260)	≥20 (988)
Education (last grade completed)											
1–9	16	86	41	16	8	3	92	59	51	28	8
10 or 11	25	14	56	69	35	11	8	39	47	35	10
12 (high school)	37	0	3	15	51	50	0	2	2	35	37
>12	23	0	0	0	7	36	0	0	0	2	44
Married at time of delivery	26	0	1	1	5	23	11	23	26	35	74
Onset of prenatal care											
1st trimester	66	43	48	57	55	70	60	62	64	65	86
2nd trimester	28	43	42	35	38	25	37	27	30	31	12
3rd trimester	5	10	7	6	5	5	3	8	6	2	2
No prenatal care	1	5	3	2	2	1	0	3	0	1	1
Number of prenatal visits—mean	10.5	8.7	9.3	9.9	9.5	10.7	10.8	10.8	11.8	11.2	11.8
(SD)	(3.9)	(4.6)	(4.3)	(4.1)	(3.7)	(3.8)	(3.9)	(4.1)	(5.1)	(3.5)	(3.0)
Certified for Medical Assistance[a]	53	66	64	69	77	54	68	57	57	58	13

[a]At time of delivery.

Table 4-9 Percent Distribution of Selected Characteristics by Race and Age at Delivery: All Resident Recorded First Order Live Births, Baltimore, 1983

	Black						White				
(Numbers)	Total (5,083)	≤15 (255)	16 (288)	17 (384)	18/19 (922)	≥20 (1,779)	≤15 (36)	16 (65)	17 (106)	18/19 (260)	≥20 (988)
Complication of pregnancy	19	27	23	23	22	19	27	14	20	19	13
Concurrent illness or condition affecting pregnancy	12	14	14	12	16	13	4	8	5	8	6
Complication of labor or delivery	44	38	43	49	43	45	50	35	45	39	42
Cesarian section	21	10	16	17	17	24	17	11	19	16	26
Mean gestational age in wk	38.8	37.6	37.7	38.2	38.4	38.8	38.7	38.8	39.1	39.6	39.7
(SD)	(3.7)	(4.6)	(4.7)	(4.2)	(4.0)	(3.7)	(4.9)	(3.6)	(3.9)	(2.6)	(2.5)
Gestational age <37 wk	17	31	31	24	20	15	21	17	15	9	9
Birth weight <2,500 g	12	16	19	15	15	13	6	15	10	5	7
Birth weight <1,500 g	3	4	4	3	3	3	3	3	3	0	1
Apgar, 1 min <7	11	12	14	13	13	12	8	11	6	11	8
Apgar, 5 min <7	3	2	3	4	3	3	0	3	1	3	1
Congenital malformation	3	4	4	3	3	3	4	0	1	3	2

births, i.e., prior to 37 weeks gestation, varied with both race and maternal age. Black infants were more frequently preterm than white, and the youngest mothers had the highest frequency of preterm babies, 31% among blacks versus 21% among white girls aged 15 or below at delivery. Among mothers aged 20 or above, 15% of blacks and 9% of whites had a preterm infant.

The frequency of low birth weight (LBW)(less than 2,500 g or 5½ pounds) also varied with race and, to a lesser extent, with maternal age. The risk of LBW was considerably higher among black women of all ages than among whites. In fact, among women aged 20 and above, it was almost twice as high among blacks (13%) as among whites (7%). In these data, 16 year olds of both races have the highest likelihood of LBW: 19% among blacks and 15% among whites. The youngest adolescents have lower frequencies, 16% and 6%, respectively. These lower frequencies may reflect the beneficial effect of being enrolled in a program providing special comprehensive services for pregnant adolescents. In our experience with such a program (Hardy et al., 1987), the youngest adolescents had the highest average weight gain in pregnancy, the infants with the highest mean birth weight, and the lowest frequency of LBW of any age group under 18 years at delivery. Our Resource Use Study (Hardy et al., 1986) also indicated that the youngest girls were overrepresented in these special programs and had the lowest frequency of LBW.

Apgar scores at 1 and 5 minutes after birth are used to assess the newborn infant's general functional integrity (Apgar, 1953). Scores of 9 and 10 are optimal; scores below 7, particularly at 5 minutes, suggest functional impairment. Black infants had minimally lower scores than white, in keeping with their average lower birth weights.

The frequency of reported congenital malformations is also shown in Table 4-6. These data must be considered unreliable for several reasons. First, bias may be introduced by the large amount of missing data from several hospitals. Second, many major malformations are not recognized at birth (Hardy, Drage, et al., 1979), and third, the birth certificate does not distinguish between malformations of clinical importance and minor anomalies, such as extra digits, skin tags, and insignificant nevi.

Summary and Implications

Pregnancy, abortion, and childbirth among teenagers living in a poor urban environment, such as Baltimore City, account for large proportions of all pregnancies (28%) and all births (26%). These proportions are more than twice those of the nation as a whole (National Center for Health Statistics, 1988). Of even more concern is the problem of adolescent childbearing; girls under 18 accounted for 47% of all teenage births and 13% of births to women of all ages in Baltimore. Nationally, on the basis of statistics cited in Chapter 3, adolescents accounted for a smaller proportion of all teenage births (38%) and for less than 5% of all births. These are striking differences that underscore the scope of the problem in poor urban centers.

Clearly, many pregnancies among teenagers are unintended, about 85% among 15- to 19-year-old adolescents, according to Zelnik and Kantner (1980). Even higher proportions of unintended pregnancies have been reported more recently in a

Baltimore urban black sample of adolescents ≤17 years of age (Zabin, Hirsch, et al., 1989). In 1983, 42% of pregnant teenagers clearly did not want to be pregnant as they elected to terminate their pregnancies. Abortion rates would probably have been much higher had Medicaid support for abortion not been severely restricted. Significant proportions of teenage mothers had been pregnant prior to their 1983 births (37%) and already had one or more children (22%).

Many teenage mothers, particularly among whites, were undereducated and poor, on the basis of their receipt of Medical Assistance to cover hospital costs. This was also true of the fathers of their babies. Lack of education reduces their prospects for satisfactory employment and income. Many received inadequate pre-natal care, had complicated pregnancies, and small infants whose development may have been compromised.

Finally, the almost universal lack of marriage among black teenage mothers and the low frequency of marriage among whites has serious implications for stable family formation and the ability of the young parents to provide the nurturing environment and resources necessary for optimal development of their children. Thus, the intergenerational cycle of disadvantage seems likely to be perpetuated and the public costs to remain high.

Appendix Table 4-1 Proportion of Birth Certificates with Missing Data, by Hospital: Resident Recorded Live Births, Baltimore, 1983

	Total (11,250)	Hospital[a] 1 (901)	2 (1,720)	3 (1,138)	4 (1,776)	5 (673)	6 (704)	7 (1,799)	8 (629)	9 (1,136)	10 (774)
(Numbers)											
Mother's age	0	0	0	0	0	0	0	0	0	0	0
Mother's race	0	0	0	0	0	0	0	0	0	0	0
Mother's education	1.6	1.9	4.0	2.8	0.2	0.4	0.1	2.4	0.2	0.6	0.0
Marital status	0	0	0	0	0	0	0	0	0	0	0
Prior pregnancies	1.8	10.9	0.8	1.3	0.3	0.6	0.6	1.1	0.8	2.4	0.8
Prior live births	1.0	7.3	0.5	0.9	0.0	0.3	0.4	0.3	0.2	1.2	0.3
Prior fetal deaths	1.5	9.2	0.8	0.9	0.3	0.6	0.3	1.0	0.6	1.7	0.6
Complications, pregnancy	14.5	1.7	39.1	0.4	0.5	0.1	89.9	0.7	1.6	23.8	0.6
Complications, labor and delivery	14.8	2.2	39.8	0.3	0.4	0.1	89.8	0.5	1.7	25.9	0.6
Concurrent illnesses	11.4	1.6	30.7	0.2	0.3	0.3	70.6	0.4	1.3	18.9	0.5
Method of delivery	1.2	1.4	15.3	0.6	0.2	1.2	1.0	1.4	0.3	1.3	0.9
Birth weight	0	0	0	0	0	0	0	0	0	0	0
Gestational age	4.2	13.7	4.8	4.7	1.5	3.1	2.0	5.5	3.0	2.1	1.0
Apgar, 1 min	1.4	1.4	0.9	1.1	0.3	1.6	0.6	2.4	0.6	3.9	0.9
Apgar, 5 min	1.5	1.3	1.0	1.1	0.5	1.5	0.7	2.6	0.8	3.7	0.6
Congenital anomalies	14.9	2.8	39.8	0.3	1.4	0.1	88.8	0.5	1.4	25.4	0.8
Initiation prenatal care	4.4	13.2	3.5	3.9	0.6	2.1	1.0	11.7	0.6	1.2	0.8
Medical assistance	10.9	86.9	18.5	0.7	0.7	1.3	0.3	3.0	0.6	2.1	1.4

[a]Excluded are 32 births at a birthing center in the city, 83 births occurring outside a hospital, and 6 births occurring at other city hospitals.

Appendix Table 4-2   Percent Distribution of Resident Recorded Live Births by Maternal Age and Race and Hospital of Delivery, Baltimore, 1983

		Black				White			
(Numbers)	Total (11,250)	Total (8,190)	≤17 (1,062)	18/19 (1,323)	≥20 (5,805)	Total (3,065)	≤17 (241)	18/19 (349)	≥20 (2,475)
Hospital[a]									
1	8	7	7	7	7	11	19	19	9
2	15	18	24	19	16	9	9	5	10
3	10	7	5	7	8	17	9	13	19
4	16	19	25	23	17	7	15	10	6
5	6	8	8	8	8	0	0	0	0
6	6	3	2	3	3	15	20	21	14
7	16	16	10	12	18	16	3	2	19
8	6	3	3	3	4	11	11	14	11
9	10	10	8	10	10	10	9	13	10
10	7	8	7	7	9	3	4	1	3

[a]Excluded are 32 births at a birthing center in the city, 83 births occurring outside a hospital, and 6 births occurring at other city hospitals.

Appendix Table 4-3   Proportion[a] of Resident Recorded Live Births with Selected Complications by Hospital and Inclusion/Exclusion[b] of Missing Data, Baltimore, 1983

Hospital	Complication of pregnancy		Complication of labor/delivery		Concurrent illness		Congenital malformation	
	Included	Excluded	Included	Excluded	Included	Excluded	Included	Excluded
1	23	23	10	10	40	40	2.1	2.2
2	14	23	6	10	40	57	2.6	4.3
3	18	18	5	5	42	42	2.5	2.5
4	40	41	36	36	56	56	5.5	5.5
5	4	4	0	0	22	22	2.8	2.8
6	1	13	0	3	23	78	0.9	7.6
7	5	5	1	1	23	23	1.9	2.0
8	8	8	1	2	26	26	2.4	2.4
9	21	27	9	12	40	50	1.5	2.0
10	8	8	2	2	36	36	2.1	2.1
Total	16	19	9	11	36	41	2.6	3.1

[a]Rounded to nearest whole percent.

[b]Included: Certificates with missing data treated as negative for the complication and included in the denominator in calculating proportion.

Excluded: Certificates with missing data excluded in calculating proportion with the complication.

5

Pregnant and
Parenting Adolescents

In this chapter we attempt to answer one of the questions raised in the introduction to this section of the book: What are the characteristics of pregnant and childbearing urban adolescents? A description of a city-wide random sample of these young women is presented, using the data and methodology described in the introduction to Part II, page 49.

Observations

Immediate Pregnancy Outcome

The immediate outcome of all recorded pregnancies among Baltimore adolescents less than 18 years at termination in 1983 is shown by race and specific year of age in Table 5-1. The number of reported spontaneous fetal deaths after 20 weeks' gestation was quite low in this age group (only 18 of the 2,428 adolescent pregnancies recorded). There were 1,302 live births and 1,108 elective abortions. Just over 45% of all adolescent pregnancies were terminated in this way (46% of the black and 42% of the white). As noted in Chapter 4, births to adolescents under 18 years of age accounted for 47% of teenage births and 13% of births to women of all ages in Baltimore.

Live Births Just over 53% of pregnant adolescents had a liveborn child. Unfortunately, data pertaining to neonatal and infant mortality are not presently available for this group of young mothers. The important point is that only about one-half of the adolescent pregnancies in this age group produced a live born child. Infant deaths, including those in the neonatal period, may have accounted for an additional attrition of 1% to 2%, the remaining pregnancies were electively terminated. Comparisons of pregnancy outcome, by specific year of age at delivery, for adolescents, older teenagers, and women aged 20 and above have been reported in Chapter 4.

Obstetrical risks and the likelihood of a low birth weight (LBW) infant are increased for second and higher order births among teenagers, and difficulties in completing education and attaining self-sufficiency are even greater than for those having a first child, often resulting in prolonged welfare dependence. As shown in

Table 5-1 Number of Resident Recorded Live Births, Reported Fetal Deaths, and Reported Induced Abortions to Adolescents, by Age and Race, Baltimore City, 1983

	Under 18	*Under 15*	*15*	*16*	*17*
All races					
Total	2,428	288	444	713	983
Live births	1,302	104	196	397	605
Fetal deaths[a]	18	2	3	2	11
Induced abortions[b]	1,108	182	245	314	367
Blacks[c]					
Total	1,999	266	374	568	775
Live births	1,060	100	161	324	475
Fetal deaths[a]	17	2	3	1	11
Induced abortions	922	164	210	243	289
Whites					
Total	419	18	68	135	198
Live births	242	4	35	73	130
Fetal deaths[a]	1	0	0	1	0
Induced abortions	176	14	33	61	68

[a]Limited to reported fetal deaths of 20 weeks or more gestation.

[b]Includes 39 induced abortions with missing data on race.

[c]Includes non-white races other than black.

Table 5-2, of the 1,060 live births to black adolescents, 141 (13.3%) were to young mothers who already had one or more children. Among whites, the frequency of prior liveborn children was similar, 15%; 35 of the 242 white adolescents who delivered in 1983 already had at least one child.

Elective Abortion As indicated above, 42% of the white and 46% of the black adolescents who became pregnant in 1983 terminated their pregnancies through abortion. The reported frequency of abortion by age and race is shown in Table

Table 5-2 Distribution of Births to Adolescents by Live Birth Order, Mother's Race and Age at Delivery: All Resident Recorded Live Births, Baltimore, 1983

Birth order and age at delivery	Total		Black		White	
	n	*(%)*	*n*	*(%)*	*n*	*(%)*
Total live births	1,302	(100)	1060	(100)	242	(100)
≤ 14	105	(8)	100	(9)	5	(2)
15	195	(15)	161	(15)	34	(14)
16	397	(30)	324	(31)	73	(30)
17	605	(47)	475	(45)	130	(54)
First live birth	1,126	(100)	919	(100)	207	(100)
≤ 14	103	(9)	99	(11)	4	(2)
15	186	(17)	154	(17)	32	(15)
16	351	(31)	287	(31)	64	(31)
17	486	(43)	379	(41)	107	(52)
Second or higher order	176	(100)	141	(100)	35	(100)
≤ 14	2	(1)	1	(1)	1	(3)
15	9	(5)	7	(5)	2	(5)
16	46	(26)	37	(26)	9	(26)
17	119	(68)	96	(68)	23	(66)

Table 5-3 Reported Induced Abortions among Baltimore Adolescents in 1983, by Age and Race

Age (yr)	Total no.	White	Black	Other or unknown
12	7	0	6	1
13	51	3	46	2
14	124	11	112	1
15	245	33	210	2
16	314	61	243	10
17	367	68	289	10
≤ 17	1,108	176	906	26
Percent	100	15.9	81.8	2.3

Data kindly provided by J. Saladini, Baltimore City Health Department, 1986.

5-3. Table 5-4 indicates the frequency of abortion by age and the duration of pregnancy at which the procedure was carried out. The well recognized relationship between young maternal age and increased frequency of abortion after the first trimester is seen in these data. Nonetheless, the great majority of abortions were carried out in the first trimester of pregnancy. It should also be noted that by 1983 there were already limitations on the availability of abortion for poor women, as federal funding for the procedure was curtailed. However, Maryland is one of the few states in which public support for abortion is provided by the state under limited circumstances such as rape, incest, congenital malformations of the fetus, and if the mother's life is jeopardized by the pregnancy.

While these pregnancy outcome data pertain to 1983, there has been little change in the number of births in the intervening years. The number of births in this age group has actually increased, from 1,302 to 1,393 (1987) and 1,452 (1988) (Governor's Council on Adolescent Pregnancy, personal communication, 1988) while the number of adolescents in the population has decreased significantly. Thus, the birth rate per 1,000 adolescent girls has increased somewhat.

Young Mothers and Their Families

We turn now to the examination of data from the city-wide random sample of 389 adolescent mothers. The observations are presented in terms of the young mother's characteristics at several points in time: during pregnancy; at delivery; and, at the

Table 5-4 Reported Induced Abortions, Baltimore Adolescents, 1983, by Age and Duration of Pregnancy at Termination

Age (yr)	Total no.	Gestation (wk)				
		< 8	9–12	13–16	17–20	> 21
≤ 13	58	13	24	10	11	0
14	124	37	58	14	15	0
15	245	75	110	29	29	2
16	314	100	147	34	31	2
17	367	114	176	35	40	2
≤ 17	1,108	339	515	122	126	6
Percent	100	30.6	46.5	11.0	11.4	0.5

Data kindly provided by J. Saladini, Baltimore City Health Department.

3- and 15- to 18-month ($\overline{X}$17.6) follow-up interviews, by mother's race, age at delivery, and number of living children, as described under "Methods," page 54. Comparisons between respondents and nonrespondents of birth certificate data suggest that the study sample was representative of all Baltimore live births in this maternal age group. Several representative cases are summarized at the end of the chapter to illustrate some of the findings in human terms.

Living Arrangements and Family Income

The family setting in which the pregnancy occurred is described using data collected at the first interview, three months after the birth of the child. Table 5-5 provides information about the adolescents' marital status, household, living arrangements, and source of income. There were highly significant differences with respect to these variables by race, number of children and, to a lesser extent, by age of mother, with 17 year olds being different from those who were younger. Large proportions of the adolescents who became pregnant and bore a child were living in female-headed households, 80% of the black versus 57% of white, with little difference by age of mother. In most instances, the head of the household was the girl's mother, but among whites it was the adolescent herself in 10% of the cases. In only 24% of the households were both the adolescent's parents present. Overall, only 6% of adolescents were married and living with their husbands, 1% of the black as compared with 25% of white ($p < .001$). In an additional 6% of black and 12% of white families, the adolescent lived with her boyfriend/father of the baby, making a total of 7% of black and 37% of white families in which mother, father, and baby were together as a family at this point in time, i.e., three months after the child's birth. White adolescents had experienced greater residential mobility than black, with 50% versus 20% having moved since onset of pregnancy. This difference in mobility resulted primarily from the higher frequency both of marriage and of cohabitation among white adolescents.

Three months after delivery, 67% of the young families were dependent on Welfare, in whole or in part, for their support, significantly more blacks than whites. In terms of gross annual income (not shown and available for only 52%), large proportions of these young women, particularly those who were white, were poor. The data suggest that 45% of blacks and 58% of whites were in households in which annual income was below $10,000; only 15% of blacks and 11% of whites had household incomes in excess of $20,000 annually. The limited financial resources available to most were further strained by the fairly large number of persons in the adolescents' households, an average of 6.3 for the black and 5.0 for the white families.

Education

Adolescents in the random sample (black and white), for the most part, attended inner city, predominantly black schools where truancy was frequent. Overall, in Baltimore, almost half of the students entering high school fail to graduate. The young mothers' schooling prior to and during pregnancy is described in Table 5-6. Marked differences were noted between black and white adolescents with respect to grades and attendance prior to pregnancy. Larger proportions of blacks reported obtaining good grades prior to pregnancy, and larger proportions of whites reported

Table 5-5 Selected Household Characteristics at Three Months after Delivery, by Adolescent Mother's Race, Number of Children, and Age at Delivery (Numbers Shown Are Percents Unless Otherwise Indicated)

Household characteristic	All adolescent mothers (n = 389)	Race Black (n = 272)	Race White (n = 117)	Number of children >2 (n = 58)	Number of children 1 (n = 331)	Age at 1983 delivery (One child only) ≤ 15 yr (n = 123)	Age at 1983 delivery (One child only) 16 yr (n = 92)	Age at 1983 delivery (One child only) 17 yr (n = 116)
Household headed by:								
Female	76	80	57***	76	75	78	77	74
Adolescent mother	2	1	10***	8	2*	1	2	1
Parents in household:								
Mother	78	83	57***	64	81***	89	83	74*
Father	26	25	30	21	27	28	28	25
Both parents	24	23	29	19	25	27	25	24
Either parent	80	86	59***	68	83**	90	86	76*
Married, living with husband	6	1	25***	7	5	1	5	8
Not married, with boyfriend	7	6	12	8	7	3	6	11
Number of members, $\bar{x}$	6.0	6.3	5.0***	6.6	5.9*	6.1	5.9	5.9
17 and younger	3.6	3.8	2.8***	4.2	3.5***	3.9	3.6	3.2*
5 and younger	1.5	1.6	1.3**	2.5	1.4***	1.4	1.4	1.4
Number residences, $\bar{x}$ past five years	2.2	2.0	3.0**	2.7	2.2	2.3	2.4	1.9
Years at current residence, $\bar{x}$	5.3	5.7	3.4***	3.9	5.5*	4.9	4.1	6.8
Since pregnancy diagnosis:								
Felt need to move	33	30	43	44	31	29	28	35
Actually moved	26	20	50***	37	24*	22	28	23
Source of family income:								
Welfare (full/part)	67	71	50***	74	66	78	68	58**
Employment	59	59	62	55	60	56	49	70***

*p < .001.
**p < .05.
***p < .01.

Table 5-6 Selected Characteristics of Mother's Schooling Prior to, during, and at Termination of Pregnancy, Percentage Distributions

	All adolescent mothers (n = 363)	Race		Number of children		Age at 1983 delivery (One child only)		
		Black (n = 257)	White (n = 106)	≥2 (n = 50)	1 (n = 313)	≤ 15 yr (n = 115)	16 yr (n = 88)	17 yr (n = 110)
Prior to pregnancy[a]								
Grades								
Good	64	67	54	55	66	63	62	72
Fair	26	24	34	32	24	27	26	22
Poor/failing	10	9	12	14	9	10	12	6
Days/month absent[a]								
≤ 1	29	32	18***	19	31	27	30	34
1–5	38	40	29	34	39	42	44	32
> 6	33	29	54	47	31	32	25	34
	(n = 389)	(n = 272)	(n = 117)	(n = 58)	(n = 331)	(n = 123)	(n = 92)	(n = 116)
In school when learned pregnant	77	85	44***	39	83***	93	88	74***
Changed school	63	61	76	77	62	68	60	59
Transferred to Paquin[b]	30	33	+[c]	27	30	43	28	22**
Dropped out during pregnancy	33	28	74	50	32	25	33	36
Education at delivery[a] (Highest grade completed)								
≤ 9	48	44	64	44	49	87	47	26***
≥ 12	5	5	0	0	5	0	2	10

[a] Data collected at Interview II.

[b] Paquin, a special school for pregnant students.

[c] Less than 0.5%.

[a] Data from birth certificates; 1% (4 girls) had progressed beyond high school.

**p < .001.

***p < .01.

78

fair or poor grades. Nearly twice as many black as white girls (32% versus 18%) reported few absences from school. Among blacks, 85%, and whites, only 44% ($p < .001$) were actually attending school when pregnancy was diagnosed. Of those who attended school, 74% of the white and 28% of the black students dropped out during the pregnancy. Not surprisingly, the educational attainment of these young women at the time of delivery was, in general, dismal. These findings are congruent with those reported in Chapter 16. Young mothers enrolled in the parenting program, The Johns Hopkins Teenage Clinic and Parenting Program (TAC), performed cognitively and academically well below national norms. High rates of chronic or repeated absence and school dropout would appear to be risk factors for pregnancy among young teens and should be useful in targeting intervention.

Adolescent Pregnancy and Environment

The influence on the occurrence of adolescent pregnancy of personal contact with female friends and relatives who were adolescent mothers (i.e., <18 years at delivery) was examined. Overall, 75% of the adolescent mothers had family members who had given birth as an adolescent; 51% of their mothers and 30% of their sisters had had a child before age 18 years; 80% had mothers who were teenagers at their first birth. In addition, 87% had friends and almost 100% had either relatives or friends who had given birth as adolescents. There were no significant differences by race or age. Thus, adolescent pregnancy and childbearing appears to be normative rather than deviant behavior among inner city residents.

Religion

Overall, 28% of the young mothers reported no religious affiliations; 60% reported being Protestant, 11% Roman Catholic, and 1% Moslem. A higher proportion of white girls was Roman Catholic, 29 versus 7% for blacks. Overall, 42% reported belonging to or regularly attending church; 44% of the black versus 36% of white adolescent mothers. There were no significant differences in these variables by age or number of children.

Onset of Sexual Activity/Pregnancy

Data pertaining to sexual activity, its age of onset, and the desirability of pregnancy are shown in Table 5-7. Sexual intercourse among these young mothers began at a very early age, for some even before puberty. Sexual intercourse occurred earlier among blacks, of whom 42% reported being sexually active by age 13, as compared with 21% of whites. Three months after delivery the pregnancy was reported to have been planned by only 5% of the black adolescents as compared with 24% of the white; 41% of the blacks versus 54% of the whites had discussed the desirability of a pregnancy with the father of the baby prior to conception. These findings suggest that more white mothers than black and more fathers than mothers wanted a pregnancy or at least were perceived by the mothers as wanting it. The small proportions of planned pregnancies notwithstanding, a method of family planning had *never* been used by more than half of the black couples (55%) and more than two-thirds (67%) of the white couples. Only 13% reported using an effective medical (prepared) method around the time of conception.

Table 5-7 Percent Distribution of Age at First Intercourse and Selected Characteristics Pertaining to the Pregnancy and Its Diagnosis, by Mother's Race, Number of Children, and Age at Delivery

Characteristic	All adolescent mothers (n = 389)	Race		Number of Children		Age at 1983 delivery (One child only)		
		Black (n = 272)	White (n = 117)	≥2 (n = 58)	1 (n = 331)	≤15 yr (n = 123)	16 yr (n = 92)	17 yr (n = 116)
Age at 1st intercourse:								
≤11	6	6	3	6	6	9	7	3
12	11	12	6	18	9	17	4	9
13	21	24	12	25	21	40	18	11
14	24	24	24	34	22	30	25	16
15	22	20	33	18	23	4	44	19
16	15	14	22	0	18	0	3	40
17	1	1	0	0	1	0	0	1
Pregnancy planned	9	5	24***	6	9	4	9	12
Desirability of pregnancy discussed with father of baby	43	41	54*	44	43	35	49	44
Pregnancy wanted by:								
Father[a]	54	52	61	54	54	38	53	63
Mother	17	12	40***	19	17	8	15	24*
Birth control at 1983 conception:								
Never used	58	55	67	23	64***	77	63	56**
Discontinued	28	29	28	47	25	14	24	32
A method used	14	16	5*	30	11***	9	13	12
Prepared method[b]	13	15	5*	28	11***	9	13	10

[a]Denominator equals the 43% of fathers with whom the desirability of pregnancy was discussed.
[b]Prepared method—pill, IUD, diaphragm, and foam/condom.

*p < .05.
**p < .01.
***p < .001.

Even though most of the young women were living with parents, only 61% had discussed with them, prior to diagnosis, the possibility that she might be pregnant. Over one-third of the adolescents suspected that they might be pregnant but did not seek care for more than one month prior to diagnosis. One-quarter did not suspect that they were pregnant prior to diagnosis.

Upon being told of the diagnosis, 60% of the adolescent mothers (58% of black and 71% of white) reported that they knew they would carry through with the pregnancy, even though only 12% overall had wanted to be pregnant. Forty percent were uncertain about what to do; of these, 70% discussed the problem with family and 33% with a professional, but 22% did not discuss it with anyone. Among those discussing the problem, the option of abortion was initially considered but discarded by 86% and adoption by 88%. However, all delivered and kept the child. These data are not shown, as the only significant group difference found was between young mothers who already had one or more children, of whom 53% were initially uncertain what to do about the pregnancy, versus those with no prior children, of whom 38% were uncertain.

Mother's Reaction to Daughter's Pregnancy

Upon learning about the pregnancy, the adolescents' mothers were reported to be angry by 35%; upset/shocked/disappointed by an additional 28%; happy by 13%; indifferent by 12%; displeased but supportive by 8%; and ambivalent by 4%. There were no significant differences by race, age, or number of prior children. Although relatively few mothers were happy to learn of the pregnancy, 88% of the adolescents reported that their families were helpful during pregnancy. A few of the adolescents were forced to move from the parents' home, but most of those who moved did so by choice.

Prenatal Care, Nutrition, and Sources of Support

Overall, many adolescents had suboptimal care during pregnancy. Only 44% began prenatal care during the first trimester, with more whites (55%) than blacks (42%) seeking early care. Older adolescents and those having a first birth were more likely to register for care in the first trimester. Larger proportions of blacks (18%) than whites (12%) and of those having higher order births (28%) versus first births (15%) registered in the third trimester or had no prenatal care. White adolescents had an average of 11.2, and black adolescents an average of 8.9 prenatal visits. Those adolescents having their first child averaged 9.6 visits, significantly more than the 7.7 visits of those who already had one or more children. Half of both black (52%) and white (50%) adolescents received Medicaid support for all of their obstetrical care, an additional 16% received partial support, and 34% had no public support for care. None was refused pregnancy care because of inability to pay (data not shown).

Because of the important relationship between inadequate weight gain in pregnancy and LBW (Niswander & Gordon, 1972; Weiss and Jackson, 1969), nutritional education and nutrition supplements play a crucial role in prenatal care (see Chapter 13). Examination of the data showed that even though larger proportions of adolescents were undoubtedly eligible, food stamps were received by only 45% of black and 40% of white adolescents during pregnancy, and nutritional supplements through the Nutritional Supplements for Women, Infant, and Children (WIC) program were received by 74% of black but only 60% of white adolescents ($p < .05$). Overall, 11% of the young women reported having difficulty obtaining adequate food during pregnancy. The majority (73%) received nutritional information from family and 88% from a professional source (data not shown). Even though the young white mothers were somewhat poorer than the black, they seem to have had less access to public support for medical care and nutritional supplements than the black. This may have been related to the higher proportion of white girls receiving care from private physicians and as a result having less contact with social service providers.

Characteristics of the Pregnancy, Labor, and Delivery

The data from interviews are supplemented here by those from the Certificates of Live Birth. As seen in the preceding chapter, complications of pregnancy were reported with considerable frequency among all teenage groups. Overall, 15% of the adolescents were admitted to a hospital during the prenatal course (14% of the black versus 18% of the white adolescents) for diagnosis and treatment, another significant item in the array of costs associated with adolescent childbearing. Anemia was reported for almost one-third of all adolescent mothers, and for 53% of those having a second or higher order pregnancy, hypertension was reported in 19%. Cesarean section was used to effect delivery in 15%. A larger proportion, 29% of the black versus 12% of the white adolescents, had a preterm delivery after a gestation of only 36 completed weeks or less, and 15% of blacks and 10% of whites had a LBW baby, weighing less than 2,500 g. Eight percent of black babies and 11% of white babies were admitted to a neonatal intensive care unit (NICU), a substantial medical care cost. The high frequency of NICU admissions and of cesarean sections notwithstanding, the average length of hospital stay was 3.6 nights for the mother and 5.6 for the child, indicating that large proportions of these young mothers and infants stayed only a short time in the hospital after delivery (data not shown).

Depression/Worry/Confusion

Emotional problems are not uncommon during pregnancy and in the early weeks postpartum, particularly when the pregnancy is unintended and unwanted. Among these young mothers 54% reported depression, worry, or a feeling of confusion. This was more frequent (62%) among those who already had one or more children. Many (69%) of those reporting emotional problems were able to discuss their problems with a family member or friend, although only 17% with a husband or boyfriend. Only 14% received professional counseling. A fairly large group (28%) received no help from any source, and among those having a second or higher order birth, 39% went without family or professional help (data not shown). The presence of maternal depression and/or other emotional problems is an important risk factor for inadequate parenting.

Number of Sex Partners and Frequency of Intercourse

Data pertaining to the number of lifetime sex partners among urban adolescents are not available in the Resource Use Study. However, this information is available from studies of the prevalence of sexually transmitted diseases in The Johns Hopkins Adolescent Pregnancy (HAC) and Adolescent Pregnancy Prevention (Self Center) Programs. These programs included urban adolescents living in East Baltimore who were similar in characteristics to those in the Resource Use Study. In each group, 37% reported only one partner. In the pregnancy prevention program 8% were virgins; 29% had two partners, and 26% had three or more. Among the pregnant adolescents enrolled in HAC, 24% reported two, and 39% three or more partners, some as many as 10 during their lifetime. Among pregnant adolescents enrolled in HAC and questioned at 32 to 34 weeks gestation, 70% reported sexual activity during pregnancy. Of those sexually active, 37% reported coitus within the prior week and 59% within the prior month. As the frequency of sexual activity and numbers of partners are related to an increased risk of cervical infection and several sexually transmitted organisms, particularly *Chlamydia trachomatis* and *Neisseria gonorrhoeae* (Hardy et al., 1984), and as transmission of STDs to the fetus can result in morbidity and mortality, these issues are of considerable concern.

Mother's Status 3 Months After Delivery

Sexual Activity

The frequency of sexual activity reported by young mothers in the Resource Use Study 3 months after delivery is shown in Table 5-8. Overall, 82% reported being sexually active. Intercourse was relatively infrequent, with 18% reporting none at all in the prior month and less than one-third reporting coitus as often as once each week or more. White adolescents reported somewhat more frequent coitus than black. Of those sexually active, 14% of the black and 27% of the white mothers were *not* using contraceptives and, thus, were at risk for repeat pregnancy, and as described later in the chapter these risks were substantial. The findings, with respect to the frequency of sexual activity, are consistent with observations reported by Zelnik and Kantner (1980) and Zabin and Clark (1981). The frequency of intercourse reported one year later, at Interview II, was essentially unchanged.

Medicaid Status

A somewhat smaller proportion of adolescents overall was receiving Medicaid at this time than during the pregnancy, but 21% had private insurance and 13% were enrolled in a Health Maintenance Organization (HMO). However, 22% had *no* support for medical expenses, including family planning. This lack of family planning service and supplies appeared to be a particularly difficult problem for young white mothers whose husbands or partners had low paying jobs. These girls could not afford to purchase contraceptives but were not eligible for Medical Assistance. Even the cost of transportation to a public clinic was a problem for some. They quickly became pregnant again after free pills provided on hospital discharge were exhausted. Use of condoms, which would have been an inexpensive alternative, was infrequently reported.

Schooling, Infant Day Care

Among blacks 60% were in school but among whites only 10% ($p < .001$), a substantial decline since the onset of pregnancy, a decline in large part related to

Table 5-8 Adolescent Mother's Status Three Months after Delivery by Race, Number of Children, and Age (Numbers Shown Are Percents)

	All adolescent mothers (n = 389)	Race		Number of Children		Age at 1983 delivery (One child only)		
		Black (n = 272)	White (n = 117)	≥2 (n = 58)	1 (n = 331)	≤15 yr (n = 123)	16 yr (n = 92)	17 yr (n = 116)
Sexually active	82	82	84	88	81	69	80	88**
Frequency of sexual activity:								
None	18	18	16**	12	19	31	20	12**
Less than once/month	16	18	7	14	16	20	18	12
Once or twice/month	26	28	19	40	24	20	25	25
Once/week	22	20	27	21	22	19	21	24
Several times/week	19	16	31	13	20	10	17	27
Of those sexually active:								
Using birth control	83	86	73*	79	84	88	88	80
Having a regular birth control site	82	84	72	78	83	88	88	77*
Source of payment for medical care:								
Medical assistance	55	55	52	59	54	65	49	51
Private insurance	21	21	24	19	22	21	22	22
HMO enrollment[a]	13	15	4*	9	14	16	18	10
None of above	22	21	24	24	21	13	22	26
Educational status:								
In school	51	60	10***	20	56***	76	58	42
Child's daytime care giver								
Mother	54	46	87***	77	50***	28	53	61***
Grandmother	21	24	8	7	23	40	25	12
Paid relative/friend	8	2	10	2	9	9	7	11
Unpaid relative/friend	12	14	1	2	13	16	12	12
Family day care	4	4	1	7	3	7	3	1
Father of baby	1	2	1	2	1	0	0	3
Foster care	1	1	1	4	0	0	1	0

[a]Some HMO fees were paid by Medicaid.

*p < .05.
**p < .01.
***p < .001.

lack of available child care. The arrangements made for the child's care during the daytime when the young mother would be expected to be at school or at work are also shown in Table 5-8. However, among whites 87% looked after their infants themselves as compared with 46% of the black mothers. Even though the population was generally poor, only 1% of whites and 4% of blacks had subsidized family day care. As many grandmothers were working, usually at low paying jobs, they could not provide day care. A small number of babies were cared for by their fathers. Other infants received care from relatives. Nonetheless, in the absence of subsidized day care, many mothers had to abandon their education to care for their infants.

Young Mother's Status at 15 to 18 Months After Delivery

Living Arrangements and Marital Status

As shown in Table 5-9, at the time of the second interview, the majority of households were still headed by a female, and the proportion headed by the adolescent mother herself had quadrupled. Six percent of the young mothers overall (2% of black and 24% of white mothers) were married and living with their husbands, the same proportion, but not necessarily the same partners, as at Interview I (Table 5-5). Also, 6% were living with boyfriends to whom they were not married. The vast majority of black adolescents (89%) had neither married nor lived with the father of their baby. While "living together" relationships were more common among whites (37%), they were unstable, with one-fifth reporting dissolution by the time of the second interview. Among those young mothers who had neither married nor lived with the baby's father, 54% perceived her relationship with the father to be less close at this time than when the child was born. Of those who were not married, 59% considered it unlikely that they would ever marry the father, and of those who had never lived with the father, 75% said that it was unlikely that they would ever live with him. The proportion living with parents had declined. Average household size had also declined slightly. There were substantial changes in residence particularly for the white girls, 66% of whom had moved since the first interview. The new residence was reported to be better or the same for most, but 10% of the black and 15% of the white girls who moved felt that the new location was worse.

Income

The annual household income (not shown) was below $10,000 for 52% of both black and white adolescents; for 17% of the black and 14% of the white adolescents household incomes averaged $20,000 or above. This does not represent any real change overall during the prior year. By any standard, most of these families, considering their relatively large size, were poor. In only 60% of families, one or more members contributed earned income to family support. As noted in Table 5-9, 92% of black and 77% of the white adolescent mothers reported Welfare dependency at some point between delivery and the 15- to 18-month interview. In addition, overall 89% had received Medical Assistance, and 70% were still eligible for coverage at Interview II.

Table 5-9 Selected Household Characteristics at Interview II ($\overline{X}$17.6 Months After Delivery) by Adolescent Mother's Race, Number of Children, and Age at Delivery (Numbers Shown Are Percents Unless Otherwise Indicated)

Household characteristics	All adolescent mothers (n = 363)	Race Black (n = 257)	Race White (n = 106)	Number of children ≥2 (n = 50)	Number of children 1 (n = 313)	Age at 1983 delivery (One child only) ≤ 15 yr (n = 115)	Age at 1983 delivery (One child only) 16 yr (n = 88)	Age at 1983 delivery (One child only) 17 yr (n = 110)
Household headed by:								
Female	76	80	56**	81	75	74	77	74
Adolescent mother	8	6	17**	20	6	2	5	10*
Other members present in relation to adolescent:								
Mother	69	73	48***	54	71*	85	78	57***
Both parents	20	19	23	19	20	21	22	18
Either parent	71	75	51***	56	73*	87	81	59***
Married, living with husband	6	2	24	4	6*	3	7	8
Not married, with boyfriend	6	5	12	11	5*	0	6	10**
Number of members: $\bar{x}$	5.8	6.1	4.5	6.1	5.7	6.2	5.7	5.5
17 and younger	3.1	3.3	2.1	3.4	3.0	3.9	3.0	2.5***
5 and younger	1.6	1.7	1.3	2.4	1.5***	1.5	1.5	1.5
Change in residence	46	42	66***	58	45	36	50	46
Change in household	28	25	42**	38	26	12	26	35
Source, family income								
Employment—one or more members employed	60	60	64	60	61	55	56	68
Welfare, currently or since delivery	90	92	77***	96	89	88	90	88
Child's daytime care giver:								
Mother	60	56	75*	79	56*	38	57	67***
Grandmother	18	18	16	5	20	29	21	13
Paid relative/friend	7	8	6	4	8	6	6	10
Unpaid relative/friend	12	14	3	6	13	16	13	10
Family day care	4	5	0	6	3	10	3	0
Foster care	2	1	6*	4	2	3	1	1

*p < .05
**p < .01
***p < .001

Child Care

Arrangements for the child's daytime care had not changed greatly in the prior year. As shown in Table 5-9, somewhat more (75%) of the white and a somewhat smaller proportion (56%) of the black teenagers were at home with their babies. Only 4% received subsidized day care to permit continued education or work. Overall, 10 children (2.5%) had received agency foster care by the time of the second interview. Foster care was much more likely for white than for black children, of whom 6% and 1%, respectively, had been or were in foster care by 15 to 18 months of age. No children had been placed for adoption.

Public Support: Welfare, Food Stamps, and WIC: Pregnancy to Interview II

Table 5-10 provides an indication of the public support received by adolescent mothers and their children in terms of general financial assistance through AFDC (Aid to Families with Dependent Children), food stamps, WIC, and Medical Assistance (MA) programs. The information presented covers the pregnancy and a mean of 17.6 months after the birth of the child. The proportion receiving financial support through AFDC increased as time went by, even though the time period covered was one during which eligibility was restricted because of reductions in the level of federal funds. It included pregnancies in the latter half of 1982, deliveries during all of 1983, and follow-up of mothers and children during 1983, 1984, and the first half of 1985.

During the 18 months after the 1983 birth, AFDC was provided to 90% of the adolescent mothers and/or their children, 92% of the black and 77% of the white. A search of the welfare records in the Department of Human Resources confirms the 90% welfare utilization figure and also indicates that, overall, 95% of mothers and/or their children received Medical Assistance coverage for health care during all or part of the period. The mothers' reports of Medical Assistance utilization (which are slightly lower) are shown in Table 5-10. There are significant differences by both race and age in rates of utilization at 3 months, but the maternal age differences are no longer discernable by 15 through 18 months after birth. Those young mothers who had a second or higher order birth in 1983 were more likely to receive public assistance than those having a first birth. Public assistance was not continuous for all of those who received it, but examination of the AFDC records suggests that a substantial number of the adolescents were in families that had a longstanding history of welfare dependence.

Nutritional supplements were used by large proportions of the young mothers and their children. This is particularly true of WIC, which by the time of the second interview had been used by 94% of the blacks and 86% of the whites and by 96% of those young women with two or more children. Unfortunately, even though more were eligible, only 60% of the white girls received WIC during pregnancy, and only 40% had food stamps. As mentioned previously, the problem may in part reflect the failure of busy private physicians to make the necessary referrals.

Young Mother's Health Since Delivery

Selected observations pertaining to the young mother's health and to the health care resources used in the first 18 months after the 1983 delivery are shown in Table 5-11. For the most part, these young women used public clinics of various

Table 5-10 Public Support: Welfare, Food Stamp, and WIC Program Status during Pregnancy and for Child at Interviews I and II, by Adolescent Mother's Race, Number of Children, and Age at Delivery (Numbers Shown Are Percents)

Program status	All adolescent mothers (n = 389)	Race		Number of children		Age at 1983 delivery (One child only)		
		Black (n = 272)	White (n = 117)	≥2 (n = 58)	1 (n = 331)	≤15 yr (n = 123)	16 yr (n = 92)	17 yr (n = 116)
Welfare support: (full or partial)								
3 mo after delivery	67	71	50***	74	66	78	68	58**
15–18 mo after delivery	90	92	77***	96	89	88	90	88
Food stamp recipient:								
During pregnancy	44	45	40	57	42*	49	43	37
At Interview I	52	56	36**	54	52	62	59	41**
At Interview II[a]	57	58	53	67	55	64	57	49
WIC Program participant:								
During pregnancy	72	74	60*	64	73	74	72	73
At Interview I	88	90	82	83	89	90	87	91
At Interview II[a]	92	94	86	96	92	95	91	90
Had difficulty getting food:								
When pregnant	11	11	10	17	10	10	11	9
Since delivery	16	16	16	20	15	18	19	10
Has had difficulty initiating or maintaining enrollment in:								
Food Stamp Program	15	15	16	21	14	11	9	21
WIC Program	29	26	48**	32	29	31	21	34
Medical assistance:								
Portion of pregnancy:								
None	34	33	36	33	34	30	36	35
Some	14	14	14	7	16	13	14	18
All	52	52	50	61	51	57	50	47
Birth to 18 months								
Mother	70	72	59	88	67*	59	63	74*
Child	84	88	68***	94	83	85	88	78

[a]Based on sample size as in Table 5-12.

$*p < .05$
$**p < .01$
$***p < .001$

kinds for their care. Eleven percent overall, 15% of the whites, had no regular source of care and, as a result, either had no care or used an emergency room. In all, 11% sought care from private physicians. The mean number of ambulatory visits was 6.5; just over three visits, on average, had included family planning services. Overall, however, 16% of the young mothers were without any family planning service, 21% of the white mothers. Eighteen percent of the young mothers were admitted to the hospital during the 18-month period; in 11% the admissions were related to repeat pregnancy.

Another point worth noting is the relatively high frequency of public transportation used for health care, particularly for family planning services. Public transportation in Baltimore is both difficult and expensive, making for difficulty in accessing care, particularly if one has children to take along and very limited financial resources.

Sexual Activity, Perceived Risk and Desirability of Pregnancy, Contraception, and Repeat Pregnancy

As shown in Table 5-12, 77% of the teenagers reported being sexually active at the second interview; of these, 24% reported infrequent intercourse (less than once per month), and only 13% reported intercourse more than once per week. These young women were fairly realistic in their assessment of the risk of pregnancy with unprotected sex. Only 10% felt that it was unlikely. While only 2% said that they would be very happy to be pregnant again, 17% appeared ambivalent, particularly among the whites. However, although most did not want another pregnancy, 32% were not using contraceptives at the time of the second interview.

Table 5-13 presents the contraceptive and repeat pregnancy experience of these young women. Contraceptive use had improved since the 1982–1983 pregnancy. Overall, 68% reported current use of birth control, and most of these reported using prepared and effective methods (pill, foam and condoms, diaphragm, or IUD); 16% reported receiving no contraceptive services, and 32% of the sexually active were not currently using contraceptives.

During the first 6 months after delivery, one girl in 10, and within 12 months one in five (22%), had conceived again. By the time of the second interview, in all, 46% of the young mothers had experienced a repeat pregnancy or a "pregnancy scare." The outcome of these repeat pregnancies is shown in Table 5-13. Where the pregnancy outcome had occurred, 61% resulted in a live birth. Recourse to abortion was more frequent among those who already had two children or were very young. The risk of spontaneous miscarriage among the whites was more than twice that among the blacks, but numbers were small.

Educational Attainment and Work History at Second Interview

Table 5-14 provides information about the young mothers' education and work experiences 15 to 18 months after the 1983 birth. Among the blacks, 47%, and the whites, 82%, had dropped out without completing high school ($p < .001$). The remainder had graduated or were still attending school.

As with their education, the adolescents' employment history also differed significantly by race. In spite of less education, the young white mothers tended to have more work experience than the blacks. However, at the time of the second

Table 5-11 Young Mother's Regular Source of Health Care, Services Received since Birth of Baby in 1983, and Method of Payment by Mother's Race, Number of Children, and Age at Delivery (Numbers Are Percents Unless Otherwise Indicated)

	All adolescent mothers (n = 389)	Race		Number of Children		Age at 1983 delivery (One child only)		
		Black (n = 272)	White (n = 117)	≥2 (n = 58)	1 (n = 331)	≤15 yr (n = 123)	16 yr (n = 92)	17 yr (n = 116)
Regular source of care:								
None or emergency room	11	9	15	16	10	8	8	13
Adolescent preg. program	16	19	3	13	16	26	21	8
Hospital-based Ob/Gyn clinic	18	20	12	14	19	13	19	22
Other hospital clinic	11	11	13	11	11	13	12	11
Neighborhood/community health center[a]	12	11	18	10	12	12	15	11
HMO	10	12	4	11	10	8	13	9
Private physician	11	8	26	16	10	6	7	15
Community FP clinic	9	10	5	8	10	13	5	10
Outside city	1	1	4	2	1	2	0	1
Mean number ambulatory visits (SD)[b]	6.5 (5.3)	6.4 (4.9)	6.9 (6.8)	6.8 (5.7)	6.5 (5.2)	7.3 (6.1)	6.0 (3.6)	6.4 (5.6)
Mean number visits that included Family Planning (SD)[b]	3.1 (2.8)	3.2 (2.7)	2.7 (2.8)	3.5 (3.2)	3.0 (2.7)	3.8 (3.4)	3.1 (2.6)	2.4 (2.1)
Proportion of girls without family planning[b]	16	15	21	18	16	11	18	17
≥1 hospitalizations since delivery[b]	18	19	15	15	19	20	18	19
Due to repeat pregnancy	11	12	7	11	11	10	13	11
Due to other reason	7	7	8	4	8	10	5	8
Source of payment[b]								
Medical assistance	70	72	59	88	67*	59	63	74*
Private insurance	15	15	16	10	16	18	24	9**
HMO enrollment	10	12	2*	14	9	6	10	10
None of above	15	13	24*	4	17*	25	10	17*
Public transportation used:								
For well child care	44	50	17***	54	42	40	41	45
For family planning	51	56	23***	62	49	46	47	53
Mean number appointments missed in past year due to lack of transportation	0.69	0.66	0.83	1.18	0.6	0.67	0.71	0.52

[a]Excludes those that are health maintenance organizations.
[b]Based on sample size at Interview II as shown in preceding table.

*p < .05.
**p < .01.
***p < .001.

Table 5-12 Reported Level of Sexual Activity at Interview II and Attitudes toward Risk and Desirability of Pregnancy by Mother's Race, Number of Children, and Age of Delivery (Numbers Shown Are Percents)

	All adolescent mothers (n = 363)	Race		Number of Children		Age at 1983 delivery (One child only)		
		Black (n = 257)	White (n = 106)	≥2 (n = 50)	1 (n = 313)	≤15 yr (n = 115)	16 yr (n = 88)	17 yr (n = 110)
Sexually active	77	75	83	85	75	68	74	79
Frequency of intercourse:								
None	23	25	17**	15	25	32	24	21
Less than once/month	24	27	13	24	24	27	23	24
Once or twice/month	23	21	30	21	23	18	30	21
Once/week	17	17	15	19	16	13	17	18
More than once/week	13	10	24	21	12	10	7	16
No sex for ≥ 1 month between Interviews I and II	76	78	66*	59	79**	89	80	72*
Perceived likelihood of pregnancy with unprotected sex:								
Almost certain	50	52	40	74	46**	48	52	40
Good chance	16	15	24	8	18	11	15	24
50/50	24	24	24	15	26	28	21	28
Probably not happen	5	5	3	0	5	9	5	3
Almost no chance	5	4	9	4	5	4	7	4
Desirability of pregnancy at Interview II[a]								
Don't want	82	85	62***	80	81	83	83	79
Not planning/would be happy anyhow	17	14	31	18	17	17	15	19
Hoping for/would be very happy	2	1	7	2	2	0	2	2
Number of children wanted (mean)	2.1	2.0	2.5**	2.7	2.0***	2.0	1.9	2.1

[a]Excludes respondents pregnant at time of interview (33/363 = 9%); of these 33% stated they had not wanted to become pregnant, 30% stated they would rather not have become pregnant, and 36% that they were not planning to be pregnant but were happy anyway. None reported desiring the pregnancy.

*p < .05.
**p < .01.
***p < .001.

Table 5-13 Birth Control Use and Repeat Pregnancies since 1983 Birth, by Mother's Race, Number of Children, and Age at Delivery (Numbers Indicate Percents)

	All adolescent mothers (n = 363)	Race		Number of children		Age at 1983 delivery (One child only)		
		Black (n = 257)	White (n = 106)	≥2 (n = 50)	1 (n = 313)	≤ 15 yr (n = 115)	16 yr (n = 88)	17 yr (n = 110)
Birth control use from 1st to 2nd interview:[a]								
None	8	8	9	12	7	11	7	5
Use discontinued	24	24	27	12	26	25	24	29
Currently using	68	69	64	76	67	64	70	66
Method(s) current:								
Pill	82	82	82	67	85*	79	82	90
Other prepared	19	20	13	25	19	30	18	11
Withdrawal	1	0	4*	0	1	1	1	1
Other	2	3	3	8	2	0	4	1
No family planning service	16	15	21	18	16	11	18	17
Repeat conception:								
Within 6 months	11	11	8	8	11	9	15	9
Within 12 months	22	23	18	25	22	23	22	21
Outcome of pregnancy by Interview II:[a]								
Live birth[b]	61	61	61	40	66	48	67	76*
Miscarriage	10	8	22	10	10	13	0	20
Abortion	28	30	17	50	24	39	33	4
Repeat pregnancy or pregnancy scare from 1983 delivery to Interview II	46	47	46	46	47	45	43	50

[a]Excludes the 22 subjects who conceived within 12 months of the 1983 birth but were still pregnant at the time of interview. Of these, 77% stated they planned to have and keep the baby, 14% stated they planned to put the baby up for adoption, and 9% were uncertain of their plans.

[b]All but one respondent had kept her child; for this case, the child (like the 1983 sibling) was living with the maternal grandmother.

*p < .05.

interview, only 17% of the whites and 9% of the blacks were actually employed. Nevertheless, the majority reported wanting to work, and it is of interest that although most had looked for work, only half had received help in their efforts from either family or friends (38%) or professionals (16%). The lack of professional help in job placement appears to have been a major disadvantage, and as with attending school, the lack of adequate and subsidized child care was a serious barrier to seeking and retaining employment.

Representative Cases: The Human Dimension

The numerical and statistical data presented above provide an objective description of adolescent childbearing in a large American city, in terms of the characteristics of the young women involved. While information of this type is essential to planning effective intervention, the quantitative approach often fails to depict the human dimensions of the problem. Pregnant and parenting adolescents are real people, caught up in a chain of events started, in some instances, by an unplanned and often unwanted pregnancy, but in most cases long before. Almost half of these young people terminated their unwanted pregnancy. A slim majority, 54%, carried on with the pregnancy, some because once pregnant they wanted a baby, others because abortion was abhorrent to them, and still others because abortion was unavailable because of its cost. Very few seriously considered adoption, even though many reported discussing this option.

The vignettes presented below were chosen from among the young mothers interviewed to illustrate the range of outcomes observed. They are not presented in any predetermined order. Some of the young mothers had more favorable outcomes than others. Some of the details that might identify individuals have been changed slightly to preserve confidentiality. There was, as shown by Furstenberg (1976) and Furstenberg et al. (1987), a diversity of outcomes. The risk involved in presenting a small number of cases is loss of objectivity. However, one should not lose sight of the fact that, in this study at least, unfavorable outcomes outnumbered those that were satisfactory for mother and child by a wide margin, at least in the short term of an 18-month follow-up.

Case 1

The young family described below seems typical of many of the young white families. The mother was just 18 years old at the time of the second interview. Her child was 16 months old. The mother had completed 8th grade in a city school; she reported having been absent, on the average, more than 10 days per month, and she "dropped out" after which she became pregnant at 16. She delivered at a community hospital and received no parenting instruction. The father was also aged 16 years. The young parents married prior to delivery; both are Roman Catholic. The mother was supported by welfare during the pregnancy and received WIC and Medical Assistance, but, soon after delivery, the father dropped out of school and became employed as a laborer at the minimum wage. The mother also worked for a few months after the birth of her child, who was cared for during the day by his maternal grandmother. With employment, AFDC and Medical Assistance support were cut off. The young parents, now aged 17 years, established their

Table 5-14 Adolescent Mother's Educational Attainment and Employment History at $\overline{X}$17.6 Months after Delivery, by Race, Number of Children, and Age at Delivery (Numbers Shown Are Percents)

	All adolescent mothers (n = 363)	Race		Number of children		Age at 1983 delivery (One child only)		
		Black (n = 257)	White (n = 106)	≥2 (n = 50)	1 (n = 313)	≤ 15 yr (n = 115)	16 yr (n = 88)	17 yr (n = 110)
Education:								
Dropped out	53	47	82***	77	50	38	51	56*
In school and/or graduated H.S.	47	53	18	23	50	62	50	44
Has worked at some time	36	31	58***	36	36	28	29	45**
Worked during pregnancy	10	8	20*	13	10	3	8	16**
Has worked since 1983 birth	29	24	51***	21	30	25	22	40**
Employment status at Interview II:								
Working	10	9	17***	6	11	6	8	16*
Deferring work until:								
School completed	5	6	2	4	5	4	4	7
Children older	10	7	24	12	10	6	5	15
Does not want to work	0ᵃ	0	2	0	0ᵃ	0	1	1
Wants to work now	74	79	54	79	74	85	82	61
Has looked for work since 1983 birth	59	56	75*	52	60	64	51	65
Mother cares for child during dayᵇ	54	46	87***	77	50***	28	53	61***

ᵃLess than 0.5%.
ᵇSee Table 6-9.
  *p < .05.
 **p < .01.
***p < .001.

own home in a rented apartment. The father's job provided no health insurance and insufficient money to cover medical and other expenses. The baby was sickly, with anemia and an elevated blood lead level. He received care in a Title V, Children and Youth Program, but by 16 months he had not yet had all required immunizations. His care was never refused because the mother could not pay.

The mother was provided with a 3-month supply of contraceptive pills at hospital discharge after delivery, but she could not afford more when these "ran out" and she became pregnant again. She had not wanted to be pregnant, but abortion was not an option for her. She had to give up her job after a few months. Their income for the 12-month period, between 3 and 15 months after delivery, was about $6,500 for a family of three (soon to be four), with no insurance. The father is supportive and helpful with child care and housekeeping chores, but life is very difficult because of their inadequate income. Their low levels of education and training reduce the likelihood of much improvement in their present status. The availability of free and accessible family planning services including contraceptives would be enormously helpful to this young family that is struggling hard to be self-sustaining.

Case 2

This young, black adolescent became pregnant at age 15. She was just 17 at Interview II. She had had three prior abortions but was refused support for her request to have this pregnancy terminated. She lived with her mother, uncle, and brother in a "nice" house that appeared to have adequate financial support. She received obstetrical care in one of the hospital programs "targeted to adolescents." Her child had a club foot and received special orthopaedic care.

The mother was not married and did not expect to be married to the baby's father, whom she considered to be "no good." He was then 18 years old and was neither in school nor employed. He had provided food and clothing for the infant, but the mother rated his support as inadequate. He did not visit often. The mother stopped contraception when she stopped "going with" the father, and she is *not* sexually active at the present.

The young mother is continuing in school; she is in 11th grade and hopes to go on to college. The grandmother, who was an adolescent mother herself, was very upset about her daughter's pregnancy at first but has been very supportive of young mother and child. The adolescent received Welfare, Medical Assistance, WIC, and a "day care mother" for the child, who is healthy and developing well. The indications seemed to be that this young mother, who was receiving the support she needs, will manage fairly well. A disturbing note, however, was that, according to the interviewer, the child did not seem attached to the mother, who made no effort to conceal the fact that the pregnancy had been unwanted. This does not bode well for the child's chances for future optimal development.

Case 3

This young mother was a young, black girl from an intact family with an income in excess of $70,000/year. Her mother is a senior professional, and her father is a mid-level administrator in a large corporation. Both she and her boyfriend were students in an elite city high school for gifted, college-bound students when she became pregnant at age 17 years. Her family was disappointed but supportive. She dropped out of school in her senior year to have her baby but, after delivery, completed the work for graduation at summer school. She was admitted to college in another state. Her parents have responsibility for her baby. She aspires to be a lawyer. The young father refuses to acknowledge the pregnancy and has not told his parents of it. He is also in college. Both young parents are Roman Catholic and did not consider abortion. The young mother, because of the support and financial resources of her family, has been able to continue pursuit of her educational goals. She is obviously concerned about her child and her responsibility toward him. The helpfulness of adequate family resources is clearly evident here.

Case 4

This young, black mother was a chronic truant from school. She dropped out after seventh grade. She became sexually active at age 15. She had known the young father only a few days before having intercourse with him. She conceived and, despite urging to terminate the pregnancy by the young father and her mother who was very angry about the pregnancy, she had the baby. She was then 16. The young mother did not get along with her own mother and stepfather, and shortly after the baby was born they "kicked her out of the house." She obtained welfare support without difficulty. The 16-year-old was established in an apartment with her baby. The young father, who preferred to spend time with other girls and their children, did not provide any help.

She was subsequently evicted for nonpayment of rent and when visited by the study interviewer, she was living alone with her child in a "filthy, dirty, trashy" room. The baby was described as "absolutely filthy." She received welfare, food stamps, and WIC. The child had apparently had little preventive health care. He had been hospitalized with acute gastroenteritis. The young mother reported being visited by protective service workers about possible child neglect.

The future appeared very bleak for this socially isolated, inexperienced young mother and for the healthy physical and socioemotional development of the child. Supportive services and parenting education are sorely needed by this young woman.

Case 5

This young white woman had her second unintended pregnancy at age 16 and had a healthy infant after prenatal care in a comprehensive adolescent program. She continued to be sexually active after delivery but had no money for birth control. Her baby received follow-up preventive health care, but the young mother has experienced major social problems. She was "thrown out" of the house by her mother and the mother's boyfriend when she became pregnant for the second time. She reported that she stayed in a different place almost every night. She also reported missing appointments for family planning and child health care because she had no money for transportation. She could not continue in school because she had to take care of her children.

By Interview II, the young mother was living alone with her two children in a small, sparsely furnished apartment. She was enrolled in an HMO. She was receiving welfare but not food stamps, and her WIC had been discontinued, presumably because the HMO in which she was enrolled had not processed the renewal form as had been done for her in the comprehensive adolescent program. She was dissatisfied with the care provided by the HMO but was unable to get back her Medical Assistance card so that she could go elsewhere.

The baby's father, who was 22 years old, helped with food and clothing. He spent time with the children. He completed high school and had a low paying job. The young mother received no help from a totally uncaring family. In fact, she reported that her mother was cited for "child neglect" when she was a child. This is a caring young woman with a good relationship with her boyfriend who is managing fairly well. However, the young family would benefit from case management services so that community services, including family planning, could be coordinated to assist family function.

Case 6

Three months after her 1983 delivery, this 17-year-old white girl was unmarried and living in a four-room apartment with her *three* children and her boyfriend. She had had no prenatal care with the last baby, and her three children had had no preventive health care. She reported being refused medical care because she owed $36 to the clinic to which she went.

She reported many changes in living arrangements. At the time of the second interview, she and her children were living with a foster mother. She now had a *fourth* baby. The household income was reported to be between $4,000 and $5,000 per year. The mother has not received WIC because she did not know how to obtain it. She has not received welfare, AFDC, or Medical Assistance for 2 years because she cannot cope with completing the necessary paperwork and has no one to help her. (The forms are formidable and require considerable reading skill.) She has delivered her babies at a community hospital. She missed many prenatal and family planning visits because she had no babysitter and no money for transportation or contraceptives.

This young family presents the problems of an uneducated, immature woman who receives no help from her own family or from community services. She had neither the knowledge nor the resources to either prevent repeated pregnancy or to provide proper parenting and health care for her children. Without appropriately planned and managed public services, which will reach out to her, the future for this family looks dismal.

Case 7

This unmarried 17-year-old black adolescent received prenatal care in an HMO. She had a LBW infant who did well. She continues to be sexually active but has side effects with oral contraceptives. She missed contraceptive appointments for lack of a babysitter. She had to leave her mother's home because her mother, who is an alcoholic, became abusive. She moved in with her boyfriend, who has graduated from high school, has a steady job, and cares for her and the child. They have a modest income and are doing well. She expects to get her graduate education diploma (GED) and to get a job to help maintain her family.

Case 8

A 17-year-old white girl from an intact, modestly affluent family delivered, after marriage, in one of the comprehensive adolescent programs. She and her husband, who completed high school and is employed in a management position, have their own comfortable home. The baby is healthy and developing well. Both sets of grandparents are supportive and loving. This case attests to the diversity in observed outcomes. Unfortunately, it was the exception rather than the rule.

Case 9

This example of a very difficult problem that is sometimes encountered comes from the TAC program. It was not a part of the random sample described above. A 17-year-old white couple was referred by the Baltimore judicial system to the Johns Hopkins Teenage Clinic and Parenting Program (TAC) for parenting instruction and health supervision for their 4-month-old daughter who allegedly had been neglected. She was a tiny, frail child. The young parents were both moderate to severely retarded. They had been released into community mental health care from a state mental health institution where they had lived since early childhood. They were established in a small apartment and supported by a monthly check from AFDC. The parents and child were brought to the clinic at frequent intervals by their social worker. Intensive parenting education improved the physical and developmental status of the child somewhat but the parents' inability to manage their money, and even the normal events of daily living, precluded adequate care for their child and, after a period of some 8 months, she was placed in agency foster care. The parents promptly carried out their expressed intent of having another child if the first was removed from their care.

This case raises some very difficult ethical questions pertaining to parental rights on the one hand and to children's rights to protection from neglect/abuse on the other. It also raises questions about the humanity and social wisdom of releasing incompetent individuals who have been in institutions for many years to community settings that lack adequate facilities for their care.

Summary and Discussion

As far as could be determined, an unbiased, city-wide, population-based body of data describing the circumstances surrounding adolescent childbearing and parenting was available to us. Although the births considered here occurred in 1983, adolescent birth rates in Baltimore were fairly stable between 1980 and 1985 and have increased somewhat in 1987 and 1988 (Governor's Council on Adolescent Pregnancy, 1989), 1983 appears representative of recent years.

The data provide a series of snapshots over a period of more than 2 years in the lives of the adolescent mothers, from the time they conceived until their children were 15 to 18 months old. The interviews with these young mothers reveal an overall picture of wasted human potential and major public cost. In this population, adolescent childbearing follows an intergenerational pattern. While significant differences were found between these young women by race, by age, and by the number of children they had, the similarities in their situations far outweighed the differences. They were, with few exceptions, poverty-stricken. In some respects, the white girls were the more disadvantaged to begin with, and marriage and moving from the parental home led to even greater disadvantages. The relationships that led to pregnancy were of longer standing than is generally realized. Sexual intercourse began at very young ages for most of these adolescents, well before entry to high school. The great majority of pregnancies were unintended; contraceptive use was low. Almost one-third of black and half of white fathers were considerably older than the mother, i.e., aged 20 and above (Hardy, Duggan, et al., 1989).

Mott and Maxwell (1981), using national data, show an improvement between 1968 and 1979 in the educational attainment of pregnant schoolgirls and a decrease in the proportion married. While our 1983 cohort is not directly comparable, our findings suggest a greater average educational disadvantage for urban white adolescent mothers, only 18% of whom had graduated or were still in school, 15 to 18 months after delivery, than for those in the national sample. Blacks did better with 54% in this category, but were at greater employment disadvantage. With respect to marriage, the urban adolescents were again at greater disadvantage; few were married as compared with national statistics (Hayes, 1987). Similarly, the work experience of the urban adolescent mothers was substantially less and their need for public support proportionally much greater.

Findings Relevant for Intervention

Findings that have particular relevance for intervention and social policy are summarized below. These findings must be considered in light of the fact that they do not include all pregnancies, only those that resulted in live births.

- The data support the view that there is a strong association between adolescent childbearing and poverty, and emphasize the fact that it is a problem of far greater magnitude in poor urban areas, such as Baltimore and other large cities, than across the United States as a whole.
- While the adolescent mothers and their families spanned a broad socioeconomic spectrum, the distribution was markedly skewed to its lower end. More than half of these rather large families have annual incomes below $10,000 and 13% below $5,000. During the more than 2 years that elapsed between conception and the termination of follow-up almost 18 months after delivery, 90% of the mother/child pairs were wholly or partially supported by welfare (during all or part of the time period) and 95% received assistance from Medicaid to cover the cost of medical care.
- The adolescent mothers spanned a broad range of developmental maturity. However, large proportions of the young mothers and the fathers of their babies, particularly among the white couples, had very low educational achievement, predicting a future characterized by continued disadvantage with respect to employment and income.
- Most of the young mothers were single parents, and where marriage occurred, it tended to be unstable. By the time of the second interview, 10 of the study children had already been placed in agency foster care for severe neglect and/ or abuse.
- The cases show the importance of support from families to the well-being of mother and baby, as described by Furstenberg (1976). They also show the important role appropriate community services can play in providing resources where families are unable to do so. They make clear the sad fact that needed public resources may not be available, even to eligible adolescents, because of difficulty with access, lack of coordination, lack of transportation, lack of referral, and other barriers including ethical considerations. Specific interventions and their effect are discussed in Part III.

• A pregnancy prevention policy that is based on "*Just Say No!*" would seem doomed to failure in an urban population of teenagers where the very early onset of coitus is normative behavior and single parenthood the rule. When these behaviors are coupled with an intergenerational pattern of early parenthood and childbearing, and with limited access to the information and preventive health services required, the inevitable result is a high prevalence of unintended pregnancy, the birth of unplanned and often unwanted children, and of STDs. The cycle of poverty with its attendant health problems is continued.

6

Partners of Adolescent Mothers

The objective of this chapter is to describe the fathers of infants born to urban adolescent mothers ($\leq$17 years at delivery) and their relationships with mother and child. Much less information generally is available about the males than about the females. The fathers are less visible, and because they do not require, or are not eligible for, some of the services received by the young mothers, they are difficult to reach. The fathers, as indicated in Chapter 4, are, in general, considerably older than the mothers, and their ages span a broad range. Few are adolescents, and many are no longer teenagers at the time their child is born. This diversity in age contributes to the difficulty in reaching them.

For those fathers who are teenagers, as Montemayor (1986) suggests, their fatherhood is a deviation from two important norms in the transition to adulthood. It is premature and it is not in the normal sequence of major life events. It would appear to offer few social advantages. For those young men who live with the young mothers and try to be responsible fathers, it may mean dropping out of school, low status, poorly paid employment, and reduced lifetime earnings (Card and Wise, 1978). It may also mean a foreshortened adolescence and social isolation from peers at a time in life when peers play a dominant role in adolescent development.

These fathers, unless they marry the young mother or establish paternity and play a father's role, will have no legal rights with respect to their child, although they may be required to provide for his or her financial support (see Chapter 10).

Recent reviews of research pertaining to teenage fatherhood and its problems (Elster and Lamb, 1986) and to the fathers of babies born to teenagers (Hanson et al., 1989; Hofferth and Hayes, 1987; Smollar and Ooms, 1987) provide information about many aspects of premature parenthood among males. In this chapter, we are concerned with the fathers of babies born to adolescents regardless of their age.

The methodology for this study is described in the introduction to Part II, page 54. In brief, the descriptions of the fathers and their relationships with mother and child are drawn from interviews with the young mother at 3 months ($n = 389$) and 15 to 18 months after delivery ($n = 363$), supplemented by data from birth certificates. The interview data are secondhand and represent the perception of the mother. In some instances, because she no longer had contact with the father, she was unable to provide information. Four fathers had died. Numbers in the tables reflect the extent of the missing information. Most tables include 355 cases; however, in the final Table 6-6, all are accounted for. Despite the problems, seemingly reliable and important information was forthcoming, and a picture of these fathers and their problems emerged.

It should be noted that 56% of the population in Baltimore was other than white in ethnic origin and that 98% of the nonwhites were black. In this study all nonwhites are considered to have been black. The mother's race was used in the analyses. In very few instances was the father's race, as reported on the birth certificate, different from that of the mother.

Father's Age

Among 1983 births to Baltimore adolescent mothers, the age of the fathers spanned from 15 to 39 years among whites and from 14 to 50 years among blacks. The white fathers were an average of four years older than the mothers. The black fathers were generally closer in age to the mothers; they were an average of two to three years older. The distribution of father's age is shown in Table 6-1 by the mothers' race, age, and parity. These data are for all 1983 adolescent births in Baltimore, used here rather than the distributions for the random sample ($n = 389$) (which were very similar) because of small numbers in some maternal age/race cells in the latter data base. Very few fathers (5%) of either race were less than 16 years of age at the births of their children. This observation is in accord with Marsiglio's (1986) report of data from the National Longitudinal Survey of Youth (NLSY). He found only 11% aged 16 and below among the 475 young men whose first child was born before they reached age 20. The low frequency of very young fathers seems rather surprising in view of the fact that sexual activity among males begins very early in this population (see Chapter 2). It suggests that males, like females, may experience some degree of subfecundity during the early years after puberty.

As indicated, many of the fathers were no longer teenagers when their child was born. Even among first births to adolescent mothers, 45% of the white and 28% of the black fathers were aged 20 or above. Among second and higher order births, the fathers were generally considerably older, 60% of the white and 58% of the black were 20 or above.

Father's Education and Employment Status

We turn now to data from the interviews with the mothers. As seen in Table 6-2, there were marked differences by race in the educational attainment of the fathers in this study sample and, within each race, by age at the time the child was 15 to 18 months old. Among white fathers age 20 and above, only 24% had completed high school, and 48% had not passed beyond ninth grade. By comparison, among older black fathers, 54% had completed high school, and 6% had post-high school education, with only 8% not having gone beyond ninth grade. As shown in Chapter 4, Table 4-6, the fathers of babies born to adolescent mothers were at significant educational disadvantage as compared with those whose partners were 20 or above when they gave birth.

When comparisons were made between the data on father's education at approximately 18 months after the child's birth, cited above, and those available from the birth certificates, very little change, beyond a minimal increase in the

Table 6-1 Father's Age: Percent Distribution by Mother's Race, Parity, and Age at Delivery

Mothers' race and age	First order births[b] Total (N)	< 15	16/17	18/19	≥20	Second and higher births[a] Total (N)	< 15	16/17	18/19	≥20
All races										
Total	(1,095)	5	26	39	31***	(162)	1	12	29	59
≤ 14	(96)	17	42	27	15					
15	(131)	10	38	33	20					
16	(336)	3	29	40	29					
17	(482)	2	16	43	41					
Black[b]										
Total	(900)	5	27	40	28***	(132)	1	12	29	58
≤ 14	(92)	17	42	26	14					
15	(152)	9	40	33	18					
16	(275)	3	30	41	26					
17	(381)	1	15	46	38					
White[b]										
Total	(195)					(30)	0	10	30	60
≤ 14	(4)	—c	—c	—c	—c					
15	(29)	10	28	31	31					
16	(61)	3	23	33	41					
17	(101)	2	18	29	52					

Data from resident recorded live births to women under 18 years of age at delivery, Baltimore, 1983.

[a] Values are percentages, which may not total 100 due to rounding.

[b] Excludes 26 births to black adolescents and 18 births to white adolescents with missing data on parity or father's age.

[c] Percentage not calculated due to denominator <10.

***χ² distribution of father's and mother's age for first order births significant at p < .001.

103

Table 6-2 Father's Education and Work Experience: Percent Distribution by Father's Age and Mother's Race

Mother's race		White				Black			
Father's age at child's birth	Total (N = 355)	Total (103)	<18 (17)	18–19 (38)	≥20 (48)	Total (252)	<18 (78)	18–19 (97)	≥20 (77)
Highest grade completed*									
Ninth or less	24	53	55	58	48	11	22	6	8††
Tenth or eleventh	37	31	37	34	28	40	49	34	37
Twelfth	36	16	8	8	24	45	29	54	49
Post-high school	3	0	0	0	0	4	0	5	6
School/work status*									
Both in school and working	1	1	0	3	0†	1	1	2	0†††
In school only	8	2	14	0	0	11	28	5	3
Working only	54	74	51	73	81	46	26	51	57
Neither in school nor working	36	23	35	24	19†	42	44	41	40
Has never worked***	26	5	6	5	4	35	50	29	29††
Is neither in school, working, nor looking for work	14	7	8	8	6	17	14	15	20

Data collected at interview $\bar{X}$17.6 months after child's birth.

***Difference by race, $p < .001$.

†Difference by age within race, $p < .05$.

††Difference by age within race, $p < .01$.

†††Difference by age within race, $p < .001$.

frequency of high school graduation among 18/19 year olds, was noted. It would seem that many of these fathers, particularly among the whites, had dropped out of school before the child was born and did not return. By the time the children in the study were almost 18 months old, only 10% of their fathers were still attending school.

Despite the fact that black fathers had received more education than white, they were at greater disadvantage in employment. A significantly greater proportion of white fathers were employed, 75% as compared with 47% of the black. Twice as many of the black fathers (42%) were neither employed nor in school as compared with the white (23%). It is important to note that 26% of all fathers had never worked and that 7% of white and 17% of black fathers who were neither in school nor working were not even seeking work.

Relationships with Baby's Mother, Marital Status, and Cohabitation

Data describing the relationship between the adolescent mother and the father of her baby are presented in Table 6-3. These couples were, for the most part, well-acquainted when conception occurred. Only 10% had known each other for fewer than 6 months, and over half had known each other for a minimum of 2 years. Instances of pregnancy occurring after a very short acquaintance were observed but were rare in this study.

Marital status differed markedly by race of mother. Very few of the black but almost one-third of the white couples were married at some point during the study. As noted in Table 6-3, the marriages tended to be unstable. An additional proportion of couples lived together at some point, but these relationships were also unstable. Among those young mothers who had neither married nor lived with the father of the 1983 baby, 60% considered marrying the father unlikely, and 74% had no expectation of living with him.

Children by Other Women

One of the problems in reaching the fathers is that one in five had a child or children by other women in addition to the study adolescent. At the second interview, 20% of the young mothers reported that the father of their 1983 baby had a child by another woman (Table 6-3). Among older fathers, 29% of the white and 36% of the black fathers were known to have children by women other than those in our 1983 sample; 12% of the mothers did not know whether the father had other children.

Relationships with Respect to the 1983 Pregnancy

As shown in Table 6-4, large proportions of the pregnancies were unplanned and unintended (89%), 95% of the black and 75% of the white. Less than half of the couples had even discussed the possibility that pregnancy might occur. Younger fathers, i.e., those closer in age to the mother, were somewhat more likely to have done so than the older fathers ($p < .05$). Among those couples who discussed a possible pregnancy, fathers desired a pregnancy significantly more often than the

Table 6-3 Characteristics Pertaining to Father's Relationship with Baby's Mother: Percent Distribution by Mother's Race and Father's Age

Mother's race		White				Black			
Father's age at child's birth	Total (N = 355)	Total (103)	<18 (17)	18–19 (38)	>19 (48)	Total (252)	<18 (78)	18–19 (97)	>19 (77)
Months known by child's mother prior to conception									
Less than 6	9	8	0	11	8	11	10	4	16
6–11	8	13	6	8	21	6	7	5	8
12–23	24	20	29	15	23	26	31	25	23
24 or more	58	58	65	66	49	57	52	66	53
Married to child's mother									
Before learning of pregnancy***	5	14	19	8	17	1	0	1	1
At child's birth***	9	27	29	24	32	1	0	1	1
3 months after birth***	8	22	27	16	26	2	0	3	2
15 months after birth***	8	23	23	18	29	2	0	3	2
Separated from child's mother at									
15 months after birth***	3	10	7	13	9	0	0	0	0
Not married to but living with child's mother:									
At child's birth*	7	12	12	11	13	4	2	7	4
3 months after birth	9	12	5	13	14	7	6	9	7
15 months after birth	8	11	6	14	11	7	6	7	8
Child's mother considers marriage unlikely[a]	60	62	55	54	69	60	57	57	64
Child's mother considers living together unlikely[b]	74	69	73	59	74	76	76	72	81
Has children by other women[c]	20	22	6	17	29†††	20	12	14	36†††

Data from interviews at 3 and 15 to 17 months after child's birth.

[a]Denominator equals fathers not married to child's mother at Interview II.

[b]Denominator equals fathers neither married to nor living with child's mother at Interview II.

[c]Denominator excludes the 12% of cases in which the child's mother reported she did not know whether the father had children by other women.

*Difference by race, $p < .05$.

***Difference by race, $p < .001$.

†††Difference by age within race, $p < .001$.

Table 6-4 Characteristics Pertaining to Desirability of Pregnancy, Use of Birth Control, and Knowledge of Pregnancy: Percent Distribution by Mother's Race and Father's Age

Mother's race		White				Black			
Father's age at child's birth	Total (N = 355)	Total (103)	<18 (17)	18–19 (38)	>19 (48)	Total (252)	<18 (78)	18–19 (97)	>19 (77)
Pregnancy unplanned***	89	75	66	78	75	95	96	94	96
Possibility of pregnancy discussed*	45	56	63	55	54	41	52	30	45
Pregnancy desired:									
By father[a]	55	61	52	71	56	52	34	64	59
By mother[a]***	39	64	51	60	72	25	13	29	33
By mother[b]****	21	41	30	45	42	13	11	12	15
Birth control used at time of conception**	13	6	0	2	10	16	10	18	18
Condoms/withdrawal ever used prior to conception[c]	26	33	19	31	40	24	20	27	22

Data from Interview II, $\bar{X}$17.6 months after child's birth.

[a]Denominator limited to cases in which mother of baby reported that she and the child's father discussed the possibility of pregnancy prior to conception.

[b]Denominator includes all cases.

[c]In relations with mother of child.

*Difference by race, $p < .05$.

**Difference by race, $p < .01$.

***Difference by race, $p < .001$.

mothers. It must be remembered that these data reflect the mother's perception of her own and the father's wishes. Furthermore, because they were collected after the birth of the child, they may not reflect accurately the status around the time of conception.

Despite the fact that 95% of the black mothers and 75% of the white reported that the pregnancy was unplanned, only 13% were using any method of contraception around the time of conception, and only 26% of the couples had ever used a male method, i.e., condoms or withdrawal, prior to conception.

Three-quarters of the fathers were informed of the pregnancy within a week of its diagnosis and an additional 10% within 1 month. One father was never told, and 12 fathers learned about it after the birth of the child. Two-thirds of the fathers who were not living with the mother were reported to have been helpful to her, in various ways, during pregnancy. Some went with her to a prenatal clinic, some provided food, and some helped with preparations for the baby.

Relationships with Mother and Child

As described in the preceding chapter about the young mothers, the relationships between mothers and fathers tended to be unstable even when the couple was married or cohabited. Over the approximately 18-month follow-up period, the fathers' contact with the mothers and children became significantly less. At the time of the second interview, 58 of the 363 fathers (16%) were living with the mother and child. These fathers were assumed to play a father's role and to have daily contact with the child. Among those not living with the child, over 90% had had some contact with him or her during the first 15 months of life. As shown in Table 6-5, during the first 3 months, half of the nonresident fathers had daily contact; only 7% had none at all. However, by the time the child was 12 to 15 months, there had been a substantial decline; less than one-quarter had contact every day and 16% had no contact.

The mothers' assessments of the fathers' enjoyment of time spent with the child and of the adequacy of his help in childrearing and financial support are also shown in Table 6-5. Two-thirds of the fathers seemed to like to spend time with their child "a lot." Black fathers appeared to enjoy it significantly more than those who were white ($p < .01$). But half of the fathers were reported to provide too little help with childrearing tasks; white fathers helped significantly less than black ($p < .05$). Over 60% were judged to provide too little financial support, with black fathers providing less support than whites ($p < .01$). In reviewing the data presented above, one is left with the impression that among whites, older fathers provide less help with childrearing ($p < .05$) and financial support than younger ones, who are closer in age to the mother.

Fathers' Living Arrangements at Interview II

Table 6-6 provides information about the fathers' living arrangements at the second interview. These data provide important insights with respect to the problems faced by adolescent mothers, their partners, and children.

Among the 363 fathers whose partners were interviewed 15 to 18 months after delivery, 58 (16%) were reported to be living with the mother and child. Of the

Table 6-5 Fathers Neither Married to Nor Living with Children's Mothers: Percent Distribution of Characteristics Pertaining to Role During Pregnancy and Following Child's Birth, by Mother's Race and Father's Age

Mother's race		White				Black			
Father's age at child's birth	Total (N = 321)	Total (76)	<18 (13)	18–19 (29)	>19 (34)	Total (245)	<18 (78)	18–19 (91)	>19 (76)
Spent time with child in first 15 mo*	90	83	84	83	84	92	94	95	87
Frequency of contact in first 3 months									
Daily	52	53	38	68	46	51	56	50	47
Weekly	27	26	26	13	37	28	27	27	29
Monthly or less often	14	14	18	10	16	14	11	17	13
None	7	7	18	9	0	7	5	6	11
Frequency of contact in months 12–15									
Daily	24	30	29	31	28	23	15	20	34
Weekly	36	33	32	32	35	36	44	34	32
Monthly or less often	24	17	19	22	12	26	29	29	21
None	16	20	19	16	25	15	13	17	14
Likes to spend time with child**									
A lot	66	54	53	64	46	69	72	65	72
Some/a little	24	24	29	18	26	25	26	24	25
Not at all	10	22	18	18	29	6	3	11	3
Helps too little in raising child**	50	33	40	12	49†	55	54	57	55
Provides too little financial support**	61	46	60	30	56	65	70	64	61

Data from Interview II, $\overline{X}$17.6 months after child's birth.

*Difference by race, $p < .05$.

**Difference by race, $p < .01$.

†Difference by age within race, $p < .05$.

Table 6-6 Percent Distribution of the Living Arrangements of Father of Baby at Second Interview by Age of Father and Race of Mother ($n = 365$)

Mother's race Father's age at child's birth	Black		White	
	≤19	≥20	≤19	≥20
Married to and/or living with baby's mother				
(Total *N*)	(58)	(14)	(8)	(17)	(19)
Living with family of baby's mother	10	17	10	17	0
Living with family of baby's father	24	48	19	23	10
Living in own household	62	36	62	55	90
Other	3	0	10	6	0
Neither married nor living with baby's mother[*,***]				
(Total *N*)[a]	(303)[a]	(156)	(72)[††]	(39)	(28)
Living with a parent	60	70	51	54	39
Living with another woman	6	5	3	8	11
Living alone	5	2	4	8	18
Other living situation	11	6	22	13	11
In jail[b]	7	8	11	3	0
In armed services	4	5	3	3	0
Unknown	10	6	6	12	21

[a]Excludes four cases where the father of the baby is deceased.

[b]An additional 5 fathers had been in jail and had been released since the birth of the baby.

*Difference by race among those ≤19 years, $p < .05$.

***Difference by race among those ≤20 years, $p < .001$.

††Difference by age among blacks, $p < .01$.

58, 35 (60%) were living in their own households as a nuclear family. That is just under 10% of those interviewed. The remaining 23 couples and their children were living, for the most part, with in-laws. Marsiglio (1987), using data from the National Longitudinal Survey of Youth, presents a rather different picture. His nationally representative data, while not directly comparable with ours because of limitation to teenage fathers, showed that substantially larger proportions of the young fathers were: 1) married to the mother (52%) either before or shortly after the child's birth; and 2) living with their children (77% of the more affluent white, 58% of the disadvantaged white, and 15% of the black).

In our sample, among those fathers who were not living with the mother and child, 60% lived with a parent, usually his mother; 6% were living with a woman other than the adolescent mother; 5% lived alone; and 4% were in the armed services. It is of interest that 7% were incarcerated and that an additional 2% had been in jail and released since the child was conceived.

Summary and Discussion

Although no direct measures of the fathers' socioeconomic status were available, certain inferences seem appropriate. Based on education, employment status, and living arrangements, and on the adolescent mothers' Welfare and Medical Assistance status, these fathers suffered serious degrees of socioeconomic disadvantage, with little hope of major improvement unless substantial job training and placement efforts were to become available to them. This social disadvantage seems in most instances to have been an antecedent and concomitant rather than a direct consequence of premature fatherhood.

Of particular concern are the older fathers. Because of the severity of their educational and employment disadvantage and because of their high frequency of children by more than one woman, the quality of their relationships with the adolescent mothers appears more deviant than that of the younger men. The fact that their infants have a higher frequency of low birth weight than those of young fathers may be indirect evidence of their greater socioeconomic disadvantage and greater social deviance (see Chapter 7).

Another indicator of deviance and disadvantage among the fathers of babies born to adolescents is the report that 26 (7.3%) of the 355 men, whose whereabouts were known, were or had been in jail. Elster et al. (1987) have reported observing an even higher frequency of judicial involvement and conduct disorders among the fathers of infants born to adolescent mothers.

The overwhelmingly negative factors notwithstanding, some of the fathers (16%) were living with their children, and 10% had established an independent nuclear family living in their own household. Even among those fathers who were not living with the mother and child, the majority remained in contact with the child and provided some support. Considering the socioeconomic disadvantages faced by these fathers, it does not seem surprising that 25% of the white and 14% of the black fathers lost contact with the mothers and their children; their inability to contribute to their support in a major way may have caused many of them great frustration and despair.

An important issue concerning the male role in adolescent pregnancy is one which is seldom raised in the popular press or elsewhere. It was not addressed in this study, but it must be mentioned. It is the role in adolescent pregnancy of sexual abuse or, if not actual physical abuse, of coercion of young girls to have intercourse with older men. Our own clinical experience and anecdotal evidence from other professionals who work with adolescents suggest that sexual abuse and coercion are not rare events. The usual perpetrators seem to be men in the adolescent's immediate environment: fathers, mothers' boyfriends, and older brothers. Also, we have encountered young girls scarcely past puberty who have become prostitutes, sometimes at the urging of their own mothers. These are situations that, unfortunately, are likely to pass unrecognized through the average prenatal or abortion clinic. Parents tend to hide the truth, the adolescents involved are often too afraid or too embarrassed to admit to abuse, and staff insensitive to the needs of adolescents fail to recognize the underlying problems.

Our data describing the characteristics of the fathers of infants born to urban, adolescent mothers are generally in accord with the results of the bivariate analyses recently reported by Hanson et al. (1989). They examined the likelihood of fatherhood over a 2-year period (1980 to 1982) among a cohort of young men who were high-school sophomores in 1980. These teenagers were included in the National High School and Beyond Survey. The finding of significant relationships between teenage fatherhood and lower educational expectations of the young fathers, their parents, and peers, and of lower academic achievement and increased disciplinary problems as compared with those who did not become fathers, extend our observations. The results of their multivariate analyses indicated that mother's education, peers' educational values, and the value put on work were significant predictors of premature fatherhood. Race, i.e., being black, and steady dating were also predictors of fatherhood. However, other family and personal characteristics did not produce significant results in the multivariate models, perhaps because of small sample size. Results from this and an earlier study (Hanson et al., 1987) suggest that attitudes toward out-of-wedlock childbearing and "going steady" are important predictors for teenage childbearing for both males and females.

In summary, our data from a city-wide, random sample of births to urban adolescents make several points with important implications for intervention to prevent unintended adolescent pregnancy; several of these points emphasize both the need to reach young men and the difficulties involved in doing so.

The fathers spanned a wide age range, and substantial proportions are not teenagers.

- The majority of the fathers and mothers had known each other for 2 years or longer.
- It was the rare father who was not informed of the birth of his child, less than 0.5%.
- These fathers, on average, exhibited substantial educational and occupational deficits, making it difficult for them to establish stable families and to support their children.
- Eighteen months after the child's birth, the majority of the fathers still lived with parents, usually a single mother.
- Contact between father and child diminished substantially during the 18-month follow-up.
- Finally, 20% of the fathers were reported by the mother to have a child by another woman; among fathers aged 20 and above, the likelihood was 29% among the whites and 36% among the blacks.

In our view, the problems associated with the male partners involved in adolescent childbearing are as socially destructive as those that jeopardize the development of the young mothers and their children. It is clear from the evidence presented above that the problems are intensified in the culture of urban poverty in which they are rooted. Needed interventions are discussed in Part IV.

7
The Infants
of Adolescent Mothers

Outcomes for children borne by adolescent mothers have been described in excellent reviews of the consequences of adolescent childbirth (Baldwin and Cain, 1980; McAnarney and Hendee, 1989; Strobino, 1987). These children may be in jeopardy because of the adverse effects of interactions between biological vulnerability (stemming from pregnancy and perinatal factors, such as inadequate maternal nutrition, STDs, substance abuse, and low birth weight [LBW]); an unfavorable, and often unstable, environment (due to poverty and social disadvantage); and poor parenting (a result of the normal characteristics of adolescent development, single parenthood, lack of requisite information, and inadequate role models). These conditions can be formidable barriers to normal child health and development. In the two preceding chapters, we have described the characteristics, during the early months after delivery, of urban adolescent mothers and the fathers of their babies, painting a generally bleak picture of the conditions in which these people and their families live. While, as described, diversity in education, family income, and other parameters was observed, the vast majority were poor as evidenced by welfare utilization for full or partial support by 90% and Medical Assistance by 95% during the 18 months that elapsed between the child's birth and the termination of the study.

We turn now to an exploration of the health and development of the children. During the course of the study "Resource Use by Pregnant and Parenting Adolescents" described in the introduction to Part II, information was collected about the babies of the adolescent mothers in the city-wide random sample from the time of birth until they were almost 18 months of age. As described under "Methods," page 55, the information sources were the Certificate of Live Birth and two interviews with the young mother in her home; the first was at 3 months and the second between 15 and 18 months ($\overline{X}$17.6) after the infant's birth.

Information was collected about the birth, the infant's health and development, and the caretaking environment. The data pertaining to infant health and health care are unusually rich, but those pertaining to the quality of parenting, child care, and development are less well-developed, as these issues were not a primary focus of the study. The child's living arrangements and relationships with his or her father have been described in the preceding chapters. Details of the methodology and findings have been reported elsewhere (Hardy, Duggan, et al., 1989). Aspects of child outcome during the 15- to 18-month follow-up are described below.

Neonatal Outcome

Birth Weight

Because of the importance of low birth weight (less than 2,500 g) to infant survival and the integrity of later physical and cognitive development among survivors (Hardy, Drage, et al., 1979; Hardy and Mellits, 1977) and to the costs of neonatal care (Schwartz, 1989), our discussion begins with a description of relationships between parental age, race, and the frequency of LBW among the infants of adolescent mothers below 18 years at delivery.

Using data from birth certificates for all first births to Baltimore adolescents in 1983, relationships among maternal age, race, and the frequency of LBW were explored. Similarly, data pertaining to age of father, when the mother was an adolescent, were also examined. The results are shown in Table 7-1. As described in many prior studies of adolescent populations, these Baltimore adolescent mothers, in general, had frequencies of LBW higher than those experienced by older teens and by mothers aged 20 and above (Chapter 4). Also, as is the case with older mothers, black adolescents had higher frequencies of LBW than did whites. An interesting and unexplained finding is that the highest frequencies of LBW for both blacks (20%) and whites (15%) were among 16-year-olds rather than among the youngest mothers. We have observed this phenomenon in other Baltimore data sets and speculate that a number of factors may be involved. In the Johns Hopkins Adolescent Pregnancy Program (HAC) (Chapter 11), girls age 15 and below had the highest average weight gain during pregnancy, babies with the highest average birth weight, and lowest frequency of LBW of any teenage group. Most were still living with parents and had more adequate care than 16-year-olds, some of whom lived with boyfriends, alone, or in makeshift arrangements with relatives or friends. Also, most adolescent mothers, age 15 or less, were first time mothers, while among 16-year-olds 26% were having a second or higher order birth. Repeated childbirth among adolescents is associated with increased risk of preterm delivery and LBW.

The significantly higher risk of LBW when the father's age was 20 or older than when he was closer in age to the young mother, particularly among blacks where the difference was highly significant ($p < .001$), was a surprise. However, as shown in the preceding chapter, these older fathers, when paired with adolescent

Table 7-1 Number and Proportion of Live Births below 2,500 g by Adolescent Mothers' Race and Age at Delivery and by Fathers' Age[a]

Age (yr)	All first births			White			Black		
	Total	N	%	Total	N	%	Total	N	%
Mothers'									
≤15	300	45	15	39	3	8	261	42	16
16	397	77	19	73	11	15	324	65	20
17	605	87	14	130	16	12	475	71	15
Fathers'									
≤17	325	48	15	48	5	10	277	43	16
18–19	419	55	13	60	6	10	359	49	14
≥20	334	61	18	86	11	13	248	50	20

[a]All resident recorded first births to adolescents, less than 18 years with known values, Baltimore, 1983.

mothers, are at high social risk in terms of low educational attainment and employment, and one-third are reported to have children by other women. The risk of LBW among these couples may reflect their high level of social deviance and disadvantage rather than the father's age per se. Little and Sing (1986) report lower birth weight among fathers who are "regular" drinkers than other fathers.

As the data just presented are for all 1983 first live births to adolescents, they include neonatal deaths. Nonetheless, the distributions of LBW by maternal and paternal age among the 389 infants in the city-wide, random study sample were not essentially different from those shown here, as may be seen for maternal age in Table 7-2. It is useful to note, also, that overall the mother's reports of infant birth weight compare quite well with weights reported on the birth certificates. As expected, white babies weighed on the average more than black babies and had a frequency of LBW less than half that of the black babies (7 versus 16%).

Gestational Age at Delivery

In combination with birth weight, gestational age at delivery provides a measure of the adequacy of fetal growth during pregnancy. Table 7-2 shows the frequency of preterm delivery (less than 37 completed weeks) among the 389 study babies. Overall, 26% of infants were preterm, significantly ($p < .01$) more among blacks (29%) than whites (12%). Comparison of mothers' estimates of the frequency of early delivery with data from birth certificates shows considerable discrepancy and suggests that the mothers' reports on this item 3 months after delivery may not be reliable.

Length of Infant's Hospital Stay

The duration of the infant's hospital stay after birth is important to the infant's development, because if the baby stays after the mother has left the hospital and the closeness required for optimal bonding is interrupted, maternal attachment may be impeded, hindering the infant's subsequent development (Klaus and Kennell, 1983). From the societal perspective, much of the expense involved in providing health care for the adolescent mother and her infant results from their utilization of inpatient hospital care. As shown in Table 7-2, on average, the babies stayed six nights after birth, two longer than their mother's average length of stay. However, while two-thirds of the infants stayed three nights or less, 23% stayed longer than 1 week, and 3% stayed longer than 1 month.

Neonatal Intensive Care

Overall, as shown in Table 7-2, 8% of the black infants and 11% of the white ones required admission to a neonatal intensive care unit (NICU). The reasons for NICU admission, as reported by the mother, are shown in Table 7-3. They reflect the usual experience that such admissions are most often associated with marked degrees of prematurity and LBW and that other kinds of neonatal pathology, such as severe congenital malformations, are relatively infrequent in this maternal age group. Neonatal intensive care has been highly successful in reducing neonatal mortality, but its complexity and intensity make it very expensive, costing on the average $30,000 to $40,000 per infant. For very small and/or sick infants, costs may amount

Table 7-2 Neonatal Outcome by Adolescent Mothers' Race, Number of Children, and Age at Delivery[a]

Infant characteristics	All adolescent mothers (n = 389)	Race		Number of children		Age at 1983 delivery (One child only)		
		Black (n = 272)	White (n = 117)	≥2 (n = 58)	1 (n = 331)	≥15 yr (n = 123)	16 yr (n = 92)	17 yr (n = 116)
Mean birth weight (g)[b]	3,091	3,044	3,292**	3,096	3,089	3,117	3,094	3,068
<2,500 (< 5–1/2 lb)	14	16	7	11	15	16	17	12
Birth weight:[c]								
< 2,500 gm	14	15	10	9	15	15	17	14
< 1,500 gm	3	3	2	0	3	3	2	4
Actual vs. expected date of delivery[b]								
>4 wk earlier	11	11	11	12	11	15	10	10
>2 wk earlier	28	30	19	29	27	31	28	25
Gestational age[c]								
< 37 wk	26	29	12**	22	26	31	35	18**
Hospital stay (mean number of nights):								
child[b]	5.6	5.8	4.7	4.7	5.7	5.2	6.7	5.4
Baby in NICU[d]	8	8	11	3	9	6	14	8

[a]Numbers shown are percents unless otherwise indicated (random sample).

[b]Mothers' reports, birth weight converted from pounds to grams.

[c]Data from birth certificates.

[d]NICU, neonatal intensive care unit.

**$p < .01$.

116

Table 7-3   Reasons for Admissions for Neonatal Intensive Care[a]

Premature (presumably also LBW)	13
Lung problems	4
Breathing difficulty	3
Underweight	2
Temperature kept dropping (low)	2
Jaundice	2
Heart stopped beating	1
"Baby swallowed liquid when born"	1
Lack of oxygen	1
Infection from mother	1
Low weight and low temperature	1
Swollen head	1
Uncertain	1

[a]Mothers' reports.

to hundreds of thousands of dollars. Using the conservative figure of $30,000 per case and an 8% frequency of utilization, one estimates that neonatal intensive care for the babies of the adolescents delivered in Baltimore in 1983 costs $3,124,500.

Perinatal and Infant Mortality

The study from which the data presented in this chapter were derived was not designed to determine risks of perinatal and infant mortality for babies born by adolescent mothers. However, this important outcome cannot be ignored. As reported by McCormick et al. (1984) experience in four regions in the United States between 1973 and 1978 showed that two groups of mothers were at unusually high risk for infant mortality and morbidity. These were mothers who delivered as adolescents, prior to age 18 and those 18- and 19-year-olds with prior births. Despite a decrease in infant mortality over the period, infants born to young mothers in these two high-risk groups were 1½ times as likely to experience neonatal mortality as those born to other mothers. The increased risk was attributable to the increased frequency of LBW in these two groups. Postneonatal mortality was also high in the infants of these mothers and appeared to be increasing over the period of the study. The high rates of infant mortality and the increased morbidity observed in surviving infants were found to be consistent with the socioeconomic disadvantage of the young mothers.

McAnarney and Hendee (1989), in a recent review of problems associated with adolescent pregnancy, comment on the greater risks of neonatal mortality among infants of mothers under age 18 and point to the postneonatal risks of these infants as being approximately twice those of other infants. The risk of SIDS (sudden infant death syndrome) is reported to be higher among the infants of young mothers; it has been reported to be between almost 2½ (Standfast et al., 1980) and 5 times (Peterson et al., 1982) that of infants of mothers 25 to 29 years of age.

Data on perinatal and infant deaths among the infants of adolescents as compared with older women in the Johns Hopkins Perinatal Study, reported in Chapter 9, also show the greater risks of the babies of adolescents. In our clinical experience in the HAC where almost 3,000 adolescents have received care during the past 10 years, perinatal deaths have been infrequent. They have occurred, for the most part, in association with very LBW and/or the presence of severe congenital malformations.

Table 7-4 Characteristics of Preventive Child Health Care at 3 Months After Birth: Percent Distribution

	All adolescent mothers (n = 389)	Race		Number of children		Age at 1983 delivery (One child only)		
		Black (n = 272)	White (n = 117)	≥2 (n = 58)	1 (n = 331)	≤ 15 yr (n = 123)	16 yr (n = 92)	17 yr (n = 116)
Regular source of well baby care	98	98	97	95	99	99	98	98
Number of well child visits by Interview I:								
None	1	1	2	4	1	1	0	2
One	1	1	2	0	1	3	1	0[a]
Two	21	20	23	14	22	26	20	20
Three or more	77	78	74	82	76	70	78	77
First visit at 2 mo or later	17	18	10	20	16	17	16	16
Had one or more immunizations by Interview I	86	85	88	72	88**	90	88	86
Breast-feeding attempted	12	12	11	14	12	10	10	14
Receiving WIC	88	90	82	83	89	90	87	91
Trouble getting food for baby	16	16	16	20	15	18	19	10

[a]Less than 0.5%

**p < .01.

Characteristics of Preventive Health Care and Infant Feeding at 3 Months After Birth

We return now to data from the Adolescent Resource Use Study. As shown in Table 7-4, almost all infants were reported to have a regular source of health care at 3 months after birth. Only four children (1% of the total) had had no care, and an additional four had had only one well-child visit. There was no significant difference in compliance with preventive health care by age of mother within the adolescent group. By 3 months of age, children should have had a minimum of two preventive visits (at 2 weeks and 2 months of age); 98% were reported to have had two or more visits; 77% had three. Overall, 86% had received one or more immunizations (the first dose of diphtheria, pertussis, and tetanus (DPT) was due at 2 months of age).

Twelve percent of the adolescents reported attempting to breast-feed their babies, but of these, few were still breast feeding 3 months after birth. Almost 90% of the infants were receiving Nutritional Supplements for Women, Infants, and Children (WIC). However, 16% of the young mothers reported difficulty in obtaining sufficient food for their babies largely because of difficulties in enrolling in and maintaining enrollment in WIC. The voucher system used in Maryland for the distribution of milk and food products is often difficult for the young mothers because of administrative "red tape" concerning appointments and visits to the distribution points where vouchers can be obtained. In addition, the adolescents report having to miss school and having difficulties in transportation to obtain the necessary vouchers. Another problem arises because the young mother using WIC may be penalized for having a healthy, well-nourished infant without anemia, and WIC supplements may then be discontinued as unnecessary. Two or 3 months later, growth may slow and/or the infant may become anemic and is eligible once more to receive WIC. We have not infrequently encountered young mothers who had to purchase milk resorting to diluting formula in order to "stretch it out" over a longer time period, a practice detrimental to good nutrition and the health and happiness of the infant. In the same vein, though not included in this data base, is the delay in changing wet and soiled diapers because of inadequate resources to purchase diapers, either cloth or disposable. This practice leads to a high frequency of severe diaper rashes and increased health care costs for the treatment of monilial infections (Hardy and Streett, 1989).

Health and Health Care at 18 Months

Information about the infant's health and health care between birth and Interview II is provided in Table 7-5. Virtually all infants were reported to have a regular source of health care. According to standards established through the EPSDT Program (Early and Periodic Screening, Diagnosis, and Treatment) paid for by Medical Assistance for poor children, a child should have eight regular well-child visits between 2 weeks and 18 months of age, including the visit at 9 months which is optional. The children in this study made an average of 7.7 well-child visits. White children averaged 8.1 visits and black children averaged 7.6. First-born children had more adequate well-child care than those who were born to adolescents who already had one or more children. In addition, during the 15- to 18-month follow-up, the children averaged 2.2 emergency room visits and 2.6 other illness visits for a total of 12.7 health care visits.

Table 7-5 Characteristics of Child's Health and Health Care from Birth to Interview II by Mother's Race, Number of Children, and Age at Delivery[a]

Utilization characteristic	All adolescent mothers (n = 363)	Race		Number of children		Age at 1983 delivery (One child only)		
		Black (n = 257)	White (n = 106)	≥2 (n = 50)	1 (n = 313)	≤15 yr (n = 115)	16 yr (n = 88)	17 yr (n = 110)
Regular source of well child care	99	99	100	96	100	98	100	100
Mean number of visits:								
Total	12.7	11.8	16.7	12.8	12.7	12.9	11.7	13.2
Well child	7.7	7.6	8.1	6.6	7.9**	7.6	7.5	8.3
Emergency room	2.2	2.0	3.1	2.3	2.2	2.0	2.7	2.0
Other illness visits	2.6	2.0	5.3*	3.8	2.5	3.0	1.4	2.9
Three or more DPTs	77	78	76	65	79*	81	73	83
Two or more OPVs	83	83	84	81	83	80	82	86
MMR	50	52	44*	33	53*	50	53	55
Used emergency room	69	69	72	61	71	69	72	71
Source of payment:[b]								
Medical assistance	84	88	68***	94	83	85	88	78
Private insurance	7	6	12	4	7	6	6	9
HMO enrollment	9	10	4	14	8	7	8	8
None of above	9	6	21***	2	10	8	7	13
Trauma requiring outpatient care	18	17	22	19	18	15	17	21
Hospitalized	18	15	31**	29	17*	14	16	19
Chronic health problems	13	11	20*	10	13	19	7	15*
Has used prescription medication >1 mo	12	10	16	8	12	12	11	13

[a]Numbers shown are percents unless otherwise indicated.

[b]Categories are not mutually exclusive as Medical Assistance paid some HMO enrollment fees.

*p < .05.

**p < .01.

***p < .001.

Another index of the adequacy of preventive health care is the receipt of immunizations against the infectious diseases of childhood. Three DPT immunizations are regularly given by 6 to 7 months of age; a booster is given at 18 months. Overall, among these infants 77% had received three or more DPT immunizations, and 83% had two or more doses of oral polio vaccine by the time they were 15 to 18 months old, which is not an ideal situation, but reports for measles, mumps, and rubella (MMR) were less adequate; 50% had received the vaccine. Because this immunization is due at 15 months (14 to 16 months) of age, some children may not have been quite old enough to have received it by the time the interview was conducted. Also, this vaccine is relatively expensive and was in short supply during the period of the study. Children cared for by private physicians may not have received it for these reasons. Only 44% of white children received MMR as compared with 52% of black ($p < .05$).

Source of Payment for Child Health Care

As shown in Table 7-5, by the second interview 84% of the infants had received Medical Assistance support for their health care, 7% had private insurance, and 9% had no health care support. There were significant differences in the availability of support by race ($p < .001$), with 21% of white versus 6% of black children without any form of health insurance.

Health Problems

Contrary to the popular perception that black children have more health problems than white children, during the follow-up white children had substantially more problems than black children, even though they weighed more at birth (on average) and had a frequency of LBW less than half that of the black infants. Twenty-two percent of white infants had accidents or injuries necessitating ambulatory care as compared with 17% of black infants. Hospitalization for illness or injury was required by 31% of white as compared with 15% of black infants ($p < .01$). In addition, 20% of white infants were reported to have chronic health problems versus 11% of the black ($p < .05$), and 16% of the whites required prescription drugs for a period greater than 1 month as compared with 10% of the black children (Table 7-5). These are high rates of illness in our experience. Middle-class children, in general, have few hospital admissions. Egbuono and Starfield (1982) note that illness among poor children is not only more frequent but more severe as well.

A preliminary chart review of the health data for 362 of the 363 children who were followed a mean of 17.6 months indicated a wide variety of current health conditions reported by the mother; 57 (16%) of the children reportedly were suffering from one or more health problems. Among the problems reported, asthma, with 14 cases, was by far the most frequent. Ear infections (five cases) and eczema (four cases) were the next most frequent. Two children had a diagnosis of cerebral palsy; two had lead poisoning, and a third such case was suspected. Two children had a diagnosis of anemia. One child was physically handicapped. In addition 10% of the children in each racial group received a diagnosis of "failure to thrive."

There were 88 hospital admissions between nursery discharge and the second interview. Accidents and/or injuries accounted for the largest number of admissions, 10; of these, four were the result of burns, three were fractures and other injuries resulting from falls, and one near drowning in the bathtub accounted for the remainder. A wide variety of illness accounted for the remaining admissions. Pneumonia or bronchopneumonia in seven cases and asthma in five were the most frequent reasons reported. Twenty-eight of the total of 74 accidents requiring medical attention resulted from falls; nine were the result of burns. Falls were more frequent among white children, and burns occurred more frequently among black infants.

Child Neglect/Abuse: Foster Care

While we do not know the true extent of child neglect and/or abuse in this population of adolescent mothers and children, 10 of the 363 mothers interviewed between 15 and 18 months reported that their children had been removed from the home to agency foster care (6% of the young white mothers and 1% of those who were black). Neglect and/or abuse are the most frequent reasons for such placement. In addition, our interviewers encountered two additional cases in which neglect/abuse was a strong possibility. These cases were reported to the Division of Protective Services for follow-up, as required by law. Thus, in this area which is recognized to be associated with social stress and disadvantage, white children were at distinctly higher risk than those in black families.

Higher than usual frequencies of illness and accidents among the children of teenage mothers have been described previously and merit further comment. Taylor et al. (1983), using data from over 16,000 British births, compared 1,031 singleton children born to teenage mothers with 10,905 children of older mothers, followed for 5 years. They noted that the children living with mothers who had delivered as teenagers were more likely than those of older mothers to be admitted to a hospital, especially following trauma and for gastroenteritis. Also, frequent less serious accidents, such as burns, lacerations, and poisoning were more common among the children of younger than older mothers. The children of mothers below age 18 at delivery were at somewhat higher risk than those of mothers age 18 and 19. As the differences by age of mother remained highly significant, even when social and biological variables that may influence outcome were taken into account, the authors concluded that low maternal age appeared to be a health hazard for children independent of socioeconomic circumstances.

McCormick et al. (1984), in the study of infants followed 1 year in four regions of the United States, mentioned above, noted higher frequencies of illness requiring hospitalization and of accidents requiring medical attention among those infants born to adolescents under 18 years at delivery and those 18- and 19-year-old women who already had one or more children than among children of older women. They attributed the excess morbidity observed to maternal inexperience and the socio-economic disadvantage characteristic of young mothers. However, Rothenberg and Varga (1981), in a detailed approximately 3-year study of the children of 282 black and Hispanic women having a first birth in New York City, failed to find any major differences in the health and developmental status of the children born to teenage mothers as compared with older mothers.

Another important reason for the differences observed may reflect the adequacy of parenting and child care. In our experience, adolescent mothers are generally woefully ignorant with respect to child development, care, and parenting, including the need for safety and accident prevention. Many have had poor role models because their own mothers were teenagers when their first child was born. Others have had no instruction from parents or professionals. The relationship between adolescent childbearing and child neglect/abuse is unclear with respect to the relative causal roles of low maternal age and the social disadvantage in which adolescent parenting usually occurs. However, in our experience, a program that provided both parenting education and social support through home visits for older mothers in the same east Baltimore population was effective in preventing both illness and accidents and neglect/abuse. The program taught us that parenting education was effective once the crises and survival problems that are so frequent among inner city mothers were resolved (Hardy and Streett, 1989).

The racial differences in health status observed in this population of adolescent mothers are contrary to the generally accepted stereotype that black infants have more problems than white infants. The finding that the white infants had more health problems than the black infants may reflect the greater educational disadvantage of white versus black adolescent mothers. It may also confirm our impression, from the income data, that the whites were generally poorer than the blacks and that, even though a larger proportion of the white fathers were working, they were in low-paying jobs without health benefits. Marriage and moving from the parental home may be an additional disadvantage to poor adolescent mothers. One of the major benefits of welfare support is that of Medical Assistance, which makes for better access to health care for impoverished families. Living with a partner employed at the minimum wage provides inadequate income to cover health care costs and, in general, no health benefits. These young couples are apt to be at a greater disadvantage than those deriving their financial support from public assistance.

One can also speculate that lack of knowledge of child care and child development when coupled with the generally greater disadvantage of the young white families may have placed their infants at greater risk of both serious health problems and neglect/abuse than black infants.

Parenting Skills Instruction

Because, as mentioned above, we had found parenting education to be highly effective, this issue was examined in the Resource Use Study. As shown in Table 7-6, there were significant differences between black and white adolescents in the receipt of parenting skills instruction as reported in Interview I. In all categories of child care queried, white adolescents received significantly less parenting education from a professional than black teenagers. The white girls also received less instruction from family and friends on each child care issue raised, and the difference between blacks and whites was significant. Conversely, the proportions of white girls receiving no instruction at all were significantly higher than for the black, with the exception of taking the baby's temperature. Only 14% of the young mothers had any instruction on this item, and there was no difference by race.

The preliminary results of examining the possible relationship between the receipt of parenting instruction by the young mother and the likelihood of the child's need for medical care for trauma or having illness of sufficient severity to warrant hospitalization suggest that such instruction may be preventive. The mothers of over 25% of children requiring medical care for an injury reported receiving no instruction on how to "make the home safe for baby" as compared with 14%

Table 7-6 Parenting Skills Instruction: Proportion at Interview I Reporting Receipt by Source by Mother's Race, Number of Children, and Age at Delivery

	All adolescent mothers (n = 389)	Race		Number of children		Age at 1983 delivery (One child only)		
		Black (n = 272)	White (n = 117)	≥2 (n = 58)	1 (n = 331)	≤ 15 yr (n = 123)	16 yr (n = 92)	17 yr (n = 116)
Received instruction from family/friends:								
Dressing baby	65	67	55	55	66	67	72	62
Telling if baby is sick	59	63	38***	49	60	58	68	56
Taking baby's temp.	54	55	52	46	56	54	55	58
Important to hold, touch, and talk to baby	46	45	43	47	42	43	52	
Making house safe for baby	46	47	44	43	47	46	48	48
What and how to feed baby	70	72	60	55	72	71	76	71
Received instruction from professional:								
Dressing baby	58	64	30***	68	56	63	64	46**
Telling if baby is sick	73	79	46***	75	72	76	74	69
Taking baby's temp.	79	81	69*	86	77	83	76	76
Important to hold, touch, and talk to baby	76	80	56***	82	75	76	81	69
Making house safe for baby	64	70	39***	70	63	70	68	56
What and how to feed baby	92	94	79***	88	92	92	93	92
No instruction received:								
Dressing baby	20	17	35**	17	21	20	11	29**
Telling if baby is sick	22	17	44***	22	22	21	19	26
Taking baby's temp.	14	14	13	9	15	11	18	15
Important to hold, touch, and talk to baby	19	15	36***	16	20	20	14	24
Making house safe for baby	28	23	46***	23	28	24	26	33
What and how to feed baby	7	5	17***	8	7	6	6	8

*p < .05.
**p < .01.
***p < .001.

of those who received instruction from a family member and 15% of those instructed by a professional. The differences with respect to the need for hospital care were of the same order of magnitude. The father's presence in the home and the adequacy of his contribution to the child's support seemed to bear little relationship to either injuries requiring medical care or to hospitalization (Jordan et al., 1990). These are complex issues, involving a multiplicity of diagnoses and a wide range of severity, which merit further investigation.

Child Care

Child care arrangements were described from the point-of-view of the mother and the daytime caregiver in Chapter 5. Here we comment on child care from the perspective of the child's needs.

Our observations suggest that the children of urban adolescents are at significant disadvantage with respect to the quality of the care received. Their care is generally substandard in the following areas:

1. The care environment is often unsafe, crowded, lacking in essential child care equipment, such as cribs, highchairs, strollers, feeding bottles, diapers, and food, and it may also lack adequate heat, cooling, and plumbing.
2. The people who provide the care, i.e., the young mother, her family members, and friends, often lack adequate information about child care and normal developmental milestones.
3. The frequent changes in place and caregivers to which the children are often subjected does not promote optimal child development. Frequently, young mothers have told us of almost daily changes in their living arrangements, as they and their babies have been shuttled about among family and friends in order to have a place to stay. Even the presence of the young mother was not always a constant for the child. Family stress and dissension were commonplace. As pointed out by Werner and Smith (1982) and Werner (1985), a stable environment, with at least one caring adult with whom the child was able to develop a secure attachment, can be protective and ensure normal development in children otherwise biologically and socially at risk.

The organized and subsidized day care that could have promoted good parenting, optimized the child's health and development, and, in some measure, compensated for the otherwise unfavorable circumstances to which many of these children were exposed, simply was not available. As described in Table 5-9, page 86, only 4% of the children had any subsidized care, and this was with a community day care mother who probably also took care of several other young children. Although, as discussed below, none of the children was found to have early signs of serious developmental retardation, suggestive signs of language delay were noted.

Developmental Status

Our resources did not permit an adequate assessment of the developmental level of each child of our study adolescents, and similar children of older mothers were not available for comparison. But, the child's developmental level was screened by the interviewer at the second home visit ($\overline{X}$17.6 months) using age-appropriate questions from the Denver Parent Questionnaire and other sources. Some interesting findings emerged. None of the 363 infants was found to be moderately or severely developmentally retarded. As seen in Table 7-7, most of the children were reported to perform the items included, with the exception of walking upstairs. Because many of these children lived in apartments without stairs, this item may have had little meaning. Some significant differences were noted between the black and the white children and between first and later born children. Several of the items where performance differed between black and white children pertained to language usage. White children were developmentally more advanced in expressive language; their speech could be understood more readily; when upset, they could be comforted by voice alone; and they pointed to body parts upon request more often than black children did. White children also fed themselves with a spoon more often than those who were black. First-born children were more willing to go to strangers than were those born later. These differences suggest that white children received more language stimulation and learning opportunities than the black, and that first-born children may have had more attention and cognitive stimulation than those later born. McAnarney et al. (1986), in a study of interactions of teenage mothers with their children during their first year, noted that the younger mothers tended not to reinforce language learning in their children and were more often insensitive to the needs of their children than were older teenagers. Our own observations of adolescent mothers and their children in the Johns Hopkins Teenage Clinic and Parenting Program (TAC) over many years are in accord. Furthermore, black adolescents, in general, talk and interact orally with their children much less often than whites and their oral offerings are more likely to be in the form of commands or demands than those of young white mothers. Zuckerman et al. (1984) suggest that the care-giving behavior of adolescent mothers, who, in general, spend less time with their children, includes fewer oral interactions with the children and less realistic expectations for their development, which may be detrimental to the development of the children.

Wadsworth et al. (1984), using data from the British 1970 national birth cohort, examined the developmental outcome of five-year-old children over the spectrum of maternal ages to assess: 1) the possible contribution of low maternal age to adverse outcomes; and 2) whether the outcomes in the child were related to biological factors or to social factors associated with the mother's age. They demonstrated, in the large sample of 1,031 children born to mothers less than 20 years and 10,950 children born to older women, that the 5-year-old children of teenage mothers had less favorable outcomes than those of older women. They did less well on tests of behavior and language. The disadvantage persisted even when a number of relevant biological and socioeconomic factors were controlled. However, there was no residual effect of maternal age on visual-motor performance and only a marginal effect on body height and head circumference. They concluded that low maternal age at delivery adversely affected the children's development through the associated social disadvantage of being born to a poor mother rather than through a biological mechanism. In our experience, the longer-term outcome for the children of adolescents was less favorable as compared with that of children of older mothers in the same population (see Chapter 9).

Reports by Brooks-Gunn and Furstenberg (1986) and Furstenberg and Brooks-Gunn (1987), on the 17-year follow-up of their predominantly black sample of Baltimore adolescent mothers and their children, indicate a high level of maladjustment and school behavior problems among the children at age 15–16 years;

Table 7-7 Proportion of Children Aged 15 to 18 Months Passing Developmental Screening Items at Interview II

Developmental screening item	All adolescent mothers (n = 363)	Race		Number of children		Age at 1983 delivery (One child only)		
		Black (n = 257)	White (n = 106)	≥2 (n = 50)	1 (n = 313)	≤ 15 yr (n = 115)	16 yr (n = 88)	17 yr (n = 110)
Walks alone	97	98	94	100	96	96	99	95
Walks backwards	93	93	92	95	93	95	97	88
Walks upstairs	68	72	52*	70	68	62	72	69
Kicks a ball forward	91	91	90	92	91	87	94	91
Throws ball overhand	86	87	85	85	86	83	93	84
Stoops and retrieves	99	99	98	100	99	100	100	98
Scribbles	95	95	94	98	94	97	95	92
Calls mother by name	98	98	95	92	98*	97	99	99
Speech understandable	81	78	97***	86	81	84	73	84
Says words besides name	76	72	97***	69	78	76	76	79
Points to body parts	73	72	78	76	72	71	72	74
Feeds self with spoon	80	78	90*	86	79	71	84	80
Drinks from cup	97	97	96	95	97	99	99	95
Removes clothing	85	85	86	88	85	87	83	85
Comforted by holding	92	91	93	88	92	90	88	96
Comforted by voice alone	69	66	83*	61	71	70	65	75
Will go to strangers	40	41	36	21	43**	38	44	46

*p < .05.
**p < .01.
***p < .001.

for example, 53% had repeated at least one grade and almost half had been suspended or expelled from school during the prior 5 years. Comparison with the black subsample in the National Study of Children (Furstenberg et al., 1983) yielded similar findings for the children of adolescent mothers but not for those of older mothers, whose children had substantially fewer school behavior problems. In a middle class and predominantly white population of 12-year-olds attending public school in Southern California, East and Felice (1990) also found the school performance of children of adolescent mothers to be less adequate than the children of older mothers. The authors speculate that the lower achievement of the children of adolescents may have been mediated through their mothers' low levels of educational attainment and expectations for their children. Both adolescent mothers and the fathers of their children felt that they provided less support for the enhancement of their children's self-esteem, as compared with older mothers and fathers.

Zuckerman et al. (1984) point to the necessity of identifying high-risk adolescents in terms of "their health status, health behavior, emotional status [especially the presence of depression] and [the availability of] social support." We would add to this list the availability of both material and information resources. On the basis of these factors, urban adolescents are, for the most part, at high risk for parenting and child care dysfunction. To paraphrase Zuckerman et al. (1984), their children are often in double jeopardy because the behavior of their mothers is associated with both poor perinatal outcome and poor parenting.

Summary and Discussion

Information from a city-wide random sample of births to adolescent mothers, followed for 18 months, indicates a high frequency of health problems among their children. The problems observed from birth to 18 months include high frequencies of LBW and utilization of neonatal intensive care; and, during the early months, of chronic and acute health problems; hospital admission for illness or injury; and accidents or injuries requiring medical care. The frequency of illness and hospital admission were significantly higher among the white than among the black children. In addition, of those followed 15 to 18 months, 6% of the white and 1% of the black children were placed in agency foster care. Placement is usually the result of parental neglect and/or abuse.

- Preventive health care appears barely adequate. Instruction in child care, accident prevention, and simple illness care—except for adolescents enrolled in special comprehensive programs (see Chapter 16)—appears to have been generally deficient, particularly for the children of white adolescents, many of whom had no medical insurance. As 16% of the young mothers reported inability to obtain sufficient food for their infants, WIC must be more accessible, regardless of the nutritional status of the child. The young mother should not have to miss school or be forced to use limited financial resources for transportation to obtain WIC vouchers. Vouchers for diapers would help to reduce health care costs. The traditional providers of health care need to be more alert to the availability of food supplements for their welfare patients through the Food Stamp and the WIC programs and should facilitate their use.

- Changes in Medicaid coverage are needed to provide reimbursement for truly comprehensive preventive health services for adolescent mothers and their infants. Both in-depth psychosocial support and health and parenting education are cost-effective as compared with crisis social work and the limited anticipatory guidance available during the traditional medical visit.
- Although the frequency of health problems in this group of children appears very high, the estimate reflects many years of experience in inner city Baltimore rather than comparison with national norms. In order to estimate the service needs within a given locale, specific population-based estimates of the prevalence of medical problems would be of value.
- The health problems that beset these children may well compromise their long-range development. Whether the high frequency of illness and injury in this population reflects, primarily, the environment of poverty, social disadvantage, and ignorance in which the children are reared, or the immaturity of their mothers, or interaction between the two, is unclear. Whatever the causal factors, intervention that reaches these young families with *both* parenting education and accessible health care is effective in improving the health and developmental status of the children. However, this alone is not sufficient.
- If these young families are to be socially healthy and self-sufficient, family and/or community support that provides child care and financial support while parents complete their education is essential. Furthermore, these services are also desperately needed by young families in which the father is working for low wages at jobs that provide no health benefits.

8

The Utilization of Services

The objectives of the "Resource Use Study" (Hardy et al., 1986), described in the introduction to Part II of this volume, were to facilitate the provision of effective services for pregnant adolescents and their children by determining: 1) the use of public and private resources by pregnant and parenting adolescents; 2) the characteristics of adolescents who used various resources; and 3) the effect of such utilization on key outcome indicators. The characteristics of the adolescent mothers, their families, infants, and the fathers of their babies have been described in the preceding chapters. Data describing the services available to the adolescents and their children were collected by means of questionnaires mailed to and completed by, and interviews with staff members of the various agencies providing services to adolescents. From these sources, services were classified and an inventory of agencies serving Baltimore adolescents and of the services described by their staff was constructed.

Our random sample of births to Baltimore adolescents below age 18 years at delivery (n = 389) included about 37% of the total in this age group in 1983. However, some of the services of agencies reporting the provision of service to adolescents were not used by any of the young people interviewed. The agencies in question seemed to be serving limited numbers of older teenagers (considered to be adolescents by agency personnel) as well as adults. Examples include several offering pregnancy testing and counseling.

Information pertaining to actual utilization was collected from the young mothers themselves by structured interviews at home at 3 and 15 to 18 months ($\overline{X}17.6$ months) after the index birth. The information covered the period from the time around conception to almost 18 months after delivery. In addition: 1) data from Certificates of Live Birth were examined; and 2) records in the Maryland State and Baltimore City Departments of Human Resources (with the exception of those in the Protective Service Division) were reviewed to identify the use of specific social services during a period of approximately four years after the birth of the index child in 1983.

The data presented in this chapter, like those described in Chapters 4 through 8, were developed in collaboration with Dr. Anne Duggan. While the analyses pertaining to use of resources are still ongoing, a number of preliminary observations are possible. Among the most important are: 1) the concordance between the mothers' reports of resources used and information obtained from other sources, such as records in the Department of Human Resources and Certificates of Live Birth; the mothers were surprisingly accurate with respect to clear-cut issues such as birth weight, method of delivery, welfare receipt, and the like; and 2) those pertaining to immediate pregnancy outcome suggest that superior results were obtained by the city's three comprehensive programs. These programs, which stress the importance of psychosocial support and health and parenting education in addition to high-quality obstetrical care, had superior results, even though adolescents receiving services from them tended to be younger and at potentially higher obstetrical risk than those served in other facilities. This latter observation lends support to findings from the evaluation of the comprehensive Johns Hopkins Adolescent Pregnancy and Parenting Programs (HAC and TAC, Chapters 11, 16, and 19). The Johns Hopkins program was the largest of the three comprehensive programs in the city.

Finally, the data point to substantial differences in the characteristics of the adolescents using the various different resources. This fact is of considerable importance because it must be taken into account in evaluating the effectiveness of services offered by various agencies.

Resource Use

Source of Prenatal Care

Of the 389 adolescents in the city-wide, random sample, 137 (35.2%) received prenatal care and inpatient hospital services for labor and delivery in one of Baltimore's three comprehensive adolescent programs. Of the remaining adolescents, 67 (17.2%) received care in a community hospital clinic that provided traditional obstetrical care targeted to teenagers. The remaining 47.6% received obstetrical services with older women. Of these, 74 (19.0% of the total) attended regular hospital prenatal clinics; 37 (9.5%) had their care in an HMO (health maintenance organization); 31 (8.0%) were attended by private physicians; and 29 (7.5%) received care in free-standing, community health centers or neighborhood health clinics. Those patients enrolled in this type of program, when found to be at high risk obstetrically, were generally referred to an appropriate level of high-risk perinatal care, for example, in a comprehensive program. Because no facilities existed in these neighborhood centers for inpatient care, all were referred to community hospitals for labor, delivery, and postpartum care. Eight of the 389 adolescents received no prenatal care, and six received care in a county clinic but delivered in Baltimore City.

Maternal Characteristics by Site of Care

Race There were differences by race in the site selected for prenatal care; 82% of the girls receiving care in a comprehensive program were black, and only 18% were white. Two of the comprehensive programs are located in teaching hospitals in predominantly black, inner city areas. The third is more peripherally located and provided care for a larger proportion of white adolescents. Larger proportions (30%) of those adolescents attending community health centers and private physicians were white. These facilities also tended to be located in somewhat more peripheral areas where many of the poor white families lived.

Maternal Age at Delivery Differences by site were also noted in the young mothers' age at delivery. Twenty percent of those enrolled in comprehensive programs were age 15 or below at delivery, and 29% were 16, as compared with only 8% and 14%, respectively, in community hospital programs targeting teenagers and 9% and 33% of those attended by private physicians.

Reasons for Enrollment and Satisfaction with Care   There were substantial differences between sites in the reasons given by the adolescents for their selection of a particular site for prenatal care. Important reasons were that the site was the same as that in which the pregnancy test was found to be positive (90% of those enrolled in HMOs; 66% of those with private physicians) and that it was close to home or to school (34%). Among those enrolled in comprehensive programs, almost half (49%) had been referred there by a professional; it was the pregnancy test site for 40%. Among those already enrolled in an HMO, that organization provided general health care, and no other choice was possible because of the conditions of enrollment.

In general, the great majority of adolescents reported being "very satisfied" or "somewhat satisfied" with their care. Of those attending comprehensive programs, 84% were very satisfied, and 2% were very dissatisfied. Among those attended by private physicians, 76%, and among those enrolled in HMOs, only 60% were very satisfied, and somewhat larger proportions than among those attending comprehensive programs were very dissatisfied.

Medical Assistance Status   Support for the cost of prenatal care and inpatient hospital costs for delivery also differed significantly by the site of prenatal care (Table 8-1). Those enrolled in a HMO had the highest frequency of full or partial Medical Assistance (MA) coverage for pregnancy care (79%); 68% of those enrolled in comprehensive programs were covered by MA as were 41% of those receiving care from a private physician; the latter group had the lowest proportion of MA coverage.

Food Stamps and WIC   The frequency of utilization of food stamps and WIC (Supplemental Nutrition for Women, Infants and Children) also differed significantly by site of care (Table 8-1). Those receiving care from private physicians had the lowest rates of utilization: 17% for food stamps and 33% for WIC even though, as 41% were eligible for MA, a considerably larger proportion should have been able to receive these benefits. By contrast, among those in the comprehensive programs, 90% received WIC, and 45% reported having food stamps. Even in these programs, it seems likely that a few eligible girls did not receive WIC, perhaps as the result of the administration difficulties often associated with enrollment or because of registration for prenatal care late in pregnancy, but in these programs great emphasis was placed on the importance of nutritional supplements and nutrition education.

Welfare support, usually through Aid to Families with Dependent Children (AFDC) (Table 8-1), was frequent 3 months after delivery among adolescents receiving all types of care; 72% of those enrolled in comprehensive programs and 68% of those attended by private physicians were receiving welfare at that time.

Education   Overall, 77% of the adolescents were attending school when their pregnancy was diagnosed (Table 8-1). Of these young people, 23% transferred to Paquin, a special public school for pregnant students. There were substantial dif-

Table 8-1 Site of Prenatal Care: Distribution of Selected Maternal Characteristics by Site

					Source of prenatal care			
Characteristic	All[a]	Comp. Adol. Preg. Pgm.	Targeted hosp. cl.	Other hosp. cl.	NHC or Non-HMO CHC	HMO	Private MD
	(n = 389)	(n = 137)	(n = 67)	(n = 74)	(n = 29)	(n = 37)	(n = 31)
Services during pregnancy:							
MA throughout***	52	58	43	53	56	74	29
MA for part***	14	10	20	23	20	5	12
Food stamps***	44	45	36	54	36	73	17
WIC***	72	90	71	57	67	87	33
Welfare recipient** 3 months after delivery	68	72	57	70	66	72	68
Education:							
In school when pregnancy diagnosed	77	77	78	77	67	77	82
Transferred to Paquin School	23	31	20	19	14	26	20

**p < .01
***p < .001

[a]Includes those with no prenatal care (n = 8) and those with source outside city (n = 6).

ferences by prenatal care site in the frequency with which adolescents transferred to Paquin. Among students in comprehensive programs, 37% transferred, the highest proportion of any group.

Unpublished data from our random sample of 1983 births were used in an attempted evaluation of the effectiveness of the Paquin School in improving outcome for adolescent mothers (Hardy and Duggan, 1988a). The site of prenatal care for the young black mothers ($n = 83$) who were still in school at the onset of pregnancy and who transferred to and attended the Paquin School during pregnancy and the immediate postpartum period was compared with that in two other groups, those ($n = 42$) who had dropped out of school prior to the diagnosis of pregnancy and those who elected to remain in their regular schools ($n = 147$) (Table 8-1). While there appeared to be substantial advantage for those who transferred to Paquin in terms of obstetrical outcome and educational attainment at 18 months after delivery, the background characteristics of the adolescents in the three groups were very different (Table 8-2). Whereas those transferring to Paquin were younger,

Table 8-2 Percent Distribution of Sociodemographic Characteristics of Adolescents by School Status During Pregnancy

Characteristic	Not in school ($n = 42$)	In regular school ($n = 147$)	Transferred to special school ($n = 83$)	p value
Age at delivery (yr)				<.001
< 15	5	9	13	
15	4	12	24	
16	17	34	31	
17	74	45	31	
One or more children born prior to 1983 index child	48	8	7	<.001
Initially uncertain whether to keep pregnancy	29	39	49	.07
First trimester prenatal care	46	42	48	.44
Comprehensive adolescent pregnancy program for prenatal care	31	33	47	.07
Medical Assistance for all of pregnancy	77	46	53	<.001
Grades before pregnancy excellent or good	30	70	81	<.001
Missed < 3 days/month from school before pregnancy	21	56	62	<.001
3 months after delivery:				
Family receiving Welfare at 3 months following index birth	80	68	75	.19
No one in household employed at 3 months following index birth	54	42	33	.07
Female head of household	78	80	81	.90

they were students reporting significantly better grades and fewer absences prior to pregnancy, and their families appeared to be slightly less disadvantaged and to provide significantly more support than those in the other two groups. Also, because of referral relationships (girls from the comprehensive programs were often referred to Paquin), a substantial proportion of Paquin students were also enrolled in comprehensive prenatal programs, which was not the case in the comparison groups (Duggan and Hardy, 1989). These differences, which are known to be associated with pregnancy outcome, make evaluation very difficult. They emphasize the importance in evaluation efforts of using comparison groups with similar background characteristics to avoid confounding by variables that are related to each other as well as to the outcome under investigation.

Two pregnancy outcome indicators (the frequencies of low birth weight [LBW] and cesarean section to effect delivery) were used to compare the effectiveness of the various prenatal programs used by the adolescents (Table 8-3). Although the results do not reach statistical significance and the numbers in some cells are too small for meaningful analysis, in general, those young mothers enrolled in comprehensive adolescent programs had superior results. It should be noted that while those adolescent patients enrolled in a community health center or neighborhood health clinic also had a relatively low frequency of LBW, this result may be biased by the referral of patients recognized to be at high risk for poor outcome to other sources of care, particularly the comprehensive adolescent programs.

Resource Use at Interview II   Table 8-4 displays selected characteristics and outcomes for the adolescent mothers at Interview II ($\overline{X}$17.6 months after delivery)

Table 8-3   Pregnancy Outcomes by Source of Prenatal Care, Controlling for Race and Number of Children

	All sources[a]	Adolescent Pregnancy Program	Targeted Ob Clinic	Other hosp.-based clinics	CHC/NHS	HMO	PMD
				Numbers			
All	376	139	67	73	29	37	31
Black	307	114	58	59	20	35	22
White	68	25	9	14	9	2	9
				Percents			
Birth weight <2,500 g							
All	13	10	14	16	9	20	14
Black	15	14	15	18	7	19	18
White	7	4	6	4	*	*	*
Birth weight <1,500 g							
All	2	2	3	6	0	0	0
Black	3	3	4	6	0	0	0
White	1	0	0	4	*	*	*
Cesarean section							
All	15	14	21	8	13	16	23
Black	14	11	22	8	16	15	24
White	16	24	12	9	*	*	*

*Denominator five or less.

[a]Those with no prenatal care or source outside city excluded.

Table 8-4 Selected Characteristics and Outcomes for Adolescent Mothers by Race and Regular Source of Medical Care Reported at X̄17.6 Months after 1983 Delivery

	None ER	Adolescent Pregnancy Program	Hosp. Ob/Gyn	Other hosp.	NHC/CHC	HMO	PMD	Comm. FP	p
Numbers	33	58	66	41	44	37	40	34	
Hospitalized:									
Due to pregnancy:									
All	8	11	14	9	8	12	14	12	.99
Black	9	12	14	8	12	11	19	13	.95
White	6	*	7	15	0	*	7	*	.85
For other reasons:									
All	12	1	12	10	10	8	0	4	.16
Black	10	1	11	8	12	9	0	3	.27
White	15	*	15	14	5	*	0	*	.75
Sexually active[a]:									
On birth control									
All	33	85	68	79	82	80	87	85	<.001
Black	28	85	68	79	80	81	93	86	<.001
White	41	*	68	80	88	*	81	*	.53
With regular FP source									
All	3	79	62	77	78	80	85	87	<.001
Black	4	79	61	76	77	81	93	86	<.001
White	0	*	68	80	82	*	80	*	<.01
In school or graduated									
All	42	57	44	48	42	43	41	53	.74
Black	53	59	46	59	50	44	66	55	.68
White	16	*	30	7	22	*	10	*	.84
Pregnant <12 months									
All	20	16	29	22	20	30	16	24	.60
Black	17	17	30	20	19	30	19	26	.65
White	28	*	22	29	21	*	11	*	.89
Has received welfare since 1983 birth									
All	91	95	84	92	91	94	88	84	.52
Black	96	96	84	95	98	95	92	87	.21
White	76	*	77	78	74	*	82	*	.99
Mean age at interview 2									
All	17.6	17.3	17.8	17.6	17.6	17.6	17.9	17.4	.12
Black	17.6	17.4	17.8	17.6	17.5	17.5	18.0	17.4	.27
White	17.8	*	18.0	17.4	17.8	*	17.8	*	.53

*Denominator five or less.

[a]Excludes those 1) pregnant at time of interview; and 2) reporting not having sex since 1983 birth.

by their reported source of regular medical care since the 1983 birth. As may be seen, there was considerable variation by site of care in the proportions reporting various characteristics. Sizable proportions of young mothers were hospitalized for both pregnancy-related and other reasons. Those continuing to receive comprehensive care infrequently required hospitalization for other reasons, suggesting that continuing care may have been effective in preventing severe illness. Reported sexual activity also varied by site, with a high frequency among those girls enrolled in a comprehensive program. However, 79% of these young women reported a regular source of reproductive health service; nonetheless, 16% of these girls were pregnant again within 12 months. This percentage is the lowest among patients at any site except that attended by private physicians, which was also 16%, and far lower than the 30% with a repeat conception reported by HMO enrollees. The low frequency of school graduation or continuation is discouraging because lack of education will be an impediment to employment that enables the young mother to become self-sustaining and independent.

Table 8-5 describes the children's health care utilization by site of care. A number of points stand out. The first is the high frequency of emergency room utilization. This is very expensive care, often for relatively minor problems. The second point concerns the high frequency of accidents requiring care, and the third point is the extraordinarily high frequency of hospital admission in this child population. In a middle-class population there would be few hospital admissions in this age group—perhaps less than 1% per year. Also striking is the fact that 30% of white children were admitted as compared with 16% of the black.

Ongoing investigations suggest that the frequency of accidents and injuries among white children in this population is higher than among blacks and may be significantly related to the fact that white adolescent mothers (who are more fre-

Table 8-5   Child's Health Care Utilization by Regular Source of Care at Interview II, Controlling for Race (Numbers Shown are Percents Unless Otherwise Indicated)

	All sources[a]	Adolescent Pregnancy Program	Other hospital-based clinics	CHC/NHS	HMO	PMD	p
All	(350)	(51)	(111)	(91)	(41)	(54)	
Black	(289)	(50)	(94)	(75)	(37)	(33)	
White (numbers)	(61)	(2)	(17)	(16)	(5)	(21)	
Has used ER*							
All	70	66	82	69	42	54	<.001
Black	69	65	82	67	48	63	<.001
White	72	*	81	79	*	65	.22
Trauma requiring outpatient care							
All	18	12	18	19	11	24	.40
Black	17	12	18	18	11	27	.37
White	21	*	23	28	*	18	.84
Hospitalized							
All	18	14	20	13	13	31	.06
Black	16	12	18	9	11	34	<.05
White	30	*	31	33	*	26	.86
Three + DPTs							
All	78	72	79	84	72	78	.41
Black	78	72	80	84	71	75	.46
White	78	*	69	87	*	82	.74
Five + well-child visits							
All	89	91	89	90	80	91	.43
Black	89	90	88	91	81	93	.49
White	88	*	93	87	*	88	.78

*Denominator five or less; ER, emergency room.

[a]Excludes those with no regular source of care or source outside city.

Table 8-6 Frequency of Selected Utilization Characteristics at Interview II, by Site of Continued Health Care

	All[a]	*None or ER*	*Adolescent Pregnancy Program*	*Hosp. Ob/Gyn Cl.*	*Other Hosp. cl.*	*NHC or CHC*	*HMO*	*Priv. M.D.*	*Comm. FP cl.*
	(n = 358)	*(n = 39)*	*(n = 58)*	*(n = 66)*	*(n = 41)*	*(n = 44)*	*(n = 37)*	*(n = 40)*	*(n = 34)*
Has had Welfare	90	91	95	84	92	91	94	88	84
Medical Assistance has or had	89	82	88	88	93	89	95	90	85
No care because unable to pay	9	17	3	12	5	12	17	3	7
Has had WIC	92	92	99	86	94	99	90	84	94
Trouble getting sufficient food	14	14	5	14	27	14	15	15	16

[a]Excludes those with no regular source of care or source outside the city.

quently attended by private physicians) have less instruction in "making home safe for baby" than black adolescents who are more often enrolled in comprehensive programs (E. Jordan, A.K. Duggan, and J.B. Hardy, in progress, 1990).

The infants' preventive health care, while leaving room for improvement, as all should have had six to seven preventive child health visits, is perhaps better than might be expected (Table 8-5) in an inner city population where survival issues, lack of transportation, lack of information about good parenting, and institutional policies may all be barriers to preventive health care. As we originally hypothesized, the young mothers are more conscientious about health care for their children than for themselves.

Information collected at Interview II pertaining to selected resource utilization characteristics is shown in Table 8-6, by site of continuing health care. The very high frequencies of public support for maintenance (i.e., welfare) and for medical care among this city-wide random sample of all Baltimore adolescent mothers bearing a child in 1983 attest to the strong relationship that exists between urban poverty and premature childbearing. The relatively high frequencies of being refused medical care because of an inability to pay for it reported by young mothers who gave certain sites as their regular source of care (for example, a hospital emergency room or an HMO) is regrettable. It should be noted that those young women who received care in a comprehensive adolescent program or from a private physician had little difficulty with this problem.

With respect to obtaining WIC, which not infrequently was difficult because of the "red tape" involved, most adolescents had received it, particularly those attending comprehensive programs (99%). Nonetheless, significant proportions of adolescent mothers reported experiencing difficulty in obtaining sufficient food for themselves and/or their children during the 18-month period, 14% overall and 27% of those attending various hospital clinics for their ongoing care. Again, those young mothers in special comprehensive programs appear to have had the fewest problems, perhaps because of the intensity of the social service and health and parenting education received.

Summary

The preliminary findings reported here support those reported elsewhere in this volume, which attest to the superior outcomes for adolescent mothers enrolled in comprehensive programs that meet their multiple medical and social needs. They reinforce the positive findings from the evaluation of the Johns Hopkins Comprehensive Programs.

9

Long-Term Outcomes
*Adolescent and Older Mothers
in an Urban Population*

It is clear from information presented elsewhere in this volume that childbirth among young urban teenagers is frequently associated with unfavorable health and social conditions detrimental to the optimal development of both the adolescent mothers and their children. Furthermore, the generally suboptimal psychosocial development of these young people results in very large personal and public costs (Burt, 1986; Hayes, 1987; Moore and Burt, 1982). These adverse conditions have been well-described by others, including the Alan Guttmacher Institute (1976), Card and Wise (1978), Baldwin and Cain (1980), Zuckerman et al. (1984), McCormick et al. (1984), Hayes (1987), Hofferth and Hayes (1987), and McAnarney and Hendee (1989). However, the important question of whether the adverse outcomes should be regarded as consequences of pregnancy and childbirth during adolescence or as ecological concomitants or even antecedents is, as yet, unresolved.

Furstenberg's report (1976) on the outcome, over a 5-year period following delivery as an adolescent, which draws comparisons between adolescent mothers and classmates who delayed childbearing beyond the teen years, suggests a substantial risk of adverse consequences for early childbearers, as do our own studies which are presented below. His later studies with Brooks-Gunn and Morgan (1987) point to considerable diversity in maternal outcome almost 20 years after delivery and suggest that no stereotypes exist. The developmental problems and antisocial behavior of the children of teenage mothers are reported by Brooks-Gunn and Furstenberg (1986) to become more severe as they enter adolescence.

The Johns Hopkins Follow-up Study

This study, which has been described in detail elsewhere (Hardy et al., 1978) used data from a large sample of adolescent pregnancies ($n = 686$) followed in the Johns Hopkins Collaborative Perinatal Study (CPS). Comparisons between the immediate and longer range outcomes of adolescent mothers and their children and those older mothers in a more optimal age range for childbearing (20 through 24 years) in the same population and their children, followed over an 8- to 12-year period, were possible in this study. In brief, the mothers in both groups delivered at The Johns Hopkins Hospital where they were enrolled in the CPS at their first visit for prenatal care. They were followed throughout pregnancy and, with their surviving children, for 8 years after delivery. Multidisciplinary observations included medical, psychological, behavioral, and family-environmental parameters. Over 88% of nursery survivors were successfully followed for the 8-year period, and in a representative subsample ($n = 466$) over 90% were followed for 12 years. In this subsample, 77 women were adolescents (<18 years) when their children were born. No special interventions were available to women and children enrolled in the CPS.

The women enrolled in the Johns Hopkins study were of lower-middle and lower-class background. Most lived in close proximity to The Johns Hopkins Hospital. Overall, 85% of the white and 69% of the black mothers were married at delivery. Seventy-seven percent of the women were black and 23% white. Their children, for the most part, attended the same inner city schools.

Adverse consequences of premature childbirth have been described in terms of both immediate and longer term outcomes. This pattern is adopted here with data from birth to 8 years for the large samples of adolescent and older mothers presented first, and then those from the smaller representative subsample followed for 4 additional years. The outcomes for 686 pregnant adolescents and their surviving children over the 8-year period were compared with those of 1,120 women aged 20 through 24 and their children; 116 of the adolescent and 285 older women were white and 570 of the blacks were adolescents and 835 were older women.

Findings from Birth to 8 Years

Maternal Characteristics at Delivery Table 9-1 displays background characteristics by race and parity, comparing adolescents and older women with respect to average age at delivery, age at the onset of menses, and education and socioeconomic status, as measured by the Perinatal Research Branch Index (Myrianthropoulos and French, 1968). This index is similar in concept to the Holingshead

Table 9-1 Maternal Characteristics at Delivery: 686 Adolescents and 1,120 Women Aged 20 to 24 years, Percent Distribution

Variable (Mean Value)	Adolescents <17 yr				Women 20–24 yr			
	White primi-para	White multi-para	Black primi-para	Black multi-para	White primi-para	White multi-para	Black primi-para	Black multi-para
Age	16.04	16.50	15.04	16.26	21.24	21.97	21.45	22.05
Age, onset of menses	12.15***	11.0	11.79	11.79	12.76***	12.63	12.55	12.68
Education (highest grade)	8.77	7.87***	8.41	8.67	10.10	9.08***	12.02	10.54
Socioeconomic index[a]	33.67	36.74[b]	23.37	28.90	44.73	40.57[b]	50.56	41.48

Reproduced, with permission, from Hardy, JB, Welcher, DW, Stanley, J, and Dallas, JR: Long-range outcome of adolescent pregnancy. *Clin Obstet Gynecol* 21(4): 1215–1232, 1978.

[a]Socioeconomic index = Perinatal Research Branch Index devised by Myrianthropoulos and French (1968).

[b]Not significant; other comparisons significant at $p < .01$.

***$p < .001$.

Index, except that maternal education has been substituted for that of the fathers. The comparisons are significant for all race and parity subgroups, with the exception of those pertaining to socioeconomic status in white mothers with more than one child. The data tell us, as one might expect, that: 1) women having a first child were younger than those having a subsequent birth (exception, black multipara, aged 20 through 24, who were slightly younger than similar blacks having a first birth); 2) the onset of menses occurred at a younger age among blacks than whites, among adolescent mothers than older mothers, and among white multiparous mothers as compared with those having a first child. However, the difference between primiparous and multiparous black women was quite small. The relationship between the early onset of menarche and premature childbearing has been described in Chapter 2. These data confirm the finding that early menarche is associated with sexual onset (Udry, 1979; Zabin, Smith, et al., 1986).

With respect to educational attainment in this population, particularly among the older women, blacks generally had more schooling than whites. Among the whites, multiparous women had significantly less education in both the adolescent and older age groups, and older mothers had more education than adolescents. Among the blacks, multiparous adolescents had slightly more education than those having a first child, but they were, on average, just over 1 year older. Among the older mothers, black multipara averaged 1½ years less schooling than those having a first child.

In terms of socioeconomic status, all groups tended to be disadvantaged. The finding that black adolescent mothers, on average, had more education than their white counterparts has been replicated in the more recent Baltimore studies reported in Chapter 4. Blacks having a first child at age 20 through 24 had the highest SES score, 50.56. This is close to the mean for the national Collaborative Perinatal Study (Myrianthropoulos and French, 1968). Adolescent mothers had much lower SES scores, particularly with a first birth and especially if black. Thus, adolescent mothers, both black and white, were seriously disadvantaged in terms of both education and family socioeconomic status when their children were born, as compared with older mothers, particularly those who delayed childbearing until reaching age 20. How did they fare?

Pregnancy Outcome through 8 Years   As shown in Table 9-2, immediate pregnancy outcome in terms of perinatal death rates, birth weight, gestational age, and

Table 9-2   Immediate Pregnancy Outcome of Adolescents and of Older Women by Age at Delivery

Age	Perinatal deaths/ 1,000 births	Mean birth weight (g)	% Birth weights <2,501 g	Mean gest. age (Completed wk)	Infant deaths/ 1,000 births
14	80	2,734	26	37	28
15	39	2,846	23	38	17
16	11	2,957	15	38	11
17	30	2,884	18	38	24
Total adolescents	40	2,855	20	38	20
Total 20–24 yr	53	2,949	17	38	21

Reproduced, with permission, from Hardy, JB, Welcher, DW, Stanley, J, and Dallas, JR: Long-range outcome of adolescent pregnancy. *Clin Obstet Gynecol* 21(4): 1215–1232, 1978.

Table 9-3   Rates of Perinatal and Infant Deaths per 1,000 Deliveries, by Parity

	Adolescent			Women 20–24 yr without pregnancy in adolescence			Women 20–24 yr with pregnancy in adolescence		
	No. of mothers	*Stillbirth neonatal deaths*	*Later infant deaths*	*No. of mothers*	*Stillbirths, neonatal deaths*	*Later infant deaths*	*No. of mothers*	*Stillbirths, neonatal deaths*	*Later infant deaths*
Black									
Primipara	478	44	21	174	51	11	—	—	—
Multipara	92	43	22	494	54	24	167	90	72
White									
Primipara	92	33	11	62	16	16	—	—	—
Multipara	24	0	42	186	22	5	37	0	27
Total	686			916			204		

Reproduced, with permission, from Hardy, JB, Welcher, DW, Stanley, J, and Dallas, JR: Long-range outcome of adolescent pregnancy. *Clin Obstet Gynecol* 21(4): 1215–1232, 1978.

infant mortality varied inversely with maternal age, with the youngest mothers at greatest risk for adverse outcome. Nonetheless, even those mothers aged 20 and above, 18% of whom had at least one child as a teenager, had substantial problems (Table 9-3), reinforcing the need to control on parity when examining outcome. It should be noted that the rates of LBW, perinatal and infant mortality shown here are very high, reflecting the high medical and social risks among women in the Johns Hopkins obstetrical population in 1959 to 1965. While these risks have been considerably reduced during the past 25 years, the relationships between maternal race, age, and parity and infant outcome remain essentially unchanged, and poor women in Baltimore face substantially increased pregnancy risk, as compared with those living under more advantageous circumstances. An exception is seen among those adolescents who receive comprehensive prenatal care in one of Baltimore's three special programs (see Chapters 5 and 8).

The outcomes, both immediate and longer range, through 8 years are compared in Table 9-4 by maternal age and parity for the 1,292 black mothers. Significant differences between age and parity groups emerged; those 20- to 24-year-old mothers with a history of one or more pregnancies when adolescent (≤17 years) had outcomes intermediate between those who were adolescent mothers and the most favored group who were 20 to 24 at their first birth. The most disadvantaged group was comprised of those young mothers who were having a second or higher order birth while still in adolescence. Findings for the white mothers and children were similar, but the differences were less marked (data not shown).

A few comments about specific findings are in order. In terms of both average gestational age and birth weight, the infants of adolescents having a second or higher order birth were smaller and had shorter gestations than those in other maternal age groups. In terms of both socioeconomic status and education, adolescents having a second birth were also at the greatest disadvantage. With respect to the children, the intergroup differences in developmental status, as measured by the Bayley Scales of Mental Development at 8 months, were small. However, the differences between groups in cognitive function at 4 and 7 years were highly significant ($p < .001$), as were those differences in academic performance, measured by the Wide Range Achievement Test administered at age 7 years. First-born children gave better average cognitive performances than those later born. Those children exhibiting the poorest average cognitive performance at ages 7 and 8 years were those born to multiparous adolescents, i.e., those young mothers who already had one or more prior children when giving birth at age 17 years or below. While the data are not shown here, the children born to adolescents had lower average performance at age 12 years than that of those of older mothers on academic testing using the Wide Range Achievement Test. Thus, in this study population, the adolescents and their children were at a disadvantage along many important outcome parameters compared with the older women and their children. Adolescents having a second or higher order birth were at a more serious disadvantage than those having a first birth. They had also repeated a grade in school more often.

Table 9-4 Pregnancy Outcome for 1292 Black Women and Children, Followed Eight Years, Percent Distribution

Maternal age Variable (Mean value)	*First birth*		*Subsequent birth*		
	≤17	20–24 yr	≤17 yr	*20–24 yr without pregnancy in adolescence*	*20–24 yr with pregnancy in adolescence*
Birth					
No. of women[a]	478	174	92	494	54
Maternal age (yr)	15.0	21.4***	16.3	22.0***	21.9***
Maternal education (yr completed)	8.4	12.6***	8.7	10.9***	9.4***
PRB index	23.6	50.6***	28.9	42.4***	38.9***
Birth weight (g)	2,820	2,869	2,784	2,970*	2,795
Gestation age (completed weeks)	37.8	38.3***	36.5	37.9**	37.4***
Neonatal hosp stay (days)	6.9	5.9	6.4	4.9	5.4
8-mo					
8-mo Bayley mental score	81.2	82.9**	79.5	81.3	80.8
4 yr					
4-yr Binet IQ	87.9	93.1***	87.4	90.9*	93**
7–8 yr					
Age at exam (months)	89.9	86.5*	91.2	88.0	91.6
WISC IQ					
Verbal	89.3	93.3***	88.4	91.0	91.5*
Performance	92.1	95.3*	89.9	93.4*	90.8
Full scale	89.7	93.8***	87.3	91.1*	90.5*
Bender gestalt error score	8.8	7.3***	9.4	8.15**	8.5
WRAT (raw scores)					
Spelling	13.63	17.73***	12.69	15.69**	14.28*
Reading	14.32	19.40***	13.18	16.08**	15.04*
Arithmetic	14.90	17.65***	14.98	16.54	15.72

Reproduced, with permission, from Hardy, JB, Welcher, DW, Stanley J, and Dallas, JR: Long-range outcome of adolescent pregnancy. *Clin Obstet Gynecol* 21(4):1215–1232, 1978.

PRB, Perinatal Research Branch socioeconomic index; WISC, Wechsler Intelligence Scale for Children; WRAT, Wide Range Achievement Test.

[a]The numbers for the follow-up examinations were slightly less, varying somewhat from group to group and reflecting about 88% successful completion.

*p ≤ .05.

**p ≤ .01.

***p < .001. Comparisons refer to difference between asterisked category and those ≤17 years.

Table 9-5 Marital Status during Follow-up, Percent Distribution

Status at:	Adolescent mothers			Mothers 20–24		
	Registration	7 yr	12 yr	Registration	7 yr	12 yr
Married	16.9	33.3	30.8	61.3	65.5	48.3
Married/divorced/ remarried		1.6	6.2			
Separated		27.0	21.6	6.5	17.2	10.3
Widowed		1.6	3.1			3.4
Divorced		6.3	7.7		3.4	20.7
Living with a man		1.6	13.8			
Single	83.1	28.6	16.9	32.3	13.8	17.2

Reproduced, with permission, from Hardy, JB, Welcher, DW, Stanley, J, and Dallas, JR: Long-range outcome of adolescent pregnancy. *Clin Obstet Gynecol* 21(4): 1215–1232, 1978.

Brooks-Gunn and Furstenberg (1986) also report that the adolescent children of early childbearers did not do as well in school as those born to older women.

Examination of certain changes in the characteristics of the adolescent mothers as compared with older mothers during the period from delivery until the children reached age 12 years may help to explain some of the developmental disadvantage shown by their children. Tables 9-5 to 9-8 report changes in marital status, education, and source of income between the time of the pregnancy, at 7 years, and at 12 years after delivery.

As seen in Table 9-5, only 16.9% of the adolescent mothers were married at registration for prenatal care as compared with 61.3% of mothers aged 20 through 24. The frequency of marriage at the birth of the child in the 1960s when these births occurred is higher than it is now. At present only about one in four white adolescents and almost none of the blacks are married. However, the frequency of change in status and the instability in relationships suggested in Table 9-5 and shown in Table 9-6 are similar to those seen among adolescents today (see Chapter 5). Family instability is not only stressful for the mother but may have disastrous effects for the development of the child.

Table 9-7 shows changes in educational attainment over time. None of the adolescents had graduated from high school at the time of registration for prenatal

Table 9-6 Changes in Marital Status over 12-Year Period after Delivery

No. of changes	Adolescent mothers (% changes)	Mothers 20–24 yr (% changes)
None	18.8	39.3
1	26.6	32.1
2	17.2	25.0
3	18.6	3.6
>3	18.8	0

Reproduced, with permission, from Hardy, JB, Welcher, DW, Stanley, J, and Dallas, JR: Long-range outcome of adolescent pregnancy. *Clin Obstet Gynecol* 21(4): 1215–1232, 1978.

Table 9-7 Maternal Educational Attainment over 12-Year Period after Delivery, Percent Distribution of High School Completion

Completion 12th grade or above	At registration	At 7 yr	At 12 yr
Adolescent mothers	0	24.3	35.3
20- to 24-yr-old mothers	64.0	77.0	77.0

Reproduced, with permission, from Hardy, JB, Welcher, DW, Stanley, J, and Dallas, JR: Long-range outcome of adolescent pregnancy. *Clin Obstet Gynecol* 21(4): 1215–1232, 1978.

care, as compared with 64% of the 20- to 24-year-old women. Seven years later, when the adolescents were for the most part in the 20- to 24-year age range, only 24% of them had completed high school, and by 12 years after delivery, 35% had done so. The older mothers also showed increases in their average educational attainment but to a lesser extent; 77% had graduated from high school by both 7 and 12 years after delivery. By the end of the period of observation, by which time the oldest of the adolescent mothers were 29 years old, less than half as many of them as the older women had completed high school. If they are ever to catch up, as has been suggested they might, it will be too late to change the environment in which their children are reared.

The source of family income at the 7- and 12-year follow-up points is shown in Table 9-8. At these points, the adolescent mothers might have been expected to be in households independent of their own parents; such was not necessarily the case. Forty-five percent of the adolescents and 67% of the women were in households that were supported by earned income (or Social Security payments); 22% of the adolescents and 17% of the older women received partial welfare support; and one-third of the adolescents and 17% of the older mothers were in families totally supported by welfare. At 12 years, the same proportion (44%) of the adolescents and a slightly larger proportion (71%) of the older mothers were in families supported by earned income, and 16% and 7%, respectively, were supported by welfare. In this generally poor population over half (56%) of the families of mothers who bore a first child as an adolescent were publicly subsidized, at least in part, as compared with 29% of the older mothers.

Another problem faced by the adolescent mothers was a higher degree of fertility than experienced by the comparison group. The differences in fertility were quite marked. The adolescent mothers averaged 3.25 surviving children during the

Table 9-8 Source of Family Income, Percent Distribution

Time after birth	Earned income or social security	Earned income and Welfare support	Welfare only
7 yr			
Adolescents	44.8	22.4	32.8
Older mothers	66.7	16.7	16.7
12 yr			
Adolescents	44.4	39.7	16.0
Older mothers	71.4	21.4	7.2

Reproduced, with permission, from Hardy, JB, Welcher, DW, Stanley, J, and Dallas, JR: Long-range outcome of adolescent pregnancy. *Clin Obstet Gynecol* 21(4): 1215–1232, 1978.

12-year period as compared with 2.35 among the older women. Among the adolescents only 3% had no subsequent children, and 46% had three or more. By contrast, among the older women 14% had no additional children, and 21% had three or more. As the adolescents were younger when follow-up ended, the differential had considerable opportunity for increase. In addition, perinatal losses during the 12-year period were higher among adolescents (46%) than among the older women (26%). The interval between births was also shorter for adolescents. Within three years of the initial delivery, 70% of the adolescents and 48% of the older women had a second child. The relationship between short birth intervals and negative birth outcomes was recognized. Furthermore, it is problems such as these that lead to high public costs for families in which the mother had her first birth as an adolescent (Moore and Burt, 1982).

Summary

There is no doubt that the adolescent mothers and their children, in this already disadvantaged east Baltimore population, fared less well over the 12-year follow-up period than the older mothers and their children. It is not clear from these data whether their continued disadvantage 12 years after delivery reflected their low maternal age, low educational attainment, and/or their generally low socioeconomic status, or some combination of these and other variables. Our experience suggests that a mix of poverty and maternal immaturity and inexperience are causally related to the adverse health and developmental outcomes observed in this population. These are important questions for research if successful intervention to prevent premature pregnancy and childbearing is to be devised and implemented.

Part III

Pregnancy and Parenting Services

It is often stated that the primary objective of pregnancy care is the safe delivery of a healthy mother of her healthy infant. Our basic intent was to show that this objective was attainable for high-risk adolescents and their infants. A major university medical center located in a high-risk area provided an excellent site for demonstration. As described in earlier chapters of this volume, the characteristics of urban adolescents and their environment put the young mothers at high risk for adverse pregnancy outcome and their children at risk for illness, accidents, and suboptimal development. In this section, we describe the characteristics of the interventions designed to offset those biological and social risk factors recognized to have an adverse effect, both immediate and longer term, on pregnancy outcome and parenting in this young maternal age group.

The legal rights of adolescents with respect to medical care and one perspective on the ethical framework for these services are discussed in Chapter 10; it is a medical model, but can be adapted to other human—and humane—services. In two chapters, we present an overview of the content and modus operandi of the intervention programs, including evaluation of their effects. In Chapter 11, the comprehensive services provided in the Johns Hopkins Adolescent Pregnancy Program (HAC) are described, and in Chapter 16 those provided to the young mother and her infant in the follow-up parenting component (TAC) are presented. The remaining chapters in this section have two purposes. The first objective is the presentation, in some detail, by the staff members who were directly involved, of the philosophy and content of major program components, such as obstetrical care, nutrition, social work, and health and parenting education. The second objective is to describe the program evaluation studies. In Chapter 19, a comparative analysis of the results of two concurrent Johns Hopkins intervention programs for pregnant and parenting adolescents are presented, one emphasizing the comprehensive services advocated in this volume, the other providing high-quality, traditional prenatal and follow-up care.

When the Adolescent Pregnancy Program was expanded in 1976 and the follow-up parenting component initiated, it was conceived as a grant-funded service demonstration program with an ongoing process evaluation to guide its evolution and an outcome evaluation to assess its effect. To this end, the following objectives were formulated and adopted by the staff.

1. Improve the health of mothers and children.
2. Reduce the frequency of:
   Complications of pregnancy, labor, and delivery;
   Maternal and child illness;
   Early, repeated conception;
   School dropout;
   Chronic Welfare dependency; and,
   Child abuse/neglect.
3. Develop and evaluate a model of successful intervention.
4. Develop appropriate educational curricula and materials for teaching health and parenting.
5. Provide staff training and consultation for other programs.
6. Provide an environment for clinical research for the study of adolescent pregnancy, its long-term consequences, and its prevention.

Chapters 11 through 19, in this section, describe the mechanisms for reaching the first three major goals. Our success in reaching other objectives is addressed during the discussion of specific subject areas. An unstated but well understood objective was the eventual institutionalization of the program so that it might become an ongoing function of the Johns Hopkins Hospital, underwritten by resources available to the Hospital.

We describe the Johns Hopkins Adolescent Pregnancy and Parenting Programs (HAC and TAC) as they evolved in the decade between 1975 and 1985. It should be noted, however, that programs change and evolve over time. Their content, quality, and effectiveness depend on a number of factors. These include the quality and dedication of the staff, the leadership, the resources, and the parent institution's support and ability to underwrite their continuation when initial demonstration funds are gone. The Johns Hopkins Pregnancy and Parenting Programs were blessed with an excellent, dedicated, and understanding staff with little turnover among key social service, educational, and nursing staff. In fact, the HAC Program has had the same social worker, Carolyn Smeton, since it began late in 1973.

However, although the worth of these programs was demonstrated, during the past few years increasing problems have been experienced with funding the social work and educational services so essential for preventing the adverse consequences of premature pregnancy and parenting. Medicaid provides some reimbursement for social service visits, particularly in crisis situations, but the amount and often the quality of service underwritten is not adequate to meet the needs of socially disadvantaged young mothers and their children. There is no reimbursement at all for preventive health and parenting education beyond the traditional one-on-one information transmitted by obstetricians, nurses, pediatricians, and nurse practitioners as part of the patient visit. As shown in the comparative evaluation of two Johns Hopkins Adolescent Pregnancy and Parenting Programs, presented in Chapter 19, the traditional program, with its crisis social service, was less effective and more costly in the long run than the special comprehensive program that offered similar medical services. In our view, the traditional medical model, which may be adequate for better informed and less needy middle-class parents, falls far short of meeting the multiple needs of disadvantaged young mothers and their children.

10

Ethical Issues in the Medical Care of Adolescents

Timothy R. B. Johnson

Ethical issues in the management and prevention of adolescent pregnancy and childbearing are subjects of controversy. They are both highly complex in their totality and are of great importance for both individuals and society. We discuss those that concern the societal context of adolescent pregnancy in the "Conclusion" on page 160. The chapters describing interventions reflect many of the ethical considerations inherent in the delivery of services to adolescents. Although an understanding of many of these issues is a major part of the training of social service professionals, it is only relatively recently that their consideration has been introduced into medical practice and into the training of medical students and house officers. This chapter focuses on one framework that has helped in the training of young clinicians as they address the often troubling management of adolescent problems.

Definitions[1]

Ethics: 1. The discipline dealing with what is good and bad and with moral duty and obligation
        2. The principles of conduct governing an individual or a group (professional ethics)
Moral: Of or relating to principles of right and wrong in behavior
Legal: 1. Deriving authority or founded on law
      2. Established by law
      3. Having a formal status from law, often without a basis in actual fact

The last decade has seen a renewed interest in ethical issues by members of the health care professions, due in part to the demand by society for an assessment of the value of medical techniques and technologies, which have grown exponentially in number and complexity in the last quarter century. This interest has had par-

---

[1]*Webster's New Collegiate Dictionary*, ed 9. Merriam Webster, Springfield, MA, 1986.

ticular relevance to the fields of obstetrics and gynecology where new interventions and manipulations have been developed that potentially alter the natural processes of conception and pregnancy. Although the new developments bring hope to many and hold out the promise of life, they are viewed by many physicians with alarm and by many consumers with dismay, as they foresee trends away from family and home. These new technologies have also caused considerable interest and controversy in the lay press and other media. New courses and texts in medical ethics have found their way into the medical school and residency curricula where previously ethical issues were seldom discussed, much less studied. Ethical discussion is relevant not only to "high tech" innovations in the field of obstetrics and gynecology, but to the provision of service, as well. In fact, it is issues that present themselves in *serving* adolescents, not in the *technology of reproduction*, that are of interest here. Many such issues can be raised with respect to adolescent sexuality and pregnancy, and we propose a framework in which to study and explore them. It is an area in which the Johns Hopkins Hospital and Medical School have been pioneers, as, in the delivery of obstetrical and gynecological service, they have focused considerable interest on such problems as autonomy, paternalism, beneficence, and many societal issues, including that of social justice in the delivery of health care. These are issues that are germane to other human service disciplines as well as to medicine.

Legal Issues

It is important to differentiate the three areas of concern outlined by the definitions at the beginning of this chapter. Many people begin exploration of ethical issues as they relate to obstetrics and gynecology, and specifically as they relate to adolescents, by raising issues of concern that are more legal than ethical in nature. To a large degree, legal practices and legal parameters define the atmosphere in which a physician can practice. For example, prior to *Roe v. Wade* (1973) it was generally illegal to perform abortions in the United States. Subsequent to that decision this practice became legal, no longer dependent on local statutes. Independent of moral and ethical decisions, legality plays a critically important role in the practice of medicine and other human services, as certain laws represent society's directions to its professionals. Thus, issues that are of ethical and moral interest throughout the world may be less pertinent in some countries because of legal proscriptions against specific practices.

In considering ethical issues as they relate to adolescents it may, therefore, be important, first and foremost, that the service provider have an understanding of the applicable law. As an illustration, Table 10-1 contains the statutes for the State of Maryland concerning medical treatment of minors. Other states may differ from Maryland in important ways, e.g., the age at majority, notification of parents, or restrictions on the timing of abortions, etc. Of particular importance, then, are legal issues that must be addressed with respect to minors' rights in the receipt of health care. Physicians and other caregivers particularly need to be aware of the adolescent's rights to a medical examination. To what extent can this examination be performed when there is a question of sexually transmitted disease or pregnancy?

Table 10-1   20-102 Annotated Code of Maryland—Medical Treatment

(a)   Minor who is married or parent—A minor has the same capacity as an adult to consent to medical treatment if the minor:

(1)   Is married; or
(2)   Is the parent of a child

(b)   Emergency treatment—A minor has the same capacity as an adult to consent to medical treatment if, in the judgment of the attending physician, the life or health of the minor would be affected adversely by delaying treatments to obtain the consent of another individual.

(c)   Specific treatment—A minor has the same capacity as an adult to consent to:
(1)   Treatment for or advice about drug abuse;
(2)   Treatment for or advice about alcoholism;
(3)   Treatment for or advice about venereal disease;
(4)   Treatment for or advice about pregnancy;
(5)   Treatment for or advice about contraception other than sterilization;
(6)   Physical examination and treatment of injuries from an alleged rape or sexual offense; and
(7)   Physical examination to obtain evidence of alleged rape or sexual offense.

(d)   Liabilities—A physician or an individual under the direction of a physician who treats a minor is not liable for civil damages or subject to any criminal or disciplinary penalty solely because the minor did not have capacity to consent under this section.

(e)   Disclosure—Without the consent of or over the express objection of a minor, the attending physician, or, on advice or direction of the attending physician, a member of the medical staff of a hospital or public clinic may, but need not, give a parent, guardian, or custodian of the minor or the spouse of the parent information about treatment needed by the minor or provided to the minor under this section, except information about an abortion. (An. Code 1957, art. 43, 135B; 1982, Ch. 21, 2).

To what extent can this examination be performed when the adolescent requires contraceptive counseling and services? Generally, an adolescent minor may consent for health care as it relates to family planning, sexually transmitted disease, pregnancy care, and substance abuse. That is to say, these services may be provided without parental notification or other legally mandated involvement. A pregnant adolescent can consent for herself and her fetus, and after birth she will act as parent for her child. The irony is that after delivery, if unemancipated, the adolescent might again be dependent on her parent or guardian for consent for her own general health care.

Many questions that are interesting ethically become less germane when the legal constraints are understood. If certain practices are illegal, then, regardless of their ethical or moral importance, they simply cannot be performed. On the other hand, the role of physicians in changing laws that do not reflect appropriate moral, ethical, or societal standards is also important to consider. In the development of the adolescent pregnancy programs at the Johns Hopkins Hospital, legal parameters and the changing legal environment have certainly been taken into consideration in establishing practice. However, consideration of the appropriateness of present legal parameters needs to continue in the evolving social and political environment in which we live, and the medical profession is in a position to understand the impact of such changes and to influence the course they take so that access to needed services is not impeded.

Informed Consent

Informed consent has become an important issue in contemporary medicine and should be for other services. A thorough understanding of legal issues involved as well as of the legal and ethical principles of informed consent are particularly important when dealing with adolescents and adolescent pregnancy. Practices of required consent are extrememly complex and are well-reviewed by Faden and Beauchamp (1986). Basically, informed consent demands that physicians or other health care providers give an adequate explanation of proposed procedures or practices to those upon whom these procedures will have an impact. Risks and benefits must be clearly elucidated. With respect to adolescents, appropriate informed consent may involve detailed medical descriptions and a significant educational component, and sometimes the involvement of others, to make sure that real understanding has been achieved. In practice, this process can further expand to educational and maturational objectives exemplified by the programs described elsewhere in this text.

Informed consent should not, however thorough, be a barrier to obtaining appropriate prenatal or intrapartum care for the adolescent, because these services fall within the limits specified by law. The adolescent can give consent for her own care. However, because these young people are usually not independent of their families, it is advisable (except in unusual circumstances) to encourage them to involve parents in the decision-making process. The Johns Hopkins Adolescent Pregnancy and Parenting Program does, in fact, encourage family involvement in these decisions, and physicians, nurses, and social workers have made themselves available to assist adolescents in "facing" their families. This has on occasion undoubtedly played a role in reestablishing important family ties. If this role is undertaken thoughtfully, it can be played while recognizing the privacy of the individual and her or his right to quality care and confidentiality.

Moral Issues

Moral beliefs and practices form the underpinnings of society's acceptance of both legal and ethical issues. In certain situations, moral practices or beliefs can be as important as legal ones. To present a prior example, it is legal in the United States (subject to certain constraints) to perform elective abortions and elective sterilizations. On the other hand, because of their particular moral and religious beliefs, certain hospitals do not allow the performance of these procedures, which are otherwise legally and ethically acceptable. Obviously, this can vary not only by hospital, but by state and country, and even by physician. For this reason relationships between legal and moral issues have practical importance. It is true that certain physicians find it morally unacceptable to perform abortions, and others find it morally unacceptable to deny them. These physician practices are crucial, and it is vital that physicians, during their training, achieve an understanding of the range of their choices, and, equally important, the effects of their choices.

The potential of using adolescent services such as prenatal clinics, sexually transmitted disease clinics, and school-based clinics to help adolescents understand moral and ethical issues is clear, but the decision of *what* to teach is extremely complicated. One of the concerns of parents and educators and, in fact, of society in general, is that, although moral values ideally should be taught at home, many parents are unable to provide the necessary instruction because they lack the knowledge or skills to do so. There is some precedent for teaching morality in schools, in the context of a curriculum in character development and personal values that often spans the elementary and secondary years. In addition to reproductive and family issues, "sex education" should also focus on personal responsibility, caring about one's self, others, and society, and planning for the future. These are value-filled areas of concern but are somewhat separate from those more controversial issues generally regarded as "moral." Only in the context of values orientation can adolescents be prepared for the decisions they will begin to make, or already are making. The teaching of morals—that is, of values generally regarded as desirable and necessary—at public institutions in our heterogeneous society remains difficult, but its potential is great, and the dialogue between parents, professionals, and religious leaders on the subject is not likely to abate. None of this should relieve the medical provider of his or her special role as educator, a role for which schools rarely prepare the practitioner. Once the provider assumes this role, it will become clear that young patients' needs often extend well beyond the medical domain and involve larger issues of human sexuality and values orientation. The physician or nurse practitioner has a unique opportunity to become the advisor and confidant of the young patient as he or she approaches puberty, well before the onset of coitus, an opportunity which few other adults have in our society.

Effective patient communication in these areas makes certain ethical demands on the health care provider. It requires that the health care provider come to terms with his or her own prejudices and biases and the value systems that underlie them. Included among the biases may be such factors as the client's race, sex, and social class, as well as the client's general demeanor and values pertaining to sexuality and childbearing. It is important to be nonjudgmental about the client's values, but, if the circumstances warrant, one should be honest about showing one's own values.

At present, it would seem from the public press that adolescence is a time when unwanted pregnancy and contraceptive or abortion issues are the primary moral issues that clinicians address (if indeed, they address them at all). However, the high frequency of certain sexually transmitted infections in this age group and the expanding epidemic of AIDS raise serious public health issues. Because education offers the only present hope of affecting behavior, hence of controlling AIDS, and is also important in preventing unwanted pregnancy, physicians and other health care professionals may have an obligation more pressing than ever before to provide information about the risks involved in premature, unprotected sexual activity.

Ethical Issues

As noted above, the practice of medicine in the 1980s is a particularly rich area for ethical discussions. Technological advances in fertility management and contraception, the correction of infertility and in vitro fertilization, as well as in the early detection of fetal and neonatal abnormalities, have put obstetricians and gynecologists at the forefront of such discussions. Discussions around these issues provide a broad avenue for the teaching of medical ethics. There is an additional complexity because we are dealing directly not only with an individual patient but, in fact, with a dyadic pair. Obstetrics deals with a female and her fetus, both of whom have rights and privileges that must be understood in an ethical framework. Infertility and the new reproductive technologies lead to discussions of families, parents, partners, and a society network that may have to deal with a new set of possibilities. The rapid advent of in vitro fertilization, for example, provides the possibility of pregnancy where it did not previously exist. This technology also leads to the possibility of surrogate parenting and new combinations in family structure that had not been thought of previously. When obstetrics and gynecology are taken to the level of the adolescent, the more important ethical issues are those that are related to patient care; they take on special significance because of the association between youthful, unintended, premarital pregnancy and the increased risk of problems, such as prematurity, low birth weight, late prenatal care, and infant mortality. There are complex ethical issues with respect to the competing interests of the pregnant adolescent and her fetus, of her parents, and, sometimes, the father of the baby as well.

With respect to ethical issues in the adolescent pregnant patient, not only do we deal with the usual obstetric combination of a woman and her fetus but, in this situation, with a young woman who is in an age group with complexities of its own. Some adolescents have been shown to be particularly mature and capable of dealing with the problems of pregnancy and parenthood. On the other hand, some adolescents are simply incapable, because of the immaturity of their psychological and physical growth, to deal with pregnancy. They need the support of their mothers, sisters, boyfriends, or other adults, and they may or may not get it. Reconciling those needs with the right of the pregnant adolescent to confidential care is a challenge to the clinician. It often requires that the clinician look closely at aspects of his or her patients' environments that may affect both treatment and outcomes. A breach of confidentiality might have disastrous consequences for the adolescent. In some cases, a careful examination of the social environment may show the pregnancy to be due to, or to result from, sexual abuse of the adolescent; this raises additional legal and moral responsibilities for the doctor. There is a recognized association between abuse in one's childhood and abuse, in later years, of one's own offspring. Therefore, in addition to serving the needs of the patient, active intervention in this situation might prevent the adolescents from becoming child abusers themselves. There may also be legal requirements for the reporting of abuse to social service agencies.

Some families demand that they have input into the gynecological and obstetrical care of their adolescent children, and this may cause problems for the physician. Under these circumstances, it is important to focus on the legal rights of minors, which were discussed above. Adolescents have a legal right to specific information, education, and confidential health services. At the same time, and despite these legal rights, the real world asks consideration of those who will not only be involved with, but will have financial and other responsibilities for, the adolescent mother and her baby for long periods after contact with the physician or acute health care system has ceased. How the clinician will balance these competing rights is both an ethical and a legal issue. It is an issue that pertains not only to the treatment of pregnancy, because the individual's right to confidential services also applies to the treatment of sexually transmitted diseases and the provision of contraception for adolescents. In resolving these conflicting needs, the counseling and educational skills of sensitive health care professionals are of paramount importance. Parents should be involved whenever possible and productive, but there are occasions when the safety and well-being of the adolescent may depend on her legal right to confidentiality. This must be upheld.

Ethical Decision Making

A general approach to ethical decision making can follow the four quadrant schema shown in Table 10-2, as proposed by Jonsen et al. (1985). This approach is the one that we use in teaching clinical ethics to 1st- and 3rd-year medical students as they rotate through the clinical services at the Johns Hopkins Hospital.

In the first quadrant, we begin with a thorough evaluation of the medical diagnoses, therapies, and decisions that are appropriate. As mentioned above, these can become extremely complex in obstetrics, where both maternal and fetal conditions and complications may exist, but, basically, in this area of medical

Table 10-2   A Four-Quadrant Approach to Ethical Decision Making in Clinical Medicine

I *Indications for Medical Intervention*	*II* *Preferences of Patients*
The ethical principles underlying this quadrant are beneficence and nonmaleficence—the duty of assisting others in need and avoiding harm. The physician has a duty to recommend interventions which have a reasonable probability of attaining clinical goals, to avoid those where risks outweigh benefits, and to refrain from those which are futile.	The ethical principle underlying this quadrant is autonomy, i.e., the patient has a right over his or her own body and mind. Competent patients have the moral and legal right to accept or refuse recommended interventions.
III *Quality of Life*	*IV* *Socioeconomic Factors*
Quality of life is the subjective physical, mental, and social satisfaction expressed or experienced by an individual. It is a concept which engenders controversy depending upon which principle one emphasizes, e.g., sanctity of life or utility. Generally, though, quality of life should be decisive in initiating, continuing, or ceasing life-sustaining interventions only when: a. No significant medical goals are attainable; b. Patient preference cannot be known; and c. Life falls below a minimal threshold.	Socioeconomic factors include: 1) the interests of parties other than the patient; 2) the costs of care; 3) the use of medical resources; 4) research; 5) medical teaching; and 6) safety and welfare of society. The major question is to what extent, if any, should burdens and benefits accruing to persons other than the patient influence clinical decisions? The consensus is that socioeconomic factors should not be decisive in clinical decisions unless: a. Achievement of significant medical goals is doubtful; b. Preferences of patient are not and cannot be known; and c. Quality of life is below or approaching a minimal threshold.

Adapted from Jonsen, AR, Siegler, M, and Winslade, WJ. *Clinical Ethics*, ed 2. Macmillan Publishing Company, New York, 1985.

decision making, we focus on the idea of beneficence. This means that the physician is trying to do the best possible for his patient. Beneficence depends on a thorough evaluation of the clinical situation and a thorough understanding of the medical issues. This approach supports the traditional medical model beginning with the history of the illness, a social, medical, and family history, physical examination, and a review of the pertinent medical textbooks and literature. By repetition of these principles, we emphasize that good ethics begin with good medicine. Any ethical discussion begins with thorough knowledge of the medical and clinical situation, and, 8 times out of 10, a thorough evaluation of the clinical situation reveals that, in fact, there is no real ethical dilemma. A thorough gathering of facts and information usually points to the one course of action that is best from a medical point of view for all those legitimately involved. Therefore, we have found it important, as we teach ethics, to stress the importance of thoroughly understanding the medical quadrant before becoming burdened with the issues of the other three quadrants.

The second quadrant concerns patient wishes or autonomy. This is an important area to address in dealing with adolescents, because, in fact, once pregnant these young women are legally autonomous in terms of their decision making. Once pregnant they are emancipated legally from the usual parental guidelines and can make personal decisions. Even marriage does not change the woman's right to make her own pregnancy outcome decisions. On the other hand, because of the patient's immaturity or other factors, the support and guidance of parents and others in making appropriate autonomous decisions may be important. Early access to a multidisciplinary team that can present options—childbearing, abortion, or adoption—optimizes the decision-making process which is a serious one, holding implications for the rest of the young woman's life. In turn, if the decision to continue the pregnancy is made, it is important to remember that even though the patient is adolescent, her fetus, in time, will develop the same rights as the fetus of any pregnant patient; these rights should in no way be affected by the fact that the parent is an adolescent, and, unfortunately, is treated by some clinicians as less autonomous than an adult patient. The ethical principle of autonomy is an important one, whatever the competitive rights may be and is, in turn, subject to legal constraints.

The third important quadrant focuses on issues of quality of life. Having stated that medical issues are primary and that patient autonomy issues are of importance, we must also consider family and quality of life issues. The home life that the baby and mother will have after delivery must unfortunately assume less importance than making a correct medical decision in response to the appropriate desire of the mother and the appropriate, hypothesized wishes of her newborn child. In some situations, the physician must deal with decisions imposed by parents or society, decisions that may not be appropriate for an adolescent who is well-advanced in sexual activity or even in pregnancy.

Finally, the fourth quadrant focuses on issues of social or societal justice, when the allocation of resources and technologies needs to be weighed. There is a clear tendency to favor the young, the newborn, and the fetus when limited medical resources are allocated, because of their long-term potential for a future in society. For example, in the area of organ transplantation, younger people have traditionally been those who would be given priority for services, and, therefore, in most medical situations, adolescents would be expected to have some kind of benefit. On the other hand, because of their minority status and the generally lower financial and socioeconomic status of those who conceive at young ages, a certain bias against adolescents has existed, which has, no doubt, formed a significant barrier to care. Barriers to care are addressed in this quadrant and are relevant to the pregnant adolescent whatever her outcome decision.

The approach to the practice of ethical decision making just described has been beneficial to patient care and to teaching at the Johns Hopkins Hospital. The case study described in the illustrative case report presented below provides insight with respect to its practical application. The case is that of a pregnant woman who presents with premature rupture of the membranes. The fact that she is an adolescent, immature, and unmarried adds complexity to the decision-making process. It raises the complex issues of the rights of adolescents who, while legally minors, have rights to autonomy and to consent to their own health care (and that of their fetus) in certain situations. Both the importance of open communication with the adolescent and her family and the adolescent's legal right to confidential services are clear. Unfortunately, they may be in conflict. The sensitive obstetrician/gynecologist is in a central position to influence the decision-making process by providing information and facilitating discussion between the adolescent and her family.

Illustrative Case

A 16-year-old adolescent, pregnant for the first time, presents with spontaneous rupture of the membranes at 31 weeks gestation. She is not in labor. She is unmarried, accompanied by her mother, with whom she lives. The pregnancy is unplanned. She has had no prenatal care. She is admitted for evaluation and management. What factors must be considered?

Issues for Discussion

1. What does the condition of premature rupture of the membrane imply? What are the management options, risks, benefits?
2. Problems of a pregnant adolescent: who will make decisions about her care, that of her baby? What are the rights of the father and of the baby: legal, moral, social?
3. Informed consent—specific issues are related to the adolescent's status and to medical/obstetrical parameters.

At admission, the amniotic fluid is noted to be discolored; the fetal heart rate is normal; the mother is afebrile without evidence of infection. Lack of prenatal care and the discolored amniotic fluid indicate the need for an ultrasound evaluation to assess fetal age and status.

Issues for Discussion

Risks and benefits of an ultrasound examination: The examination reveals multiple fetal abnormalities, including kyphoscoliosis, gastroschisis, abnormal intracranial structures consistent with porencephaly, and facial clefting is noted.

Issues for Discussion

1. What is the prognosis for the baby? How will the anomalies (syndrome) affect the care of the mother and her outlook on the pregnancy? What should the parents be told? What further diagnostic steps and/or consultations are indicated?
2. Who will provide support (social, psychological, and financial) to the mother—her family, the father?

In consultation with perinatologists, geneticists, and neonatologists, the sonographic findings are found consistent with amniotic band syndrome, a syndrome inconsistent with survival for more than a short time.

Issues for Discussion

1. Prognosis for mother, for fetus?
2. Management options. How does the diagnosis change the risk/benefit ratio with respect to an adolescent with premature rupture of membranes?
3. What are the risks of inducing labor to affect delivery?
4. How do you inform the patient and her mother of the situation and the issues raised? Who gives informed consent?
5. How do you monitor fetal status during labor? Who decides?

After informed consent, labor is induced with prostaglandin priming of the unfavorable cervix and intravenous oxytocin; the fetus is not monitored during labor. After 18 hours, a stillborn infant with stigmata of amniotic band syndrome is delivered.

Issues for Discussion

1. How is the grief process handled for multiple anomalies? For a dead baby? Who decides about anesthesia during delivery, viewing of the infant, the value of an autopsy?
2. The need for counseling the adolescent and her family regarding assurance of diagnosing genetic aspects and the likelihood of recurrence?
3. The need for sexuality and contraceptive counseling and continuing reproductive health to prevent a recurrence of unintended pregnancy.
4. The need for family counseling/therapy.

Not all cases present with medical considerations so compelling. Whereas this example puts the emphasis upon the patient's and her family's adjustment to a medical decision, other situations leave more room for choice. The model should not suggest that one quadrant *supercedes* the others in importance even if, in an appreciation of each case, one may *precede* the other in the decision-making process.

Conclusion

The purpose of this chapter has been to outline briefly some of the legal, ethical, and moral issues involved in providing medical care to adolescents and to describe the approach to ethical teaching for professionals that is used at the Johns Hopkins

Hospital. Opportunities abound for teaching ethical decision making using this adolescent model. In addition, the possibility of using adolescent pregnancy and sexually transmitted disease clinics to explore moral values with other care providers, counselors, educators, and clinicians, should not be underestimated. The issues involved are important ones with dilemmas at all levels of intervention.

Many of the issues touched upon in the preceding discussion are common to any discipline as its professionals interact with the adolescent, but clearly the emphasis will differ. The four quadrant framework proposed here (Table 10-2) is specific to medical decision making, especially the component that emphasizes the objective medical and physiological data upon which the physician's decisions are predicated. Effective guidance in the informed consent process depends even more on the interaction between counselor and client and demands a delicate balance between direction and support of the client's decision, whatever it may be.

The dilemmas faced by those providing services to adolescents, with barriers that are placed by the family, society in general, the educational system, and the medical community, are many, and services described in this book have addressed many of them. Although the services were designed within the framework of that which is legal, they have sought to do that which is morally right to promote a level of service that is ethically incumbent on a caring society to deliver to those who are most dependent upon it.

11

The Johns Hopkins Adolescent Pregnancy Program (HAC)
Services and Evaluation

As described in Chapter 1, the recognition of the high pregnancy risks for child-bearing adolescents and their infants and the difficulties involved in managing the labor and delivery of an unprepared, often terrified and uncooperative young patient, led to the initiation of a separate program to meet their multiple needs. The program design drew on the experience of the "Young Mothers' Program," which had been initiated at the Grace New Haven Hospital some years earlier (Sarrel and Klerman, 1969). The program established at Johns Hopkins in 1973 became known as HAC, Hopkins Adolescent Clinic. Results for patients enrolled during the first two years of operation have been described by Youngs et al. (1977). In 1976, with additional grant funds, the program was increased in size and extended in scope.

Program Characteristics

It was postulated that the obstetrical needs of urban adolescents would be met most effectively: 1) in a clinic setting separate from that serving older pregnant patients; 2) by a caring staff who liked and understood inner city adolescents; 3) when the adolescents' parent(s), usually a single mother, and/or the father of the baby could be included; and 4) where an evaluation process was in place to monitor progress and to assess and improve program effectiveness.

Given the setting described above, we hypothesized that the programmatic ingredients listed below would be necessary to enhance compliance and participation by the adolescent and to meet her special needs.

Program Ingredients

- High-quality medical and obstetrical care directed toward meeting the special needs of the adolescent patient
- An emphasis on nutritional needs and supplements
- Special nursing service to provide continuity between prenatal clinic sessions and between outpatient and inpatient care

- Social work to provide psychosocial support and link the adolescents and their families with a wide range of community services for financial support, nutritional supplements, continued schooling, and crisis intervention, which was frequently needed
- Education in health, pregnancy, nutrition, early parenting, and family planning, to assist the adolescent and her significant others to participate in her pregnancy care and to prevent an early repetition of unintended pregnancy
- A team approach to patient care, including all professional and support staff members, brought together to coordinate their efforts through an individual case management system
- An approach that takes into account the developmental level and cognitive maturity of the adolescent
- Access to consultation for specific medical problems in the high-risk pregnancy clinic and other specialty services in the Hospital

Patient Characteristics

Between 1976, when the initial program was augmented and extended, and July of 1982, when it was institutionalized within the Johns Hopkins Hospital services, 300 to 350 pregnant adolescents were enrolled each year. They were enrolled after the pregnancy diagnosis had been made elsewhere and after they had been counseled with respect to pregnancy options and had reached a decision to carry on with the pregnancy.

Of the 1,780 adolescents discussed in this chapter, all were age 17 or below at registration and all but 238 (13%) were below age 18 at delivery. Just over 21% were 15 or below and 27% were age 16 at delivery. Of the 1,780, 167 (9%) had one or more prior liveborn children. It should be noted that the outcome evaluation was limited to girls aged 17 or below at delivery between January 1, 1979 and December 30, 1981.

In the early years, 20% to 25% of the adolescents were white, but as the population of East Baltimore became predominantly black, the proportion of whites declined to about 10%. Most of the adolescents lived in East Baltimore, where rates of pregnancy among adolescents have been extremely high; in some census tracts rates were above 150/1,000 adolescents aged 15 through 17 years (AK Duggan

Table 11-1   Age of Maternal Grandmother at Birth of Her First Child

Grandmother's age (yr)	No.	%	
13–14	8	6	
15–16	40	30	51%
17	20	15	
18–19	29	22	
20–29	27	20	
30–35	2	2	
Unknown	8	6	

Data are from the first 134 young mothers enrolled in the follow-up program.

and JB Hardy, unpublished data, 1989). For the most part, they lived in single-parent families where a majority of mothers had started childbearing at an early age (see Table 11-1). As in the random sample of adolescent mothers described in Chapter 5, approximately 51% of the grandmothers also had their first child as an adolescent.

Because the background characteristics of these young people were similar to those described in detail in Chapter 5, suffice it to say here that they were, almost without exception, poor; 95% were eligible for Medical Assistance (MA) to cover the cost of both prenatal and inpatient hospital care for mothers and neonates. These costs were augmented by those resulting from antenatal hospital admission, required by 15% of the young mothers, and when required, by neonatal intensive care for about 8% of the infants.

Program Components

Medical and Obstetrical Care

The HAC Program was designed to render high-quality obstetrical care, while providing the learning and teaching opportunities for house staff required in a major teaching hospital. It provided obstetrical care by residents, working under the close supervision of a faculty member, the director of the pregnancy component. This obstetrician, with the team of full-time nurses, a social worker, a health educator, and support staff, provided the continuity of care that facilitates patient compliance and an early identification of emergent problems. Care during labor and delivery and the inpatient hospital stay was provided by the faculty and house staff assigned to the care of all patients in those areas.

Nursing Care

Two obstetrical nurses assigned full-time to the program played a central role in the continuity of patient care. They provided nursing service in the clinic and a link between the outpatient and inpatient services, both by exchanging information and maintaining patient contact with daily visits to the labor and delivery floor and patient wards. In addition, they were available in the clinic, between regular sessions, on a daily basis, to follow-up on recognized problems, manage new problems, and, at certain hours each day, by telephone to provide advice and answer questions. Many telephone calls served to reduce the adolescent's anxiety and save unnecessary trips to the hospital.

Routine nursing duties included conducting a private *exit interview* with each girl as she completed her clinic visit. The purpose of this interview was to make certain that: 1) all her questions had been answered in a way she could understand; 2) instructions given to her by the physicians had been understood; 3) arrangements made for laboratory tests and/or consultations were understood, both in terms of their contribution to her care and the practicalities involved (i.e., where, when, and any special preparations that were required); and 4) she was supplied with free vitamins and iron supplements and was receiving WIC without problems.

Important to the success of the nurses was their ability to assess the developmental level of the adolescent and to use this skill to direct their teaching to the maturity level and needs of individual girls. They developed warm, friendly relationships with each patient, which carried over from prenatal care to inpatient care and to postnatal follow-up of each patient.

The nurses also participated in the program's educational component, leading or coleading groups in areas such as the physiology of reproduction, fetal growth, preparation for labor and delivery, and sexually transmitted disease. In addition, virtually every individual patient contact had its appropriate educational aspects. For example, the visit to the mother in her room, during the postpartum period, reviewed her knowledge about her own care and that of her baby when she went home and provided her with foam and condoms as a temporary family planning method until more definitive plans could be made at the postpartum visit. The ongoing process evaluation showed us, early in the program, that contraceptive service delayed until the postpartum visit 4 to 6 weeks after delivery could be too late for some girls; they had already conceived. The nurses also made sure that the need for continuing care for both mother and baby was understood and that appropriate follow-up appointments had been made.

A *nurse midwife*, employed on a part-time basis, saw most of the patients at their postpartum visit. She also provided continuity of care for certain unusually high-risk adolescents during their prenatal course. She was able to give the increased time required by these patients (for details see Chapter 15).

During the early years of the program, three nurses and an obstetrical technical assistant were employed. In addition to the nursing duties already described, they were on call around the clock to attend each adolescent as she was admitted in labor. They provided coaching and psychosocial support during labor and delivery. This service, although appreciated by the adolescents and the staff on the labor floor, was disruptive of the nurses' daytime activities and expensive. With the expansion of the program in 1976, resources were reallocated. The nursing staff was reduced to two, assisted on clinic days by a licensed practical nurse. The adolescents were asked to identify a support person to help them during labor and this person, usually the girl's mother, or sometimes the baby's father, was asked to participate with the adolescent in the activities that prepared her for labor (see Chapter 14). This person came with her to the hospital and stayed with her until the baby was delivered.

Social Service

A full-time social worker screened each adolescent at registration and arranged for follow-up counseling as needed, with the adolescent and her mother and/or the putative father, with respect to decisions about health care, plans for continued schooling, and for the arrival and care of the baby. Her role is described in detail in Chapter 17.

The social worker also participated in the educational groups as leader or coleader and took responsibility for conducting the tours of the labor and delivery and inpatient facilities that were part of the preparation for labor. She described admission procedures so that the adolescent and her support person would know where to go and what would happen on admission. She also took responsibility for organizing the weekly staff conference at which new patients were discussed and information on current ones brought up-to-date so optimal plans could be made for patient care.

Community Outreach Worker

The community outreach worker was an integral part of the team. She assisted in the clinic, visited on the wards, and extended the work of the social worker into the community. She routinely visited the homes of the youngest and most high-risk patients because most of their mothers did not come to the clinic with them. She interacted with community groups to meet the special needs of pregnant adolescents. For the adolescents themselves, she was a special friend and role model. Several adolescents took up nursing careers "to be like Miss Carrie."

Health and Pregnancy Education

A full-time health educator has served as program coordinator since the program's inception, freeing the time of the obstetrical director for clinical care and other duties. The content and modus operandi of this important component are described in Chapter 14. Nutrition and nutrition education are discussed in Chapter 13.

Supporting Staff

A full-time *registrar* had responsibility for answering the telephone, making appointments, registration, general clerical work, and maintaining patient records. She has been a member of the team and is also a friend and role model for the patients.

A part-time *licensed practical nurse* or nurse's aide has assisted with routine work during clinic sessions. She, too, has been part of the team, getting to know each adolescent and helping her to manage her pregnancy.

Case Management

Individual case management has been an integral part of each of the three major programs described in this volume. While it has differed somewhat with the specific needs of each program, two basic mechanisms have been employed: 1) Regular, weekly, clinical staff conferences have been utilized, at which new patients are discussed and the progress of current patients monitored. Thus, each staff member is able to contribute her insights about each patient and to be informed of plans for care and who would implement them. 2) At the end of each prenatal clinic session, the record of each patient appointed that day was reviewed by the obstetrical director and the nurses. The review of all records had two functions. One, it monitored the work of the residents and the patient's medical needs. The patient's course and the appropriateness and adequacy of laboratory tests and referrals were checked to assure high-quality patient care. Unmet needs were identified and provided for. Two, the review also included the charts of patients who failed to keep their appointments, about 20% on any given day, to determine the action needed to facilitate their prompt return. Telephone calls, letters, or home visits were used as indicated. The registrar was responsible for routine appointments; the social worker or outreach worker was responsible for those in which difficulties might have been anticipated or in which further delay might jeopardize patient care.

Evaluation

We turn now to consideration of measurement of the program's success. Evaluation efforts were both outcome- and process-oriented. The outcome evaluation was directed toward determining whether the program was effective, that is, whether it met its objectives for improving pregnancy outcome. The ongoing process evaluation monitored the operation of the program in terms of annual goals for numbers of patients served, their characteristics, and outcomes.

Outcome Evaluation: Did the Program Work?

The outcome evaluation was facilitated by the availability of: 1) a computerized database that included detailed, structured summaries of all deliveries at the Johns Hopkins Hospital, maintained by personnel in the Department of Obstetrics and Gynecology, and additional data collected specifically by the program; and 2) a comparison group of similar, adolescent obstetrical patients who, although delivered concurrently in the same facilities by members of the same staff as the HAC patients, received their prenatal care in other more traditional Johns Hopkins-related programs. These "control" patients did not receive the psychosocial support and intensive health, nutrition, and early parenting education and individual case management that were the hallmark of HAC.

The results of a preliminary evaluation suggested that the program was effective in reducing complications of pregnancy and the need for cesarean section as compared with similar controls. Averted costs for savings in hospital care of mothers and infants for the pregnancy and a 2-year follow-up period amounted to $1,440 per mother/child pair (Hardy and Flagle, 1979) as compared with incremental costs for the special services (beyond traditional medical care) of $775 per pair.

The results of a more extensive outcome evaluation for two successive time periods, 1976 through 1978 and 1979 through 1981, have been published elsewhere (Hardy et al., 1987). Data from the second period are discussed below. These data were limited to patients aged 17 years or less at delivery. After exclusion of those enrollees who had become 18 by the time of delivery, 744 HAC patients were compared with the "controls."

Population Characteristics

For meaningful results it was necessary to determine that the adolescent patients in the two groups were comparable with respect to certain characteristics recognized to be associated with pregnancy outcome. Adolescents in both groups were predominantly black, unmarried, and poor. Approximately 95% were eligible for Medicaid coverage for obstetrical care. Cigarette smoking was reported by approximately half of each group, but most were occasional smokers; few reported smoking as many as 10 cigarettes per day. Reports of drug use were rare, with alcohol use somewhat more frequent than illicit drugs.

Comparisons between groups with respect to selected demographic and physical characteristics and prior pregnancy history are shown in Table 11-2. No statistically significant differences were noted, with one exception. The HAC patients were slightly shorter than those in the comparison group, a difference not considered to be of clinical importance.

Table 11-2 Selected Characteristics of Adolescents Enrolled in the Comprehensive HAC Program Compared with Those of Controls Receiving Prenatal Care in Other Johns Hopkins Related Programs (1979 to 1981)

Maternal characteristics	HAC (n = 744)		Controls (n = 744)	
	Mean	%	Mean	%
Education, highest grade completed	8.3		8.4	
History of				
prior birth		7.3		10.3
prior abortion		11.6		11.4
Gestation at registration (completed wk)	17.3		17.0	
Registration in 1st trimester		16.5		17.0
Pregnant weight (lbs)	121.8		120.7	
Height (inches)*	62.6		63.3	
Age at delivery (yr)	16.1		16.0	

*$p < .01$.

Obstetrical Course and Outcome

There were no significant differences between groups in the average duration of pregnancy at registration for prenatal care: 17.3 completed weeks for HAC patients and 17 for those in the comparison group, or in the proportions registering during the first trimester. However, as seen in Tables 11-3 and 11-4, important differences between groups in pregnancy course and outcome were noted. On average, HAC patients made more prenatal visits, 9.2 (exclusive of the pregnancy diagnostic visit that had been made elsewhere prior to referral), as compared with the controls who made an average of 8.7 visits, usually including the diagnostic visit. The HAC adolescents gained an average of almost 29 pounds during pregnancy as compared with 23.5 pounds by the controls ($p = .0001$). Both anemia and preeclamptic toxemia, problems of some frequency and concern among pregnant adolescents, occurred significantly less frequently among the HAC patients than controls. These findings suggest that HAC patients were more compliant with program directions and took better care of themselves than the controls. No significant differences were observed between groups in the average gestation at delivery, in the frequency of preterm delivery (<37 completed weeks), or in the frequency of cesarean section among the youngest patients. However, two labor and delivery complications were significantly less frequent among HAC patients than controls; these were premature rupture of the membranes (more than 12 hours prior to the onset of labor) and lacerations of the cervix during delivery.

Fetal Outcome

Significant differences were also observed between groups in fetal outcome (Table 11-4). The infants of HAC mothers were healthier and had fewer neonatal problems than those of the control mothers. On average, HAC babies were heavier, and

Table 11-3 Obstetrical Course and Outcome: Adolescents Enrolled in HAC versus Controls (1979–1981)

	HAC (n = 744)			Controls (n = 744)			
	Mean	*SD*	*%*	*Mean*	*SD*	*%*	*p value*
Prenatal characteristics							
Weight gain (lbs)	28.9	12.8		23.5	15.1		.0001
Visits (no.)[a]	9.2	3.5		8.7	4.1		.006
Anemia (hematocrit <30 mm)			10.9 (81)			15.6 (116)	.002
Preeclampsia			3.5 (26)			5.9 (44)	.02
Gonorrhea			7.9 (59)			5.4 (40)	NS
Labor and delivery							
Gestation (wk completed)	38.5	3.0		38.4	3.5		NS
Gestation (≤36 wk)			18.7 (139)			21.5 (160)	NS
Premature rupture membranes, (>12 hr)			3.5 (26)			5.5 (44)	.03
Cervical laceration			2.8 (21)			4.2 (31)	.05
Cesarean section at ≤14 yr			17.1 (127)			19.5 (144)	NS

NS, not significant.

[a]Johns Hopkins Adolescent Pregnancy Program visits do not include initial visit for pregnancy diagnosis and counseling; controls include diagnostic visit.

there were highly significant differences in the frequencies of low birth weight (LBW, <2,500 g) and very low birth weight (VLBW, <1,500 g). Among HAC patients, 9.9% of infants were LBW and 1.9% were VLBW as compared with 16.4% and 3.9%, respectively, among the controls. The status of HAC babies at birth as measured by Apgar score (Apgar, 1953) was more favorable than that of controls. Not surprisingly, as the risk of neonatal mortality is strongly related to

Table 11-4 Fetal Outcome for HAC Patients as Compared with Controls

Fetal outcome	HAC (n = 744)		Controls (n = 744)		
	Mean	*%*	*Mean*	*%*	*p value*
Birth weight (g)	3,083		3,038		NS
<2500		9.9		16.4	.0006
<1500		1.9		3.9	.02
Apgar score					
1 min	7.87		7.68		.03
3 min	8.81		8.71		.04
≤6 at 5 min		4.0		6.7	.02
Congenital malformation[a]		4.9		7.0	NS
Stillbirth		1.2		1.0	NS
Neonatal death		0.4		1.2	.08
Hospital days	4.9		6.0		.05

Reprinted with permission from *Risking the Future* © 1987 by the National Academy of Sciences, National Academy Press, Washington, DC.

NS, not significant.

[a]Includes minor malformations.

low birth weight, "control" infants experienced a neonatal mortality three times that of the HAC infants. Similarly, the increased hospital stay of "control" infants, an average of 6 days, as compared with HAC babies (4.9 days), is a likely reflection of the higher frequency of LBW among the controls.

Data from Process Evaluation

Examination of data for the larger cohort of 1,780 consecutive HAC patients enrolled between 1976 and 1981 provided insight as to possible relationships of certain maternal characteristics to prenatal care and pregnancy outcome. The relationships between maternal race, age, and prior pregnancy history and the duration of gestation at registration for prenatal care are shown in Table 11-5. Those who were younger and black registered significantly later than those who were older or white. Those with a history of prior abortion registered earlier than those without such a history, perhaps a reflection of slightly less social disadvantage among those electing abortion. While those without a history of prior childbearing registered, on average, almost one week earlier than those with one or more prior births, this finding was not statistically significant.

In Table 11-6, the results of a comparison between early (i.e., first trimester) and late registration (i.e., after 28 completed weeks gestation) are presented. Early registrants were slightly older, gained more weight during pregnancy, and had slightly larger infants. Their infants stayed, on average, somewhat longer in the newborn nursery because, in most cases, the opportunity for delivery of premature infants of very low birth weight had passed by 28 completed weeks of gestation and was not likely to be a problem among late registrants.

In Table 11-7, infant outcome is displayed by maternal age and parity. In the comprehensive program, infant outcome, in terms of mean birth weight, percentage

Table 11-5 Adolescents Receiving Comprehensive Care in HAC: Time of Registration for Prenatal Care by Certain Maternal Characteristics

| Variable | No. | Registration time | | Significance |
		Mean/wk	SD	p value
Age (yr)				
≤15	371	18.2	6.5	.0001
≥16	1,388	16.5	7.0	
Race				
Black	1,388	17.0	6.9	.003
White	240	15.6	7.3	
Prior live birth				
None	1,594	16.8	7.0	NS
≥1	165	17.7	6.5	
Prior abortions				
None	787	17.0	7.1	.009
≥1	231	15.7	6.6	

Adapted from Hardy, JB, et al. The Johns Hopkins adolescent pregnancy program: an evaluation. *Obstet Gynecol* 69: 300–306, 1987.

Variations in numbers reflect missing data points and some adolescents may have had both prior births and abortions.

NS, not significant.

Table 11-6 Adolescents Receiving Comprehensive Obstetrical Care in HAC: Comparison of Certain Maternal and Infant Characteristics by Early and Late Registration

	Early registration[a]			*Late registration*[b]			
	No.	*Mean*	*SD*	*No.*	*Mean*	*SD*	*p value*
Maternal age (yr)	415	16.1	1.1	85	16.0	1.2	.0001
Pregnancy weight gain (lbs)	399	29.5	12.4	77	23.6	11.9	.0002
Gestation age at delivery (wk)	414	39.4	2.8	84	39.5	2.1	NS
Infant birth weight (g)	415	3053	618	84	2989	459	NS
Days in hospital (infant)	122	5.1[c]	9.6	28	3.7[c]	2.3	NS

Adapted from Hardy, JB, et al. The Johns Hopkins adolescent pregnancy program: an evaluation. *Obstet Gynecol* 69: 300–306, 1987.

Discrepancies in numbers reflect missing data points.

NS, not significant.

[a]Registration by 13 weeks gestation or less.

[b]Registration after 28 weeks gestation.

[c]Range 1 to 84 days for early and 2 to 12 days for late registrants.

below 2,500 g, and risk of perinatal mortality, was generally most favorable for the youngest mothers, i.e., those age 15 and below and for those having a first birth regardless of age. While the small number of infants of adolescents having a second birth at age 15 or below had the most favorable outcome of all, the number is very small, making the importance of the observation uncertain. Older adolescents having a second or higher order birth fared distinctly less well obstetrically

Table 11-7 Adolescents Receiving Comprehensive Obstetrical Care in HAC: Infant Outcome by Maternal Age and Parity (*n* = 1780)

Age (yr)	No.	Birth weight (g)			Gestational age (wk)		Perinatal death	
		Mean	*SD*	*%<2,500 g*	*Mean*	*SD*	*No.*	*%*
No. prior births								
≤ 15	366	3,066	572	11.5	39.9	2.8	6	1.6
16	439	3,039	592	12.8	39.0	3.1	3	0.7
17	609	3,043	611	12.5	39.1	3.1	17	2.8
18	199	3,029	593	14.6	39.4	3.0	4	2.0
Total	1,613	3,045	595	12.6*	39.1	3.0	30	1.9
One or more prior births								
≤ 15	12	3,176	587	8.3	38.8	2.5	0	0
16	37	2,842	941	21.6	37.8	4.8	4	10.8
17	79	2,996	697	17.7	38.9	3.5	2	2.5
18	39	3,039	540	12.8	39.7	2.8	0	0
Total	167	2,985	720	16.8*	38.9	3.7	6	3.6

Adapted from Hardy, JB, et al. The Johns Hopkins adolescent pregnancy program: an evaluation. *Obstet Gynecol* 69: 300–306, 1987.

*$p < .001$.

than those having a first child despite the intervention. Sixteen year olds, having a second or higher order birth, had the highest frequency of LBW and perinatal mortality.

Reduction of Low Birth Weight

It may be noted that the frequency of LBW is somewhat higher for the total group of 1,780 enrollees than for the 744 enrolled from 1978 through 1981 included in the outcome evaluation reported above. During the 1976 through 1978 period there was a substantial reduction in pregnancy complications, very low birth weight, and perinatal mortality but no significant reduction, as compared with controls, in LBW in general. During the second period, nutritional education and counseling and the use of WIC were intensified with a concomitant reduction in the frequency of LBW to less than 10%. When the program was institutionalized in 1982 to include all adolescents (excepting those enrolled in the Johns Hopkins HMO), the frequency of LBW increased for that year as the result of deliveries of patients who transferred late in pregnancy from other prenatal programs to HAC, but in 1983 it dropped back below 10%, where it has since remained.

Summary and Discussion

The services provided by the Johns Hopkins Adolescent Pregnancy Program and the program's effectiveness in meeting its primary objectives have been described. As compared with a comparison group of similar adolescents delivered in the same facilities, the HAC program's adolescent mothers and their infants experienced superior pregnancy outcomes. As shown in Chapter 19, we believe the superior results and averted costs reflect not only the separate and caring environment in which HAC patients received their care, but the importance of integrating case management, intensive psychosocial support, and health education into the medical care setting.

12

Medical Management of Pregnant Adolescents

John T. Repke

Teenage pregnancy represents a significant health problem in the United States. It is a problem not only because of the large number of teenagers becoming pregnant and the sociological consequences accompanying this phenomenon but because of the medical complications associated with pregnancy in younger teens, i.e., adolescents below 18 years at delivery. Many attempts have been made to address the issue of adolescent pregnancy, with some of these appropriately centered in the area of preventing teenage pregnancies from occurring in the first place. Facilitating the learning of responsible sexual behavior among young people is no easy task, and even when coupled with provision of contraceptive services, failures happen. The dilemma remains as to what is the best approach to the teenager when these preventive services have failed and pregnancy has occurred. Clearly, this is a very controversial area with regard to what choices might be made available to the adolescent. Pregnancy option counseling, including understanding the implications of choices among childbirth, adoption, and abortion, should follow pregnancy diagnosis and should involve, if at all possible, not only the adolescent but her parents and the father of the baby (for discussion of legal aspects, see Chapter 10).

For the current discussion, we presume that the pregnant adolescent has been professionally counseled, offered real alternatives, and has chosen to continue her pregnancy to term. The importance of prompt referral for prenatal care to meet the special needs and counter the pregnancy risks of adolescents cannot be overemphasized, if she and her infant are to have an optimal outcome. The usual clinic or private physician care available to poor, urban adolescents is generally inadequate. A comprehensive, case-managed approach, such as described in the previous chapter, is required to provide the medical, pregnancy-related health education and psychosocial support needs of most inner city adolescents. The medical management that will improve her chances for having the best possible pregnancy outcome is outlined in the pages that follow.

Prenatal Care

History and Physical Examination: The First Visit

Seeing an adolescent pregnant patient for the first time is not easy for either clinician or patient. It is important to recognize not only the adolescent's right to confidentiality but also her right to confide in those family members whom she feels would be supportive of her pregnancy. Familial support, when present, can play a major role in optimizing both the prenatal care of the patient and her intrapartum experience and even early childrearing. This type of support becomes extremely important when one considers current trends that suggest that as many as 40% of today's 14-year-olds will become pregnant before they reach age 20 (Hayes, 1987).

Not uncommonly, the first prenatal visit represents the first time that the adolescent girl has undergone a gynecological examination. Thus, it is imperative that she be reassured of her right to confidentiality and supported as she attempts to develop her own sexual identity. The first pelvic examination is also an extremely important event that may sensitize her positively or negatively toward subsequent visits (Niebyl and Youngs, 1975). It is best accomplished by an experienced clinician. A detailed explanation of what to expect during the examination can greatly reduce anxiety as well as facilitate the examination itself. A complete sexual history is also essential. Once again this underlines the need for reassurance of the adolescent of her right to confidentiality. Prior pregnancy history as well as number of sexual partners, illicit drug use, and any previously acquired sexually transmitted diseases will play a major role in subsequent obstetrical decision making and assigning patients to high-risk groups for subsequent care.

The antepartum care of the pregnant adolescent is extremely important. In addition to what we have said about the experience of the first pelvic examination, the first prenatal examination also requires sensitivity and compassion. It will set the stage for subsequent care and compliance. At the Johns Hopkins Hospital, we have advocated for many years a comprehensive programmatic approach to pregnancy in the adolescent population (Hardy et al., 1987; Youngs et al., 1977). This programmatic approach includes medical care provided by faculty and resident staff, as well as intervention by obstetrical nurses and a full-time social worker, a full time health educator, and supporting personnel working together as a team, using a case management process through which specific medical and social problems are identified and management strategies individualized. This individualization is important for several reasons. Clearly, the care of a 13-year-old patient will be different than that of a 17-year-old one, as issues of medical care, education, support, and familial involvement are all dependent to some degree on age and individual socioemotional maturity. Likewise, the physiology of the 13-year-old will be different from the 17-year-old in areas ranging from nutritional requirements to skeletal maturation.

At this first examination, it is important to consider the possibility that pregnancy resulted from sexual abuse, especially among the younger adolescents, pointing to an increased need for sensitivity in patient/caregiver interaction and social work intervention in these younger patients.

Routine Laboratory Tests

The medical care component of the initial visit consists primarily of the initial history and physical examination and the performance of routine laboratory tests.

These tests include a complete blood count, a Pap smear, and tests for gonorrhea and chlamydia, a serological test for syphilis, a rubella screen, and blood typing, including Rh typing with a screen for atypical antibodies. In black patients a hemoglobin electrophoresis is also carried out to detect the presence or absence of abnormal hemoglobins (i.e., hemoglobin "S" or hemoglobin "C"). Additionally, all patients are screened for tuberculosis and for urinary tract infections.

One of the most important aspects of the medical care component of the first prenatal visit is establishment of correct gestational age. Not uncommonly, adolescents are uncertain of the date of their last menstrual period or have such irregular cycles that the last menstrual period may not be reliable in establishing the time of conception. In fact, we have encountered a few 10- to 13-year-old patients who have become pregnant prior to their first recognized period. As a result of difficulty in establishing the date of conception, it may be equally difficult to establish the gestational age of the fetus. For this reason, careful clinical examination with corroboration by ultrasound examination is essential in establishing correct gestational age. This will become an extremely important baseline, if in the third trimester, the diagnosis of intrauterine growth retardation is suspected. Additional recent concerns have resulted from the high prevalence of HIV infection (AIDS) and of maternal cocaine abuse and their potentially devastating fetal effects.

Involving the Patient in Her Own Care

After the initial history and physical examination, aspects of her health care are discussed with the patient by the physician. These principles are then reinforced by the health educator in a group discussion and individual sessions and by the nurses conducting the patient exit interviews. At the time of their first prenatal visit, all patients are required to meet with the social worker in order to discuss situations that might benefit from social work intervention. If the adolescent is less than 18 years old and unmarried, as she usually is, she is urged to bring her mother, or other close relative, to this session. Discussions include the role of the father, her continued education, and the availability of social support. The adolescent is given assistance in completing the application for Medicaid, which can help to facilitate the availability of other health care throughout the course of the pregnancy. Also at this first visit, the adolescent is introduced to the group education program. The group education experience serves to allow the girl to form a bond not only with her health care providers and staff, but with the other girls who are sharing a similar experience. It encourages participatory learning about the course of pregnancy and prenatal care, the importance of nutrition and avoiding substance use, such as cigarettes, alcohol, and drugs, in optimizing fetal development, and, later in pregnancy, about neonatal care and parenting.

Problem Identification and Screening

Adolescent pregnancy has been associated with an increased risk of low birth weight (LBW) and preterm delivery (Hardy et al., 1978; Horon et al., 1983). Some studies have suggested that many of the perinatal losses were due to amniotic fluid infection, placental abruption, and intrauterine growth retardation (Merritt et al., 1980; Naeye, 1978; Naeye and Peters, 1978; Naeye et al., 1977). It has also been proposed that nutritional factors may play a role in the pathogenesis of some of these events. With these possibilities in mind, the adolescent pregnant patient must be observed very carefully for signs of intrauterine growth retardation and sexually transmitted diseases. In addition to this screening, nutritional education should be afforded a high priority, because there is a very high frequency of anemia and other nutritional problems among adolescent pregnant patients, and weight gain during pregnancy has been strongly correlated with infant birth weight (Scholl et al., 1987) (see Chapter 13). With these issues in mind, data from our Adolescent Pregnancy Program (HAC) demonstrate that the comprehensive approach to health care can significantly reduce the frequency of some of these pregnancy-associated complications (see evaluation, Chapter 11).

Previous data reported by Weiss and Jackson (1969) have demonstrated that weight gain during pregnancy is the strongest determinant of birth weight, but factors such as prepregnant weight, birth weight of the last prior child, and cigarette smoking also have significant effects. Contrary to some reports, their data failed to show any meaningful correlation between birth weight and maternal age or height, presumably because of the strong correlation between maternal age and height and socioeconomic factors that have a marked effect on birth weight. It is of interest that in looking at population-based data, the prepregnant weight for whites is slightly lower than the prepregnant weight for blacks, although the weight gain during pregnancy for whites is slightly greater (Hardy and Mellits, 1977). Despite this, babies born to black mothers are, in general, larger than those born to white mothers prior to the 35th week of gestation, with female infants larger than males (Hardy, Drage, et al., 1979), accounting in part for the somewhat lower risks of perinatal mortality among black and female infants at low gestational ages (<35 weeks). Once again, the issue of LBW versus prematurity is a confusing one and is best addressed by accurate determination of gestational age at the earliest point possible in pregnancy.

Sexually Transmitted Diseases

Screening for sexually transmitted diseases is performed at the initial visit and again between the 30th and the 34th week of gestation. Additional screening and treatment is warranted if suggestive symptoms appear and/or a history of exposure is provided by the patient.

The importance of screening for sexually transmitted diseases goes beyond mere public health concerns. Some of the classic sexually transmitted agents clearly have implications for both mother and infant. Gonorrhea may result in gonococcal ophthalmia neonatorum as well as increasing the risk of postpartum endometritis. Likewise, syphilis may result in not only sequelae in the mother but the occurrence of congenital syphilis in the neonate. Additionally, attention has been paid to *Chlamydia trachomatis, Trichomonas vaginalis*, and the *Mycoplasma hominis* and *Ureaplasma ureolyticum* as agents potentially responsible for adverse pregnancy outcome among adolescents (DiMusto et al., 1973; Frommell et al., 1979; Martin et al., 1982; Thompson et al., 1982). Chlamydia, for example, clearly has been shown to cause conjunctivitis, pneumonia, or both, in newborns. However, the presence of chlamydia during pregnancy has less certain implications. Some studies have associated chlamydia positivity with adverse pregnancy outcome, while others have not (Hardy et al., 1984; Harrison et al., 1983; Heggie et al., 1981). This type of inconsistency has also held for the genital mycoplasmas (Braun et al., 1971; Embree et al., 1980; Foy et al., 1970; Harrison et al., 1979; Klein et al., 1969;

Tafari et al., 1976). Interestingly, at least one study has demonstrated an unexpected association of *Trichomonas vaginalis* infection and adverse pregnancy outcome (Hardy et al., 1984). This study failed to show any independent association with chlamydia. The problem in applying much of these data to an adolescent population is that the very high frequency of multiple infections with trichomonas, mycoplasma, ureaplasma, and chlamydia, makes it difficult to interpret which organism, if any, plays the major role in adverse pregnancy outcome. An additional problem is the high frequency of inapparent infection.

Hepatitis B is a frequently ignored but not infrequently sexually transmitted disease organism. In an indigent population, we have found that screening for hepatitis B during pregnancy is indicated, either in the third trimester or at the time of admission in labor (McQuillan et al., 1987). Identification of hepatitis B surface antigen carriers will allow for prompt treatment of the neonate with hepatitis B immune globulin and hepatitis B vaccine. In this way, the carrier state in the neonate can potentially be avoided, thus significantly reducing the risk of that infant becoming a chronic carrier at risk of subsequent development of chronic hepatitis or hepatocellular carcinoma.

Interest in *group B streptococcal infections* has increased considerably over the past several years. Such infections have been implicated as a cause of premature delivery and LBW. Surveys would suggest a prevalence ranging from approximately 8% to 31% among women, with vertical transmission from mother to infant at the time of delivery being significant, especially in preterm deliveries (Ancona et al., 1980). It has been suggested that selective administration of antibiotics to group B streptococcus-positive mothers during labor would interrupt the transmission of group B streptococcus infection from mother to fetus (Boyer et al., 1983 a-c) but more controlled studies are needed in this area in order to understand better which patients would most benefit from this type of intervention. Presently, at the Johns Hopkins Hospital, our policy is not to screen women routinely for group B streptococci. However, if a patient has a positive group B strep culture, intrapartum administration of antibiotics is given to those women delivering preterm. In the term infants, antibiotics are withheld unless treatment of maternal chorioamnionitis during the intrapartum period becomes necessary.

Other Complications of Pregnancy

Urinary Tract Infections   These are a frequent complication of adolescent pregnancy. Pregnant women are predisposed to urinary tract infection as a result of physiological hydronephrosis and hydroureter and displacement of the bladder, allowing for increased vesicoureteral reflux, increased capacity, incomplete emptying, and hypotonia of the vesicle musculature. An elevated urinary pH, glycosuria, and increased urinary excretion of estrogens may also contribute to development of a medium more susceptible to bacterial colonization. Approximately 4% to 7% of pregnant patients will develop asymptomatic bacteriuria, with approximately 10% among indigent patients (Whalley, 1967). This figure is roughly doubled in patients with sickle cell trait. Screening patients for asymptomatic bacteriuria at the initial visit is imperative as 20% to 40% of pregnant patients with asymptomatic bacteriuria will go on to develop symptomatic acute pyelonephritis, if untreated. Although asymptomatic bacteriuria, when carefully studied, has not been shown to predispose to premature delivery, there is an increased risk of premature deliveries in those bacteriuric patients who develop acute pyelonephritis prior to the onset of labor (Kincaid-Smith and Bullen, 1965; Monzon et al., 1963; Whalley, 1967).

Acute Pyelonephritis   Acute pyelonephritis occurs in only 1% to 3% of pregnant patients, with the incidence increasing as the gestation advances. Approximately 25% to 30% of these cases will occur in women who had sterile urine cultures on the first prenatal visit, suggesting that it will be impossible to eliminate all cases of pregnancy-associated pyelonephritis (Cunningham et al., 1973). However, 60% to 70% of these cases should be preventable. Treatment of pyelonephritis during pregnancy should be aggressive, including hospital admission for treatment with parenteral antibiotics. Antipyretics may be used as needed in the initial phases of treatment in order to minimize endogenous prostaglandin production, with its concomitant theoretical risk of initiation of parturition (i.e., preterm labor). Once the patient has responded appropriately to parenteral antibiotic therapy, oral antibiotic therapy should be initiated and continued through the rest of the pregnancy until six weeks post partum. Macrodantin or trimethoprim/sulfamethoxazole, in a once a day regimen, is appropriate for antibiotic suppression of urinary tract infection. (Harris and Gilstrap, 1974; Stamey et al., 1977).

Preeclampsia   Preeclampsia (toxemia of pregnancy) is another disorder more common among adolescent patients than among older gravidas. Evidence of increasing blood pressure or sudden unexplained rapid weight gain may be early signs of the development of this condition. Additionally, progressive proteinuria and edema may further suggest to the obstetrician the development of preeclampsia. Preeclampsia, while placing the fetus at risk for intrauterine growth retardation, also increases the risk of placental abruption.

Preeclampsia will develop in approximately 5% to 7% of all pregnancies. In the adolescent population, the risk is roughly twice that in the general population (10% to 15%). Many hypotheses have been put forth regarding the pathophysiology and pathogenesis of preeclampsia. Abnormalities in prostaglandin production as well as an interaction with the renin angiotensin aldosterone system seem to play a role in its pathogenesis. Gant and co-workers (1973) have demonstrated that the physiological changes of preeclampsia occur well before clinical signs are manifest. In our adolescent population, preeclampsia occurs with a frequency of approximately 12%. Close attention is paid at each visit to evidence for rapid weight gain, elevation in blood pressure, and/or proteinuria. In addition to looking for blood pressure levels in excess of 140/90, it is important to recall that an increase in the systolic pressure of 30 mm of mercury above the baseline or an increase in diastolic pressure of 15 mm of mercury above the baseline represents a significant increase and may justify the diagnosis of preeclampsia. The rollover test has been employed clinically to try to identify those patients at risk for preeclampsia. To accomplish this test, the patient is asked to lie on her left side. Her blood pressure is then taken in the nondependent arm and recorded. The patient is then placed in the supine position, and the blood pressure is retaken in the same arm. A rise in the diastolic blood pressure of 20 mm of mercury or greater is indicative of a positive test. Although not every woman with a positive rollover test will go on to develop preeclampsia, almost all women who go on to develop preeclampsia will have had a positive rollover test, thus making it a useful, albeit simple, clinical tool. It has been hypothesized that nutritional interventions potentially provide a way to reduce the frequency of preeclampsia. The details of these clinical trials are recorded elsewhere in this book (see Chapter 13).

Intrauterine Fetal Growth Retardation   This is also a frequent problem among pregnant adolescents. Intrauterine growth retardation is usually defined on the basis of a fetal weight estimated to be below the 10th percentile for race, sex and gestational age, where known. As mentioned above, the importance of correctly establishing gestational age at the earliest possible time in order to evaluate possible intrauterine growth retardation later in pregnancy cannot be overemphasized. When intrauterine growth retardation is suspected, sonographic evaluation of the fetus is indicated. This should include morphometric measurements, as well as an overall estimate of fetal weight and gestational age. Suggestive but inconclusive evidence for intrauterine growth retardation should lead the obstetrician to the initiation of regular fetal surveillance, utilizing either contraction stress testing or biophysical profile scoring. Utilization of umbilical Doppler velocimetry may also aid in the diagnosis of intrauterine growth retardation (Fleischer et al., 1985). Evidence of fetal distress demands consideration of immediate delivery. A conservative approach should lead to an improved outcome for these high-risk pregnancies by permitting continued gestation with reassessment testing and appropriate intervention when test results suggest uteroplacental insufficiency.

Depression   Depression is a common finding among pregnant adolescents, especially those experiencing a second or higher order pregnancy (see Chapter 5). It may lead to lack of compliance with prenatal care, inadequate nutrition, failure to gain weight, academic problems, and other problems. Sensitivity on the part of health care professionals and supporting staff and appropriate counseling are usually sufficient to manage the situation, but psychiatric referral will occasionally be indicated.

Intrapartum Care

With the successful negotiation of the antepartum period, attention is now turned to the management of the adolescent through her intrapartum experience. The adolescent should be encouraged to have the infant's father or a family member as a support person during labor and delivery. Childbirth education classes, with the support person participating, movies of normal deliveries, and tours of the labor and delivery area prior to the onset of labor all serve to minimize the anxiety that may accompany the onset of labor and the imminent delivery of her child. A more mature adolescent who has had childbirth education may be able to negotiate labor and delivery without aid of anesthesia or analgesia. However, most adolescents will require some type of intrapartum anesthesia. Our experience suggests that regional anesthesia is an optimal way of managing the labor and delivery of the very young adolescent. Utilizing these approaches, it is clear that indications for cesarean section in the adolescent population are the same as in the adult population, and that adolescence in and of itself may not increase the risk for delivery by cesarean section (JT Repke and JB Hardy, unpublished data, 1986). In the HAC program, about 15% of adolescents are delivered by section each year.

Postpartum Care

Once the not inconsiderable tasks of successfully completing antepartum and intra-partum care have been accomplished, an even more monumental task lies ahead. The postpartum care of the adolescent patient represents a unique challenge. In addition to supporting her bonding efforts with her new child, much patient education in family planning, child care, and parenting must take place. Data from the HAC program suggest that risks of repeat pregnancy are high and that many of these young mothers, if not properly educated, will become pregnant again within 18 months. As repeat pregnancy may occur within the first month after delivery, it is imperative that the new adolescent mother be given contraceptive counseling and education and contraceptive supplies before hospital discharge. Recent data suggest that it is the inner city clinic patients who are at the highest risk of noncompliance with contraceptive methods and who subsequently have unplanned pregnancies (Emans et al., 1987). Recent studies suggest that school- and community-based education programs may assist in reducing teenage pregnancy rates in the United States (Edwards et al., 1980; Zabin, Hirsch, et al., 1986). In any event, postpartum education and close patient follow-up are essential in order to optimize the outcome for the mother and her baby and to minimize the risk of an untimely new pregnancy.

Conclusions

Adolescent pregnancy remains a major problem in the United States. At this time, however, several observations may be made. Most adolescent pregnancies are unintended and unwanted (Chapter 5). Therefore, clearly, the first priority needs to be in the area of prevention (see Chapters 23 and 24). Second, prenatal care tends to begin later for adolescents than for older women; the average of nine prenatal visits for girls in our program reflects late onset of care and is far from optimal. Reproductive health education as part of a pregnancy prevention program should underline the need for early prenatal care to those women who go on to become pregnant and choose to continue their pregnancies. Third, complications of pregnancy are frequent in this age group, and the health care provider should screen patients in this population carefully for anemia, sexually transmitted diseases, AIDS, substance abuse, preeclampsia, and intrauterine growth retardation. Finally, in general, up to 20% of urban adolescents will have a repeat pregnancy within 12 months. These pregnancies are, for the most part, unintended and undesired, thus emphasizing the need soon after delivery for effective contraceptive counseling and services.

The problems of adolescent pregnancy will not be easily solved. However, a comprehensive program of care can serve to aid in the resolution of serious health problems by improving the obstetric and neonatal outcome for those patients who participate. Development of such programs, emphasizing education, social services, and a team approach, is clearly the best way to achieve these goals.

13

Nutrition and the Pregnant Adolescent

John T. Repke and Linda Carr Watkinson

Throughout history, it has been recognized that nutrition during pregnancy is an important issue, one that might, in fact, alter the outcome of the pregnancy itself (Tannahill, 1973). Different dietary recommendations for the pregnant patient have been in vogue at different times. Initial observations in the more socioeconomically privileged classes suggested that abundance of food was in part responsible for the larger birth weights seen in this more affluent group of women. On the other hand, dietary restriction during the third trimester of pregnancy has occasionally been recommended to women thought to have a small pelvis, in an effort to reduce the size of the infant, thereby effecting an easier vaginal delivery (Hirst, 1906). Although at one time, when maternal mortality was relatively high, the philosophy that held "the smaller the baby, the easier the birth" may have had merit, as maternal mortality risks diminished, it was noted that lower birth weights tended to be associated with higher risks of morbidity and mortality among newborns and to relate to higher risks of neurological deficits and mental retardation among survivors (Broman et al., 1975; Hardy and Mellits, 1977; Little, 1862).

As stated elsewhere, the adolescent pregnant patient is at particular risk for low birth weight (LBW). Adolescents, in general, are still growing themselves and are often the victims of a poorly balanced diet, thus contributing to their risk of low infant birth weight. In this chapter, the issue of maternal-fetal competition for nutrients is discussed, and the effect of some individual nutritional components on pregnancy outcome is examined, followed by discussion of the practical aspect of implementing good nutrition. There is evidence that pregnancy frequently is a time when women will abandon bad habits (e.g., cigarette smoking) and establish new ones for the sake of their unborn child and that these changes in behavior not infrequently persist beyond the pregnancy itself, providing dividends for the mother as well. Prepregnancy nutrition is also becoming an increasingly popular subject for public education. Suggestions that neural tube defects may be associated with folic acid deficiencies have prompted the resurgence of interest in prenatal vitamin supplementation for at-risk populations. Preconceptional control of diabetes as measured by normal levels of hemoglobin A_1C has been demonstrated to reduce the incidence of congenital malformations among insulin-requiring diabetics. In short, nutrition during pregnancy is an extremely important issue, and in the adolescent pregnancy, its importance is enhanced.

Finally, in learning about nutrition in pregnancy, the adolescent begins to develop an understanding about nutrition for her soon to be born child. Recognition of the importance of nutrition may allow the mother to help her child develop good eating habits, thereby reducing the risk of childhood obesity and all of the long-term risks that may have their genesis in childhood obesity. In short, the nutritional education component of any comprehensive adolescent pregnancy program should be a strong one because of the impact nutrition can have on the developing adolescent, on her child, and on their continued development in the postpartum period.

Epidemiology of Pregnancy and Nutrition

Perhaps, one of the most often quoted studies demonstrating a relationship between pregnancy and nutrition is that of Smith (1947), describing the Dutch famine, which was most severe from September 1944 to May, 1945, in western Holland. As mothers' caloric intake dropped, it was clearly noted that infant birth weight dropped sharply as well. In 1975, data were presented demonstrating that not only birth weight but also placental weight decreased among these Dutch famine patients, and this decrease was evident by the end of the second trimester (Stein et al., 1975). If the nutritional intake was markedly reduced over a longer period, as in the famine in Leningrad, amenorrhea occurred and fertility ceased until adequate food was available (Antonov, 1947).

By the late 1960s, results from the Collaborative Perinatal Study (CPS) of the National Institute of Neurological Diseases and Blindness (Hardy, Drage, et al., 1979; Niswander and Gordon, 1972; Niswander et al., 1969; Singer et al., 1968), from the President's Panel on Mental Retardation (1962), and the British Perinatal Study (Butler and Alberman, 1969) clearly demonstrated the adverse effects of LBW, in terms of increased risks of perinatal and infant mortality and neurological and cognitive deficits in later childhood. Furthermore, relationships between gestational age and birth weight and the importance of intrauterine growth retardation in determining long-range outcome have become clearer (Hardy and Mellits, 1977). Data from the CPS suggest that an average weight gain of about 30 to 35 pounds was associated with optimal fetal outcome. By comparison, LBW occurred four times as often among infants of women gaining less than 16 pounds (Singer et al., 1968). Weiss and Jackson (1969), using a multivariate analysis, demonstrated that among the 32 variables entered into the analysis, maternal weight gain was most strongly associated with infant birth weight. Prepregnant weight and cigarette smoking were almost as influential. These studies were followed by others in which attempts were made to increase birth weight among infants of undernourished mothers by means of providing nutritional supplements to the pregnant woman. Many such studies (e.g., Higgins, 1976; Stein et al., 1978) demonstrated that food supplements given to disadvantaged pregnant women were effective in increasing the birth weight of infants as compared with those of unsupplemented mothers, in similar socioeconomic circumstances, who were receiving similar medical care.

It was exactly these types of data that contributed to the institution of the program known as WIC (Special Supplementary Food Program for Women, Infants, and Children of the United States Department of Agriculture). The evaluation of a large service program involving hundreds of thousands of women and children is extremely difficult because of lack of detailed nutritional and socioeconomic information about individuals. However, past evaluations of WIC have provided favorable but inconclusive evidence of effectiveness (General Accounting Office, 1984). In essence, although the role of nutrition in pregnancy is clear, the exact means by which good nutrition exerts its effects remains elusive.

Relationship of Nutrition to Low Birth Weight (LBW) and Prematurity

As stated elsewhere, pregnant adolescents are at very high risk for both LBW and prematurity. Some of the factors that have been related to low birth weight and prematurity include low prepregnancy weight, low maternal weight gain during pregnancy, short maternal height, physical activity of the mother, cigarette smoking, and alcohol consumption (Niswander and Gordon, 1972; Villar and Cossio, 1987). Although a direct relationship has not been clearly established that inadequate nutrition plays a role in the birth of low weight infants, the relationships among nutrition, maternal body weight, weight gain during pregnancy, and birth weight have been known for years. Several reports have demonstrated that women of normal weight who gain less than the recommended weight during pregnancy tend to have smaller infants. In contrast, women who are overweight may have larger than average infants even when their weight gain is less than the recommended 11 kg (Eastman and Jackson, 1968; Niswander et al., 1969; Simpson et al., 1975). Because of adolescent eating patterns, it is not uncommon to have both ends of the nutritional spectrum overrepresented in the adolescent pregnant patient population, that is, those who are underweight and those who are obese.

In taking into account the nutritional requirements for the adolescent, it should be recognized that: 1) In general, the younger the adolescent, the greater are the nutritional requirements for her own growth; and 2) Most weight charts are based on information for adult women (those more than 20-years-of-age) who have completed their physical growth in height. Therefore, the applicability of these types of recommendations, i.e., those based on adult data, to the adolescent population remains in serious question. A notable exception are the recommendations in a booklet entitled *Working with the Pregnant Teenager* produced by the Department of Agriculture in collaboration with the Office of Maternal and Child Health, Public Health Service and the March of Dimes Birth Defects Foundation (see Table 13-1). In the pregnant adolescent, optimal weight gain includes consideration of: 1) her initial weight deficit or excess; 2) her estimated growth during gestation, which, depending on the stage of her physical development, may be well in excess of 1 kg (Rosso and Lederman, 1982); and 3) the gain needed to meet the requirements of fetal growth and of supporting structures, such as the uterus and breasts.

Although inadequate nutrition, with its associated low caloric intake, may contribute to low birth weight, poor nutrition may also have other indirect effects on pregnancy outcome, such as an increased frequency of preeclampsia and perhaps of some birth defects. We move next to a consideration of individual nutrients in the diet and their effects on the mother and the fetus.

Table 13-1 Estimated Daily Nutrient Needs of Pregnant Adolescents Based on the Increment Suggested for Pregnancy in Mature Women

Nutrient and units	Pregnancy increment	Total estimated need	
		11–14 yr	*15–18 yr*
Energy (kcal)	300	2,500	2,400
Protein (g)	30	78 (1.7 g/kg)	82 (1.5 g/kg)
Vitamin A (μg RE)	200	1,000	1,000
Vitamin D (μg)	5	15	15
Vitamin E (mg TE)	2	10	10
Vitamin C (mg)	20	70	80
Thiamin (mg)	0.4	1.5	1.5
Riboflavin (mg)	0.3	1.6	1.6
Niacin (mg NE)	2	17	16
Vitamin B_6 (mg)	0.6	2.4	2.6
Folacin (μg)	400	800	800
Vitamin B_{12} (μg)	1.0	4.0	4.0
Calcium (mg)	400	1,600	1,600
Phosphorus (mg)	400	1,600	1,600
Magnesium (mg)	150	450	450
Iron (mg)	30–60[a]	30–60[a]	30–60[a]
Zinc (mg)	5	20	20
Iodine (μg)	25	175	175

Recommended Dietary Allowances for Pregnant Women. Reprinted from *Working with the Pregnant Teenager*. U.S. Department of Agriculture, Program Aid No. 1303. National Academy Press, Washington DC, 1981.

[a]This intake cannot be met by the iron content of habitual American diets; the use of a supplement is recommended.

Prenatal Vitamins

The need for prenatal vitamins as part of routine prenatal care remains controversial. In general, a woman who is eating a well-balanced diet can usually fulfill her nutritional needs without supplementation, with the possible exception of iron (Johnson et al., 1986). Those individuals who are at high nutritional risk, for example, underweight or significantly overweight women and adolescents, may benefit from the addition of vitamin and mineral supplements.

Additionally, it has been suggested that women who take multiple vitamins periconceptionally, specifically vitamins containing folic acid, may be at reduced risk for having an infant with a neural tube defect (Smithells et al., 1981). These findings have not been confirmed by a recent study of United States women (Mills et al., 1989).

Suffice it to say that adolescents are an extremely high-risk group from a nutritional standpoint. Routine prenatal vitamins should help to avoid some of the nutritional deficiencies that adolescents may be at risk for developing. The practitioner should be aware that while prenatal vitamins are generally similar from one brand to another, some differences do exist, specifically with respect to mineral content. There are also substantial differences in cost among products that are otherwise quite similar; this can be important in situations where funds are limited.

Calcium

Pregnancy is a time of increased calcium demand. This is primarily due to fetal requirements that result in a deposition of 30 gm of calcium in the fetal skeleton by term. The most important time for calcium to be available to the developing fetus is in the third trimester of gestation, when more than 80% of the total fetal calcium is deposited (Pitkin, 1975). While pregnancy is a time of increased demand for calcium intake, certain maternal adaptations allow for an increased efficiency of calcium absorption. In the normal pregnancy, bone turnover increases with a rise in reabsorption of calcium, intestinal absorption of calcium is enhanced, and renal tubular reabsorption of calcium is diminished, with no apparent change in fecal calcium levels (Villar and Belizan, 1986).

The adolescent pregnant patient has a particular need for calcium during pregnancy. First and foremost is the fact that as an adolescent, her own skeleton is still developing and her own nutritional needs must be met so that not only is her diet adequate in calcium for the nonpregnant state, but also for the additional demands placed on her by pregnancy. Additionally, with a look toward the future, it has been suggested that exercise, balanced nutrition, and adequate calcium intake, especially in the adolescent period and early adult period, may be the best methods for prevention of postmenopausal osteoporosis (*The Medical Letter*, 1987). An added benefit to adequate calcium intake may be lower blood pressure. Investigators have recently suggested that calcium supplementation lowers blood pressure in men, nonpregnant women, and pregnant women (Villar, Repke, et al., 1986). Utilizing 2 g of elemental calcium as a supplement per day, these investigators have also hypothesized that calcium supplementation could perhaps play a role in reducing the incidence of pregnancy-induced hypertension (Villar et al., 1987).

Iron

Iron requirements increase markedly during pregnancy, not only to accommodate the expanding maternal blood volume, but also to fulfill the needs of fetal and placental development. Approximately 600 mg of additional iron are needed for the expanding red cell mass (Lind, 1983). The need for iron increases as the pregnancy progresses, with the greatest need being in the third trimester. Because of other nutritional deficiencies in the adolescent diet and because of needs related to their own growth requirements, adolescent patients are at particular risk for the development of iron deficiency anemia during pregnancy. In the Johns Hopkins Adolescent Pregnancy Program (HAC), 11% of adolescents in this comprehensive program, as compared with 16% of controls, had anemia when it was defined as a hematocrit of ≤30% (Hardy et al., 1987). Maternal anemia has been associated with adverse outcome and low birth weight. In a recent large-scale study of risk factors accounting for racial differences in low birth weight, Lieberman et al. (1987) found that maternal hematocrit level (or some related factor) accounted for 60% of the increased rate of premature births among black women. It was the only medical risk factor that, with the socioeconomic characteristics examined, showed a relationship with prematurity. Low levels of iron and hemoglobin in the placenta and umbilical cord and a reduction in the vascularity of the placental villi have also been associated with low birth weight (Agarwal et al., 1981). Pregnancy itself will alter red cell indices. The hematocrit will generally fall somewhat, as a function of the increased maternal intravascular volume that naturally occurs during pregnancy. This will result in a concomitant reduction of mean cell hemoglobin and mean cell hemoglobin concentration. Additionally, in normal pregnancies, serum iron and iron-binding capacity may decrease, as may transferrin saturation. Although the optimal dose of iron to be given to a pregnant woman as a supplement remains unclear, in general, the recommendation has been to provide at least 100 mg of elemental iron per day as a supplement (Taylor et al., 1982). Most prenatal vitamin supplements will provide between 30 and 60 mg of elemental iron, in combination with other vitamins and minerals. It should be remembered, however, that administration of iron in conjunction with calcium carbonate or magnesium oxide may inhibit iron absorption by the gut, thus necessitating the larger iron supplements.

Recently, interest has been generated regarding the relationship of iron and zinc. There is a competitive interaction of iron and zinc, and experimental evidence exists for a common intestinal absorption pathway of both iron and zinc. This information was first elucidated by means of animal studies (Evans and Johnson, 1980; Forth and Rummel, 1973; Hamilton et al., 1978; Pollack et al., 1965). The interaction was later demonstrated in nonpregnant humans, with evidence being presented that the presence of inorganic ferrous iron interfered with zinc uptake into the plasma (Solomons and Jacob, 1981; Solomons et al., 1983). At this point, one can conclude that there is ample evidence to support the interaction between oral iron and zinc and the absorption of each element. Whether or not this association is of practical significance is not clear at the present time. But, in the adolescent pregnant patient, iron supplementation is an absolute necessity, given not only the high incidence of iron deficiency anemia in these patients, but also the strong association between iron deficiency anemia and adverse pregnancy outcome (Lieberman et al., 1987).

Trace Elements

There is a surprising lack of information with regard to trace elements, such as copper, chromium, lead, and zinc, and their possible relationship to pregnancy outcome. It is only recently that trace elements have been recognized as playing an important role in human nutrition and in maintenance of physical well being.

Zinc Recognition of the importance of zinc in the diet of the pregnant patient has grown in recent years. There are 2 to 3 g of zinc in the body of the average adult, and it is present in almost all human tissues, being responsible for helping to catalyze several steps in oxidative metabolism (Sandstead, 1978). For example, zinc is a necessary requirement for the proper function of DNA polymerase and RNA polymerase (Solomons et al., 1986). It has also been demonstrated to play a role in membrane stabilization and immune function (Bettger and O'dell, 1981; Keusch et al., 1983). Also of interest has been experimental evidence linking zinc deficiency to birth defects. A molecular mechanism for zinc's teratogenic effect has been based on the disruption of proper RNA and DNA synthesis (Hurley and Baly, 1982).

With regard to the adolescent patient, the zinc-iron interaction has already been discussed. However, adolescent pregnant patients, especially in an indigent population, are at very high risk for sexually transmitted disease and the subsequent development of in utero infections, i.e., chorioamnionitis. There is evidence to suggest that amniotic fluid levels of zinc are reduced in cases of intrauterine infection

(Warkany and Petering, 1972). Reduced levels of zinc have also been associated with pregnancies complicated by intrauterine growth retardation and preeclampsia, as well as in those which are postmature (Antoniou et al., 1982; Kynast et al., 1979; Orlando et al., 1978). Other investigations have demonstrated an association between abnormal pregnancy outcome and increased concentrations of amniotic fluid zinc (Chez et al., 1978; Dura-Trave et al., 1984; Favier et al., 1972). A recent study has suggested that, in fact, amniotic fluid zinc levels were of no predictive value with regard to pregnancy outcome (Rosick et al., 1983).

Copper   Pregnancy results in an increased concentration of ceruloplasmin, thereby increasing the concentration of copper. While there is considerable evidence to suggest that copper deficiency will cause abnormalities and fetal wastage in animals, there is no evidence to date to suggest that copper deficiency is a problem in human reproduction (Allen, 1986).

Chromium   Little is known about chromium deficiency in pregnancy, although it has been suggested that chromium deficiency may result in an increased frequency of low birth weight (Allen, 1986). At least one study has demonstrated that both premature infants and growth-retarded infants have lower than normal concentrations of chromium in hair (Hambidgh and Baum, 1970). It seems probable that a relative chromium deficiency is a common occurrence in most pregnant women and is of no clinical significance.

Lead   In general, exposure to lead is environmental and usually is secondary to ingestion of water transported through lead pipes, inhalation of automobile or industrial pollutants, or ingestion of paint chips of lead-based paints. In an indigent adolescent population, this may represent a not insignificant problem. The placenta is readily permeable to lead, and maternal and cord blood concentrations of lead tend to be similar. At least one study has suggested that, as a past exposure to lead correlates better with cord blood lead levels than current exposure, lead stores may in fact be mobilized during pregnancy and lead transferred to the fetus (Buchet et al., 1978). Higher placental lead concentrations have been reported among fetuses with congenital anomalies and stillborn fetuses (Wibberley et al., 1977). An even stronger association between congenital anomalies and lead level has been reported by Needleman et al. (1984). In this investigation, variables such as coffee, alcohol, marijuana, and tobacco use were also taken into account. Beattie et al. (1975) have demonstrated that even a moderately elevated blood lead level in the newborn period may increase the risk for subsequent development of mental retardation. In a population such as ours, these concerns should have been addressed well before puberty.

Fluoride   Fluoride is an important trace element. Fluoride supplementation has been used for years in the prevention of dental caries. Many adolescents who have not been exposed to long-term supplementation are still at risk for dental caries and may benefit from fluoride supplementation. In one study, 1 mg of fluoride daily was administered to pregnant women during the last two trimesters of their pregnancy. Follow-up of the children born to these women revealed a decreased incidence of dental caries as well as tooth crowns that contained up to 600% more fluoride than those of nonsupplemented children (Glenn et al., 1982). As with all elements, there is always a concern about possible toxic side effects of exposure. The placenta clearly does provide some protection against fluoride transfer to the fetus, with cord blood levels approximately only 75% of maternal levels (Rapaport, 1956). In general, however, normal supplementation of fluoride as in fluorinated drinking water or supplemental fluoride in vitamin and mineral tablets has not been associated with adverse effects for either mother or newborn. Although there had been a suggestion that an increased incidence of Down syndrome was associated with the fluoride content of drinking water (Rapaport, 1956), this finding has not been supported by more recent studies (Erickson et al., 1976; Needleman et al., 1974).

Referral for Nutritional Services

In our programs, we have chosen to have the nutrition educational groups taught by health educators who are well-grounded in adolescent development as well as in nutrition. However, some adolescents have nutritional needs that also require the attention of a registered dietician or professional nutritionist. Adolescents requiring referral for individual nutrition counseling include those who are markedly undernourished or obese, those who fail to gain adequate weight in pregnancy, and those who require special diets for diabetes and other conditions. Medical Assistance (MA) provides reimbursement for nutritional services of this type. We refer such adolescents to registered dieticians in the hospital's nutrition department.

Let us turn now to the second part of this chapter, i.e., to consideration of teaching good nutrition to pregnant adolescents.

Teaching the Pregnant Adolescent About Nutrition in Pregnancy

The pregnant adolescent presents unique challenges to health care professionals in the area of nutrition education. How do we, as educators, reach and teach pregnant teens about diet and nutrition? How do we promote dietary changes in their life styles that we hope will become a permanent part of their health behavior?

First, and most importantly, we must always be aware that we are dealing with adolescents—adolescents who may be experiencing the stressful stages and events of their own adolescent development. There are three key issues regarding the characteristics and developmental tasks of the adolescent period that can lead to serious problems in bringing about positive change in the dietary behaviors of the pregnant teenager.

Adolescent Developmental Issues

The first issue is that teenagers are primarily present-oriented, viewing events and situations in their lives concretely rather than abstractly. It is very difficult for a pregnant teen to visualize realistically the developing fetus inside her or the placental transfer of nutrients to her baby. Therefore, it is essential that educators and nutritionists provide learning opportunities that help the pregnant adolescent to conceptualize this abstract link between her own body and the developing fetus. Concrete visual aids, such as fetal and placental models and diagrams, are most helpful in demonstrating this concept, so that teens fully understand that whatever substances, healthy or unhealthy, they consume will eventually be transferred to their babies.

A second issue is that the pregnant adolescent is very much concerned with her own body image and is often appalled by, and rejects, the recommendation that she should gain 25 to 30 pounds or more during her pregnancy. Many teens firmly state, "I don't want to gain all that weight. I'll be fat." Here, it is important to teach the teen exactly where the weight gain will occur and why. By stressing that she will return to her normal weight soon after delivery and encouraging her to become or remain active with frequent exercise, some of these fears regarding body image and fatness may be allayed.

A third issue pertinent to adolescent development is that many teens are in a state of denial regarding the pregnancy and are depressed that they are pregnant. When a patient is referred for poor weight gain, it is extremely important that the health educator or nutritionist determine the pregnant teen's feelings about the pregnancy and the adequacy of her and her family's adjustment to the pregnancy. Frequently, it is not a matter of teaching her what to eat or recommending a high-protein, high-calorie diet; it is primarily a matter of referring her to the team social worker or counselor who can help her resolve some of the conflicts regarding an unplanned pregnancy. Depression should always be considered in teen patients who are experiencing excessive or insufficient weight gain during their pregnancies.

Once these issues are resolved, the adolescent is able to focus better on nutrition and follow through on the diet recommendations given to her.

Availability of Food

Not only is it important to help the pregnant adolescent through the issues and concerns regarding adolescent development and her pregnancy, but it is also important to determine if food is readily available to her. Some teens, both inner city and rural, have problems getting enough to eat, especially where there are large families or several families living together under economically deprived circumstances. (Some patients have even told this health educator that they have their own refrigerators that they keep locked so that other members of the household will not eat their food or drink their milk.) It is also important to teach the adolescent about community resources that may be available to her and her family and to empower her in obtaining WIC, food stamps, or other potential resources.

Recommended Daily Food Intake: Suggestions for Pregnant Adolescents

Adolescents, and their parents if they live at home, are helped to improve their diet by practical, simple, and concrete instruction as to daily food requirements during pregnancy. These requirements are laid out in the nutrition chart displayed as Figure 13-1.

Common Problems and Suggestions

In teaching pregnant adolescents about nutrition, there are five problem behaviors that are detrimental to the health of the adolescent as well as to the health of the developing fetus. These behaviors can often result in anemia or low birth weight, two serious medical risks of adolescent pregnancy; they are discussed below.

1. *Skipping Meals*—Teens are notorious for skipping meals, especially breakfast and often lunch, waiting to eat their first meal of the day after school. It is extremely important to help the pregnant adolescent realize that when she

Milk and milk products	Protein foods	Fruits and vegetables	Breads and cereals
4–6 Servings	4 Servings	4 Servings[2]	4–6 Servings
Include: Milk, powdered milk, yogurt, cheeses, cottage cheese, orange juice with calcium Ice cream,[1] foods made with milk, such as macaroni and cheese, pudding[1]	Include: Beef, hamburger, liver, pork, chicken, turkey, fish, tuna fish, salmon, nuts, peanut butter, dry beans	Include: All fruits and vegetables such as: apples, citrus fruits, other green leafy vegetables, broccoli, beans, bean sprouts, carrots, peas, potatoes, others	Includes: Breads, whole grain breads Cereals[3] Rice, oats, grits, cornbread Crepes Pasta Rice, noodles, spaghetti, macaroni, lasagna, other
Serving size Milk or yogurt = 1 cup Calcium equivalent: 1½ slices cheddar cheese 1 cup pudding 2 cups cottage cheese 1¾ cup ice cream	Serving size 2 ounces meat 4 tablespoons peanut butter	Serving size ½ cup cooked vegetables Medium sized apple, orange, banana	Serving size 1 slice bread 1 cup ready-to-eat cereal ½ cup pasta
	Encourage patient to: Bake and broil meats instead of frying Cut off visible fat	Pregnant teens who are "picky eaters" tend to avoid vegetables. Encourage them to be adventuresome and try new food items or to put cheese over broccoli or cauliflower.	
[1]Encourage the pregnant teen *not* to consume 4–6 servings of this product per day as her calcium requirements will not be met.		[2]Encourage teens to choose nutritious snacks from this group instead of candy or other junk food. Patient may consume more than 4 servings.	[3]Encourage teen to avoid sugar-coated cereals. Suggest alternatives and compare costs of sugar-coated with other cereals.

Figure 13-1 Nutrition chart: recommended daily food intake and suggestions for pregnant adolescents. These recommendations provide for the 300 to 500 additional calories required to meet the adolescent's own growth needs as well as the energy requirements for pregnancy. *Other suggestions*—Always be aware of cultural preferences and differences in selection of food items. Utilize this knowledge in your teaching. Learn favorite food items of your patients and incorporate these in your suggestions.

skips her meals, her baby skips meals too. Guidelines and recommendations can be given to the adolescent in helping her to prepare quick, nutritious foods for breakfast and lunch if she doesn't like the school lunches. Teens can be given permission to eat a small breakfast; many believe that only a large breakfast is a nutritious breakfast. The important thing is for them to develop the habit of eating regularly. A teenager can even be advised to eat four to six small meals per day. This is important in helping her through periods of nausea or in the third trimester of pregnancy when her enlarged uterus makes it difficult for her to eat a large quantity of food at one meal.

2. *Junk Foods*—Adolescents (and most adults as well) like some form of junk food. However, all too frequently adolescents substitute junk foods for nutritious foods. It is unrealistic to advise teens to stop eating all junk foods, so three recommendations are given to adolescents in the HAC program:
    a. Decrease junk food to no more than one to two junk foods per day. (A "big bag of chips" is not one junk food). Whenever possible, substitute fruit or something nutritious for junk food.
    b. *Never* substitute junk food for the daily requirements, which include: four to six servings of milk and milk products; four servings of protein foods; four servings of fruits and vegetables; and four to six servings from the bread and cereal group. Always "make sure that you have given yourself and your baby what you both need *before* eating any junk food." A list of food groups and required amounts is provided to the pregnant adolescent, and she is asked to check each evening to make sure she has eaten well that day.
    c. Whenever you do eat junk foods, choose ones that are more nutritious for you; such foods include those with peanuts or peanut butter or oatmeal raisin cookies instead of candy or chocolate cookies.

3. *Fast Foods*—From preference or because meals are not available at home, some teens visit fast food places several times or more each week. Frequently when an adolescent is referred for excessive weight gain, she reports a pattern of eating frequently from fast food restaurants or carry-out establishments. We encourage pregnant adolescents to decrease their visits to fast food places, and when they must choose to eat fast food, to choose from the more nutritious items on the menus. Adolescents need to know that pizza can be nutritious; most think of it as junk food. Fast foods are a problem because, despite the expense, eating them has become a common practice among impoverished, inner city adolescents who have inadequate facilities and knowledge to prepare meals at home.

4. *Poor Compliance with Iron and Vitamins*—Many adolescents have difficulty swallowing pills or are afraid of pills. In fact, many teens become pregnant because they discontinue their oral contraceptives due to nausea or simply to not wanting to take them. The pregnant adolescent must feel comfortable with the health care team members to disclose the fact that she is not taking her iron or vitamin pills. Two things can be suggested to her if she has difficulty swallowing pills; she can take the pills in applesauce, orange juice, or some other food product, or she can ask the medical provider for a prescription for liquid iron and vitamins. It is important for the adolescent to know how to take her medication correctly in order to avoid nausea.

5. *The Younger Teen and the "Picky Eater"*—It may be important to involve parental support in helping the younger pregnant teen and the "picky eater"

to improve dietary behaviors. It is strongly recommended that parents or guardians of pregnant adolescents be made aware of the daily recommended requirements and the recommended weight gain for their daughters. They should be involved as soon as possible after the teen registers for prenatal care. It is especially important to attempt to involve the parent in this education process if the patient is very young, immature, or has learning disabilities or problems.

6. *Breast-Feeding and Its Advantages*—Issues such as breast-feeding and the nutritional advantages of breast-feeding over bottle-feeding may be reinforced and the reluctance of many adolescents to breast-feed infants overcome during question and answer periods in nutrition education sessions. Unfortunately, few inaugurate and even fewer continue for more than a month or two.

Finally, in meeting the challenges of teaching pregnant adolescents about their pregnancies and about nutrition, the following suggestions have proved successful in the HAC program:

1. Teaching methodologies adapted to specific levels of adolescent development should be emphasized. Group education, which offers numerous opportunities for peer interaction and peer influence, is highly recommended in addition to individual nutrition counseling, which is especially important when weight problems or anemia occur.

2. Teaching aids adapted to adolescent development and needs are essential if we are to affect knowledge, attitude, and behavior in the pregnant adolescent. These include concrete visual aids, pamphlets, and booklets developed specifically for adolescents at their reading levels, and stimulating games and activities that can be conducted in large or small group settings by a trained facilitator.

3. A sense of humor and a bit of creativity are necessary components if one truly wants to change health behaviors in pregnant teens. Didactic teaching alone will not produce results. Adolescents relate to staff members who show a sense of caring, who are nonjudgmental, who do not appear hurried, and who can use humor to teach even the most serious topics.

4. Expect the best from your patients. Children, as well as adults, often do what is expected of them, and sadly, in our society, expectations for our children have been low. All health care team members—physicians, nurses, social workers, health educators, nutritionists, and registrars—need to share this philosophy. There will always be those few adolescents who are noncompliant, but for the most part, when an entire staff shares a mutual philosophy in setting expectations, young people become aware of what is expected, and it is meaningful to them because someone cares about them.

In teaching pregnant adolescents, there will always be frustrations along with challenges. However, there will also be rewards when patients demonstrate that we, as professionals, did make a difference, that changes and growth did occur, and that healthy pregnancy outcomes did result for both the young mother and her baby.

Conclusions

The importance of good nutrition and adequate weight gain in any pregnancy cannot be overemphasized. They are probably the two most important factors in preventing low birth weight and perinatal mortality, problems of particular importance among adolescents because of their high frequency in this age group.

- Specific nutritional factors are essential in the prevention of specific health conditions to which pregnant adolescents are particularly prone, for example, iron in the prevention of anemia and calcium in the prevention of preeclampsia (toxemia of pregnancy).
- Pregnant adolescents, unlike older women, need a nutritional intake sufficient to supply the nutritional requirements for their own physical growth, in addition to those required for fetal growth and the maintenance of the pregnancy and for lactation if the baby is breast-fed. This means that a larger daily food intake is required by pregnant and nursing adolescents.
- Special professional nutritional counseling is required by adolescents with certain medical problems, such as diabetes, and those who are anemic, obese, or who fail to gain adequate weight in pregnancy.
- Because most pregnant adolescents come from disadvantaged homes and have little knowledge about nutrition, appropriate education is essential to their proper utilization of available food resources. This education should be directed to the developmental level of adolescent patients, taking into account their eating habits, preferences, and socioeconomic level. It should be provided in a format that will enhance learning and motivation.
- Because young adolescents are generally part of a family group and dependent on family resources, it is important that parent(s) understand the nutritional needs of their pregnant daughter.
- The socioeconomic background of most pregnant adolescents mandates access to the WIC and Food Stamp Programs if they are to have adequate nutrition. Private physicians, hospital, and agency personnel need to make sure that the necessary referrals are made, and the WIC and Food Stamp Programs need to facilitate enrollment rather than to set rules that require adolescents to miss school in order to obtain vouchers and/or to receive delivery of food products. Vitamin and mineral supplements should be made available at prenatal visits, free of charge if necessary.

14

Health Education
Teaching the Pregnant Adolescent

Linda Carr Watkinson

For optimal pregnancy outcome, patient participation in both prenatal care and the process of labor and delivery is essential. All too often such cooperation is not forthcoming because the special needs of poorly informed, depressed, and frightened adolescents are overlooked by those providing traditional obstetrical care. Meeting the information needs and raising the morale of pregnant adolescents so that they are able to participate in their own care presents a major challenge to professional caregivers and community workers alike. Whether the educational setting is a health care facility, a residential or community agency, or a more traditional school classroom, the challenge and the opportunity for successful intervention exist.

Several characteristics of adolescents have important implications for the educational process. For example, as described in Chapter 2, young people in early and middle adolescence are generally egocentric, or "me oriented." Not only is their attention centered on themselves, but they often believe that the attention of the rest of the world is also focused on them. They tend to be self-conscious to a marked degree, and body image may be a preoccupation. For example, the idea that, for optimal fetal outcome, they should gain about 30 pounds during pregnancy is often both frightening and disgusting to them. Another characteristic of adolescents is their tendency to be present-oriented, failing to realize the future consequences of their behavior: sexual, parenting, or other. A third characteristic is difficulty with abstract thinking. Many adolescents are still in the stage of concrete operations, thinking and functioning on a concrete level.

Educators and health professionals must utilize their knowledge of the level of adolescent development in designing curricula and teaching methods that are effective in teaching pregnant urban adolescents, many of whom have very limited reading skills and may have dropped out of school. Key decisions in the planning of health and pregnancy education programs concern finding appropriate answers to the following questions.

- What is the essential subject matter (content)?
- How can the material be effectively presented (methods, teaching strategies)?
- Who will be the teachers (staffing issues)?

• What resources can be made available (teaching aids, space, time, etc.)?
• How will success (or failure) be determined (evaluation issues)?

Curriculum Development

The time available for teaching is a key factor in determining what is to be taught and how it should be presented. For example, in a school setting, a family life course, extending over a period of several months, with classes several times each week, provides an opportunity for including a wide range of subject matter. It also provides the luxury of utilizing different methods of presenting the material to be covered and ample opportunity for reinforcement. The content of such a course is usually determined by school personnel and is accompanied by a set of guidelines for its use. The school setting is advantageous in that, in some programs, males are also reached.

In a community setting, on the other hand, teaching opportunities depend on the frequency of contact with the pregnant adolescent and the time available at each visit. Because almost all adolescents have some prenatal care, the prenatal clinic provides an unparalleled opportunity to reach them to help prepare them for a successful pregnancy outcome. The content and methods suggested here are based on experience in a hospital prenatal clinic specially designed to serve adolescents who are less than 18 years old. The average number of prenatal visits is 10 to 12. The program's philosophy places a strong emphasis on patient education.

Educational Methods

Two basic methods are employed. The first is the traditional one-on-one, patient education by medical and nursing staff. In this adolescent pregnancy program, it involves virtually every patient-staff contact. The relevance of each procedure, examination, and laboratory test is made clear to the adolescent in simple, concrete terms before or during its performance so that she understands what is happening to her and to her fetus as pregnancy progresses. From an understanding of the course of events comes a sense of control and a reduction in anxiety and fear.

Education by Group Process

The second strategy is education by group process. The one-on-one teaching is reinforced and extended by participation in an educational group session at each prenatal visit. These sessions are part of the program expectations. The girls are encouraged to bring the father of their baby. Participation in the group process not only facilitates learning, it provides emotional support and enhances self-esteem. It is efficient, permitting education of a number of patients at one time. However, for optimal success in meeting patient needs for information in a timely fashion, both careful planning and a well defined curriculum are essential. The curriculum topics are listed in the Appendix to this chapter, followed by sample lesson plans for group discussion of exercise, substance abuse, and family planning. The scheduling of both routine prenatal visits and of the educational sessions must be coordinated so that each patient receives the maximal educational exposure without experiencing gaps in some areas and duplication in others. To facilitate the group process, and to help in the warm-up process during which the young people are helped to participate, each group has a group leader and a backup leader. The curriculum is organized as shown in Table 14-1. The group process is designed to assist the adolescent in identifying her goals by fostering responsible decision making with reference to caring about herself and her baby. This involves the development of responsible behavior with respect to the objectives of a good pregnancy outcome, parenthood, completion of education, and the prevention of unintended conception. The caring attitudes and behavior of staff members can be valuable models for the adolescent.

Educational Issues

Many adolescents have very limited understanding of events leading to conception and pregnancy; therefore, they need to understand how they *really* become pregnant. A section on human reproduction should be included, perhaps as part of a fetal development class and definitely as part of a family planning class.

Pregnant teens have little information and a great curiosity about the growth and development of their babies and a concern about their own body changes. This is a group that always sparks interest and initiates questions. It should help to improve motivation with respect to self-care in order to optimize fetal development.

Nutrition education is one of the most crucial components in any adolescent pregnancy program curriculum (see Chapter 13). Both group and individual sessions in which individual problems and needs can be addressed are required. It is equally essential that information about sexually transmitted diseases (STDs), including AIDS, be presented; some pregnant teenagers are testing HIV-positive, and there is a high prevalence of chlamydia and gonorrhea in urban populations. Sexually active teens need to be aware of the dangers of STDs for the developing fetus as well as for themselves; information about the methods of spreading sexually transmitted diseases and personal protection are particularly important with respect to AIDS. Adolescents must be made aware that while STDs such as gonorrhea and chlamydial infections can be successfully treated, AIDS is an ultimately fatal disease for which there is no effective treatment, making prevention of paramount importance.

Adolescents must be prepa.ed for the labor and delivery process, which is often very frightening to them. They should understand what to expect through each stage of labor and what options for pain relief and anesthesia are available. They should have the opportunity during pregnancy to tour the labor and delivery facilities with their support person. Parenting groups should be available, and when possible, a parent educator with expertise in early childhood education should facilitate the groups. Adolescents frequently have unrealistic expectations of their babies' capabilities; prenatal parenting classes may begin the educational process required to change these expectations.

Because of the high risk for "repeat" pregnancies among young mothers, pregnancy prevention is a crucial topic in any adolescent pregnancy educational program. This should not simply be a didactic "these are the choices you have" group, but a group in which goals and aspirations are explored, and the reasons teens frequently do not use birth control or discontinue their methods of contra-

Table 14-1   Educational Content for Pregnant Adolescents in a Health Care Setting

Basic reproduction
   A. Anatomy—male and female
   B. General physiology of reproduction

Maternal and fetal development
   A. Changes in the mother
       1. Physiological changes
       2. Discomforts
   B. Development of the fetus

Nutrition
   A. Requirements for adolescence and pregnancy
   B. Compliance with iron and vitamins
   C. Common problems (nausea, anemia, poor weight gain, too rapid weight gain, junk foods, constipation, skipping meals)

Harmful substances during pregnancy[a]
   A. Alcohol (fetal alcohol syndrome)
   B. Drugs (illegal and over the counter) and their potential for fetal damage (crack babies)

Sexually transmitted diseases, including AIDS
   A. Various diseases (causes, symptoms)
   B. Modes of transmission to patient and fetus
   C. Effect on patient and fetus
   D. Prevention

Prenatal exercises[a]

Preparation for labor and delivery
   A. Introduction and expectations
       1. Labor warnings, planning for labor and delivery (when, what, where, who)
       2. What to expect in the admitting exam room, labor room, delivery room, recovery room
   B. Film—"Have A Healthy Baby"
   C. Options in labor
   D. Tour of labor and delivery suite and nursery area

Parenting groups
   A. What to expect from your newborn (needs)
   B. Falling in love with your baby (film)
   C. Decisions, decisions
       1. Naming your child
       2. Well child care
       3. Crib or bed
       4. Feeding: breast or bottle
       5. Circumcision

Family Planning
   A. Future hopes and goals
   B. Options in birth control
   C. Making a decision and a commitment
   D. Who's in control?

Myths of pregnancy[b]

---

[a]See suggested lesson plan in Appendix to this chapter.

[b]Can be incorporated into another group if time does not permit for a separate group.

ception are examined. The emphasis in this group is on *responsibility, decision making*, and the concept of *taking control* of one's sexuality and of one's future.

Finally, as stated previously, the amount of time and the number of staff available to teach will determine what topics are discussed and to what extent they can be explored or elaborated.

Teaching Methods and the Group Process

Effective Teaching

Employing a variety of methods promotes learning and learner participation in any educational process. Try to seat the group members in a circle so that they can see each other. Know everyone's name, and have each person introduce her- or himself to the rest of the group. A list of guidelines follow that will enhance the group process.

General Guidelines for Facilitating Group Education

1. Set the tone and expectations for the group in the initial part of the group session (establish "ground rules," such as respect for others' opinions, the right to disagree with any group member, etc.).
2. Be a facilitator, not a "lecturer."
3. Employ a variety of teaching methods and aids.
4. Be a good listener (communicator).
5. Use humor to teach (every good teacher should be able to "ham it up" occasionally).
6. Allow adequate time for patient participation and for feedback to the group.
7. Always be aware of the nonverbal communication in the group. It sometimes speaks louder than the spoken words.
8. Be aware of individual needs, such as shy patients who may need several sessions before they feel comfortable responding orally in the presence of other patients.
9. Be appreciative of contributions to the discussion but allow for individual differences in beliefs, values, and opinions.
10. Allow time for a brief closure and/or summation at the end of the group.
11. Praise group members for their participation (e.g., I like the way you responded today; I like the eye contact you gave me today; I appreciated the way you listened today).

Effective Teaching Methods

Effective teaching methods are determined by several factors, many of which are discussed below. The determinants are: 1) style and personality of the educator; 2) group size (it is much easier to have an intimate group discussion with six patients than with 22 patients); 3) learner readiness and capabilities; and 4) resources and monies available to the educator. As noted, space and time allocations are important, as are funds for movies, handouts, and other aids.

Based on this educator's experience in teaching pregnant adolescents in three different settings, school, residential, and hospital, the following methods and strategies have proved most useful:

1. Discussion Format—learner participation reinforces the incorporation of information and its subsequent utilization:
    a. Interjecting information with discussion
    b. Utilizing inquiry/discussion method to encourage group participation
2. Use of Audiovisual Aids—this strategy can enhance learning if the material is well-chosen to illustrate specific points and is incorporated into the lesson plan:
    a. Use films, videos, and film strips.
    b. Try to limit films or videos to 15 to 20 minutes to allow for introductory activities and group discussion and participation.
    c. *Always* preview materials for accuracy and appropriateness for the intended patient/student population prior to its use in teaching.
    Note: Showing a film without preliminary introduction and follow-up discussion is no substitute for a properly planned educational group.
3. Visual Aids—including:
    a. Concrete visual aids such as fetal models with placenta and umbilical cord in utero
    b. Teaching boards such as the Magnell 77, which can be used to teach reproduction, fetal development, and family planning
    c. Games that can be purchased or developed by staff, for example, a game developed at Johns Hopkins, which demonstrates fetal development in very concrete terms
4. Pen and Paper Tasks—Having the pregnant teens, in a group, write or draw. For example, this is useful in the beginning of the maternal and fetal development group session, when teens are asked to draw what they think their baby looks like and what their baby can do in utero, and then again at the end of the group after the information has been presented and discussed.
5. Role Playing—when group size and personalities are conducive to this method.
6. Education Handouts and Pamphlets—adapted to the needs and reading abilities of pregnant teens. (Few urban adolescents read above a fifth grade level.)
7. Humor—(not enough can be said about this method of relating to other human beings).

Combining a variety of these methods is most effective in providing an environment that fosters learning. Also, one should remember that according to Scott and Carlo (1980) in *On Becoming a Health Educator*, "For the preprofessional who has been brainwashed into believing that the factual information he has gathered throughout his career is the most important of his equipment, it can be traumatic to realize that his personality, the way he relates to his students, and his becoming a superior teacher will have a greater impact on the students whose lives he touches than will the content of what he teaches."

Who Will Teach the Pregnant Teen?

Scott and Carlo's thoughts bring us to a brief discussion on who should teach pregnant adolescents. The person who is fortunate to be chosen for this task must be aware of the enormous responsibilities and the great rewards of working with patients who have such well documented and demonstrated learning needs. The educator must be flexible and open-minded, providing a positive, caring role model to her or his patients. She or he must be able to respond honestly to the patients; children of all ages are very quick to recognize dishonesty in adults. Credibility is an important basis of the learning process.

Program administrators cannot afford financially, educationally, or emotionally to employ educators or health care professionals who are punitive in their approach or attitudes in providing care for pregnant adolescents. It is permissible for professionals to transmit and impart their own values, although they may differ greatly from the values of the pregnant adolescents, in a nonpunitive and nonjudgmental way when appropriate in providing patient care or in serving as a positive role model. Those who cannot or who find it difficult to remain kind, caring, and nonjudgmental should seriously consider working with a different patient/ student population.

Resources

Numerous resources, in terms of films, film strips, videos, books, pamphlets, and posters have become available in recent years to assist in the development of effective educational programs for pregnant adolescents. In selecting resources, it is important to choose those appropriate for the age and ethnic background of adolescent patients. Many resources designed for adult and middle-class women may seem attractive to staff members but are ineffective when used with adolescents because the teens do not relate to them and, therefore, are not interested by them. Among educational programs that provide excellent resource materials are: 1) *A Community of Caring*, a publication of the J. P. Kennedy, Jr. Foundation, Washington, DC (1980). This program was developed for the parents and teachers of pregnant adolescents to help them have an optimal pregnancy outcome and to achieve a happy and healthy life. This curriculum is broadly based, covering a wide range of relevant material, with teaching modules on pregnancy, early parenting, and much more. Detailed lesson plans and resource materials are presented. While the curriculum is generally too long for use in a prenatal clinic setting, some of the modules are highly relevant. 2) *Growing-up Caring*, a publication from the Kennedy Foundation, by Glenco-McGraw-Hill, 1990. This book is intended for use in junior and senior high schools. Its objective is the provision of information to assist students with wise decision making, leading to responsible behavior, in many areas important to their future development. This volume and its teachers' guide are valuable resources for those developing educational curricula for pregnant and parenting adolescents. 3) Another excellent resource is the curriculum *Teenage Pregnancy: A New Beginning* developed by staff at the New Futures School in Albuquerque, New Mexico (1980 and 1989). Parts of this volume have been updated and the teachers' manual "Working with Childbearing Adolescents" is currently under revision.

Evaluation

The overall goal of health and prenatal education is to empower the adolescent patient to incorporate the recommended health behaviors into her life style and, thus, improve the likelihood of optimal pregnancy outcome. As suggested in Chapter 19, Figure 19-1, this may involve a sequence; gains in *knowledge* leading to changes in *attitudes* that in turn lead to changes in *practice* (KAP). There are formal and informal means by which such changes may be evaluated.

Informal Evaluation

The following suggestions have value both for purposes of informal and formal process evaluation:

- Brief oral pre- and posttesting during group sessions to assess changes in knowledge (and possibly in attitudes) in the subject area and enhance both client motivation and learning
- Oral evaluation and feedback at the end of the group sessions in which patients review main concepts and/or assess the effectiveness of the teaching method(s) used
- Informal surveys to determine compliance with the medical regimen, for example, with taking iron and vitamins as prescribed (patient self-report)
- Informal feedback from other hospital personnel (such as residents and nurses), for example, reports of patients' knowledge and behavior during labor and delivery as an indication of effective preparation for these events
- Oral feedback from patients at the postpartum visit that assesses their perceived value and/or shortcomings of the educational group process

Formal Evaluation

In the Johns Hopkins programs, described elsewhere in this volume, formal evaluation has focused on meeting certain objectives concerned with improving the health of pregnant and parenting adolescents and their children. Health indicators used have included such items as the frequency of pregnancy complications, for example, anemia, maternal weight gain in pregnancy, the frequency of low birth weight, the length of hospital stay, and subsequent conception. With the exception of preliminary studies in the Adolescent Teenage Clinic and Parenting Program (TAC) (Chapter 18), there has been no direct assessment of the educational component per se. However, there has been formal assessment of changes in knowledge in a pregnancy prevention program and they were significant (Chapter 25). As an integral part of the special comprehensive services provided and on the basis of the ongoing informal process described above, the group and individual education received by each patient during her prenatal course appear to contribute in a major way to improved pregnancy outcome. Those patients exposed to a program that included group educational sessions among its comprehensive services fared better than those in a program designed for adolescents that was more traditional in its orientation (Chapter 19).

Conclusion and Recommendations

Our experience suggests that the following points are important in developing an effective prenatal educational component that will enhance compliance by pregnant adolescents and improve pregnancy outcome.

1. *Set expectations.* Clearly established expectations, which have the *total* support of all program staff, should be conveyed to the patient (and her significant

others) as she enters the program. It is important that she: a) understands her rights and responsibilities; b) is aware of expectations for her behavior, i.e., that she will become an active participant in her own health care (including health education), complying with clinic routines for her care; and c) is aware of the basic philosophy of the program and its responsibilities to help her to have a successful pregnancy.

Attendance at the group educational sessions is virtually 100% because all staff members expect each girl to participate in the learning experience.

2. *Provide a structured and supportive environment in the clinic.* To facilitate compliance, a patient flow-sheet is prepared for each visit. It informs the patient of the things to be accomplished that day. As each item is completed, the sheet is initialed by the appropriate staff member and, at the end of the visit, it is returned to the registrar who checks to assure that all has been completed.

3. Keep clearly in mind, that *the success of a comprehensive program lies in its team approach to meeting the multiple needs of pregnant adolescents.* Thus, each component, such as health education, social services, and medical care, must work together to meet these needs in an environment that encourages caring and the development of trust between patients and staff.

APPENDIX
The Johns Hopkins Adolescent Pregnancy Program

Group Education Outline for First and Second Trimester

Posted on clinic bulletin board with dates and names

Date	Group—Topic	Leader	Co-Leader or Backup Staff
	Orientation: Clinic Routines & Expectations		
	Maternal & Fetal Development I		
	Feeling Good & Looking Great: Exercise in Pregnancy		
	Feelings & Thoughts about Being Pregnant		
	Eating Well & Feeling Good		
	Smoking, Drugs & Alcohol in Pregnancy		
	Making Decisions about Sex		
	Sexually Transmitted Diseases & AIDS		
	Families		

Please Note: Small group and individual nutrition sessions will be provided after the large groups are completed.

Group Education Outline for Third Trimester

Date	Group–Topic	Leader	Co-Leader or Backup Staff
	Being a Parent I Expectations & needs, getting to know your newborn Being a Parent II Making choices about your baby Being a Parent III Mother-infant communication Maternal & Fetal Development II Brief review of Maternal & Fetal Development I Debunking myths of pregnancy Labor & Delivery I Introduction, expectations Labor & Delivery II Having a Healthy Baby (Discussion of film) Labor & Delivery III Choices in labor & delivery Family Development (Family planning and contraception) Tours of Labor & Delivery Suite, In-patient Rooms & Nursery (Conducted for small groups so the adolescents know what to expect).		

Outline for Postpartum Group Session

Labor and Delivery Experience
Changes in Life Style and Coping
Well Child Care, Reinforcement

Return to School
Birth Control Decisions/"Safer Sex"

Lesson Plan: "Drugs, Smoking, and Alcohol During Pregnancy"

I. *General Objectives*: Upon completion of the group, the adolescent will be able to:
   A. Identify the placenta as the link between mother and baby.
   B. Identify four substances harmful to the fetus.
   C. Describe two effects of smoking on the fetus.
   D. Describe one effect of alcohol on the fetus.
   E. Can also focus on STDs and AIDS

II. *Basic Content*:
   A. The Role of the Placenta. Can transport harmful as well as beneficial substances to the fetus.
   B. Harmful Substances
      1. Alcohol (beer, wine, liquor)
      2. Drugs (general)
         Stimulants, depressants, narcotics, marijuana, cocaine (crack)
      3. Over-the-counter drugs
      4. Cigarettes (nicotine, a stimulant)
      5. Caffeine
      6. Excesses in general (too much salt or sugar)
   C. The Responsibility factor in being a Parent
      1. When does one become a parent?
      2. Emphasis on the positive—"You're here today because you care."
      3. Encouragement—offering to assist if one wishes to quit smoking or other forms of drug use.

III. *Conducting the Session*:
   A. Initiatory Activities
      1. What have you done today that was good for your baby? (Make list on the board and discuss as responses are given.) What decisions have you made for your baby today?
      2. How do things both helpful and harmful get to the baby?
         a) Explain role of placenta—use birth atlas.
         b) Stress that the placenta cannot be selective, it allows both harmful and beneficial things to cross.
   B. Developmental Activities
      1. What are some things that are harmful to the baby? List them beside the list in (A1).
      2. Try to find out if patients know how substances are harmful.
      3. Show film "Pregnant Teens—Taking Care."
      4. Discussion of the film.
   C. Culminating Activities
      1. Discussion—focus on:
         a) When does one become a parent?
         b) It's tougher being pregnant now because doctors know so much more than when your moms were pregnant. It's a big responsibility.
         c) You are making decisions for two in so many ways.
      2. Distribute smoking badges and "I Quit" kits. (Emphasize the positive.)

IV. *Materials Needed*:
   A. Film: "Pregnant Teens—Taking Care"
   B. Film Projector
   C. Smoking Badges—3 types
   D. "I Quit" Kits
   E. Various Pamphlets
      1. "Smoking During Pregnancy"
      2. "So you want to quit cigarettes"
      3. "Can they stop smoking?"
      4. "Why Start Life Under a Cloud?"
      5. "The Decision is Yours"
      6. "Drugs and You"
      7. "Before You Drink . . . Think"
   F. Supplementary Materials
      1. Film—"Alcohol Crisis for the Unborn"
      2. *The Why Quit Book*

Lesson Plan: "Feeling Good and Looking Great" (Essential Exercises)

I. *General Objectives*:
   A. To develop an understanding of the need for and benefits of exercise
   B. To present six basic exercises for the antepartum and postpartum periods
   C. To develop a general exercise routine* (optimal)
   D. To present two basic relaxation techniques
   E. To encourage the patient to accept responsibility for her health and well being

II. *Behavioral Objectives*: At completion of the group, the patient will be able to:
   A. List five benefits of pre- and postnatal exercising
   B. Demonstrate five pre- and postnatal exercises
   C. Participate in a general routine set to music (if time permits)
   D. Utilize one relaxation technique that can aid in the labor and delivery process

III. *Basic Content—Demonstration*:   *Materials*
   A. Introduction (appox. 5–10 min)   Newsprint or chalkboard,
      1. Explanation   magic markers, tape
      2. List Advantages
      3. Why Exercise? (The Benefits)
         a. Decrease backaches
         b. Decrease constipation
         c. Decrease hemorrhoids
         d. Improve posture
         e. Decrease abdominal (lower) pain
         f. May help to shorten labor
         g. Help to decrease leg cramps
         h. Get back in shape after birth
   B. The Best Exercises during Pregnancy:
      1. Walking
      2. Swimming
      3. Bicycling
   C. The Muscles That Need Most Work:
      1. Abdomen
      2. Back
      3. Buttocks
      4. Pelvic Floor—Helps in labor and helps decrease hemorrhoids
   D. Demonstration (approx. 15 min)   Chair, tape, & tape player
      1. Tailor-sitting (demonstrate how to get to sitting position)
      2. Bending and lifting
      3. Sitting in chair
      4. Kegels
      5. Getting up and down
      6. Abdominal breathing
      7. Pelvic tilting
      8. Curl ups (straight & diagonal)
      9. Routine (approx. 10 min—optimal)   Tape & recorder chart
         a. Arm circles
         b. Side bends
         c. Pelvic tilting
         d. Curl ups
         (Relaxation part of routine)   Soft music
         e. Head circles
         f. Shoulder shrugs
         g. Foot exercises
         h. Tightening and relaxing body parts
         i. Visualization of peaceful scenes

E. Actual Exercises: (Do each exercise 2–5 times, twice daily)
1. Deep breathing with abdominal wall tightening
2. Foot exercises
3. Pelvic tilting
4. Tailor-sit (Chicken-flop)
5. Straight curl ups
6. Diagonal curl ups

F. Some Good Tips:
1. Tighten the abdominal wall while standing or sitting
2. Squat, don't bend forward
3. Sit in tailor-style on the floor to watch television
4. Check posture when passing mirrors
5. Don't hold your breath while you are exercising
6. Never do double leg raises

IV. *Remember*:
1. Posture check when passing mirrors
2. Pelvic floor exercises in the bathroom
3. Your hard work and efforts will pay off. Good Luck!!!

V. *Materials Needed*:
A. Mats
B. Comfortable clothing
C. Music (tape)
D. Handouts:
1. "Comfort in Pregnancy"
2. "Feeling Good and Looking Great"
E. Film, "Essential Exercises for the Childbearing Years"
F. Chart, "Pre- and Postnatal Exercises"

*If it is impossible to conduct exercises, the film "Essential Exercises for the Child-bearing Years" can be shown and handouts can be distributed.

Lesson Plan: Family Planning (For Individual or Group Session)

I. *General Objectives*: At completion of the group, the patient will be able to:
   A. Identify the major parts and functions of the male and female reproductive systems
   B. Identify five types of effective birth control devices
   C. Explore birth control alternatives in relation to:
      1. Personal preference
      2. Advantages and disadvantages
      3. Life style
   D. Explain the proper use and management of the chosen method
   E. Review concept of "safer sex" and prevention of AIDS and other STDs

II. *Basic Content*:
   A. Review of female reproductive system:
      1. Ovaries
      2. Fallopian tubes
      3. Uterus
      4. Cervix
      5. Vagina
      6. Hormones
      7. Ovulation
      8. Fertilization
      9. Menstruation
   B. Review of male reproductive system:
      1. Penis
      2. Scrotum
      3. Testicles
      4. Vas deferens
      5. Prostate gland
      6. Semen
      7. Sperm
      8. Ejaculation
   C. Review of methods of birth control:
      1. Abstinence
      2. Diaphragm
      3. Foam
      4. Undesirable methods, i.e., withdrawal, douching
      5. Condom
      6. Contraceptive sponge
      7. Pill (oral contraceptives)
      8. Natural family planning
   D. Decision making: (Helping the patient to arrive at the best decision for her at this point in her life for not only contraception but also AIDS and STD prevention.)

III. *Educational Procedure*:
   A. Initiatory Activities:
      1. Introduction to build a level of comfort
         a. Introduce yourself and explain your function
         b. Find out why the patient is there and whose idea it was
         c. Use positive reinforcement for decision to come to clinic
      2. Assess personal and educational needs of patient
   B. Developmental Activities:
      1. Have the patient identify as many parts of the female reproductive system as she can using a visual aid. (Example, Lindi Model)
      2. Using magnetic board, explain ovulation and fertilization (this is a key point in explaining how birth control methods work)
      3. Discussion of myths concerning birth control
      4. Utilizing examples of birth control devices ask patient to *identify* method, *explair* how it works, basic advantages and disadvantages

15

The Role of the Nurse Midwife and Pediatric Nurse Practitioner in Pregnancy Care and Prevention

Marcia Gratton

This chapter describes the roles of the nurse midwife (CNM) and pediatric nurse practitioner (PNP) in the adolescent health care setting and illustrates the diverse functions of these midlevel health care providers. This is not a statistical survey, but rather an individual perspective drawing on five years' personal experience in the Johns Hopkins Programs. These midlevel professionals have successfully provided rather major portions of adolescent health care in these programs, even though, as a general rule, CNMs deliver only about 2% of all prenatal care in the United States as compared with 96% in Norway and 70% in England (Institute of Medicine, 1985).

Because details of adolescent health care are well-described in this and other texts, for example, Neinstein (1991), no attempt has been made to do so here. The emphasis is on describing the functions of the CNMs and the PNPs and the contributions they make within our own programs.

The training of the nurse midwife/practitioner is built upon a broad definition of health that encompasses the biological and psychosocial domains of function. A sound understanding of the growth and development of the adolescent coupled with a "feelings"-oriented perspective provides the nurse practitioner with the breadth of understanding of adolescent behavior required for effective performance. The adolescent is then accorded the opportunity to relate positively to an objective, caring adult, and compliance is enhanced. The training and experience required for the pediatric nurse practitioner are, in many ways, quite similar, except that her expertise emphasizes the pediatric aspects because she is required to provide preventive and acute primary medical care for the infant, child, and adolescent rather than obstetrical care for the mother. Both professionals provide primary reproductive gynecological care, including family planning.

The multidisciplinary team approach to the delivery of health care for adolescents has been the model used in the Johns Hopkins Adolescent Pregnancy, Parenting and Pregnancy Prevention Programs. As team members, the CNM and the PNP wear many hats. Their roles are versatile. Major responsibilities are discussed below.

Provision of Primary Adolescent Health Care

As a health care provider, the nurse practitioner working in the Johns Hopkins Programs has responsibilities for both preventive and acute ambulatory care, working in concert with obstetricians and pediatricians, depending upon the context. (See specific programs below). Her role in physical assessment, with referral as indicated, is technical in scope and is a basic expectation of her function. Training is based on identification of normal versus abnormal findings, with the point when referral should be made being well-recognized. When caring for adolescents, the development of physical assessment and medical management skills demands additional training and a broadly based body of knowledge. Adolescent health care incorporates aspects of the specialities of pediatrics, obstetrics, gynecology, mental health, and sexually transmitted diseases (STDs), and training and experience in these specialized areas are essential to the provision of high quality care. However, technical skill and professional knowledge by themselves are not enough, particularly for those adolescents who come from disadvantaged backgrounds. These young people require caring and sensitivity in their management, with attention to the building of a trust relationship between provider and patient. The CNM or PNP may be the first adult with whom such a relationship has developed. They may become surrogate mothers and adult role models. A number of our adolescent patients have sought to emulate them and have entered nursing careers over the years.

Communications

Good communication skills are a necessity for the CNM or PNP working in adolescent programs. Adolescents, because of their inability to, or fear of, communicating with adults and their shyness and embarrassment relative to issues of sexuality, place the burden of communication squarely on the health care provider. A kind, direct, matter-of-fact, and nonjudgmental approach works best. Once the protective shell is penetrated and rapport established, most adolescents are extraordinarily frank. They are often hungry for information, particularly about sexual matters that may be taboo at home. As a result, they may ask seemingly outrageous personal questions. Keeping cool and providing honest answers are both important. These young people are seeking both information and satisfactory adult role models. Many of them have little access to either.

Contracting is another way of assuring positive communication. The roles of the health care provider and of the patient are clearly defined as a basis for positive interaction and to encourage compliance. In their quest for independence, adolescents respond beautifully when encouraged to participate in decisions affecting themselves. Striking an agreement in a contractual format is a valuable learning experience for the young person, teaching him/her to solve problems and to make responsible decisions. Young people learn that they have choices. The consequences of a broken contract must be clearly communicated and then followed through. Teenagers need and accept guidance and must know their limits. This may be their only exposure to adult limit setting. It is good to know someone cares enough to be firm and then to take the time to explain why. Never make assumptions. Assumptions, unfortunately, may take the place of communication. Common assumptions, misconceptions, and examples to illustrate them include:

1. *Teen pregnancies are unplanned!* While it is true that most teen pregnancies are unplanned, others are planned! Most youngsters will not admit this. It takes time and skill to elicit the truth and the reason for the desire for a child.

   Andrea finally admitted that her 18-year-old boyfriend was unhappy and embarrassed that he was the only one out of a group of eight regular friends who did not have a child. She wanted to please him.

2. *A parent would not want a 14-year-old daughter on contraception.* An irate single parent, a father, called to express his irritation and frustration that Nichole was *not* given oral contraceptives. He had his hands full and could not deal with a baby in the house. The fact that his daughter was not sexually active and had menarche only 6 months before did not impress him. He truly believed in prevention. After a counseling session, he had a better understanding of how to communicate with his daughter, and she knew where to go when the need presented itself.

3. *A parent of a 15-year-old adolescent would not want a grandchild.* A 36-year-old mother was unable to bear a second child. Her daughter, Tracy, got double messages from an early age. Mom wanted a baby so badly, it was "okay" to bring a child into the world, especially for mom. Tracy delivered at 15 years old, and within 9 months, her mom wanted to know when Tracy was going to "give her another grandchild!"

In these examples, without good communication the true feelings of none of the participants would have been recognized. Intergenerational communication should be encouraged, not only between parent and teen but between provider and teen. At its best, the education goes in two directions. The clinician knew she had reached a level of acceptance when two 17-year-old patients laughed and informed her that, "You don't say 'making love'—you say 'having sex'! Kids don't make love!" This provider was educated that day!

Parents, too, often need understanding and support. When working with adolescents, it should be expected that the provider will often be a diplomat and serve as a liaison between the generations. It is important not to be too critical of seemingly uninvolved parents, without understanding their situation. It may be difficult for a parent to be involved in children's growing pains when living in extreme poverty and when survival is a daily issue. Parents are also victims of misconceptions, myths, and superstitions. The practitioner can help to clarify issues for parents as she can for their children. Parents must be educated before they can educate their children; most welcome new information and admit to wishing they had known more 20 years earlier. Getting parents into group discussions can be enlightening—for them and the provider. Suggest role reversal—do they remember themselves as teens? Do they have a double standard? Have they given different messages to daughters and to sons?

Communication within the community is an important way to increase the awareness of the problems of teen pregnancy. Public discussions may mobilize citizens to create jobs or activities for young people. School officials often welcome talks from experts to increase faculty awareness and knowledge regarding teenage problems. In reaching out into the community, it is important to identify supportive factions as well as to identify those who are hostile, and to establish a dialogue. For example, conflicting, ambivalent feelings may prevent teachers from referring students to a pregnancy prevention clinic; they may hear it referred to as the "sex" clinic by the students and misconstrue its services. An open house or personal invitation to see the clinic and talk with its staff may change the teacher's perceptions and remove a potentially destructive obstacle.

Last but not least, good communication practices within the program staff itself enhance the team approach to adolescent health care and promote optimal programmatic outcome. Good communications are vital in a case management system. Because the issue of teen sexuality is fraught with moral and ethical dilemmas (see Chapter 10), the staff must be free to express their concerns and frustrations in an ongoing fashion to prevent burnout. Regular ventilation also increases self-awareness; knowledge of personal beliefs, strengths, and weaknesses surrounding issues of sexuality, especially adolescent sexuality, makes one a better counselor. With free communication comes an improved level of understanding of the problems surrounding teen pregnancy and of the role of each professional in addressing those problems.

Confidentiality and Informed Consent

Issues of confidentiality and informed consent are central to the delivery of medical care to patients in any age group. However, they pose particular and sometimes difficult problems when the patients are adolescents. These young people, because they are minors, experience limitations in their rights to confidentiality, as far as their parents are concerned, and in the legal right to give informed consent for their own medical care (see Chapter 10). In Maryland, adolescents under age 18 years of age have the same rights as adults and may give consent for the diagnosis and management of: 1) pregnancy, including abortion, and contraceptive services; 2) substance abuse, including alcohol; and 3) sexually transmitted diseases. Minors may not give informed consent for any other types of medical care except in a life-threatening emergency. A further limitation is that the right to elective abortion may be severely limited by its cost; the ability of Medicaid to pay for it is highly restricted.

Adolescents need to understand these limitations and to understand that professionals will help them exercise their rights to the fullest. In addition, they need to be aware that in a comprehensive program, while patient information is not released without consent to anyone outside the program, it may be shared among members of the staff. Being told that different points of view and expertise enhance the quality of the care they receive is helpful to the adolescent's acceptance of the case management approach. Similarly, they need to be informed and give consent, on a voluntary basis, before their data can be used for research or evaluation. Assurance that no information that specifically identifies them will be divulged usually suffices to obtain their cooperation.

Having discussed adolescents' legal rights to give informed consent and to receive confidential medical services, it is important to point out that program philosophy requires that the adolescent be seen as part of a family unit. To this end, the value of communication between adolescent and parent is emphasized. Parents should, ideally, know what their children are doing about sexual activity and contraceptive and other services received. Adolescent patients may be helped by role modeling, for example, to discuss these issues with their parents. However, within the legal limits discussed above, they are entitled to, and must be assured of, confidentiality. In the few instances in which adolescents receiving confidential services chose not to tell their parents that they were attending the clinic after one to three visits, it was usually with good reason. They must be trusted to make that decision.

Young people in an inner city environment may have very limited access to medical services and they sometimes come to a pregnancy prevention clinic with a serious medical problem or have one that comes to light during a physical examination. Immediate medical attention may be required for such conditions as pelvic abscess or a suspected ectopic pregnancy. When these problems were encountered in the Self Center, the findings were discussed with the adolescent, and her permission to tell her parents was obtained; permission was always granted. The CNM or PNP usually talked with a parent on the telephone, but sometimes the social worker returned with the adolescent to his or her home to help resolve the problem.

Medical Examination and History Taking

The medical examination and its preliminary history taking is another area for the practitioner wherein confidentiality and sensitivity are important. It is here that the trust relationship so necessary to adequate and continuing compliance has its genesis. The adolescent must be told what to expect during his or her visit, the kinds of questions that will be asked, the details of the examination, including the genital exam, and any procedures, with the reasons for them. CNMs and PNPs by training and temperament are usually very successful at this work.

History taking presents several problems when the patient is an adolescent. The young patient requesting confidentiality may be unfamiliar with certain historical details, and the parent cannot be queried. Sometimes, asking for details such as "nights spent in a hospital" or using some event or time period, such as "the summer before you started seventh grade," as an anchor will stimulate memory and help elicit useful information.

A more troublesome and important problem is the youngster who presents himself or herself with a vague or even bizarre complaint. As such a situation may be an attempt to mask embarrassment and/or fear of pregnancy or an STD and be simply an excuse to get in the door, it is important for the provider to have a high index of suspicion, and to be thorough whatever the presenting reason. The girl who has missed a period and who is afraid that she might be pregnant may fail to volunteer this information. If it is not elicited, and she is assured that her ostensible complaint is nothing to worry about, she is likely to go away reinforced in denying her pregnancy; prenatal care will be delayed, or the opportunity to terminate an undesired pregnancy may be lost.

Another kind of problem in history taking arises when the young patient becomes resentful about the number and depth of questions asked because she perceives them as unnecessary prying. A complaint that staff is "getting into my business" is sometimes voiced. A direct approach to history taking, explaining at the beginning why the information is needed, is productive and is appreciated by both adolescents and their parents.

Role as Health Educator

A major objective has been to teach the adolescents to be knowledgeable consumers of medical care. This involves encouraging them to ask questions (what and why) of their medical providers. A demonstration of success was an irate call from a nurse in an intensive care unit of another hospital complaining that one of our young black mothers (age 17 years) kept asking questions about her 2-year-old son who had been injured in an auto accident. "She wants to know if he had a head X-ray and what it showed." "I told her the boy was all right and that should be enough!"

As an educator, the nurse practitioner provides service to adolescent clients and program staff, as well as to medical and nursing students within a teaching institution. In fact, the entire client/provider experience should be educational, and, not surprisingly, the flow of education is in both directions. Staff teaching by the nurse practitioner is vital to the growth and expertise of other providers and may cover topics such as adolescent growth and development, group process, communication skills, counseling skills, and medical/legal implications. A useful impact can be made when the nurse midwife has the opportunity to teach and demonstrate clinical skills such as the pelvic examination. A gentle and sensitive approach to this embarrassing and humiliating examination can be a determining factor for the adolescent's decision to return to a family planning center. Few women forget their first pelvic examination.

The PNPs also play an important role as educators as they follow the young mother and her infant, providing preventive and acute primary health care for each member of the dyad. Not only do they monitor the mother's health, particularly the family planning aspects, but they also share with the program's educator the teaching of child care and parenting.

Consultations

The nurse midwife often finds herself in the role of OB/GYN consultant to the pediatric staff. The midwife may find she is accepting referrals to perform examinations on young clients who have been sexually abused or who refuse a pelvic examination for various reasons. Mentally retarded and physically handicapped clients are particularly challenging. Parents also may require intensive support in dealing with the sexuality and vulnerability of their youngsters. Pregnancies occurring in the adolescent age group can be devastating to them.

Case Management

As a case manager, the nurse practitioner, with a global view of primary health care, can be effective in the coordination of comprehensive care for a young client receiving services from a team of providers, such as a social worker, nutritionist, and health educator. Follow-up, an important component of good medical care, can be a challenge in the adolescent population where confidentiality is an important issue and motivation often lacking. Its success often depends on a friendly, trusting relationship with the provider.

Thoughts on Cost Effectiveness

The cost effectiveness of the nurse practitioner is a debatable and often controversial issue. It is frequently examined in terms of increased time spent with individual clients (Slome et al., 1976). The psychosocial orientation of the midlevel provider and her role as educator does require more time spent with the client than the examination itself. Those who support a preventive philosophy of health care accept the implications of this approach. Meeting the particular needs of the adolescent, as compared with the adult client, for psychosocial support and extensive education requires considerable staff time. These considerations should be built into the structure of a youth program. A useful trade-off is that the use of the practitioner can release more expensive physician time for more complicated or acute cases.

Another consideration in planning for the use of nurse practitioner's time is the program's funding source. A grant-funded, demonstration project permits the development of philosophy and protocol that allows for more time to be spent with each client. A busy, cost-conscious, comprehensive clinic, with a never-ending stream of medically needy adolescents, is more likely to lack resources and to be concerned with making maximal use of provider time and facilities. It is in just such a setting that preventive services, particularly education and regular case management, will prove most cost-effective by preventing costly complications of pregnancy, low birth weight, and unnecessary illness and accidents among the children of adolescents (see Chapter 7), or by preventing pregnancy (see Chapter 23).

Nurse Midwife and Nurse Practitioner in Specific Programs

Adolescent Pregnancy Program

The management of adolescent pregnancy has been described in Chapters 11 and 12. As medical care is provided by obstetrical residents, under the direction of the program's medical director, the nurse midwife provides some continuity of medical service by following those patients with the more severe psychosocial problems. She also participates, with other members of the comprehensive team, in the development and implementation of the educational program, mandatory at each prenatal visit for all the adolescents registered in the program. An important contribution of the nurse midwife is the care provided to each adolescent at her 4-week, postpartum visit. Each young woman is not only examined to assure the adequacy of her recovery from pregnancy and delivery, but she is also provided with detailed counseling and education directed at the prevention of an unintended, early repetition of pregnancy. If continued sexual activity is likely, the young mother is helped to choose a suitable contraceptive method, instructed in its use, and given supplies. Adolescents frequently make sudden decisions to stop taking oral contraceptives because of imagined adverse side effects, therefore each is provided with contraceptive foam and condoms as a "backup" method.

Follow-Up Parenting Program

Approximately half of the young mothers and their infants, usually the most high-risk mother/child pairs, entered this program. Intensive services were provided for three years. Health care was provided by one or more PNPs, working under the direction of a faculty pediatrician. The PNPs provided the bulk of the routine care for both mothers and infants, working with the mother/child pair as a unit to maximize efficiency of care and to minimize loss of time from school. Close patient/provider relationships developed. Preventive health care for both mothers and infants was emphasized.

Pregnancy Prevention Programs

Children and Youth Program Adolescent Clinic   Because pregnancy (and its complications) was noted, in 1982, to be the most frequent reason for hospital admission among females aged 12 to 18 years enrolled in the Johns Hopkins Children and Youth (C&Y) Program, an adolescent clinic was established as part of that program. Its major intent was to provide reproductive health services and to prevent pregnancy. The clinic was staffed by the CNM and PNPs from the C&Y modules working under the direction of C&Y pediatricians. Health education was a major concern, and both group and individual education was provided. Other health needs were provided within the general pediatric module within which individual patients were registered. Youngsters were seen at their parents' instigation as well as on a confidential, self-initiated basis. Most of these young people were sexually active, and contraceptives were supplied by the CNM and PNP, both of whom were involved, with the assistance of a health educator, in the guidance components.

School-Linked "Self Center" Program   As described in Chapter 23, this program was a research and demonstration program organized in collaboration with a public junior and senior high school. A nurse midwife and a nurse practitioner were the routine, full-time health care providers in this program. Physicians and medical students were rotated through the clinic; medical backup was provided by attending physicians in obstetrics, gynecology, and pediatrics. Referrals for abnormal findings were made to the appropriate place in the institution or to the private physician of the family's choice. Because confidentiality issues were a cornerstone of the clinic philosophy, referral for health problems often created serious dilemmas. The teenagers knew that under some circumstances, such as an acute medical problem, they would have to confide in their parents in order to resolve the problem. The nurse practitioner often made this happen by helping the student talk with her parents. For less acute problems, confidentiality was not an issue when the nurse could act as liaison between the client and parents.

The practitioners spent half of each work day in either a junior or senior high school and the other half in the storefront clinic (the Self Center) serving appointed as well as walk-in clients. In the school to which she was regularly assigned, the practitioner had several responsibilities. She provided classroom instruction with respect to issues concerned with human reproduction and contraception. She served as a resource and consultant for teachers and other school staff, and she was readily available to students during lunch breaks. Students were free to drop in to her office, individually or in small groups, to seek answers to questions or to receive counseling or make appointments for clinic visits. The opportunity to talk with the program's nurse or social worker was much used by students, particularly in the junior high school where students, both male and female, had many questions and anxieties about puberty and sexual and other health issues.

In the clinic, after attending an educational session and seeing a social worker, the clients met with the practitioner for physical examination or revisit exam usually related to contraceptive use. Minor gynecological problems and sexually transmitted diseases were diagnosed and treated. Pregnancies were also diagnosed; options were discussed, and referrals made. The practitioners had access to students in the schools if follow-up for medical problems was necessary.

Before and after each clinic, records were reviewed, and multidisciplinary plans were developed for each client by members of the team, who kept each other informed of the youngsters' well being. Information was exchanged at weekly staff meetings or on an individual, need-to-know, basis.

The nurse practitioners were called upon to speak formally and informally to various community groups regarding issues of teen sexuality and pregnancy prevention. The education of parents and the raising of community awareness of the problem of teen pregnancy were major goals of the project.

For this practitioner, 5 years' experience in an adolescent pregnancy prevention clinic created respect for the enormous scope and challenge presented by the issues of adolescent sexuality and the consequences of premature intercourse. The evaluation of information and experiences at weekly staff conferences resulted in frequent revision of techniques and approaches. As solutions were devised, new problems emerged. The challenges occurred daily; the experiences were bittersweet. The students were a joy and a sorrow. As the staff became wiser, the task seemed more monumental. A staff that began the project with zeal and naiveté soon learned to measure success in smaller increments. For some high-risk patients, the simple delay of pregnancy became a goal. The entire staff, including registrars, functioned as a team; all were recognized to have an impact on the success of the program. They were facilitators, advisors, counselors, providers, and advocates. There was at the outset some ambivalence among the staff members regarding the ethics and morality of adolescent sexuality. In time, a consistent philosophy emerged. Abstinence was encouraged and promoted as healthy, acceptable, and the most effective way of preventing pregnancy and STDs. (AIDS was not a recognized problem then.) However, practicality demanded a realistic approach; the major goal was responsible sexual behavior, including use of effective contraception by those who chose to be sexually active. An educational program evolved based on personal responsibility and incorporated exercises to develop decision-making skills and values clarification. The clients knew that they had choices and that they made them every day.

Involvement of the male was important. The staff learned that the male was not always the instigator for intercourse; the males also often felt victimized, powerless, and helpless. The boys needed help in learning to say "no" effectively. They, too, had many questions and many anxieties as to the normalcy of their development, and, in fact, it was these questions and concerns they often brought to the practitioners because there was no one else in their lives to whom to turn.

There were daily rap groups in the clinic as well as in the school, and class sessions were led by the staff in the schools. The presentations were incorporated into the schools' Family Life Curriculum. Interestingly, the younger teens took these groups more seriously. Why? Did the older teens need to save face because they "knew it all?" Following a values clarification exercise, in which the topic of sexual abuse was raised, several youngsters identified themselves as victims of incest. The nurse practitioners who functioned in the school setting as well as the clinic provided the continuity of provider/client relationships needed to match clues leading to the diagnosis of sexual abuse. An outspoken, seemingly sophisticated young woman who sought help raised a red flag when she refused a pelvic examination. When sexual abuse was suspected, the nurses worked with the program social workers and appropriate school staff to bring the matter to the appropriate local authorities.

The narcissistic attitude, normal in the adolescent, was used and developed in counseling. What does it mean that you are a woman or you are a man? How does being a woman or a man interface with being a parent? The lesson was that being biologically capable of parenting does not qualify you to be a parent; other attributes are required.

There were sexual identity issues to be addressed. Youngsters, male or female, had preferences as to the sex of the provider. Some females did not want a male provider; some did not want a female provider because they questioned the provider's sexual identity. What an opportunity this provided to discuss sexual identity issues! A prominent lesson for staff was the adolescents' continuing need for information and reassurance of normalcy. Misinformation and belief in myths were widespread.

Conclusion

Adolescents are a medically underserved group with many health problems stemming from premature sexual activity. The adolescent years are difficult and trying times for the young people themselves as well as those who love and care for them. Adolescents are neither child or adult; they may be capable of reproduction but not, on a consistent basis, of formal thought leading to sound reasoning and decision making. They are likely to demonstrate inconsistencies between attitude and behavior. Issues relating to an emerging identity are tied into intimacy, sexuality, and sexual expression. These topics are not confronted comfortably by even the most sophisticated adolescent and his/her parents. The nurse practitioner, with the unique blend of biopsychosocial orientation, seems ideally equipped to assist the adolescent and his/her parents through these years.

The multiple roles of the nurse practitioner have been discussed; she is provider, educator, consultant, manager, advocate, and friend. In all areas, the practitioner, by virtue of training and philosophy, makes a contribution to the provision of quality adolescent care.

16

The Johns Hopkins Parenting Program (TAC)
Services and Evaluation

By the end of the second year of the Adolescent Pregnancy Program (HAC), two circumstances called attention to the need for follow-up care of these high-risk young mothers and their children despite their improved pregnancy outcomes. The first was the return to the prenatal clinic, within the early months after delivery, of adolescents with another unintended pregnancy, even though family planning education had been included in the prenatal program. The second circumstance concerned the infants, many of whom became ill and/or showed evidence of neglect during the early months after birth; some required hospital admission and some died. Continued comprehensive care was imperative. Plans were made to develop a follow-up program using the same basic principles that guided the implementation of HAC.

The follow-up program, which began in 1976, was designed to provide comprehensive services to the young mother and infant as a *unit*, usually at the same visit. A major difficulty in providing health care, including family planning, for inner city adolescents has been patient motivation and compliance. We postulated that the young mother would be more compliant with preventive health care for her infant than for herself and that she would be more compliant as the result of her interaction with one set of health care providers than she was with two. Furthermore, because one of the program's objectives was to encourage the completion of schooling by the young mothers, the less time missed from school the better. Except after hours, when emergency services were available in the hospital, adolescents and their infants received care in a special and separate teenage clinic (TAC).

Characteristics of Population Served

During the early years, only 100 to 150 mother/child dyads of the 300 delivering in HAC were enrolled in TAC. A major consideration underlying this decision was the desire for a comparison group against which to measure the effects of the new services. However, those young mothers who enrolled were, on the average, younger, at higher social and medical risk, and with less education than those referred to other sources of continuing care. When major problems were recognized during the obstetrical course, staff were more likely to encourage enrollment in the comprehensive follow-up program.

Among the first 244 patients enrolled, those in 1976 and 1977, 8% were age 14 or below, 11% were 15, 21% were 16, 37% were 17 years old, and 23% had turned 18 by the time of delivery. Their cognitive skills and academic achievement were tested routinely by a staff psychologist. Figure 16-1 shows the distributions of reading, spelling, and math scores obtained by these young women. The distributions were generally very low, with skewing of the curves toward the lower end. Scores obtained on the Peabody Picture Vocabulary Test were also well below the norm and similarly skewed. Interestingly, self-esteem, as measured by the Coopersmith Inventory of Self-Esteem, was within the normal range (Table 16-1). The suggestion that low self-esteem is a frequent finding among pregnant and parenting adolescents was not borne out in this population of young mothers. However, low academic skills and high rates of school dropout were also characteristic of the random sample of adolescent mothers who delivered in 1983 (see Chapter 5).

These families were poor. The source of family income for 247 patients consecutively interviewed by the TAC social worker between January and June 1979 is shown in Table 16-2. The percentage (85.5) who received welfare was not very different from that reported for the city-wide, random sample in Chapter 5; the proportion of families with earned income was very small. Table 16-3 shows the occupation of the father of the baby where known to the mother: 26% were in school; 8% were enrolled in a work-study program; 17% were in the Job Corps; 43% were employed; 6% were in the Armed Services; and 16% were unemployed. Twenty percent of young mothers did not know the father's occupation or even whether he was employed. These findings, while discouraging in terms of unemployment and absent fatherhood, are considerably more favorable than those for 1983 to 1985 reported in Chapter 6; then 36% were neither in school nor employed.

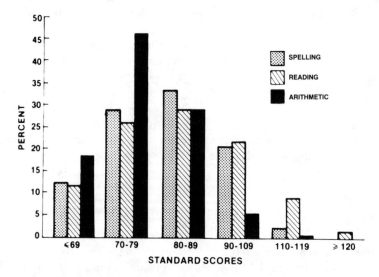

Figure 16-1 Adolescent mothers in follow-up program. Distribution of academic performance in spelling, reading, and math, as measured by the Wide Range Achievement Test administered to 244 young mothers followed in TAC.

Table 16-1 Results of Assessment of Self-Esteem, Using the Coopersmith Inventory,[a] of 244 Young Mothers Followed in the TAC Program for 18 to 24 Months[b]

Total raw score	Classification	No.	%
≥84	Above average	43	17.6
59–83	Average	153	62.7
≤58	Below average	48	19.7
Mean total score = 70.49	SD (15.26)		

	Mean subscale scores			
	Self	*Home*	*Social*	*School*
$\overline{X}$ Score	18.67	5.18	6.63	4.86
SD	(8.13)	(2.06)	(1.43)	(1.74)

[a]Coopersmith Inventory of Self-esteem.

[b]Unpublished data from the Final Report on the Johns Hopkins Center For Teenage Parents to the Health Care Financing Agency (1977 to 1980).

Table 16-2 Source of Income/Financial Support for 247 Consecutive Adolescents Interviewed by Social Worker Between January and June 1979

Source	No.	%
DSS, both mother and/or child	118	85.5
DSS, mother and/or child	69	50.0
DSS, child only	40	35.5
Earned income, family or husband	20	14.4

DSS, Department of Social Services. DSS included financial assistance and Medical Assistance.

Table 16-3 Occupation of Father of the Baby[a]

Occupation	No.	% of those known[b]
In school	28	26
Employed	46	42
Work-study program	8	8
U.S. Armed Services	6	6
Job corps	2	2
Unemployed	17	16
Totals	107	100

[a]Data from interview with 134 young mothers enrolled in TAC, 24 months after delivery.

[b]Percents have been rounded. The whereabouts of 27 fathers were unknown.

Program Characteristics

As the follow-up program matured, as described in Chapter 1, a comprehensive program that provided around-the-clock primary care evolved, with crisis medical and/or social service management on weekends through available hospital facilities. The program provided preventive and acute primary care on an outpatient basis, inpatient hospital care, and consultation as needed in the hospital's specialty clinics. The program's pediatrician was the faculty member who was also responsible for the dyad's inpatient hospital care. The clinic, like the obstetrical component, had its own social worker, educator, and support staff. Like HAC, it provided comprehensive services, organized and monitored by an individual case management system. The social and educational services are described in detail in Chapters 17 and 18.

Medical Services

Intensive primary care was provided at routine visits of decreasing frequency for the first 3 years after delivery: six routine visits in the first year, four in the second, and two in the third, after which mothers and children were referred to other programs for continuing care. The regimen for the infant's preventive health care followed, in general, that required in the EPSDT Program (Early and Periodic Screening, Diagnosis and Treatment) for Medical Assistance reimbursement (for further detail see Chapter 19). The regime for the young mothers also provided complete primary care but was directed mainly toward their family planning needs. The need to avoid an unintended pregnancy was emphasized by every staff member, at each visit. Preventive health visits, and acute care visits when possible, were by appointment. An attempt was made to group these appointments by the age of the child, to facilitate the mothers' attendance at educational groups appropriate to the age of their children. Attendance at a group educational session at each preventive health visit was mandatory, as it had been in HAC. Until the program was institutionalized in July 1982, no charges were made for services; contraceptive supplies were dispensed at a cost of 25 cents, or at no charge for those who could not pay. We did not want cost to be a barrier to access in this demonstration program. Bus tokens were provided for transportation when necessary, and an occasional taxi coupon was available when the young mother or her infant was sick.

Vocational Counseling

During the period 1978 to 1981, a vocational counselor was employed to assist the young mothers, and those of their partners who wished to avail themselves of her help, in remaining in school or finding jobs. This program component was popular with both the mothers and the fathers. The assistance involved individual counseling, providing instruction on how to fill out job applications and make appointments for interviews, as well as guidance on behavior, dress, and the like. We well remember one 16-year-old with an appointment for an interview at McDonalds. She stopped in on her way to show the counselor how she had "fixed herself up" for this momentous and highly sought-after occasion. She had put on extraordinarily long, false eyelashes, rouge, and lipstick, and bright butterfly pasties were stuck on her face and upper arms. She was helped to clean up and tone down her appearance and was taken to the place of the interview. After a while, she reappeared to tell us that she had gotten the job—to her surprise after her misguided attempt to enhance her appearance had been undone. She worked after school all through that year.

The counselor's job involved getting out into the community to find entry-level jobs and job-training opportunities. She also helped the young people to make suitable day care arrangements for their babies. She tried to make them aware of how important education was to success in life and how detrimental an unintended pregnancy could be. She helped a number of older adolescent mothers obtain tuition grants permitting them to attend local colleges and universities or to obtain technical training. Several of those mothers have become teachers, nurses, computer experts, and the like. One severely dyslexic 17-year-old mother who had dropped out of school entered a work-study program which supplied day care for her child. She became a telephone operator, working in a local police department since finishing school. She changes out of uniform before going home, as she lives in a crime- and drug-ridden part of Baltimore where the police are unloved. Another welfare-supported young woman with two children was helped to obtain her GED certificate, a tuition grant, and day care for her children. She completed 4 years of college and has been teaching in a local school system for several years.

Those were good days for the teenagers and staff alike. Many opportunities were realized. However, in 1980, jobs, job training, and subsidized day care began to disappear, and by 1981, there were virtually none for our clients. In 1981, with great regret, the vocational counselor was dropped from the program. The program continued, but the lives of the adolescents became more difficult and the opportunities for improvement much less frequent. Repeat pregnancies seemed to occur with greater frequency. As the holes in the "safety-net" under the poor grew ever larger, we sensed a disappearance of the optimism of the 1970s and an increasing pessimism and depression. Unfortunately, we did not document these changes. With the institutionalization of the programs in 1982, the girls in the comparison groups that had facilitated evaluation also became enrolled in the HAC and TAC programs, with the exception of those whose families were members of the Johns Hopkins HMO.

Evaluation

Presented below are selected results from an early outcome evaluation of the comprehensive follow-up program, TAC. Dr. Charles Flagle assisted with this evaluation in which the outcomes for TAC enrollees and their children were compared with those of similar HAC enrollees and their children who had been referred to other community clinics for follow-up family planning and well-child care. One hundred young mothers enrolled and followed for 2 years in TAC were matched on race, age and education at delivery, and Medicaid status with control patients from HAC who had not been followed. Young mothers in each group were interviewed by an experienced interviewer using a structured interview. Eighty-seven of the TAC mothers were interviewed as compared with only 54 of the control group. Many of the latter group had moved and could not be located with the limited resources available. The two groups are not strictly comparable because, as explained above, assignment to TAC was voluntary, and those young mothers perceived to be at higher risk for adverse consequences were encouraged to enroll. Furthermore, the greater attrition to follow-up of the control group may have introduced biases of which we were unaware. Nonetheless, the two groups who were followed-up appeared reasonably comparable. Just over 80% of each group were black, 21 of the 87 TAC mothers were age 15 or below, and 20 were 18 years of age at delivery, as compared with 10 and 14, respectively, of the 54 controls who were interviewed. Selected outcomes for the two groups of mothers are discussed below.

Social, Educational, and Health Status

As shown in Table 16-4, young mothers enrolled in the comprehensive program, even though younger and at higher medical and social risk at the time of delivery, had more favorable outcomes along several parameters when compared with the controls. High school graduation had been achieved by 42% of TAC patients, and 40% were still attending school, as compared with 20% and 35%, respectively, among controls. Among TAC girls, 77% were or had been employed, compared with 52% of the controls; 46% of those in TAC reported welfare dependence compared with 68% of controls. Among TAC patients, less than one-half were at home with their infants during the day, compared with three-fourths of the controls. Almost 20% of TAC mothers had subsidized day care while they attended school; grandmothers and a few fathers of the babies helped out. Subsidized day care was unusual among controls (3% or 5.5%), and fewer grandmothers provided day care. Almost 20% of the TAC mothers were married 24 months after the birth of their child, as compared with 11% of controls; this was a higher frequency of marriage than is found in the 1983 random sample of adolescent births in Baltimore City (see Chapter 5). The more favorable circumstances of the TAC mothers appears to be reflected in their lower frequency of welfare dependence as compared with those in the control group.

Table 16-4   Preliminary Outcome Evaluation: Comparison of Selected Characteristics of Adolescent Mothers Followed 24 Months in a Comprehensive Program with Similar Mothers Referred after Delivery to Community Clinics

Selected maternal characteristics	Followed in TAC (n = 87)		Comparison group (n = 54)	
	No.	%	No.	%
Education				
High school grad.	36	42.1	11	20.3
Attending school	35	40.0	19	35.2
Welfare-dependent	40	46.0	37	68.5
Ever worked	67	77.0	28	52.0
Married	17	19.5	6	11.1
Child care				
Mother at night	70	80.5	47	87.0
Mother in day	42	48.2	40	74.0
Grandmother in day	26	29.3	8	14.8
Other day care	18	22.0	5	9.5

Table 16-5 Selected Medical Variables from a Preliminary Outcome Evaluation of the Comprehensive Follow-up and Parenting Program for Adolescent Mothers and their Children (TAC)

	Followed in TAC (n = 87)			Comparison group (n = 54)		
	No.	%	Mean	No.	%	Mean
Medical care: mother						
Acute OPD care	34	35.0		25	45.7	
Hospital admission	19	22.0		21	39.1	
Family planning	86	98.7		35	65.0	
Never used family planning	1	1.3		6	11.1	
Medical care: child						
All immunizations	86	98.8		45	83.3	
Acute OPD visits			4.2			6.1
Hospital admission	18	20.7		20	38.3	

Mothers in both groups received obstetrical care in HAC; the controls received follow-up care in community clinics.

Table 16-5 shows selected health outcomes for mothers and babies in the two comparison groups. Interesting differences are seen. During the 24-month period, substantially more control mothers than those receiving comprehensive care in TAC required acute outpatient care and hospitalization. Almost all TAC mothers received family planning services (the one who did not was not sexually active) as compared with fewer than two-thirds of the controls. As shown in Figure 16-2, within 12 months, 7%, and within 24 months, 25% of TAC mothers had a repeat pregnancy as compared with 22% and 39%, respectively, for the controls. Of the babies born, 29% of those born to the TAC mothers who became pregnant again had a different father from the index birth, as compared with 43% of the controls. Data from the first 118 patients followed for 24 months in TAC were used to

Table 16-6 Data from the 24-Month Follow-up of the First 118 Mothers Enrolled in TAC, Comparing Those Who Became Pregnant Again and Those Who Did Not

Maternal characteristics	Repeated pregnancy (n = 40) %	No repetition (n = 78) %
Age ≤ 15 yr at index delivery	32.5	25.0
Married	10.0	1.3
Medical assistance	65.0	38.0
H/O prior pregnancy		
Index only	42.5	86.8
1 additional	47.5	13.2
≥2 additional	10.0	0.0
WRAT Reading ≤ 80	46.0	33.0
Peabody Vocabulary Test score ≤ 80	82.0	69.0
Low self-esteem (Coopersmith)	30.8	12.0

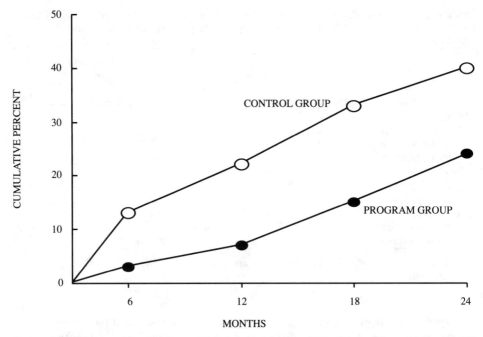

Figure 16-2 Percent distribution of repeat pregnancy within 24 months of index HAC delivery for those young mothers enrolled in the TAC follow-up progam as compared with controls referred to community family planning clinics.

Table 16-7 Contraceptive Experience of Repeaters and Those with No Repetition of Pregnancy

	Repeated pregnancy (n = 40)	No repetition (n = 76)
	%	%
No contraceptive use before index pregnancy	73.0	80.3
Contraceptive use following index pregnancy	81.5	98.6
Oral	42.5	60.5
IUD	12.0[a]	21.0
Other	27.0	17.1
Unknown	5.0	1.3
None	19.5	.0
Method changes in follow-up		
None	13.2	54.0
One	13.2	23.7
Two	10.5	15.8
Three or more	63.2	6.2

[a]Two girls became pregnant with IUD in place. The use of IUDs has been discontinued because of the high risk of infection in this population.

compare the characteristics of those having a subsequent pregnancy with those who did not. As may be seen in Table 16-6, those who became pregnant again were, on the average, younger and poorer. They had less adequate cognitive performance and a lower self-esteem, and they had had more prior pregnancies than those who did not become pregnant again. Also, a larger proportion (10% versus 1.3%) were married when the subsequent pregnancy occurred.

The contraceptive experience of the two groups is of considerable interest (Table 16-7). Not surprisingly, those young women who had no repetition of pregnancy in the 2-year period appeared to be more effective users of contraception than those who became pregnant again. Our clinical impression was that those who had difficulty settling down to one or two methods were at greater risk for conception. Among those with a repeat pregnancy, 63% changed contraceptive method three or more times during the period before they conceived again, as compared with 6% of those who did not have a repeat pregnancy during the 2-year period.

Among the babies followed for 24 months, 99% of those enrolled in TAC had received all the immunizations appropriate for age as compared with 85% of the controls; TAC babies made fewer acute outpatient visits and had fewer hospital admissions than the controls (Table 16-5)—a very satisfactory outcome in a disadvantaged population.

Conclusion

The health and social outcomes for the young mothers and their children enrolled in the comprehensive program were superior to those of similar mothers who were also enrolled prenatally in HAC but who were referred after delivery to community clinics for follow-up care. The results of this preliminary evaluation are similar in many respects to those reported by Duggan et al. in Chapter 19.

17

Psychosocial Support for Pregnant and Parenting Adolescents

Babette R. Bierman

The objective of this chapter is to describe the role of the social worker and the contribution of professional social services to the effectiveness of comprehensive adolescent health programs. The material presented here is drawn from experience in concurrent Johns Hopkins programs providing services for inner city adolescents. These programs, which shared overall direction, management style, and philosophical approach, were separately organized and funded, and each had its own social work staff. The social workers, while responsible to the program in which each worked, were members of the Social Work Department of the Johns Hopkins Hospital. Two programs, the Adolescent Pregnancy Program (HAC) and the Parenting Program (TAC), provided preventive and acute primary health care, including inpatient hospital care, as appropriate, in separate clinical sites. The Pregnancy Prevention Program (Self Center) was a research and service demonstration organized in collaboration with two Baltimore public schools (see Chapter 23). This program had its own "store front" clinic, "The Self Center," close to the schools, which served as a base for the social work and nursing staff who worked in both school and clinic.

While the specific social work tasks differed somewhat in each program component, in accord with the demands of its mission, the basic approaches were similar, as were many of the problems encountered. For example, counseling with respect to the occurrence of pregnancy was a crucial component of each.

In an adolescent program, be it one to improve health outcomes or to prevent unintended pregnancy and its adverse consequences, the social worker plays a vital and special role in the health care team. Her training, her communication skills, and her knowledge of family dynamics and community resources enable her to assess the social background and needs of each client and to help implement the socially comprehensive aspects of the program. The social workers have played a major role in emphasizing the human and social aspects of adolescent problems and the importance of a "caring" environment to their solution.

Specific aspects of the social work component of each program and the special tasks common to all programs are discussed below. In general, however, the social worker was the primary advocate for the adolescent and her channel to community services. In staff meetings and in-service education, it was the social worker who was responsible for providing information about the adolescent in her family and community setting. In this role, she made a major contribution to individual case management decisions.

The adolescent advocacy role has been particularly important in the parenting component (TAC) where the adolescent not infrequently perceived the primary focus of interest among physicians, nurses, and educators to be the baby. The expression by the social worker of interest in, and appreciation for, problems faced by the young mother herself, was critical in establishing rapport and helping her to cope with rearing a child, from a usually unintended and often unwanted pregnancy, while still a child herself.

In addition to advocacy, social workers were required to provide services for the adolescent and her family in four general areas. The first area was concerned with problems of maintenance, i.e., those pertaining to the basic requirements for food, shelter, financial assistance, and medical insurance. The second included the adolescent's need for continued education and/or job training and placement so that she could become self-sufficient and provide for herself and her baby, as marriage was seldom an option. The third involved the provision of education and information, particularly with respect to health, parenting, family planning, and sexuality issues. Finally, and most important, were psychosocial assessment and counseling covering a multitude of concerns. These were brought to the attention of the social worker by routine screening, as in the prenatal and parenting programs, by referral from other staff members, or by the adolescents themselves, a frequent occurrence once the adolescent realized what the program had to offer.

In general, referrals to the social worker were made when: 1) there was a breakdown in family support through illness, alcoholism, drug abuse, death, or desertion; 2) medical care providers perceived interpersonal problems between adolescent and family, adolescent and child, or adolescent and peers or school; 3) when neglect and/or abuse of the adolescent or the child were suspected. Sexual abuse of the adolescent was not an infrequent problem, particularly in the pregnancy prevention school-linked program; and finally 4) in a medical setting, adolescents were frequently referred for counseling because they were resistant to, or unable to follow, medical advice or failed to keep appointments. Counseling was provided to those girls who exhibited attitudes of denial of a medical diagnosis such as pregnancy, a sexually transmitted infection, or a handicap or malformation in the child. A special challenge were the girls who were physically or mentally handicapped themselves. The social worker took responsibility for the necessary referrals for services and for following through to see that these were received and utilized.

Social Work Tasks in Special Situations

Pregnancy Option Counseling

Pregnancy diagnosis was available in all three programs. However, all adolescents enrolled in the Adolescent Pregnancy Program had been diagnosed as pregnant, had been counseled, and had decided to continue the pregnancy prior to their first visits. Nonetheless, a few changed their minds and required further counseling. While various staff members counseled adolescents found to be pregnant, it was primarily the responsibility of the social workers to do so. Information about their options for pregnancy resolution and their legal rights and obligations (Chapter

10) were made available to the adolescent, preferably in the company of her mother and/or the putative father. The reality, however, was that the adolescent was usually counseled alone. In part this was because of issues of confidentiality and in part because of the possibility that she might not return with her mother in a timely fashion. The options included having the baby and raising the child herself, placing him/her for adoption, and terminating the pregnancy by abortion (within the existing legal and financial constraints). The pros and cons associated with each option were presented objectively, and questions were answered so that the adolescent had a basis for rational decision making. The first hurdle for some pregnant adolescents was to tell their parents about the pregnancy. As the vast majority were unmarried, parental support was essential to their well-being. The social worker not infrequently acted as an intermediary in this difficult situation.

Once the pregnancy decision was made by the adolescent, usually in consultation with her family, referral for appropriate care was promptly made, with continued support provided afterward.

Adolescent Pregnancy Program

In the prenatal component of the Johns Hopkins program, as described in Chapter 11, a full-time social worker screened each adolescent. Usually she talked with the adolescent's mother and often with the father-to-be. She provided counseling to the adolescent and family where indicated and helped in resolving conflict around the pregnancy, planning for the future so that the adolescent was able to remain in, or return to, school to complete her education. Referrals were often made to the special school for pregnant girls, the Paquin School. Referrals were also made to other agencies for needed services, both prenatally and after delivery, and a network of community services was developed, with the channels of communication necessary for their proper functioning. This necessitated attending many meetings in the community to facilitate linkage. As an advocate for the adolescent within her family, the hospital, and the community, the social worker visited on the maternity floor to help in discharge planning. In addition, she played an important role in the educational program, serving as leader or coleader of a number of educational groups and providing guided tours of the labor and delivery suite and the rooms where the adolescent might stay during her hospital admission. She dispensed emergency funds for transportation, food, and other needs, on a short-term basis, until other community resources could take over. Social work referrals were considered when any of the medical and/or social risk factors listed below were present:

1. Maternal age, 15 years or under
2. Negative attitude toward the pregnancy
3. Adoption or foster care planning
4. Repeat pregnancy, particularly when the adolescent already had one or more children
5. Family/interpersonal relationship problems (history of abuse/neglect)
6. Significant age discrepancy between patient and father of baby (suspicion of sexual abuse)
7. Noncompliance regarding appointments/medical regimen
8. Late prenatal registration
9. Fear/anxiety/depression

10. Psychiatric problems (current or by history)
11. Mental retardation and/or physical handicap
12. Alcohol or drug abuse, personal or parental
13. Antisocial behavior
14. Maternal disease; fetal or infant anomalies or death
15. Prenatal admission
16. Inappropriate maternal/infant bonding
17. Environmental/economic constraints
18. Crisis situations, for example, need for shelter

A full-time community outreach worker was part of the program. She extended the work of the social worker and other staff, making home visits to all the pregnant girls of 14 years and below and to others judged to be at unusually high risk or who failed to keep clinic appointments. She worked with family members, the schools, churches, and other community agencies, as well as working in the clinic and on the wards. She became advocate, friend, and role model for the adolescents.

Illustrative Case Report

The following case illustrates the presence of several of the above indicators and follows an adolescent through the prenatal program (HAC) and her transition into the follow-up parenting program (TAC).

Carol, a 15-year-old girl, was a pediatric patient in the Children and Youth Program who became upset and sad when her pregnancy was diagnosed and at that time said that she wanted an abortion. However, Carol was not a very articulate or aggressive youngster and allowed her older sister to speak for her during subsequent examinations. A sonogram confirmed not only that she was pregnant but also that she was carrying twins. Carol's mother was excited to hear that she would be the grandmother of twins and strongly encouraged Carol to continue with the pregnancy. The family unanimously offered to help with the babies. Carol was swept up in their enthusiasm and unable to make an independent decision.

She entered the HAC, and during the ensuing months the social worker and outreach worker got to know the family and Carol better as they worked on some specific problems and Carol's adjustment to having twins. Toward the last trimester Carol needed to remain on bed rest and was admitted antenatally to the hospital for preeclampsia. A home teacher was obtained to aid her in keeping up with her school work. The family needed the social worker to intervene and be an advocate for getting emergency fuel and enrollment in the WIC program, which provides supplemental nutrition for women, infants, and children who are at risk. At the time of the infants' delivery, the family was not prepared with adequate clothing, equipment, or milk. Although the family continued to be overjoyed at the birth of the twins, Michael and Larry, Carol remained withdrawn, silent, and uncommunicative throughout the last trimester, birth, and during the postpartum hospital stay. Michael spent a short time in the Intensive Care Nursery because of low birth weight. It was noted in the medical chart that his mother seemed depressed, with flat affect.

The outreach worker was called on to help with the transition from the prenatal program to the follow-up component, but even so, Carol missed the first well-child clinic appointment for her twins. Four days later she brought Michael in to be seen for nasal congestion, but again missed the next appointment of well-child care. The staff became concerned; here we had a 15-year-old mother who, by report, appeared depressed and unhappy about being pregnant, who had verbalized a desire for an abortion, whose family verbalized their desire for her to continue with the pregnancy, but at the time of discharge from the hospital were not prepared with adequate supplies and equipment for the children.

Carol and her mother agreed to a home visit by the social worker and outreach worker, for they knew and trusted the outreach worker. When they arrived at the home, they were surprised to see a well furnished and recently painted house. They were met by both grandparents and several of Carol's siblings. The twins were in the living room snuggled together in one bassinet. The crib, which the prenatal staff had helped the family to acquire, was not being used for lack of a mattresss. The bassinet had a mattress, but it was too small, leaving a 6-inch gap that no one had thought to fill. Carol was noticeably absent from the room while the family showed off the twins, and it was only after several requests and a lapse of 10 minutes that she appeared, a small, sad looking girl, who in contrast to her family, looked unkempt. She walked slowly into the room, sat with eyes cast down, and only talked when prodded by her mother.

With effort, the social worker was able to engage her in conversation and learned that she was involved in school, had some close friends, and had been having difficulty with the father of her children, who was denying paternity. She began to make eye contact and had a few infrequent smiles as a result of keeping the attention on her rather than on the babies. Several observations became apparent and were confirmed in later interviews. Her style of interacting and communicating was grossly different from her gregarious family. She seemed overwhelmed as she spoke about her feelings during pregnancy and now as a mother of twins. Lack of money and the task of taking two infants out alone kept her from keeping clinic appointments, but more important, she was not feeling well. In response to our concern about her physical discomfort, she agreed to return with us to the hospital to be seen by the nurse practitioner in the follow-up TAC program.

Some 40 minutes passed before Carol was ready to talk about her children's needs. With her mother, we discussed community resources for obtaining the safe equipment and clothing needed. Carol brought up questions about the umbilical cord and the dryness of the twins' skin. A call to the hospital put her in touch with the nurse practitioner and allowed for her to make an appointment for well-child care.

Subsequent interviews took place in the clinic, during which time Carol was allowed to talk about her feelings and plans for herself. As a result of our reaching out and paying attention to the emotional needs of this very quiet, somewhat sullen 15-year-old mother, she was able to keep most of her appointments, and her infants progressed and thrived. She returned to school, the family assumed the task of babysitting and, at our request, agreed to have one family member accompany her for clinic visits. However, the twins continued with one crib without a mattress; as a result, they no longer slept in the small bassinet but began to share the bed with Carol. From all outward appearances, Carol gave the impression of enjoying her children. However, from our experience, we anticipated that the next crucial time might come when the babies began to separate from her as they became more mobile and entered toddlerhood. This continued to be considered a family at risk and surveillance was maintained.

Follow-up Parenting Program (TAC)

TAC also had its own full-time social worker. The case described above helps to illustrate her role as social worker in the follow-up component of the program. It is essential that the social worker have the ability to be flexible and ready to move from one area of her expertise to another, for example, from changing diapers to obtaining emergency food, to evaluating parent-child interaction, to offering ego-supportive, insight-oriented counseling. She must be willing to move away from the security of an office to interact with a client in a hallway, sitting on the floor of a waiting room, in an examination room, or in the home. Very often, instead of a quiet background, there was an infant crying or a toddler demanding to be played with or fed. There were frequently other family members or boyfriends present, with their own agendas.

In the follow-up program, the social worker talked with all new adolescent mothers on their first visit, 2 weeks after delivery, for a psychosocial assessment, to ascertain her family support and to begin to understand something of her relationships with her parents (especially her mother), her siblings, and the father of her baby. At that time, a preliminary assessment of her ego strength and object relationships was obtained. She was seen again for a brief screening when her child was 6, 12, and 24 months old, and on her last visit when the child was 3 years old. These were the only mandatory interviews, but it was made clear in the initial interview that advocacy and counseling were available at any time and that members of the team might refer her to social work, if they felt it would be helpful. Such referrals were often made for the evaluation of problems perceived by other staff members to require more exploration or because of crisis situations. Some young mothers often sought help from the social worker on their own initiative.

Along with usual "tools of the social work trade," knowledge of adolescent developmental stages and infant/toddler development is imperative. This aspect is discussed at some length later in the chapter. The tools most frequently used are the ability to make assessments, to communicate a good knowledge of community resources, and an abundance of tolerance and patience.

Social work referrals in an adolescent parent/child follow-up program were made for the following reasons:

1. Maintenance problems
    a. Financial, including food stamps
    b. Medical Assistance/insurance coverage
    c. WIC (Supplemental food, Women, Infants, and Children)
2. Concerns about abuse/neglect (adolescent or child)
    a. Repeated accidents to the child
    b. Consistent low weight gain/failure to thrive in the child, without medical explanation
    c. Dramatic shift in behavior or affect of either child or parent
3. Adolescent health problems, e.g., depression, difficulty with family planning, sexually transmitted diseases
4. Breakdown in family support: illness; death; desertion; alcoholism; and/or drug abuse
5. Problems with interpersonal relationships
    a. Between family members, including the baby's father
    b. Between parent and child
    c. With community agencies

6. Counseling for medical problems
    a. When there was an inability or resistance to keeping medical appointments
    b. For denial of implications of a medical diagnosis
    c. For support in dealing with a medical diagnosis
7. Where the mother was mentally retarded or physically handicapped

In our experience, most contacts with the social worker were crisis-oriented. At least 75% of our patients sought or had been referred for specific acute problems; the contact was usually brief, although it was not unusual for our patients to make frequent contacts over the 3-year period. Only 5% to 10% of girls receiving help were involved in ongoing counseling at any given time, with an average of three to five visits each. Very few, perhaps 2%, were able to engage in sustained therapy focused on insight. The average age of our patients when they entered the follow-up component was just over 15 years, a difficult age group to involve in sustained therapy or counseling under any circumstances.

It was important to understand the psychodynamics and characteristics of the population we served, and it was the social worker's task to help contribute this understanding to the team. In this context, it is important to be familiar with the normal characteristics of adolescence (see Chapter 2). Some of these characteristics, as they may affect parenting, are discussed below.

Characteristics of Adolescence

The characteristics of adolescent development may conflict with the adolescent mother's ability to mother her child adequately, especially her toddler. A good working description of adolescent development is given by Anna Freud (1958). She states that: "Adolescence is by its nature an interruption of peaceful growth; the upholding of a steady equilibrium during the adolescent process is in itself abnormal. It is normal for an adolescent to behave for a considerable length of time in an inconsistent and unpredictable manner, to fight his impulses and to accept them; to love his parents and to hate them, to revolt against them and to be dependent on them; to be deeply ashamed to acknowledge his mother before others and, unexpectedly, to desire heart to heart talks with her; to thrive on imitation of and identification with others while searching unceasingly for his own identity; to be more idealistic, artistic, generous and unselfish than he will ever be again, but also the opposite; self-centered, egotistic, calculating" (Freud, 1958). She speaks of the adolescent's inability to bear frustrations, especially in feelings of love-hate, the experience of isolating words from affect, the narcissistic withdrawal, the tendency for projection, the intermittent feelings of destructive hopelessness, acting out tendencies, and lack of insight. She comments that (1959), "adolescents may change rapidly from one of these emotional positions to the next, exhibit all simultaneously or in quick succession." Adolescents are normally inconsistent or unpredictable. However, consistency and predictability are essential to successful mothering.

Characteristics of Mothering

The ability to mother, as defined by Teresa Benedek (1956), refers "to the many and practical attitudes necessary to take care of a child and guide its maturation and primary learning. Motherliness is the characteristic quality of a woman's personality which supplies the emotional energy for maintaining the tasks of mothering. However, motherliness is not a function of childbearing alone." Benedek states further "that the psychodynamic tendencies which motivate maternal behavior, the wish to feed the infant, to succor, originate in the symbiotic relationship which the mother individual has experienced with her own mother. The term symbiosis signifies a continual reciprocal interaction between mother and child." This symbiosis is necessary in the early stages of a child's development—the first few weeks and months of life. Therefore, it is important to consider the adolescent's relationship to her own mother, which will help shape the way in which the teenager establishes this early symbiotic relationship with her own child. This process bonds mother and baby in a loving, trusting relationship that provides the baby with the security and self-confidence he or she needs to develop into a competent toddler. Only then will the child be comfortable in exploring and experiencing the process of separation and individuation.

It has been further theorized that the mother's ability to take care of her offspring and guide its maturation and primary learning has a direct relation to her maturity. The amount and kind of maternal care any mother is able to provide for an infant is dependent on her conscious and unconscious feelings and attitudes about having a baby, her knowledge of child care and child development, being a mother, and the growing child itself. Various stages in her child's development arouse fantasies, conflicts, and anxieties and are linked with the same period in the mother's childhood, and thus play a role in determining her relationship with her baby. The mother who delighted in the care of her young infant may react with withdrawal when her toddler becomes active and begins to show independence. Conversely, when the toddler does become more independent, he or she may gain admiration from the mother who did not find satisfaction in caring for the child in infancy.

From our experience, the young mothers showed more problems in mothering when the infant become a toddler, i.e., no longer dependent, but beginning to walk and to attempt separation from his mother. This is not to say that the first year of life was problem-free. In fact, we saw our patients interpret their infants' age-appropriate behaviors such as whining, spitting-up, and throwing toys as deliberate and hostile acts. Furthermore, some young mothers who had not wanted to be pregnant and have a child were seen to be resentful of the constraints imposed by the responsibilities of childrearing.

When this happened we found it helpful to listen carefully to their complaints, to reflect back on their wishes and hopes, and then to offer our support and encouragement as they looked realistically at what they might be able to do to achieve their goals. This frequently could not be done in just a few interviews but came about after a relationship of trust was established. As adolescents tend to be very concrete and see situations in their totality, our help often took the form of helping them break things down into smaller segments, for example, accepting a part-time job versus working full-time, agreeing to an abbreviated nurses' aide course versus a full-time 2-year nursing course, or attending a school for just a few courses, perhaps in the evening rather than on a full-time basis. When it came to constraints on their social lives, we tried to counsel them to agree to go out for a prescribed period of time versus the freedom of staying away from home for an undetermined number of hours. In essence, our help was directed toward assisting the teenage mothers we worked with to accept and learn the skill of compromise.

As we witnessed it, the young mother's anger displayed toward the child—for example, anger at whining, spitting, and throwing of toys, all appropriate behavior for infants—is often misplaced anger, projected onto the infant but derived from anger at her own parents or even at herself.

Helping a young mother to understand and deal with this anger and her negative reactions to her child's behavior took a period of time and could only be achieved after a trusting relationship was formed. We found that efforts to correct her or to give her didactic material on child development were usually not effective until the young woman felt her own frustration was understood and some of her needs for nurturance and acceptance were met. The behaviors of the young child are primitive in nature and often stirred up the same primitive responses in the young mother. If her hold over her own aggressive impulses was not secure, she was inclined to meet her child's aggression in kind.

Role Modeling   Having the adolescent watch staff interact with the whining, spitting child and their demonstration of diversion techniques were very effective, along with giving the young mother a chance to share, without fear of retribution or criticism, understanding of how her child's behaviors made her feel. Letting her know that the role of mothering can be a frustrating, nerve-wracking job, but that there are techniques that can be used to modify her child's behavior, will help her to achieve the appropriate feeling of power needed in the mother-child relationship. Letting her see the pleasure that can be derived from mutually satisfying mother-child relationships can be reinforcing and can encourage more effective parental behavior.

The Adolescent as a Mother

Many teenagers may have the potential for motherliness that Benedek speaks of; however, for some, resolution of their adolescent problems may have to be more completely achieved before motherliness is possible. The normal task for the adolescent girl is to establish her own identity, detach herself from her own parents, especially to work through her dependent feelings with respect to her mother and cathect a new object. Usually, she displaces these feelings to parent substitutes, i.e., to persons older than herself (caring professionals become effective role models), to peer leaders, or peer groups. A few adolescent girls deal with the anxieties over their dependent feelings by fleeing into premature pregnancies. They want a feeling of freedom, a new sense of independence from the parent; yet, unfortunately, a greater dependence for the necessities of life often follows. Too frequently the young mother finds she has lost what little independence she had and has become even more dependent on her mother, particularly for child care so that she can return to school. Now she is no longer free to linger after school with her friends, stop off for a soda, or go to a party on an impulse—she has a child to take care of, and she must make child care plans.

Developmental Tasks of the Toddler and the Associated Problems for Adolescent Mothers

Looking now at the infant and his or her development, we know that the period of one to three years is marked by major maturational events that affect the closeness and quality of the relationship with the mother, upon whom the child remains quite dependent for both physical and emotional support. Two of the well-known events that are often distorted or misunderstood by the young mothers we see are walking, with its obvious potential for physical independence, and talking, which allows the child some beginning control over its environment. At times there is an exaggeration, by the mother, of the child's ability to walk, with expectations beyond his or her capacities in the areas of endurance and speed or in the unattended use of steps and stairs. Some mothers no longer feel the necessity to carry their infant once it is walking. They are tired of the infant's dependence on them. Fourteen-year-old Andria came to clinic laughing and talking with a friend, with her 14-month-old son, Calvin, trailing, falling, and wailing half a block behind. He had been walking alone only 6 to 8 weeks. When it was suggested that she might carry him, she said, "He can walk, can't he? He's heavy and I'm tired." This young woman had no baby carriage. We listened to how tired she was carrying him around all the time, but at the same time she was helped to understand his immaturity and discomfort. She was also helped to obtain a stroller.

In contrast, we see mothers like Mary, who could not tolerate separation from her toddler and kept her daughter passive on her lap and close to her breasts most of the day. The child had few toys and little verbal interaction, but sucked a pacifier and kneaded her mother's breasts during many of her waking hours. Mary needed her child to remain in this infantile stage to meet her own needs and only allowed appropriate separation after intensive intervention focused on her own great need for nurturance.

Ruby, a 14-year-old mother with an IQ score of 50, did not like her baby, held her away from her, and pinched her to make her cry. Intensive social service support and parenting education, including child development, helped to establish rapport and trust between mother and child and a mutually reinforcing and enjoyable relationship.

Especially significant is the development of the comprehension of the word "*no*" at around 16 months and the use of language to express aggression. Defiance is then made easier for the toddler. Unfortunately, this is often interpreted by the young mother as bad or evil behavior, willfully executed. Those who find their toddler's defiance intolerable often react with a physical rather than an oral reprimand and slap, spank, or threaten the child with a belt. Telling the young mother not to hit is not sufficient. Letting her talk about how she feels when her youngster defies her and modeling other techniques for modifying behavior were found to be more successful.

Bowel training, which becomes physiologically possible at roughly the same time as comprehension of the word "*no*," gives the child more control over his or her body but also leads to defying mother in the classical bowel struggle. It is often very hard for young mothers to tolerate the child who sits on the pot and then gets up and has a bowel movement in its pants. They also find it difficult to have patience with the toddler who verbalizes the need to sit on the pot frequently but then cannot produce. Often the pot is used for punishment, which is counterproductive. The child is made to sit upon it for long periods as punishment for messing in the diaper.

One of the tasks of the child during the period from 1 to 3 years is to gain more control over impulses—the messing and sadistic but especially the aggressive ones. The temper tantrums of the "terrible twos" is an example of how difficult this task may be. Most adolescent mothers do not know what to do with a tantrum, even though, and perhaps because, they may still be having them with their own mothers. The toddler continues to demand closeness from the mother in the area of feeding and desires to be soothed and carried, at the same time demonstrating an ability to tolerate some absence. These rapid shifts between dependence and independence are often confusing to young mothers who lack information about child development and who are expressing similar feelings with respect to achieving independence from their own parents.

Similarities Between Adolescent and Toddler

Let us look now at the similarities between an adolescent and a toddler. The adolescent, like the toddler, is undergoing significant and rapid maturational changes, both hormonal and psychosocial. In preadolescence and early adolescence there is a rapid increase in the quantity of impulses, not only sexual but also aggressive, and a rekindling of the messing impulses (cluttered rooms, etc.) from the toddler stage. The major task of early adolescence, for the female, is the painful severance of the tie to her mother. We are asking that, at the same time as the adolescent mother severs the bond with her mother, she establish a bond with her infant. Perhaps this conflict is among the reasons why very young adolescent mothers usually have so much difficulty in mothering.

Some potential interlocking points between an adolescent mother and her toddler might be the following:

1. The very imperfectly controlled impulses of the toddler threaten the teenager, especially the young adolescent who is threatened by her own shaky controls. At times she might not find it possible to allow the toddler to express him- or herself and would tend to be harshly prohibiting.

    For instance, Andria, the 16-year-old mother of a 15-month-old toddler, decided one day she could not stand to change diapers anymore. She told her son he had to use the pot and beat him each time he soiled his pants. He quickly learned to use the potty, but then we observed that he fell off his growth curve because he refused to eat.

2. When the teenager has to help her toddler to form his conscience about body control during toilet training, she is at the same time often struggling with her own conscience and the controls she feels were put upon her by her own mother. This raises the possibility that she might unconsciously foster rebellion or lack of training in her child, especially if her mother is helping her to bowel train the toddler.

3. Care of the hygiene or health of the toddler may also present difficulties to the teenage mother, whose mother may still be very involved in doing these things for her. Edna was never able to bring her new daughter to the Cardiology Clinic for evaluation of a probable congenital heart defect. She broke at least seven appointments over a 21-month period. Her own mother had had a similar pattern of failing to bring Edna into the Cardiology Clinic for her own cardiac difficulty. Some mothers care for their children the way they were cared for by their own mothers, who also may have been teenage mothers. They have ghosts in their nurseries, to borrow Selma Fraiberg's apt phrase (Fraiberg et al., 1975). The delay in taking full responsibility for the care of the body is often the last residue of infantilism between child and mother, and gets resolved late in adolescence. It is difficult to take care of someone else's body when

you are trying to resolve your own conflicts and to take proper care of your own.

A study involving 23 young mothers, age 15 years and under, who delivered their babies in 1980 and were registered in our follow-up program provided insight into the problems of very young mothers (Bierman and Bierman, 1985). We reviewed medical staff notes, observations, diagnoses, and comments that provided information on the child care provided by these mothers. It should be kept in mind that they had received prenatal instruction and were continuing to have postnatal instruction on infant feeding. Twelve mothers were recorded as giving inappropriate feedings to their infants. Five children were judged overweight and six underweight. One child developed pica and another failure to thrive. Fourteen developed nutritional anemia. Three developed sleep difficulties, and there was evidence of lack of adequate skin and body care in eight.

Only one of the 23 girls kept all 10 of the scheduled appointments for her child. Eleven missed two. Ten missed four or more. Two girls missed 10 and 11 initial and rescheduled appointments. Several of the children were behind on routine immunizations because of missed appointments. One problem of great concern was the lack of compliance with care for acute illness, for example, failure to give antibiotics according to directions, for conditions such as acute otitis media.

The pattern of inconsistent care, for baby and self, was already evident before delivery, as it was noted that only 9 of the 23 girls had registered for prenatal care during their first trimester, 9 waited until the fifth or sixth month, and 2 until the last trimester. Clearly, very young mothers with limited knowledge, resources, and good role models, in an inner city population are at extraordinary risk for inadequate parenting, perhaps because they were and are, themselves, poorly parented and poorly supervised by their own mothers. There seemed to be a correlation between those mothers who appeared at the clinic dirty and disheveled and the babies who were also unclean. Some of these mothers, who, after 3 years in the program, were no longer as deeply involved in the adolescent development struggle, were observed to dress themselves and their children with more care and cleanliness and to provide more considerate care for their toddlers.

4. The teenager may shift her dependency feelings from her mother to her toddler and thus not let the toddler be independent enough for optimal development. Conversely, during the clinging phase of the toddler, the clinging may pose too much of a threat to the mother, and she may force the child to a degree of independence inappropriate for his age. For example, Tina, whose child was walking at 11 months, could not understand why she became tired after a short distance and needed to be carried. She was often seen walking down the street dragging her by the arm. At the office she expected the child to be examined and receive immunizations without any need to be comforted by her. Very concrete explanations and examples from her own experience helped to modify her behavior.

The young child and the adolescent share a common problem, the inability to control impulses, the child over his or her motor outflow and the adolescent over her emotional outflow. Ernest Jones (1950), in a pioneer paper on adolescence, expressed his feeling that adolescence recapitulates infancy and stated that the precise way in which a given person will pass through the necessary stages in adolescent development is, to a great extent, determined by the form of his or her infantile development. These are two very vulnerable ages. The adolescent mother's developmental tasks are such that, theoretically, they make it difficult for her to give optimal mothering to her child to assure adequate development for both the child and herself. Professional intervention, parenting education, and psychosocial support are frequently needed during the first few years after the infant's birth. This is an important investment in the future of both mother and child.

As noted, an important intervention is supportive counseling, directed toward interpretation of behavior and feelings, which helps the adolescent develop insight and define goals. Guiding and allowing the adolescent to think about herself, as well as her child, are necessary for the optimal growth of both parent and child. We must let her know that she is important, and we must attend to and understand her dual role, a young woman in the midst of adolescent development and a young mother carrying the responsibility of a new life.

Summary

The role of the social worker in a comprehensive adolescent health program is a challenging one, requiring many skills, including the ability to be both a role model and a surrogate parent to the adolescent.

This chapter has included some of our thinking, which evolved as a result of our experience with many hundreds of urban adolescents, as well as some interventions we found to be helpful. The social worker's daily observations can contribute to the ongoing preventive and primary health care of these young people and their children, the education of staff members, and to research efforts directed toward a greater understanding of the interventions needed to assist the optimal physical and psychological growth of this vulnerable population.

Social workers are essential to effective, comprehensive adolescent pregnancy and parenting programs. They assist in the resolution of crisis situations, which are of frequent occurrence in disadvantaged, urban populations. Of even greater and longer-lasting benefit is the personal support and counseling provided to pregnant and parenting adolescents and their parents. This can have long-lasting effects in optimizing the development of both the adolescents and their children. There is limited reimbursement for crisis oriented social service through Medicaid, but none at all for the *preventive* education and counseling aspects of their work. This is yet another example of the bias in our society and government toward emergency services in crisis situations rather than toward prevention, which would improve the quality of life and cost less, in the long run.

18

Parenting Education

Rosalie Streett

The objective of this chapter is to describe the educational component of the comprehensive Johns Hopkins Adolescent Parenting Program (TAC) described in Chapter 16. Here we attempt to address some of the questions raised over the years as to how such an education program can be integrated into a hospital clinic setting that provides preventive and acute health care, including inpatient services, for its adolescent and infant patients. It should be emphasized that the TAC program was designed with a broad preventive focus, based on our perception that health and development are strongly affected by interactions between biological/health and family/environmental factors (see Chapter 2). A socially impoverished environment puts many of the children and adolescents who live within it at developmental risk. They are, on the one hand, at risk for more frequent and more serious illness (Egbuonu and Starfield, 1982), and, on the other, resources in terms of information and material needs available to their mothers are likely to be inadequate to either prevent or manage health and developmental problems if they arise. Thus, to help offset these problems, a special clinic was established in which health and parenting education and social services were equal partners with medical care, coordinated by an individual case management system. As shown in Chapter 16 and by Duggan et al. in Chapter 19, comparison of health care indicators demonstrated that this approach produced results superior to those of a concurrent, more traditional Johns Hopkins program serving other pregnant adolescents and teenage mothers and their infants. Whereas Chapter 17 dealt with psychosocial screening and special intervention for those with individual problems requiring a social worker's skills, the education described here reached all young mothers in the program.

Background

In 1977, with funding from grants from the Office of Child Development and the Health Care Financing Agencies, parenting education and social services were added to the follow-up component of the Johns Hopkins Adolescent Pregnancy and Parenting (TAC) Program. Prior to this time, adolescent parents who had delivered in the Johns Hopkins Adolescent Pregnancy Program (HAC) were encouraged to continue their own and their children's primary care at Hopkins, and a limited program of parenting education was put into place. It soon became apparent that in order to support and strengthen young people in their often conflicting dual roles of parents and adolescents, a more carefully crafted, intensive effort was needed. Therefore, an educator with extensive background both in early childhood and adolescent educational program design and implementation was hired to develop a curriculum for use with teen parents in the clinic. The program would consist of group and individual sessions and would occur at the time of the young parent's primary care/preventive health visit. The research question to be answered was whether or not a program of parenting education offered during clinic visits could be effective enough to offset what was in many cases a lifetime of negative parenting experiences.

Because all of the parents enrolled in the clinic were 18 years or younger at the time their children were delivered, it was particularly challenging to develop and implement a program that would take into account both their youth and the fact of their status as parents to their own children while they were children still in their own parents' homes. However, if the services were to be successful, this fact of life had to serve as the underpinning of the program, guiding the development of the curriculum and its implementation. As a result, the parent education program included:

- Information and services that all adolescents needed in order to negotiate their own teen years effectively
- Materials presented in a manner that would support and respect the grand-parents, whose authority in their own homes must be maintained
- Teaching methods that recognized and capitalized upon the developmental stages of young parents
- A curriculum that encouraged the healthy social, emotional, cognitive, and physical development of babies, 0 to 3 years

In examining other attempts to educate young parents in a clinic setting, we noted that, for the most part, the health care provider was assigned the task. It seemed to become an expanded form of anticipatory guidance, occurring in the examining room at the time of the well-child check. Occasionally, a program brought together a group of parents for special group sessions. Furthermore, it seemed that most programs provided special services to young parents until their children were between six weeks and six months old. After that time, the parents became a part of a regular clinic population, with no additional preventive services.

The TAC program was different in many respects, including coverage. The clinic accepted adolescents who had delivered in the prenatal program and provided them and their children primary and acute care until the children reached three years of age. Occasionally an adolescent parent who had not delivered within the HAC program was permitted to enroll in the program, but this was rare. Fathers were encouraged to come to clinic visits with the mothers and babies, and to participate in the educational sessions.

How Educational Services Were Integrated into the Clinic Visit

It is extremely difficult to provide meaningful educational services to parents within the context of a busy clinic that serves the health care needs both of adolescents and their children. In order to achieve this goal, careful planning, a dedicated staff, and additional resources were needed. The basic preventive health service provided for the young parents and their children included:

1. Preventive health examination for children at 2 weeks, 2, 4, 6, 9, 12, 15, 18, 21, 24, 30, and 36 months, including immunizations as needed
2. Family planning visits for mothers every 6 months and whenever needed, with sexual activity and contraceptive use explored at each well-child visit
3. An intake interview with a social worker; additional interviews every 6 months and as needed
4. Access to the WIC Program, i.e., the Supplemental Nutrition Program for Women, Infants, and Children, screening, nutritional counseling, and referral every 6 months
5. Health and parenting education groups at each preventive health care visit and individual sessions as needed
6. Referrals for acute and chronic social, emotional, nutritional, and physical problems to program staff and to other resources as needed

The health and parenting educator assisted in the delivery of this more comprehensive service and ensured that parents would be able to participate in an educational group experience at each preventive health visit. The educator was also responsible for providing individual educational sessions on an as-needed basis to parents who had limited ability to learn, who were particularly at risk for some reason, were experiencing a crisis, or whose children had a developmental or chronic health problem. Education was delivered in the waiting room, classroom, office, home, or any other site that afforded an opportunity for intervention. Materials were developed on a reading and interest level appropriate for young parents, and new techniques were tried in order to maximize learning in the busy, often threatening, clinic setting.

The way in which parents were scheduled for appointments had to be rethought and revised. This was achieved through scheduling babies of similar ages at the same time and making the appointed time for the visit 45 minutes before the children would be seen by the health care provider. Thus, a typical morning's schedule might be:

8:30 AM: Four 2-month-old babies and their parents arrive in the clinic and are registered. The first two pairs, in addition to being registered, receive laboratory services required for the particular visit.

9:00 AM: All four pairs come into the educational group. While this group is occurring, other patients who do not require a group that day are being registered (for example, for acute problems or their follow-up).

9:45 AM: The group ends, and the two patients whose lab work is completed are given physical examinations; the other two patients receive lab work prior to seeing a health care provider. If a member of the group needs private consultation with the educator, or if the educator wants to refer the parent to another professional, the educator sees the patient after the group or makes another appointment for her to return, depending upon the circumstances.

10:00 AM:	The educator begins a second morning group, perhaps this time consisting of two to five parents and their 1-year-old babies. (These children would have been given appointments at 9:45 AM and would have completed the laboratory tests needed).
10:45 AM:	The group ends; some parents linger, or are asked to stay on as described earlier. After the group session, the parents and children visit their pediatrician or pediatric nurse practitioner.
11:00 AM:	The educator checks the schedule to find stragglers who did not fit into either of the groups or who may have come in for an acute problem that requires additional educational intervention.

Examples of mothers who might be sent to the educator for extra individual attention include those whose babies had chronic diaper rash, chronic ear infections, or eating problems; these mothers were sent to the educator for additional reinforcement, beginning with an in-depth interview. A referral might also be indicated for a parent who is a first time oral contraceptive user in need of family planning education or a young mother the social worker or educator identified as in need of individual attention. In the unlikely event that there were no referrals or parents in need of individual education, the educator might go into the clinic waiting room with play materials to engage parents and children in developmentally appropriate play.

As illustrated by the schedule of events of a typical morning, one can see that the role of the educator in a clinic is varied and requires a multitude of skills. The educator enhances and supports the work of the physician, nurse, and social worker, as well as filling the otherwise vacant role of provider of health and parenting education.

Why Groups?

Health and parenting education was offered in small groups, rather than on an individual basis, because group sessions were both cost- and time-efficient. In addition, and perhaps most important to the decision, is the fact that teens learn well from their peers, they like to be with people of the same age and they benefit from knowing that the problems facing them as parents are not uniquely theirs. Individual sessions between an adult authority figure and one adolescent parent take a longer time to show benefits, because the teens are at first somewhat shy and fearful of showing any areas of inadequacy as parents. The inequality of status often hinders the smooth development of an open relationship, and while this can be achieved, it takes more time than one typically has in this setting.

In a group, on the other hand, the atmosphere is more informal, the teen does not feel as much "on the spot," and there are many opportunities to learn from the situations of others. Frequently, the more outgoing parents share their trials and successes fairly readily, and the more introverted teen can maintain an observer status until she feels more comfortable and less threatened. Another advantage of the group setting is that one can readily observe differences in child-rearing styles. When one parent is particularly impatient or particularly understanding, or employs a technique that others would benefit from noting, the group is the ideal vehicle to communicate the advantages or disadvantages of that approach.

For many of the patients who attended the HAC and TAC programs, reading and other conventional methods of teaching were simply ineffective. In small groups, it is natural to use audiovisual materials, practice some role-playing, and engage in lively discussions. In addition, there are always babies with whom the leader can demonstrate various techniques, such as encouraging a baby to vocalize, reach for a rattle, attend to sounds coming from different places, self-feed, and countless other important developmental activities. After the leader demonstrates, the parents can practice the newly learned techniques on their own and others' children. The group is dynamic, and often a lot of fun.

What to Teach and How to Teach It

As stated earlier, among the challenges faced by an educator in a clinic are setting her teaching priorities. If one were teaching in a school or another environment in which the parents attended on a more frequent and regular basis, curriculum design would be much simpler. However, in a well-child clinic, if all goes smoothly, one can count on seeing a parent only 12 times over the course of 3 years. The limitations of the intervention are obvious, but the importance of the contacts is immeasurable. Educational sessions in the clinic were, for most of the young participants, the only formal health and parenting education received during their children's first 3 years. After that, there were some opportunities if a child was enrolled in a Head Start program or when the child enrolled in kindergarten. However, in these urban populations, the entire first 3 years, perhaps the most important years for setting the stage for later learning and relationship formation, are usually left to chance.

Compounding the difficulty of coping with a new baby and young toddler is the parent's own youth, inexperience, lack of information, and immature state of social and emotional development. Because her developmental stage is one that demands a great deal of her energy, it often competes with her child's needs. In addition, the young mother may not be receiving optimal support from the father of the baby or from her own parents. It is, therefore, imperative that the few adults who see adolescent parents early in the baby's life provide guidance, information, support, and role models for caring about others.

A curriculum was developed that covered topics relevant to the age of the child as well as to the age of the parents. In the curriculum, care was taken not to overwhelm the parent with too much information at one time, despite the realization that the parent would only participate in 12 such sessions during the next 3 years. It was important, therefore, to capitalize on the time together by covering some basic areas and encouraging a relationship of trust and caring between the educator and the parents. During all of the group sessions, the parents' needs for support and information were paramount and always superseded the prescribed curriculum. Following are examples of subjects that were emphasized at the 2-week, 2-, 4-, 6-, and 18-month visits (similar, age-appropriate topics were discussed at other visits):

2 Weeks: The birth experience and the first 2 weeks at home, emphasizing emotional aspects of parenting; soliciting questions from parents; reinforcing basic baby care (particularly feeding, safety, and issues around comforting); supporting mothers who are breast-feeding; how to use the primary health care system and proper use of the emergency room; developing a support system at home; how to access WIC

2 Months: Basic care and feeding of the baby; demonstrations of how to encourage the baby's language development and why this is so important; reinforcing proper feeding, comforting, and safety issues; how to read a thermometer and what to do if a baby is sick (particular emphasis on vomiting and diarrhea and simple home care for mild bouts); topics relevant for the parents themselves, including returning to school or work, finding good child care, and how to balance the baby's needs with their own

4 Months: Reinforcing basic child care, physical, emotional, and cognitive; early child development; how to introduce solid foods; reproductive health care for parents (covered in depth and including teaching about the methods of contraception); the importance of completing one's education

6 Months: Basic care and feeding, reinforcing how to introduce new solid foods; WIC; babyproofing the house for the crawling baby; activities to play with the baby that encourage language and cognitive growth; introducing the concept of stranger anxiety and debunking the myth that a baby who cries when his mother leaves him is "spoiled"; sick child care; discussion of parents' needs and feelings; nutrition for parents on the go

18 Months: All aspects of babyproofing the house for the active toddler, with particular emphasis on preventing accidental injury; ingestion of toxic substances; toilet training and why to postpone it; nutrition and self-feeding; dealing with aggressive behavior and techniques for setting limits; encouraging language; relationship with the father of the baby and/or current male interest in the mother's life (as it relates to issues of discipline and child care)

Education for Health Care

The challenges of providing health and parenting education to adolescent parents are many. The first reality is that most adolescents do not take full responsibility for their *own* health care; unfortunately, teen parents must assume that very adult role both for a baby and frequently for themselves as well. They need to become excellent consumers in the health care system, knowing when to seek out services, what questions to ask of the provider, how to administer medicine, take a temperature, comfort and care for a sick child, and provide proper nutrition. Part of the role of health and parenting education, then, must be to empower the young parent and teach her techniques that will make her a better health care consumer. Here issues of compliance with preventive health visits, appropriate use of the emergency room, communicating with a busy health care provider, keeping a list of nagging nonemergency questions and insisting that they be answered, as well as teaching how to care for a well or sick child, must be dealt with.

Confounding the health education process even further is the necessity of reinforcing the need for young parents to take care of their own health, educational, and social needs. A portion of each session must therefore be devoted to reproductive health issues, both supporting and encouraging the teens to use effective methods of birth control, comply with regular family planning and other preventive health care visits, and teaching them about STDs and AIDS and how their bodies work. In addition, information about resources in the community that will help them return to school, find a job, or provide other support is given in the formal group sessions. Follow-up is done individually, and whenever necessary, referrals are made to the clinic social worker or to an outside agency.

Perspective-Taking

The second reality is that a normal characteristic of adolescence is egocentricity. Under other circumstances, society simply accepts this as a fact of life; we do not, however, admire or see this trait as appropriate in a parent. In providing an educational program for young parents, one must figure their egocentricity into the equation and recognize that information might best be learned if taught from the teen's perspective. This method of teaching, called perspective-taking, is most effective with adolescents; it asks that the teacher, whenever possible, construct the learning from the learner's point of view. For example, an issue of "discipline and the 2-year-old" might begin with a discussion of what makes the teen listen to a teacher. Who are the teachers that she most respects, wants to be with, and listens to? How do "mean" teachers make her feel about herself? How does she act when she resents how she is being treated? The educator then pulls from the discussion those behaviors and characteristics that the teen feels are most unpleasant. These are then translated into parental behaviors, and the session continues from there.

Educational and Home Environment

A third truth is that many of the youngsters who become parents too soon have poor reading skills, live in poverty, and are unmarried. This means that information must be developed that is appropriate to both the reading and interest levels of young parents. Most of the pamphlets that are available from major drug and baby food companies are written at too high a reading level and are illustrated with pictures of adults who appear to live rather mainstream middle-class lives. Teens do not relate to these materials.

To address this problem, we developed many of our own reading materials and posters. The pamphlets developed by the clinic staff were written on a fourth grade reading level, illustrated with simple and appropriate drawings and duplicated on paper of a different color for each topic. They dealt with the issues most commonly confronted by new parents in the first 2 years. A total of 36 pamphlets were developed, each one covering one topic. Some of the topics in the single issue pamphlets were: making a decision about breast-feeding; how to breast-feed or bottle-feed; toilet training; how to take a baby's temperature; how to deal with diarrhea, vomiting, and the common cold; introducing solid foods; how to set limits; how to encourage language development; what are good foods for toddlers; finding child care; and the role of fathers. We felt it was important to have easy-to-read materials for the parents to take home both as a reference for them and to share with their parents and others. The pamphlets were often the only child care and child development resource materials available to the families. Other appropriate books, pamphlets, and articles were also used. Sometimes clinic staff would put together collages, make posters, or write other short booklets to convey a message. The waiting room was the repository for learning materials and provided good wall space for bright, colorful, interesting posters that addressed adolescent as well as infant issues.

A fourth important fact that must be addressed is that most teens live in their parents' homes. Frequently, information and ideas promulgated by the clinic staff are in direct conflict with childbearing techniques used in the teen's home. The educator must be skillful enough to respect the values and ideas of the grandparents while introducing a new way of providing care for children. Simply written, single topic, educational pamphlets given to the adolescent to take home not only reinforce her own learning but help her to counter the often outmoded practices of her mother.

Over the course of time, the clinic collected a number of movies, slides, and filmstrips on topics such as parenting, child development, and sexuality. These were used in group sessions and were always followed by a discussion. Audiovisual materials were never considered a substitute for a group session, but were seen as a means of initiating discussion or as a supplementary means of imparting information.

Support Systems and Reinforcement

Another challenge faced by educators in clinic settings is that there may be long gaps between visits and a resultant lack of follow-through or reinforcement. It is critical that, whenever possible, the young parent is linked to a support system within the community. At other times, sending the parent a short note, a reinforcing article, or merely telephoning can make a great deal of difference. Whenever possible, a system of home visits can help in significant ways.

Home visits are an effective and cost-effective means of delivering services to high-risk families. "Kitchen sink" education has been used successfully throughout history by public health nurses, social workers, and educators. These visits provide the worker with the opportunity to see the child in the context of the family and the family in the context of its community. Too often, office-bound service providers forget how insignificant their agenda is in the lives of high-risk, multiproblem families. Through home visiting, the educator can understand better the many forces that have an impact on the life of the family and can structure more effectively the educational program, make meaningful referrals, and in turn, be viewed more as a friend and ally than as a clinic employee. Olds et al. (1986a and b) have shown that home visits can be helpful in securing compliance with pregnant adolescents. In a different Johns Hopkins demonstration that provided family support and health education to older mothers between routine well-child visits, home visits not only improved compliance with health care for children but significantly reduced hospitalization and neglect/abuse and also reduced health care costs as compared with similar, unvisited controls (Hardy and Streett, 1989).

Role Modeling

An important teaching tool for all parents is role modeling. At all times, therefore, the clinic educator was aware that her interactions with parents and children must be exemplary and reflect nurturing, thoughtful child-rearing practices. As a result, the educator spent a great deal of time in the clinic waiting room when she was not leading a group or conducting an individual session. In this way, all assembled— parents (mothers and fathers), grandparents, and visitors—were able to witness methods of interacting with children that the clinic wished to support.

To ensure that follow-up occurred, educators maintained their own records on each patient, in addition to entering notes in the parents' central clinic records. A satisfactory system utilized large file cards kept in a box in the educator's office. Thus, when a patient came in or called, the information was immediately available and did not require the hospital chart. With today's computerized hospital records, this process may be simplified, but there still may be anecdotal information inappropriate for a hospital chart, yet critical to working effectively with adolescent parents.

How Were the Services Coordinated?

A key to the success of a comprehensive program, delivered in a nontraditional manner, is coordinating services and recognizing the unique talents and abilities of various team members. In addition to the case management system described elsewhere in this volume, the Johns Hopkins model used both a multidisciplinary and transdisciplinary internal referral approach. There were times when it was most effective to refer a patient to another service provider in order to ensure optimal care and make full use of the provider's expertise. At other times, however, the best system was to use another service provider as a consultant. This permitted an adolescent parent who was reluctant to trust others or who had formed a particularly strong attachment to a particular staff person to obtain the information from a "trusted friend."

In order to operationalize this system and continue the case management system that worked well in the HAC program, case conferences were held before each clinic session. All of the patients who were scheduled for that day's clinic were discussed, either briefly or in detail, depending upon the needs of the individual. Each provider came to the conference with her personal notes on the adolescent, in addition to the hospital chart. Service plans were coordinated at that time.

To maintain continuity and to ensure that all adolescent parents would receive all of the services necessary during that visit, a yellow tracking sheet was developed. This sheet consisted of a listing of all possible services provided in the clinic. During the case conference, one of the members of the team checked the appropriate services needed by that parent/child that day and placed the "yellow sheet" on the young mother's/child's chart. Upon registration, the mother was given the form, which was "signed-off" by each provider as a service was delivered. The patient returned the sheet to the registrar at the end of the visit, while making her next appointment. The sheets were checked at the end of the day to ascertain whether or not the patients received the comprehensive, coordinated care planned. The yellow sheet became a familiar tool to both clinic staff and young mothers, and although it seemed cumbersome initially, over time it became a critical part of patient management.

Evaluation of the Educational Component

Prior to introducing the educational program, a needs assessment was carried out to determine the level of parenting and family planning information possessed by young mothers as compared with older teenage mothers and older women in the same population. Adolescent mothers were woefully lacking in information about child development, child care, pregnancy risk and contraception, as were the older individuals tested, to a considerable but lesser extent. These results were used in the design and determination of the content of the TAC educational program. Once the program began, its effectiveness was assessed by a system of pre- and posttests. New mothers were pretested in a group setting. The young teens learned how little they knew and were provided with motivation for learning. Periodically thereafter, at 6 and 12 months after delivery, they were retested, as were mothers in the comparison groups not exposed to the educational program. By the time their children reached 12 months of age, the TAC program mothers' responses indicated considerably greater knowledge in the areas mentioned than that of young mothers in a comparison group, who received only the traditional one-on-one education provided by physicians and nurses at the well-child visit (R Streett and DW Welcher, unpublished data, 1980). The comparisons between the knowledge gained by the first 100 young mothers exposed to the educational program during the year after delivery and controls who had received only traditional instruction from pediatrician and pediatric nurse practitioner were a revelation to the latter providers who had prided themselves on their attention to parent education. The young mothers who had participated in the group educational process were far ahead of the others in knowledge of child care and child development.

Summary

It was possible to design and implement an adolescent and parenting education program as an integral part of a comprehensive primary care program for adolescent mothers and their children. It was well-accepted by patients and staff and contributed in a major way to the effectiveness of the overall project. Unfortunately, educational programs such as this, which both prevent the occurrence of costly medical problems and promote healthy child development during the critical early years, are difficult to carry out. Educational efforts of this kind are not reimbursed by Medicaid as part of a preventive health care program for poor people. Almost all parents, young and old, affluent and poor, recognize the value of preventive health care for their infants and young children; thus, the public clinic, hospital or community-based, is one of the best, if not the best, portal of entry for intervention with poor mothers and their children. Medicaid funding in pediatric and adolescent care must be redirected from more traditional patterns of medical care toward the support of more comprehensive services, which are preventive. Not only is the prevention of problems more humane, it is also cost-effective and, in the long run, less expensive.

19

Comprehensive Versus Traditional Services for Pregnant and Parenting Adolescents
A Comparative Analysis

Anne K. Duggan, Catherine DeAngelis, and Janet B. Hardy

Chapters 11 and 16 describe and evaluate the results of special comprehensive programs for pregnant and parenting adolescents. In this chapter, we compare the results obtained when comprehensive services were provided with those obtained by adolescents served in a special clinic based on a traditional medical care model.

Background

At the time this evaluation was conducted, there were within the Johns Hopkins Medical Institutions two special programs providing prenatal and follow-up services to high-risk pregnant adolescents and their children: the Johns Hopkins Adolescent Pregnancy and Parenting Program (APP, a combination of HAC and TAC) already described, and the Children and Youth Program (C&Y). Inpatient obstetrical care was the same for both groups.

The APP programs provided multiphasic screening and used a multidisciplinary approach to the management of high-risk pregnant adolescents less than 18 years of age (300 to 350/year) and young mothers and their infants up to age 3 years (approximately 470 pairs/year). The program was administered as a single unit with two closely related service components. The Obstetrical Component (HAC) provided care during the prenatal period, ending with the mother's 4-week postpartum visit. The Follow-Up Component (TAC) provided all health care to mothers and their infants beginning at the child's birth and continuing until the infant reached 3 years of age. Their objectives and modus operandi are described in Chapters 11 and 16. Approximately half of the girls enrolled in the HAC program received follow-up care for themselves and their children in the TAC program. They were, in general, the "high-risk" young mothers. The remainder elected to receive follow-up care in their own communities.

The C&Y program was a Title V Children and Youth Project providing continuing, comprehensive care to children and youth residing in a defined 13-census tract area surrounding the Johns Hopkins Hospital. In total, the clinic had an active enrollment of approximately 17,000. Ambulatory care for both medical and dental problems was provided by the program. Routine preventive services, acute illness, and chronic disease care as well as periodic dental screening and dental care were included. Social work staff were an integral part of the program, providing service for acute problems. On a regular basis, specialty consultants visited the primary clinic area to see patients and discuss their problems with the primary care provider. These on-site specialty services included cardiology, orthopaedics, ophthalmology, surgery, dermatology, and otolaryngology.

Annually, about 125 C&Y program enrollees required prenatal and postpartum care from the program's obstetrics and gynecology service, which was staffed by an obstetrician, nurse midwife, family planning nurse, and a licensed nurse practitioner. Continuity of follow-up care was provided to the young mother and her children, at separate visits, through the program's four pediatrician-nurse practitioner teams.

The services that the APP program provided were comprehensive, including psychosocial support and education as well as medical care. The service configuration represents the major distinction between the two programs. The C&Y program, like other more conventional health care resources, provided a wide range of traditional medical services with social service back-up. Physicians and nursing staff provided routine instructions and education during patient visits. The C&Y program was comprehensive in the traditional medical sense. The comprehensive approach used in the HAC and TAC programs was designed to meet the individual developmental needs of pregnant and parenting adolescents and their infants within a clinical environment that emphasized human, educational, and family needs while providing excellent medical care.

In addition to the services themselves, there were differences in the way in which the services were provided. In HAC and TAC but not the C&Y program:

1. A case management system was an integral part of the program, assuring a planned, comprehensive team approach;
2. Health and parenting education services included group discussions using a values clarification format in addition to the standard one-on-one education provided by physicians and nurses; and
3. The Follow-Up Component (TAC) was arranged to provide continuing preventive health care to mother and infant as a unit, at the same visit.

The last major distinction between the two programs was basic to their orientation. While the APP program was developed and implemented specifically for adolescent mothers and their children, the C&Y program served a much larger target population, of which only a small portion (less than 5%) was comprised of adolescent mothers and their children.

Research Objectives

In 1979, the APP program conducted a preliminary evaluation of its effectiveness in meeting program objectives. The results of this evaluation were presented in preceding chapters. Financial constraints limited the size of this preliminary study, and variation in the resources used by control group subjects precluded a detailed cost/benefit analysis of the APP program's services. In contrast, the similarity of APP and C&Y program objectives and their parenting adolescent populations, coupled with their organizational differences, provide the ideal elements for a "natural experiment", i.e., evaluation of the impact of the APP program's special services and organization on both immediate and longer-term adolescent pregnancy outcomes (Campbell and Stanley, 1963). This was the primary goal of this APP-C&Y program comparative evaluation. A secondary goal was to replicate and extend the preliminary evaluation.

Program evaluation research can have many applications. Among those cited by Rossi et al (1979) are process evaluation, including program planning and program monitoring, and outcome, i.e., client impact assessment and economic efficiency. The APP-C&Y program comparative evaluation is limited to the areas of outcome assessment and economic efficiency.

Outcome Evaluation

Relative program impact is assessed through measurement of patient outcomes associated with four of the stated objectives of the APP program:

1. To optimize adolescent and infant health and development (so that these young families may become well adjusted, independent, and self-sustaining)
2. To prevent "repeated" pregnancy until a more favorable maternal age and until the child is wanted
3. To prevent school dropout with its subsequent limitation on employment
4. To prevent child neglect and abuse, including abuse of the adolescent mother herself

Suchman (1973) has noted that program objectives can be classified in numerous ways, one of which is in terms of their generality. This is evident in the APP program objectives. While the last three objectives are precise, the first is quite general. Implied in it is a series of assumptions linking program efforts (immediate goals) to patient behaviors (intermediate goals) and, finally, to patient health status, social, and economic outcomes (ultimate goals). An example of this implied progression for one program effort, i.e., nutrition education, is shown in Figure 19-1.

An evaluation can focus on any level of program objective. Generally, it is easier to study lower-level process objectives, and this is the most common type of evaluation. The primary danger here is that the means to the ultimate goal will be viewed as ends in themselves, and the linkage from effort to effect will be patently assumed without rigorous testing. On the other hand, evaluation of ultimate goals may lead to erroneous conclusions if the measured effects result from efforts or forces outside the program. This threat can be controlled for or minimized through study design and/or analysis.

For the most part, the APP-C&Y program comparative evaluation focuses on ultimate goals. This is shown in Table 19-1, which displays the relationship between program objectives, the null hypotheses to be tested in measuring relative program effectiveness in meeting the objectives, and selected dependent variables and indicators for each outcome.

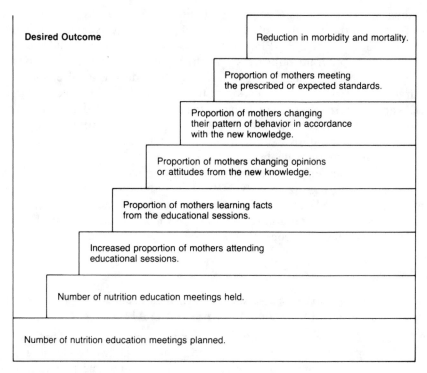

Desired Outcome

Reduction in morbidity and mortality.

Proportion of mothers meeting the prescribed or expected standards.

Proportion of mothers changing their pattern of behavior in accordance with the new knowledge.

Proportion of mothers changing opinions or attitudes from the new knowledge.

Proportion of mothers learning facts from the educational sessions.

Increased proportion of mothers attending educational sessions.

Number of nutrition education meetings held.

Number of nutrition education meetings planned.

Figure 19-1   The stepwise progression of program goals from specific process objectives to the desired outcome objective is presented using nutrition as an example.

Economic Efficiency

The second portion of the evaluation addresses the issue of economic efficiency. This is approached through measurement and comparison of the costs to deliver medical, social, and educational services in the APP and C&Y programs, and the benefits received by enrollees in the two programs.

Relative economic efficiency of the APP and C&Y programs is assessed through comparison of their estimated program costs and the benefits to their enrollees. Benefits are measured in terms of illness visits and adequacy of preventive health care (indicators of health status) and likelihood of repeat pregnancy, school completion, and welfare dependency.

Methods

Study Design

This comparative study of the structure, process, and outcomes of the APP and C&Y programs utilized a posttest only and a nonequivalent control group or static group design. Although this design does not control for some sources of invalidity (e.g., maturation, selection, mortality, and interaction of selection and mortality), it does control for history, testing, instrumentation, and regression, and represents the most powerful design available, given the inability to assign subjects randomly to the two programs.

Table 19-1   Program Objectives, Study Hypotheses, and Dependent Variables/Indicators

Program objective	Study hypothesis	Dependent variables/indicators
To optimize adolescent and infant health and development so that these young families may become well-adjusted, independent, and self-sustaining.	H_1: *There is no difference in the incidence of adverse pregnancy outcomes between APP and C&Y program enrollees*	Frequency of: Perinatal mortality Gestation less than 37 wk Birthweight less than 2,500 g Resuscitation Length of stay following delivery
	H_2: *There is no difference in the incidence of complications of pregnancy, labor, and delivery between APP and C&Y program enrollees.*	Complications of pregnancy Number of hospitalizations prior to delivery Frequency of: Preeclampsia Pyelonephritis Urinary tract infection Venereal disease Insufficient weight gain Low hematocrit (<32 mm) Complications of labor delivery Frequency of: Cesarean section Dystocia Premature rupture of the membranes Use of oxytocin Fetal monitoring Umbilical cord complications Excessive postpartum hemorrhage
	H_3: *There is no difference in morbidity between APP and C&Y program enrollees following delivery*	Mother and child Frequency of: Hospitalizations Emergency room visits Hospitalization(s), length of stay
	H_4: *There is no difference in preventive health care use by APP and C&Y program enrollees*	Mother Number family planning visits Method of contraception used Completeness of contraception use Child Number of well-child visits
To prevent "repeated" pregnancy until a more favorable age and the child is wanted	H_5: *There is no difference in the rate of repeat pregnancy between APP and C&Y program enrollees*	Number of repeat pregnancies at 1, 2, and 3 years postpartum
To prevent school dropout with its subsequent limitation on employment	H_6: *There is no difference in the school completion rate of APP and C&Y program enrollees*	Last grade completed at time of delivery and at 2 years postpartum Educational aspirations at time of delivery and at 2 years postpartum School status at 2 years postpartum Employment status since birth of index child Sources of income at 2 years postpartum Medical Assistance (MA) status of mother and child since birth of index child
To prevent child neglect and abuse, including abuse of adolescent	H_7: *There is no difference in the incidence of child neglect and abuse between APP and C&Y program enrollees*	Number of reports to the Maryland State Department of Social Services for: Child abuse Child neglect

Selection of Subjects

A precise definition of the available sample was developed, limiting selection to those enrollees who met the following criteria:

1. The pregnancy terminated between January 1, 1979 and December 31, 1980.
2. The APP or C&Y program enrollee had at least one visit for prenatal care within the program.
3. The enrollee was 18 years of age or younger at the time of pregnancy termination.
4. The pregnancy was not terminated by a therapeutic abortion.

The final sample of 867 black adolescents consisted of 623 APP program enrollees and 244 C&Y program enrollees. Within the APP program group, 343 adolescent mothers were enrolled for prenatal care only, and 280 were enrolled in both the program's prenatal and follow-up component. While all subjects in each group had delivered by the end of the study, periods of follow-up varied, depending on date of delivery. The clinic samples did not differ significantly by age at delivery. They did, however, differ by race ($p < .001$), with a larger proportion of white adolescents in the APP program group than in the C&Y program group (12.0% and 2.9%, respectively), which led to the decision to limit the analyses to black subjects only. There were 542 in the APP program group and 236 in the C&Y. Previous research in the area of adolescent pregnancy has demonstrated the importance of controlling for race. The small number of white adolescents in the C&Y program group ($n = 7$) precluded meaningful clinic group comparisons within this racial group.

Sources of Data

Data were collected in two major activities: review and abstracting of existing sources of information and interviews with a subsample of mothers in each of the two clinic programs; record review was conducted from January 1982 through January 1983 and patient interviews in the last portion of the study period.

Although numerous existing sources of information were identified and used in the record review process, none of them had been developed specifically for research purposes. Because of this, and because patient health resource utilization extended to facilities outside the Johns Hopkins Hospital, the interview was of particular value, both to validate the completeness and accuracy of information contained in existing sources and to gather data not otherwise available.

Existing Sources of Data   A variety of existing data sources was used, as displayed in Table 19-2. The computerized information system of the Department of Obstetrics and Gynecology provided the information needed to test hypotheses related to prenatal care, labor, delivery, and pregnancy outcome. Pregnancies terminating in fetal death at less than 20 weeks gestation are not included in the system; for these, data were obtained from medical records.

Hospital utilization and its associated costs were measured using information gathered for the hospital's in- and outpatient billing systems, the computer system of the Department of Pediatrics (C&Y program), clinic appointment logs, and medical records.

Table 19-2   Sources of Data for Major Variable Groups

Variable Group	Computer information systems						Medical records	APP program appt. log	Social worker
	Ob-gyn summary	Inpt billing	Outpt billing	Fertility control clinic	Pediatric records C&Y	APP program	Medical records	APP program appt. log	Social worker
Complications of pregnancy	X						X		
Complications of labor and delivery	X						X		
Adverse pregnancy outcomes	X						X		
Hospitalizations		X					X		
Inpatient utilization costs		X							
Clinic use			X		X		X	X	
Emergency room use			X		X		X		
Outpatient utilization costs			X						
Family planning/contraceptive use						X	X	X	X
Well-child care			X			X	X	X	
Immunization/screening status					X		X		
Repeat pregnancies	X			X		X	X		
School enrollment						X	X		X
Employment/sources of income							X		X
Reported child abuse/neglect							X		X

For each adolescent mother, repeat pregnancies were identified using the OB-GYN computer system, the APP program computer file of repeat pregnancies, patient medical records, and the computer files of the hospital's Fertility Control Clinic (abortion data).

The only existing sources of information on school enrollment, employment, and sources of income were the medical record and social work records. The completeness of information contained in the former varied widely by source and by enrollee. Overall, more information was routinely documented for the APP program enrollees. This was particularly true for social work records. The APP program enrollees saw their social worker on a regular basis, and her records were both standardized and highly detailed. The C&Y program enrollees, on the other hand, saw a social worker only when they so requested or when referred by a physician or nurse practitioner. As a result, social work records existed for only a portion of the C&Y program sample, and those that were available were usually limited to information relating to a specific episode or problem.

Finally, child abuse and neglect were operationally defined as instances reported to the state's Department of Social Services. Such instances were identified from medical records, the files of individual social workers, and a log of reported instances maintained by the social worker staff of the Department of Pediatrics.

Interviews with Adolescent Mothers   A major objective of the interview procedure was to collect information on the pregnancy experience subsequent to the index birth, schooling, employment, and sources of income, particularly welfare utilization. Existing data tended to be unreliable in these areas. In addition, health care utilization, sexual activity, and contraceptive use were queried.

As resources for interviewing were limited, subsamples of program enrollees were selected. These included young mothers who, between November 1, 1981 and January 31, 1982, had been followed 31 to 36 months since their 1979 index delivery. There were 97 APP and 104 C&Y enrollees who met these criteria. The interviews were conducted by personnel separate from the clinics, at home visits, following informed consent in writing. Because of a high degree of residential mobility, it was not possible to make contact with all subjects. One APP and two C&Y mothers refused to be interviewed. The overall response rates were 85% (82 of 97) APP and 81% (84 of 104) C&Y adolescents. Within each clinic sample, chi-square analysis was used to test for differences between respondents and nonrespondents with regard to age at delivery, school status, and parity. No significant differences were found.

Results

Description of the Study Sample

Although the study subjects were not randomly assigned to the two clinic programs for their prenatal care, they were found to be very similar in terms of age at delivery and pregnancy history. There was no significant difference in the age distributions of the two clinics, although the C&Y program enrollees tended to be slightly younger, with 11.0% 14 years of age or less at the time of delivery as opposed to only 6.5% within this age group in the APP program sample.

The two clinic samples were remarkably similar with regard to pregnancy history. Among study subjects, approximately one-quarter in each clinic sample had had at least one prior conception. The proportion of subjects who had a prior live birth was small in each clinic, 9.3% in the APP program and 9.7% in the C&Y program. Within the APP program, 3.8% of enrollees had a prior fetal death. This is not significantly different from the corresponding rate for the C&Y program, 3.4%. Finally, the clinic samples were virtually identical with regard to abortion history. Within the APP program sample of subjects, 13.7% had had a prior induced abortion as compared to 13.5% in the C&Y program sample.

The two clinic samples were also compared on height, prepregnant weight, and level of schooling at the time of delivery. No significant differences between the clinic samples were found. They were all residents of poor, socially disadvantaged neighborhoods.

Health Outcomes

Pregnancy Outcomes   The first study hypothesis relates to the incidence of adverse pregnancy outcomes between APP and C&Y program enrollees.

The hypothesis was tested first by comparing the proportion of pregnancies in each clinic group that resulted in fetal death, neonatal death, and perinatal death. Multiple births ($n = 8$) were excluded because of their small frequency.

The small numbers of fetal and neonatal deaths in both groups mandate caution in the interpretation of results.

For each outcome, two rates were calculated. For the first rate, the denominator was defined as all pregnancies, and for the second rate the denominator was defined as all pregnancies of 20 weeks or longer gestation. The major objective of calculating the second set of rates was to provide data comparable to national statistics. The first set of rates, however, is felt to represent the pregnancy outcome experience of the subjects more accurately. The results of the analysis are presented in Table 19-3. When all pregnancies are included in the analysis, the overall fetal death rate, as well as the neonatal and perinatal mortality rates, are lower among APP program enrollees than C&Y program enrollees. The early fetal death rate is significantly lower ($p < .02$) for APP program enrollees (9.2/1,000 versus 33.9/1,000). The C&Y program enrollees had a lower, but not statistically significant, rate of late fetal death. It should be noted that the C&Y adolescents were long-term enrollees in their program and often sought care for miscarriages, whereas the APP program enrollees did not register until pregnancy was well-established. Therefore, early abortions were infrequently observed.

Within each clinic, the fetal and perinatal mortality rates are markedly different, depending on whether early deaths are included. The rates also vary greatly between clinics, but in opposite directions, for the same reason. As shown in the table, only one-third of the fetal deaths to APP program enrollees occurred prior to 30 weeks gestation, whereas four-fifths of the fetal deaths to C&Y program enrollees occurred during this period.

Table 19-3 Frequency and Rate of Fetal, Neonatal and Perinatal Death in Single Pregnancies of Black Enrollees, by Program

| | *All pregnancies* | | | | |
| | *APP program (N = 542)* | | *C&Y program (N = 236)* | | |
	N	*Rate/1,000*	*N*	*Rate/1,000*	
All fetal deaths	15	27.7	10	42.4	NS
Early[a]	5	9.2	8	33.9	$p < .02$
Late[b]	10	18.4	2	8.5	NS
Neonatal deaths[c]	4	7.4	2	8.5	NS
Perinatal deaths[d]	19	35.1	12	50.8	NS
	All pregnancies >20 wk gestation				
	APP program (N = 537)		*C&Y program (N = 228)*		
	N	*Rate/1,000*	*N*	*Rate/1,000*	
Fetal deaths[b]	10	18.6	2	8.8	NS
Neonatal deaths	4	7.4	2	8.8	NS
Perinatal deaths	14	26.1	4	17.5	NS

NS, not significant.

[a]Fetal deaths occurring prior to 20 weeks gestation.

[b]Fetal deaths occurring at 20 weeks gestation or later.

[c]Infant deaths occurring within the first 28 days after birth.

[d]The total of fetal deaths and neonatal deaths.

Table 19-4   Frequency and Proportion of Selected Indicators of Adverse Pregnancy Outcome in Single Live Births to Black Enrollees, by Program

Indicator	APP program		C&Y program		
	n	*(%)*	*n*	*(%)*	
Birth weight less than 2,500 g	52	(9.9)	37	(16.4)	*p* < .05
Gestational age less than 37 wk	80	(15.4)	33	(14.8)	NS
Resuscitation	39	(7.4)	14	(6.2)	NS

NS, not significant.

Several other indicators of pregnancy outcome were examined, including birth weight, gestational age, and infant resuscitation. The results of this analysis are displayed in Table 19-4. While there was no difference in mean birth weight by program, a significantly larger proportion, 16.4%, of babies born to C&Y program enrollees were less than 2,500 g at birth (*p* < .05). Among APP program enrollees, 9.9% had babies weighing less than 2,500 g, an important difference between groups because of the well recognized relationship between low birth weight (LBW) and adverse outcome for the infant. No differences between the two clinic groups were found with respect to gestational age or the use of resuscitation.

Length of infant hospital stay following delivery was calculated for all single live births to enrollees within each clinic. Preliminary analysis indicated a significantly longer mean length of stay for children born to C&Y program enrollees (6.7 days) than APP program enrollees (4.7 days) (*p* < .01). Within each clinic group, there were several infants with extremely long lengths of stay, but even when such outliers were excluded, the significant difference in mean length of stay remained. Furthermore, at 4 days and at 1, 2, and 3 weeks postbirth, larger proportions of C&Y versus APP program enrollees remained hospitalized (see Table 19-5).

As discussed later, there was a larger proportion of cesarean sections among C&Y program enrollees. Because an infant is usually kept in the hospital until the mother can be discharged, and because mothers with cesarean sections are usually

Table 19-5   Infant Length of Stay following Birth and Single Live Births to Black Enrollees, by Program and Method of Delivery

All deliveries	APP program (n = 526)		C&Y program (n = 226)		
	Mean	(SD)	Mean	(SD)	
Length of stay in days	4.7	(5.6)	6.7	(10.9)	*p* < .01
Length of stay					
>4 days		(36.1)[a]		(43.4)[a]	NS
>7 days		(15.6)		(23.5)	NS
>14 days		(3.8)		(8.4)	NS
>21 days		(2.5)		(6.2)	NS
Vaginal deliveries					
Length of stay in days, $\overline{X}$	3.9	(4.9)	5.2	(9.2)	NS
Cesarean section					
Length of stay in days, $\overline{X}$	8.6	(6.9)	11.5	(14.5)	NS

NS, not significant.

[a]Numbers in parentheses are percentages.

Table 19-6 Frequency and Proportion of Black Enrollees with Selected Indicators of Complications of Pregnancy, by Program

Indicator	APP program		C&Y program		
	n	*(%)*	*n*	*(%)*	
More than 12 prenatal visits	79	(15.2)	41	(18.3)	NS
Hospitalization during pregnancy	29	(5.5)	12	(5.3)	NS
Severe preeclampsia	5	(1.0)	9	(4.0)	$p < .05$
Pyelonephritis	3	(0.6)	3	(1.3)	NS
Urinary tract infection	25	(4.8)	20	(8.8)	$p < .05$
Venereal disease	45	(8.6)	20	(8.8)	NS
Insufficient weight gain[a]	24	(4.7)	8	(5.9)	NS
Hematocrit <32.0 mm	251	(48.0)	148	(65.5)	$p < .001$

NS, not significant.

[a]Insufficient weight gain is defined as a gain of ten pounds or less.

hospitalized longer than those with vaginal deliveries, the analysis was repeated, controlling for the method of delivery. The same, though less pronounced, relationship between program enrollment and length of stay was found, with longer hospitalizations for infants born to C&Y versus APP program enrollees. These findings are consistent with the larger proportion of LBW infants born to C&Y program mothers.

Prenatal Care, Labor, and Delivery The second study hypothesis relates to the incidence of complications of pregnancy, labor, and delivery between APP and C&Y program enrollees.

The first two indicators of complications of pregnancy to be examined were the number of prenatal visits and hospitalizations during pregnancy. As shown in Table 19-6, the two clinic groups did not differ with respect to these variables. A slightly larger proportion of C&Y program enrollees made more than 12 prenatal care visits. The proportion of enrollees admitted to the hospital prior to the onset of labor was virtually the same in the two settings, 5.5% in the APP program and 5.3% in the C&Y program.

Six other complications of pregnancy were examined: severe preeclampsia, pyelonephritis, urinary tract infection, venereal disease, weight gain of ten pounds or less, and a hematocrit of less than 32 mm. Although the clinic groups had similar rates of pyelonephritis, venereal disease, and insufficient weight gain, there were marked differences in their rates for the other three complications. In the APP program, 1.0% of the enrollees suffered severe preeclampsia, as opposed to 4.0% in the C&Y program ($p < .05$). The APP program rate for urinary tract infection was a little over half that of the C&Y program (4.8% versus 8.8%, $p < .05$). Finally, anemia, as measured by low hematocrit levels (<32 mm), was found in 48% of the APP program enrollees and 65.5% of the C&Y enrollees ($p < .001$).

Cesarean section was less frequent among enrollees of the APP program; 16.9% of APP program enrollees had a cesarean section, as opposed to 22.6% of C&Y program enrollees. When repeat cesarean sections are excluded, the rates are 14.8% for the APP program and 19.9% for the C&Y program. Though not statistically significant, these rates suggest a reduced number of complications among APP program enrollees as a whole.

The clinics' rates for six complications associated with vaginal delivery were also examined: dystocia, premature rupture of the membranes, use of oxytocin, fetal monitoring, umbilical cord complications, and excessive postpartum hemorrhage. No significant differences between the two programs were found, with the exception of postpartum hemorrhage. In the APP program, only 4.2% of the enrollees experienced a blood loss in excess of 500 ml in the first 24 hours following delivery. For the C&Y program enrollees, the rate was 10.1% ($p < .05$).

In summary, the prenatal course of enrollees in the APP and C&Y programs was similar in most of the areas studied. Where there were differences, however, their direction was consistent and supported the alternative hypothesis of fewer adverse pregnancy outcomes and complications of pregnancy, labor, and delivery among APP than among C&Y program enrollees.

Morbidity During Follow-Up   The third study hypothesis relates to differences in morbidity between APP and C&Y program enrollees following delivery.

Hospitalizations and emergency department visits over the 3 years following the child's birth were used as indicators of morbidity for both adolescent mothers and their children. In- and outpatient billing files served as the data sources. For this portion of the evaluation, the APP program study group was limited to those mother-child pairs who enrolled in the program's follow-up component.

To standardize and maximize the period of observation, the study samples were divided into three groups, based on the child's date of birth. For children born in the first 6 months of 1979, utilization data were collected for the first 3 years of life. The period of observation for births occurring between July 1, 1979 and June 30, 1980 was 2 years. Only one year of utilization data were collected for births occurring in the latter half of 1980.

Hospital Admission   For the adolescent mothers, marked differences between the programs were found with respect to inpatient service utilization. Table 19-7 presents a summary of the hospitalization data. In each year following the birth of the index child, the overall hospitalization rate was lower for APP program mothers than for C&Y program mothers. In the first year following delivery, 6.8% of the APP program patients were admitted to the hospital one or more times. During the same period, 13.3% of the C&Y program mothers were admitted. Hospitalization rates for both groups increased in the second year following delivery, to 13.7% for the APP program and 21.8% for the C&Y program. Finally, in year 3, 11.6% of the APP program mothers experienced one or more hospitalizations, less than half the C&Y program rate of 23.7% for that period. During the full 3-year period following the birth of the index child, 30.4% of the APP program mothers were admitted at least once. In the C&Y program, nearly one-half of the mothers (47.5%) were hospitalized.

Each hospitalization was categorized as either pregnancy-related or not related to pregnancy. The categorization was based on the service to which the enrollee was admitted. Admissions to the Fertility Control Clinic (for abortion) and the Obstetrical Service were categorized as pregnancy-related, and all others as not related to pregnancy. Within both categories, the C&Y program enrollees were

Table 19-7   Inpatient Utilization by Adolescent Mothers, by Year and Program

	APP program			*C&Y program*			
	N	*n*	*(%)*	*N*	*n*	*(%)*	
First year following index birth	266			233			
One or more admissions		18	(6.8)		31	(13.3)	$p < .02$
One or more pregnancy-related admissions[a]		11	(4.1)		16	(6.9)	NS
One or more admissions not related to pregnancy		8	(3.0)		15	(6.4)	$p < .10$
Second year following index birth	197			174			
One or more admissions		27	(13.7)		38	(21.8)	$p < .05$
One or more pregnancy-related admissions[a]		22	(11.2)		28	(16.1)	NS
One or more admissions not related to pregnancy		6	(3.1)		11	(6.3)	NS
Third year following index birth	69			59			
One or more admissions		8	(11.6)		14	(23.7)	$p < .10$
One or more pregnancy-related admissions[a]		7	(10.1)		13	(22.0)	$p < .10$
One or more admissions not related to pregnancy		1	(1.5)		2	(3.4)	NS
First 3 years following index birth	69			59			
One or more admissions		21	(30.4)		28	(47.5)	$p < .05$
One or more pregnancy-related admissions[a]		16	(23.2)		19	(32.2)	NS
One or more admissions not related to pregnancy		6	(8.7)		11	(18.7)	$p < .10$

NS, not significant.

[a]Pregnancy-related admissions are defined as those to the Obstetric Service and those to the Fertility Control Clinic (therapeutic abortions).

found to have higher hospitalization rates than did the APP program enrollees, in each year following the index birth.

In contrast to their mothers, the children enrolled in the two programs were found not to differ significantly in terms of their inpatient utilization. Over the full 3 years following birth, 17.4% of APP program children were admitted to the hospital at least once, as opposed to 13.6% of C&Y program children.

Emergency Department Utilization   The two clinic groups differed greatly in their use of the emergency department. Both programs offered walk-in care during regular clinic hours. Thus, emergency department use can be attributed to either true emergency problems or misuse (i.e., inappropriate use for problems more properly and economically treated within the clinic). As shown in Table 19-8, the adolescent mothers in the APP program made significantly fewer emergency department visits than did the C&Y program mothers. This holds true in each of the 3 years following the birth of the index child. In each successive year, the mean difference in emergency department visits increased. A possible explanation for this trend is that the APP program mothers were instructed in appropriate use of emergency room service and were seen as patients along with their children, at clinic well-child visits; the C&Y program mothers were not. As a consequence, the APP program mothers were more likely to view the APP program as their regular

Table 19-8   Mean Number of Emergency Department Visits Made by Mothers and Children, by Year and Program Affiliation

	APP program			*C&Y program*			
	N	*Mean*	*SD*	*N*	*Mean*	*SD*	
Adolescent mothers							
First year after							
index birth	260	0.67	1.1	238	1.04	1.9	*p* < .02
Second year after							
index birth	194	0.73	1.1	182	1.42	2.8	*p* < .01
Third year after							
index birth	65	0.61	1.0	64	1.44	2.2	*p* < .01
Children							
First year of life	264	3.1	3.3	227	2.6	2.9	NS
Second year of life	192	1.6	2.3	179	2.2	3.3	*p* < .05
Third year of life	67	1.2	1.5	54	1.3	1.5	NS

NS, not significant.

source of care and hence were less likely to use the emergency department for nonurgent problems. The C&Y program mothers, in contrast, had less contact with their program as patients over time. Over time, the APP program mothers decreased their use of the emergency department, while the opposite trend was noted for the C&Y program mothers.

In their first year of life, children enrolled in the APP program made slightly more emergency department visits than did the children enrolled in the C&Y program (3.1 versus 2.6 visits per enrollee). In contrast, APP program children used the emergency room significantly less often than did C&Y program children in the second year of life (1.6 versus 2.2 visits per enrollee, *p* < .05). No difference in emergency department utilization was found for the third year of life. In both clinic groups, the mean numbers of visits declined as the child grew older.

Outpatient Clinic Utilization   It was planned originally to measure outpatient utilization through the interview activity. A comparison of interview and medical record data revealed, however, that the adolescent mothers seriously underreported the number of clinic illness visits their children had made in their first 2 years of life. Because of this, a thorough study of medical records, the computerized pediatric system, and outpatient billing files was conducted for all subjects who were eligible for the interview. The review was limited to utilization by the children in their first two years of life.

Table 19-9   Mean Number of Outpatient Illness-Related Visits Made by Children in the First 2 Years of Life, by Program

Program site	*APP program* (n = 97)	*C&Y program* (n = 104)
TAC/C&Y program	5.4	12.4
Other	0.9	0.3
All clinics	6.3	12.7

As shown in Table 19-9, outpatient utilization by C&Y program enrollees for illness and injury was more than twice that of the children enrolled in the APP program. Children in the latter program were more likely to have been referred to specialty clinics than were those in the C&Y program, where specialty consultations were available on site, but the utilization rates for both groups were quite low.

Preventive Care

The fourth study hypothesis relates to differences in preventive health care use by APP versus C&Y program enrollees.

Adolescent Mothers   For the adolescent mothers, examination of preventive health care was limited to the use of contraceptives as reported in the patient interviews. Respondents were first asked if they had been sexually active in the 6 months prior to the time of the interview. As shown in Table 19-10, a substantial proportion of enrollees in each program denied being sexually active (38.0% in the APP program and 42.7% in the C&Y program). Striking differences by clinic were found with regard to the consistency of contraceptive use by those who reported they were sexually active ($p < .01$). Over half of the C&Y program enrollees (53.7%) stated that they did not use any birth control method, as opposed to only 15.2% of the APP program enrollees, and of those who did use birth control, more APP program enrollees did so consistently. Nonetheless, virtually all of the respondents said that they sometimes forgot to take their pills, or that it was sometimes inconvenient to use the diaphragm or condoms.

The clinic groups were not found to vary in the methods of birth control they used. In both settings, the pill was by far the most widely used method, followed by the IUD. Respondents were also asked how long they had been using their current method of birth control. In the APP program group, nearly half responded that they had used their current method less than 1 year (46.2%), and nearly half had used it over 2 years (43.6%). In contrast, only about one-quarter (26.3%) of the C&Y program respondents reported using their current method less than 1 year and nearly two-thirds over 2 years (63.2%). The majority of respondents in both programs still considered their program the main site for family planning services. Nearly all of those who named another site stated that they had been referred there by staff in their original program.

Table 19-10   Reported Sexual Activity and Use of Contraceptives at Time of Interview

	APP program			C&Y program			
	N	n	(%)	N	n	(%)	
Sexually active?	79			82			
Yes		49	(62.0)		47	(57.3)	
No		30	(38.0)		35	(42.7)	
Contraceptives used?	49			47			$p < .01$
Yes—consistent use		17	(37.0)		15	(37.0)	
Yes—inconsistent use		22	(47.8)		4	(9.8)	
No		7	(15.2)		22	(53.7)	
NA (pregnant)		3			6		

In summary, APP and C&Y program enrollees were found not to differ with respect to sexual activity. Of those who were sexually active, birth control use was reported much more frequently among APP than among C&Y program enrollees. Users in clinic groups did not differ with respect to type of contraceptive used.

Children For children, the adequacy of preventive care was measured in relation to EPSDT (Early and Periodic Screening Diagnosis and Treatment) guidelines for well-child care and immunizations. This standard specifies that well-child visits should be made at specific intervals, as shown in Table 19-11. In addition, four DPT/OPV (diphtheria, pertussis, and tetanus/oral polio vaccine) immunizations should be received within the first two years of life, as well as one MMR (measles, mumps, and rubella) immunization at 15 months.

During the interview, the adolescent mothers were asked whether their children had missed any appointments for well-child care and whether they were up-to-date on their immunizations. Virtually every respondent indicated that her child had missed no appointments and was up-to-date. Because failure to keep well-child visits is known to be one of the biggest problems in clinic programs, there was good reason to question the reliability of the mothers' responses in this area. Consequently, as indicated earlier, an exhaustive review of medical records was conducted to ascertain the preventive health care received by the children.

A child was considered to have had a well-child visit at the time specified if such a visit was made within 1 to 2 months of the scheduled time. As shown in Table 19-11, a larger proportion of APP than C&Y program enrollees had each required well-child visit, excepting those at 2 weeks and at 4 months. The difference

Table 19-11 Completeness of Well Child Care and Immunization Status of Children in First 2 Years of Life, by Program

	APP program	C&Y program	
	(n = 97)	(n = 104)	
Proportion of children having a well-child visit at:			
2 weeks	(89.7)	(98.1)	$p < .02$
2 months	(98.9)	(97.1)	
4 months	(91.8)	(92.3)	
6 months	(94.8)	(86.5)	$p < .05$
9 months	(91.8)	(76.0)	$p < .005$
12 months	(95.9)	(79.8)	$p < .001$
15 months	(83.5)	(79.8)	
18 months	(90.7)	(74.0)	$p < .01$
21 months	(77.3)	not required	
24 months	(92.8)	(56.7)	$p < .001$
Proportion of children who missed well-child visits:[a]			
None	(60.8)	(31.7)	
One	(26.8)	(27.9)	
Two	(7.2)	(19.2)	
Three or more	(5.2)	(21.2)	
Proportion having all immunizations required in first two years of life	(89.4)	(74.0)	$p < .005$

[a]Twenty-one month visit excluded. (This visit was not required in the C&Y program.)

in proportions increases by age. With few exceptions, well-child appointments at each age were kept by over 90% of the APP program children. In the C&Y program, the proportion of children having well-child visits decreased dramatically as they grew older. As a result, there was also a marked difference between the two clinic groups in the overall completeness of well-child care in the first two years of life. In the APP program sample, only 5.2% of the enrollees missed three or more of the required well-child visits. In contrast, 21.2% of the C&Y program enrollees were found to have missed three or more visits. It should be noted that care in each program was subsidized and, thus, essentially free to the parent.

Finally, the two groups differed substantially in terms of immunization status. While 89.4% of the APP program were found to be up-to-date on their immunizations at two years of age, only 74.0% of the C&Y program enrollees had all four DPT/OPVs and the MMR immunization by that age.

Repeat Pregnancy

The fifth study hypothesis relates to differences in the rate of repeat pregnancy between APP and C&Y program enrollees.

Repeat pregnancy was measured for enrollees in the interview subsample. Thus, the interview was the primary source of repeat pregnancy information. Because of the sensitivity of questions on miscarriages and abortions, the interview data were compared with medical records and computer files of the Department of Obstetrics and Gynecology, the Fertility Control Clinic, and the APP program. The reliability of the interview data was found to be high, with virtually no underreporting of repeat pregnancies and little error in the dates of termination. Where there was a discrepancy between reported and documented date of pregnancy termination, the documented date was used.

Table 19-12 summarizes the repeat pregnancy experience of the two clinic groups. Within the first year following birth of the index child, 22.0% and 27.4% of APP and C&Y program enrollees, respectively, experienced a repeat pregnancy. There was no significant difference in the overall repeat pregnancy rate, nor were there any significant differences by program in the rates of repeat pregnancies terminating in live birth, fetal death, or abortion. Over the full 2-year period following the birth of the index child, about one-third of the enrollees in each program had a repeat pregnancy. Again, the clinic distributions by type of termination were markedly similar.

As noted earlier, approximately 25% of all enrollees in each program had had another pregnancy prior to the index birth, and 10% had had a prior live birth. To determine if gravidity and parity influenced the rate of repeat pregnancy differentially by program, the analysis was repeated, controlling for these variables. No significant differences by program were found.

Educational, Vocational, and Social Outcomes

The sixth hypothesis relates to differences in the school completion rate of APP and C&Y program enrollees.

The hypothesis is based on the APP program's stated objective "to prevent school dropout with its subsequent limitation on employment." The evaluation was not limited to school completion rates, but incorporated variables relating to

Table 19-12   Repeat Pregnancies Conceived in the First, Second, and First 2 years
Following the Index Birth, by Program

	APP program (n = 82)		C&Y program (n = 84)		
	n	(%)	n	(%)	
First year following index birth					
No conceptions	64	(78.0)	61	(72.6)	NS
One or more conceptions	18	(22.0)	23	(27.4)	
Terminating in live birth	7	(8.5)	9	(10.7)	NS
Terminating in fetal death	3	(3.6)	3	(3.6)	NS
Terminating in abortion	10	(12.2)	12	(14.3)	NS
Second year following index birth					
No conceptions	61	(74.4)	69	(82.1)	NS
One or more conceptions	21	(25.6)	15	(17.9)	
Terminating in live birth	12	(14.6)	5	(6.0)	NS
Terminating in fetal death	2	(2.4)	2	(2.4)	NS
Terminating in abortion	10	(12.2)	10	(11.9)	NS
First 2 years following index birth					
No conceptions	52	(63.4)	55	(65.5)	NS
One or more conceptions	30	(36.6)	29	(34.5)	
Terminating in live birth	16	(19.5)	13	(15.5)	NS
Terminating in fetal death	4	(4.9)	4	(4.8)	NS
Terminating in abortion	18	(22.0)	17	(20.2)	NS

NS, not significant.

employment and sources of income as well. All data were collected in the two-
year postpartum interview activity.

Schooling   Respondents were asked a series of questions about their schooling
and educational aspirations at both the time of delivery and the time of the interview. The last grade completed at the time of delivery ranged from 7th to 12th in
each program. Overall, the C&Y program enrollees had not progressed as far in
school for their age as the APP program enrollees at the time of delivery. At the
time of the interview, 48.8% of the APP program enrollees had finished at least
high school or had earned a Graduate Equivalent Degree. The corresponding rate
for C&Y program enrollees was 38.1%. In addition, 30.8% of APP program versus
22.8% of C&Y mothers were still in school. Thus, 79.6% of APP program enrollees
were still in school or had graduated as compared with 60.9% of those in the C&Y
program. The clinic groups also differed in their stated educational goals at the
time of the interview. In the APP program, 35.1% of the enrollees planned to go
beyond high school, whereas in the C&Y program, only 27.4% had such plans.

Employment   At the time of the interview, 15.8% of APP program enrollees
reported they were working as opposed to 12.0% of C&Y program enrollees.
Similarly, a slightly larger proportion of APP program enrollees than C&Y program
enrollees were going to school. Within both programs, a high proportion of enrollees were neither working nor attending school (62.2% and 71.1% for the APP and
C&Y programs, respectively). Of those who were neither working nor attending

school, over half within each program had worked at some time since the birth of their child. Among those not working, 72% in the APP program and 60% in the C&Y program stopped working because the job was temporary. Other reasons given by enrollees in both programs included quitting, health, pregnancy, lack of child care, and return to school. The respondents varied greatly by program with regard to their reasons for not working at the time of the interview. Inability to find a job and lack of child care were the reasons given most frequently by enrollees in both programs. In the C&Y program, however, over twice as many enrollees as in the APP program cited inability to find a job (62.5% versus 30.6%). Lack of child care was the reason most frequently given by APP program enrollees (38.8%). Small proportions of enrollees in each program stated they did not want to work at the time of the interview.

Respondents citing reasons other than "do not want to work" as the major reason for their not working were asked whether they would like to work now, or to wait awhile, if their stated reason for not working was alleviated. Four APP program enrollees and nine from the C&Y program stated they would prefer waiting. A large proportion of those not working in each program had not received any vocational counseling (60.0% in the APP program and 75.0% in the C&Y program). Slightly over half of those who did receive counseling cited a friend or relative as the source, rather than a professional. It is interesting to note, however, that a much larger proportion of APP program enrollees reported counseling by program staff than did C&Y program enrollees. Overall, most enrollees felt they needed more information on how to find a job. Again, however, there was a significant difference between the two program groups ($p < .05$). While only one-quarter of the APP program enrollees felt they had all the information they needed, virtually none of the C&Y program enrollees (4.7%) did. Finally, the APP program enrollees were more likely than their C&Y program counterparts to view success in finding a job as dependent upon knowing how to seek employment or on the effort made, rather than on luck. Nearly twice as many C&Y program enrollees (61.9%) as APP program enrollees (34.2%) stated they believed finding a job was a "matter of luck."

In summary, the APP and C&Y program enrollees did not differ significantly in terms of their current and past employment experience. It should be borne in mind that 1982 was in the depths of the recession, and entry-level jobs were scarce. Furthermore, these mothers were for the most part still teenagers, some still in school.

Sources of Income   The final indicator of self-sufficiency was sources of income. As shown in Table 19-13, enrollees in both programs were receiving financial assistance from a variety of sources at the time of the interview. The clinic groups did not differ significantly with regard to the proportion of enrollees receiving income or assistance from their own employment, social security, parents, or the Department of Social Services. There was, however, a marked difference ($p < .02$) in the proportion of cases in which the father of the baby provided financial assistance. In the APP program, nearly one-fifth of the young mothers reported aid from their child's father. In contrast, only 6.0% of C&Y program mothers stated they received financial assistance from the child's father. The APP program made a concerted effort to include fathers in the educational and counseling services.

Table 19-13   Reported Sources of Income[a] at the Time of Interview, by Program

Source	APP program (n = 82)		C&Y program (n = 84)		
	n	%	n	%	
Respondent's employment	13	(15.8)	10	(11.9)	
Unemployment compensation	0	(—)	2	(2.4)	
Husband's employment	1	(1.2)	3	(3.6)	
Father of the baby	16	(19.5)	5	(6.0)	$p < .02$
Respondent's parent(s)	13	(15.9)	16	(19.0)	
Other relatives	2	(2.4)	2	(2.4)	
Social security	3	(3.7)	7	(8.3)	
Department of Social Services (Welfare)	71	(86.6)	66	(78.6)	

[a]Sources of income are not mutually exclusive.

Child Abuse and Neglect

The fourth APP program objective was to prevent child neglect and abuse, including abuse of the adolescent. The last study hypothesis reported here is based upon this objective, and relates to differences in the incidence of child neglect and abuse between APP and C&Y program enrollees.

This hypothesis could not be adequately tested because of differences inherent both in the programs and in the records they kept. To test the hypothesis, all available hospital sources of information on reported instances of child neglect and abuse were reviewed. For APP program enrollees, there were three sources of this information: patient records, pediatric social work logs of reported instances of abuse and neglect, and the case records maintained by the TAC program social worker. For C&Y program enrollees, only the first two sources existed. This distinction is important because the case records kept by the TAC program social workers were far more complete than either of the other two sources.

Another important distinction between the two programs and their record-keeping practices pertains specifically to child neglect. In the APP program, careful records were maintained on the regularity with which scheduled well-child visits were kept. If a mother failed to keep three consecutive appointments for well-child care, the TAC program social worker filed a report of suspected child neglect with the Department of Social Services. This was done only after contacting the mother, notifying her of the clinic's policy on repeated failure to keep well-child visits, and offering her every opportunity to either bring her child in for well-child care or demonstrate that her child had received such care at another site. No such policy was in effect for the C&Y program. (This difference, no doubt, was largely responsible for the differentials reported above in levels of well-baby care.)

In the area of child neglect, as was expected, there were many more reports filed for APP than for C&Y program enrollees in each of the first 3 years of life (21 and 4 reports, respectively). Much of this can be attributed to the APP program policy described above; of the 21 reports filed, thirteen were for medical neglect. The remaining eight APP program reports were for a variety of reasons, including potential for neglect and lack of supervision, more easily identified here than in the C&Y program. Virtually every TAC clinic session was preceded by a staff conference in which each scheduled mother-child pair was discussed. These conferences enabled staff members to exchange views and observations on enrollees and facilitated the identification of problems, real and potential. In the C&Y program, social workers became involved in a case only on a crisis basis, upon the request of a medical professional. Hence, the frequency of child neglect reports was dependent not only on the actual prevalence of child neglect, but on the medical professionals' ability to identify such cases.

In the areas of child abuse, the programs were found to be quite similar. Within the first three years of life, reports of suspected child abuse were made for eight children in each program. In the C&Y program, two reports were filed on each of two children in their first year of life. Other than these two cases, there was only one report per child. Once again, it must be noted that while APP program records are known to be complete, the same cannot be said of the C&Y program records for abuse and neglect. No reports of neglect or abuse of the adolescent mother were identified in either program.

Economic Efficiency   In this portion of the evaluation, two research questions pertaining to economic efficiency are addressed:

1. What were the costs of delivering services and the benefits to program participants?
2. Was the program an efficient use of resources compared with alternative uses of the resources?

Two major factors limited the extent to which actual program costs could be measured. First of all, the study period for this analysis extended over several years, beginning in 1978 (the prenatal period for sample subjects who delivered in 1979). During this period, the APP program was greatly extended. Clearly, as the number and types of services provided within the APP program setting changed, so too did program costs.

The second constraint on assessment of economic efficiency was the inability to measure actual *costs*. Costs were estimated by the *charges* applied to hospitalizations and the outpatient visits. Charges for hospitalization can be compared readily between groups because they are determined in the same way; the charge for an outpatient visit, however, was determined in part by the method of payment. For C&Y program visits, for example, the charge was set at $30 per visit, the amount the C&Y program was reimbursed by the Medicaid (Title XIX) Program. This amount had not changed in ten years, despite the increase in actual costs over that period. While the per visit cost of $30 undoubtedly fell far short of covering the hospital cost for prenatal care, it was reasonably adequate for well-child care. TAC program payments more nearly reflected actual costs.

Because of these limitations, this portion of the evaluation does not include costs associated with provision of services to the adolescent mother (such as prenatal care), other than hospitalizations and emergency room visits which were usually paid by Medicaid at a higher rate than C&Y prenatal visits, the only areas for which complete and accurate cost and utilization data were available. Second, it must be emphasized that the correspondence between service charge and cost is not perfect and may vary over time, by enrollee and by service delivery site.

In- and outpatient billing files were used to measure the charges associated with provision of selected services in each clinic program. For each adolescent mother and child, a listing of the date, clinic site, and charges for each outpatient visit made in the two years following the child's birth was obtained. From this list, mean utilization rates and charges were derived, while computer-generated listings of hospital admissions provided data on number of hospitalizations, length of stay, admitting service, and total charges for each enrollee.

Table 19-14 summarizes differences in program charges for the services examined. Birth hospitalization charges include those for admissions during pregnancy and at delivery. The mean charge for APP program enrollees was $2,029 and that for C&Y program enrollees, $2,426. The $397 difference can be attributed to increased length of stay for both C&Y program mothers and infants resulting from that program's higher rates of cesarean section and low birth weight. These were charges based on prevailing Medicaid rates and did not include reimbursement for physician's services.

In the first 2 years of life, children in the two programs were not found to differ substantially with regard to inpatient utilization. Consequently, the per enrollee difference in charges for this service was only $22. In contrast, C&Y program adolescent mothers were found to have significantly higher rates of hospital admissions than did APP program mothers in the first 2 years following their child's birth. Overall, the per enrollee charge for these hospitalizations was $261 higher in the C&Y program than the APP program.

Emergency department utilization rates paralleled hospitalization rates, in that substantial program differences were found for the adolescent mothers, but not for their children. In the first 2 years following birth of the index child, the C&Y program mothers were found to make an average of 2.46 such visits per enrollee. For the APP program mothers, the average was 1.40 visits. The mean emergency room visit charge was $85, resulting in per enrollee costs of $119 for the APP program and $209 for the C&Y program.

Outpatient utilization was defined as all visits to Johns Hopkins Hospital clinics (excluding the emergency room), for reasons other than well-child care. For children enrolled in the APP program, the average charge for a TAC program illness visit was $36, and the mean visit rate was 5.4 visits per enrollee. In addition, TAC program children averaged 0.9 visits to specialty clinics where the mean charge was $49. Thus, in the APP program, the overall per enrollee charge for illness-related outpatient utilization was $243.

Table 19-14   Program Difference in per Enrollee Charges for Selected Services[a]

Service	Difference in charges (C&Y minus APP program)
Birth hospitalization	$397
Hospitalizations—child	22
Hospitalizations—mother	261
Emergency services—mother	90
Outpatient illness use—child	143
Well-child care	−66
Net difference	$847

[a]For the prenatal period and the first 2 years following birth of the index child.

For children enrolled in the C&Y program, $30 was the fee reimbursed for illness and well-child care visits alike. The C&Y program illness visit rate was 12.4 visits per enrollee. In addition, C&Y program children averaged 0.2 visits to specialty clinics, at an average of $45 per visit. The charge per C&Y program enrollee for illness-related visits was $386, over 1.5 times the charge for children enrolled in the APP program. The charges for C&Y patients are underestimates, as the program was reimbursed on an all-inclusive per visit fee basis, which included X-rays and all laboratory tests.

There was a slight differential in the charge per enrollee for well-child care. On average, APP program enrollees made 8.9 well-child visits in the first two years of life, at $34 per visit, for a total per enrollee charge of $303. In the C&Y program, the charge was $30 per visit. Enrollees made an average of 7.9 visits, for a total charge of $237 per enrollee for well-child care. Thus, APP program children cost an average of $66 each more than C&Y enrollees.

Thus, the estimated total average medical care utilization charges for each mother-child pair were $3,725 for APP program enrollees and $4,580 for C&Y program enrollees (as defined for this study) for a net difference of $855 less for APP program enrollees (Table 19-14).

It is not possible to document the overall cost-effectiveness of the APP program. This would require examination of the costs per enrollee involved in operating both programs and comparisons between them. Between 1979 and 1982, the APP program's outpatient services were entirely supported by a service demonstration grant; the costs of the C&Y prenatal program cannot be separated from those of the rest of the C&Y program. However, it is possible to estimate the costs involved in those APP program prenatal and immediate postnatal services that differentiated it from those provided in C&Y. For 1980, the estimated costs for the additional medical and nursing time involved in case management, social service and counseling, health and parenting education and outreach amounted to approximately $108,000 in salaries, including 20% fringe benefits. For the 300 adolescents enrolled that year, averted costs for obstetrical inpatient services are estimated, in 1980 dollars, to be $119,100 (397 × 300). This estimate is based on comparison with the experience of C&Y adolescents, whose per enrollee hospital cost for these services were, on the average, $397 greater than those of APP program mothers. Thus, the obstetrical portion of the APP program was cost-effective.

Estimation of overall costs during the follow-up period is far more complex. Nonetheless, these would appear to be additional averted costs for the mother-child dyads in the APP program, as compared with the experience of those in the C&Y clinic, for inpatient hospital care and emergency and acute illness outpatient services. These averted savings of approximately $213,000 would have adequately covered the additional services provided to the 450 dyads enrolled over the 2-year period in which the savings were realized.

Whether the APP program represents an efficient use of resources as compared to the C&Y program may best be addressed by focusing on the benefits to enrollees. For the adolescent mothers, enrollment in the APP program was associated with lower rates of hospitalization and emergency room use. Children enrolled in the APP program experienced significantly less morbidity (as indicated by illness visits) than did their C&Y program counterparts. In addition, they were more likely to have received complete well-child care and to be fully immunized at 2 years of age.

Conclusion

Despite unavoidable methodological problems, which included utilization of non-equivalent control groups and of existing data that, in some areas, differed between programs, data from multiple sources were consistent, and valid comparisons between the two programs were possible. The results indicate significant health advantages for both mothers and children enrolled in the comprehensive APP program model as compared with the more traditional medical model employed in the C&Y program. The averted costs for APP program enrollees, calculated on the basis of comparison with the experience of C&Y enrollees, more than offset incremental costs for the added services provided in the APP program, attesting to its cost-effectiveness. Substantial but lesser gains were realized in educational attainment and employment for APP program mothers. As the quality and availability of medical care were not different between the two programs, it seems likely that the success of the APP program model can be attributed in large part to the addition of the individually case-managed, comprehensive psychosocial support and educational services, which were not available in the C&Y program. The implications for public policy should be clear; not only were the comprehensive programs more effective in terms of their human outcomes, in the long run, they were more economical as well.

Part IV

Fertility Control Services

The programs discussed in the previous section were designed for pregnant and parenting adolescents. As has been shown, their needs are many and varied and require the services of a team of caring professionals dedicated to their well-being and that of their children. One of their most pressing needs is the need to prevent another conception. Indeed, family planning is an important part of the education and guidance they are offered in the course of their pregnancies and as part of their medical services in the postpartum program. Providing contraception to adolescents who have already conceived is widely accepted as an appropriate part of follow-up care; little of the ambivalence that plagues preventive programs for nulliparous young women is focused on these interventions.

But there are many other adolescents to consider. Young people who need reproductive health care present not only at different developmental ages but at different stages in their sexual histories. Some are sexually active, and some are not; some are pregnant, and some are not; some elect to carry to term, and others choose to terminate their pregnancies. Many who present for routine care or for other medical problems are in need of educational and medical services if they are to avoid premature childbearing. Sometimes their presenting reasons are a not-too-subtle pretense, an excuse for coming in to ask the questions that worry them. In that case, the clinician's role is to create a climate in which the real questions can surface. However, sometimes the adolescent (male or female) is not aware of the need for guidance in human sexuality or the prevention of pregnancy and sexually transmitted disease; it is then the responsibility of the clinician to discover those needs and to address them.

There is general agreement that programs should seek, wherever possible, to influence young people to postpone sexual activity and to discourage coitus during the adolescent years. There is also general agreement that the United States must seek to reduce reliance on elective abortion and must find ways to reduce the level of unwanted conception; rates in this country for unintended pregnancy and for abortion greatly exceed the rates in similar, developed countries in the Western world (Jones et al., 1986). Clearly, the best way to reduce reliance on abortion among those who are sexually active would be the provision of universal contraceptive services, with sufficient education and follow-up to increase continuation rates and effective use. Among the many young people who are not abstinent, the need for these services is great and, because their risk is early as explained in the introduction to Part V, cannot wait until their first visit to a reproductive health clinic.

Frequently, the only physician who has access to young patients in time to prevent their first accidental pregnancy is the pediatrician or the family practitioner. Whether in a private or a clinic situation, the pediatric nurse practitioner or physician may well be in contact with a young boy or girl as he or she approaches puberty, begins to experience puberty, and, all too often, becomes sexually active. Unless in a crisis situation, no other medical professionals, and only an occasional guidance professional, will have similar opportunities for contact. Until members of pediatric and family health disciplines are willing to accept the responsibility for sexuality counseling and contraceptive counseling, and the provision of contraceptive service where it is indicated, we will continue to see children bearing children before they have discussed the possibility with any adult.

Other clinicians who need to be on the alert for problems related to sexuality, pregnancy prevention, and pregnancy testing and referral are those who serve in sexually transmitted disease clinics, which all too often offer no family planning at all. Yet other professionals are those who staff counseling and medical facilities concerned with the prevention of substance abuse. In a study of data collected from four Baltimore schools in connection with the program described in Part V, the association between early sexual onset and substance use is discussed (Zabin, Hardy, et al., 1986). Because early coitus is more frequent in the black community and early substance use in the white, that relationship has sometimes been masked. Females more frequently smoke cigarettes; males more frequently drink alcohol. White females initiate substance use earlier, perhaps because they are dating older males. However, when sex/race groups are controlled, the association is clear: those who initiate coitus at early ages are likely to score higher than their peers on an index that includes *type* of substance (cigarettes, alcohol, marijuana, hard drugs) and *frequency* of use. The implications of these findings for the desirability of combining initiatives in these high-risk areas should be apparent.

The next two chapters deal with the medical aspects of fertility control for adolescents, i.e., contraception and elective abortion. Chapter 22 reports the findings of a recent prospective study of the sequelae of pregnancy termination among a sample of urban black adolescents, many of whom were enrolled in the study when they presented for pregnancy tests at the Johns Hopkins Children and Youth Clinic. Chapters 20 and 21 are written by gynecologists/obstetricians who have functioned in the setting of reproductive health clinics. As suggested above, the information they impart, information that has often required specialized training in their disciplines, should also be imparted to other medical professionals if they are to be equipped to treat young people in a variety of health settings.

Counseling and Support

Young women who adopt contraception often fail to continue its use; except in the case of those who attend a program such as the TAC program, few receive follow-up attention. It is hardly surprising that continuation rates are low when the developmental ages of these young women are taken into account, and when other barriers to use are considered: their lack of privacy, their intermittent coital experiences, their fear of discovery, and their ambivalent or negative perceptions of contraception. New approaches to contraceptive education are attempting to present contraception in the context of a more positive understanding of the sexual behavior of young people in order to improve acceptance and continuation.

As seen in Chapter 22, even when support and counseling are provided, many young women conceive again following childbearing, abortion, and especially following a negative pregnancy test. The implications of recidivism for counseling are discussed in that chapter. Those who terminated their pregnancies have the lowest rate, but with 37% conceiving again within 18 months, their rate is still too high. These young women rarely receive the support that is given to childbearers, even when counselors are sympathetic to their desire to abort their unintended conceptions. They generally have less opportunity to receive that support for several reasons. First, when they come for pregnancy tests, even when all options are presented, those who elect to abort are rarely given the help in scheduling the procedure that their peers receive in arranging for prenatal care. Second, the abortion process entails minimal contact compared to the prenatal process, even when counseling is offered. Concern is focused on the immediate problem, more than it is on the future. Third, postabortion contacts are minimal compared with postpartum contacts, and, again, the discussion of family planning is a one-time rather than an ongoing affair. Finally, when young women are involved in a continuing program such as TAC, they receive continuing contraceptive advice and support that is not available to the girl who terminates her pregnancy, unless she has sought out a separate family planning clinic. In view of these difficulties, the fact that recidivism is considerably lower among aborters than it is among childbearers or those with negative pregnancy tests testifies to their higher motivation.

That may be in part because at the Johns Hopkins Hospital during part of the time these data were collected, counselors had the opportunity to help young women through the abortion process. They were able to bring them back several times, if necessary, to discuss their outcome options, and when they decided to abort, were able to help them with their appointments. A Fertility Control Clinic was available as part of the Department of Gynecology and Obstetrics, within the same hospital facility. Once the appointment was made, the counselor would often go with the young woman to her first meeting with the fertility control staff; at times, that first consultation was a joint one, with both counselors present. When the counselor perceived that a young woman did not have a family support system around her, she would return to be present when the procedure took place. Unfortunately, with the Fertility Control Clinic moved away from the hospital in 1986, that option was closed to the counselor. The lack of a facility at the hospital, and the need to refer these patients elsewhere, erected a further barrier to their care. The importance of quality, comprehensive care for pregnant and parenting teenagers, using a case-management system, has been emphasized throughout; it is regrettable that those who seek to prevent a first unwanted birth, or better yet, to avoid a first unintended conception, rarely are given the same level of support as those who do not.

The Ethical Context

In Chapter 10, a model was presented that is used to teach concepts of medical ethics to physicians in training at the Johns Hopkins School of Medicine. The author stresses the importance of good medicine, medicine that minimizes health risks to the patient, as a first premise upon which ethical judgments must be made. He also emphasizes autonomy, the primacy of the patient's option, as another cornerstone of ethical treatment. After these are considered, the social concerns that allow consideration of the patient in his or her family environment are relevant concerns. And the author points out that, in Maryland as in many other states, the minor can consent to reproductive health services legally, without parental involvement, if she so desires.

Considered in this framework, how does contraception look as a medical option? And elective abortion? The safety of the oral contraceptive for teenagers with appropriate screening is well-documented. We know, on the basis of work at the Centers for Disease Control, that elective abortion for teens, as for women of other ages, is a safe procedure, especially in the first trimester (Grimes and Cates, 1979). At every stage of gestation, it remains safer than childbearing. We also know that more than 80% of the young women who become pregnant each year in the United States do not intend to conceive. Furthermore, there is evidence that unwanted children, specifically children of women denied abortion, fare less well as children and young adults than those of women similar in all other respects (David, 1986; Dytrych et al., 1975; Forssman and Thuwe, 1966; Reiterman, 1971). Over 96% of the girls who bore children after presenting for pregnancy tests and enrolling in our study did not want a child; consequences to these young women are reported in Chapter 22. As a result of that study, we know something of the consequences of both outcomes, childbearing and abortion, and there is no doubt that those who terminated their pregnancies are less adversely affected by the experience than those who carried their pregnancies to term.

If the ethical model is taken seriously, we must also take seriously the question: why is the procedure that is associated with least medical risk not more readily available to those whose pregnancies are unwanted? To what extent has the option to choose elective abortion been voluntarily rejected by the young women in our community, and to what extent have barriers—economic, consensual, and emotional—been erected to steer them away from the outcome that carries least medical and social risk? Finally, and of greatest importance, where have we failed when the safest course of all, prevention of unwanted pregnancy with effective and consistent contraception, is so often rejected, even by sexually active young women who are informed about reliable contraception and who have reasonable access to it? What is the appropriate role of the clinician, of the social worker, and of the educator when those choices are being made? Are all the options being presented fairly, is equal access to all options assured, and do the young women who are making their choices know the relative safety and differential consequences of the choices they make?

20

Contraception and the Adolescent

John T. Repke and Theodore M. King

Sexual activity, family planning, contraception, and adolescents are words that not infrequently provoke moralistic debates. As health care providers, our responsibility is to assist our patients in best meeting their health care needs, leaving debates to the theologians and philosophers. However, it is legitimate to ask: What are the health care needs of the adolescent and how might these needs optimally be met?

Adolescent Sexual Behavior

Adolescent sexual activity is not a phenomenon unique to the 1960s, 1970s, and 1980s. In fact, adolescent pregnancy occurred in the 1950s and before, but some major differences have occurred since those years. First and foremost, there were relatively few contraceptive options available to women then. Additionally, pregnancies were more likely to occur in the late teens, with almost 80% of those teens married by the time the child was born. In the 1980s, more teenagers are becoming pregnant at 16, 15, 14, or even earlier, and on the national level 75% of these women are unmarried at the time of the delivery. In poor urban areas, the frequency of out-of-wedlock pregnancy is much higher. This change in patient profile has profound sociological implications, ranging from educational opportunity to family structure. Furthermore, as the great majority of these pregnancies are unintended, it would seem that their prevention would be an important goal for professionals to pursue. However, much misinformation exists about family planning, its effect on sexual behavior, and the methods available and appropriate to nulliparous teens. The Baltimore experience has demonstrated that health education, including sex education, in combination with family planning services, can postpone the age at which sexual activity is initiated (Zabin, Hirsch, et al., 1986). In fact, the absence of such educational programs and family planning services leads to increased rates of unwanted pregnancies at tremendous social, economic, and emotional costs. This is not only true in the United States, but worldwide (Centers for Disease Control, 1983).

If unintended pregnancy, abortion, and the spread of sexually transmitted diseases, including AIDS, are to be prevented, adolescents must have the information required for making wise choices about their sexual behavior, and those who are sexually active need access to contraceptive services. Because most adolescents receiving ongoing health care are served by pediatricians or family practitioners in their offices, these professionals can play an important role in providing the counseling and needed services. In addition to providing information and contraceptive services, counseling objectives should be to delay the onset of intercourse until the adolescent has completed his or her education, and a monogamous relationship can be established (Hardy, 1988). These professionals should consider their obligation, as part of the patient-physician informed consent process, to make adolescents aware of the potentially adverse consequences, for themselves and any children they may have, of premature sexual activity (Elkins et al., 1987) and other potentially self-destructive behaviors such as drug abuse. School health clinics and other reproductive health clinics can also be a source of counseling, education, and reproductive health service for adolescents who lack continuing preventive care.

Family Planning Services and Methods: Role of the Family Planning Clinic

In an effort to meet the needs of adolescents, access to health care should be easily obtained. As women move from childhood to adolescence, primary health care not infrequently is provided as an adjunct to sought-after gynecological care. A Hopkins school-linked program was successful in part because of its accessibility (Zabin, Hirsch, et al., 1986). While the initial visit may be for the purpose of seeking contraception, it has been recognized that reproductive health clinics are not infrequently responsible for identifying other significant health problems (JB Hardy, personal communication, 1986). Indeed, they are often the adolescent's point of entry into the health system. In this way, they serve as excellent screening clinics for disorders that would go unrecognized until they become acute. Therefore, in order to fulfill their true health care role, family planning centers should provide not just for gynecological care, but complete adolescent health care as well. Complete history taking and physical examinations should be part of the reproductive health visit and, only after this has been completed, should the focus shift to contraception, if in fact contraception was the major reason for the visit.

Additionally, such centers should provide an educational service for both sexes. Many adolescents, by the time of their first health care visit, have already asked themselves key questions about their sexuality. Commonly, these are questions about normalcy (am I normal?), desire for sexual intimacy (should I have intercourse?), contraception (is it safe? do I need to use it? where is it available?), and about fears—fears of pregnancy and fears about sexually transmitted diseases and more recently, fear of AIDS. In many cases, the adolescent may feel that she or he has satisfactorily answered these questions for her- or himself. However, these questions can only be satisfactorily answered if the answers are based on correct information. It is surprising that even in the "enlightened eighties" much misinformation prevails with regard to women's health and to contraception (Grubb, 1987; Liskin, 1984). Family planning clinics may serve a major role in eliminating much of this misinformation and, in so doing, more completely fulfill their potential role as a health care service.

Family Planning Methods

Oral Contraceptives and Health Risks

Most adolescents desiring contraception prefer to use oral contraceptives. Oral contraceptives have been in widespread use for over 25 years, yet many myths persist regarding their use; moreover, many concerns about oral contraceptives seem to be based on misinformation. Health care providers can play a key role in dispelling these myths, thereby not only serving the health care needs of the patient, but also fulfilling their role as educators.

Cancer of the Breast or Reproductive Tract   One of the most serious misconceptions about oral contraceptives is that they increase a woman's chance of developing cancer of either the reproductive tract or breast. In one study (Grubb, 1987), up to 40% of women surveyed thought that the pill was associated with an increased risk of developing breast cancer. In fact, although some studies have reported an association between oral contraceptive use and breast cancer (McPherson et al., 1987; Pike et al., 1981), the majority of data do not support this association (C.A.S.H. Study Group, 1986; Schlesselman et al., 1988; Shaw, 1987), and so at best, results linking pill use to breast cancer are inconclusive. The data on oral contraceptive use and female reproductive tract cancers are somewhat more conclusive and, in general, very reassuring that there is no increased risk.

Cervical, Uterine (Corpus), and Ovarian Cancer   Oral contraceptive use has been thought to increase the risk of uterine cancer by as many as 50% of the women surveyed (Grubb, 1987). In fact, oral contraceptive use reduces the risk of uterine corpus cancer by as much as 50%, with this protective effect lasting for at least five years after stopping oral contraceptives (C.A.S.H. Study Group, 1987a; Kols et al., 1982).

The effect of oral contraceptives on the risk of developing cervical cancer has been more difficult to measure. This difficulty stems from possible differences in sexual behavior among pill users, or more frequent cancer screening among pill users, both of which may result in increasing the apparent relative risk of developing cervical cancer when compared to nonusers. Regardless, it seems unlikely that pill use in and of itself increases the risk of developing cervical cancer but rather may promote the diagnosis of cervical cancer in patients at risk for other reasons.

The risk of ovarian cancer is clearly reduced by oral contraceptive use, with the protective effect increasing as duration of use increases and the protective effect lasting long after discontinuation of the pill (C.A.S.H. Study Group, 1987b).

Other effects of oral contraceptives, beneficial and adverse, have been established but, again, are often clouded by myth. Oral contraceptives may account for several benefits to the patient besides the prevention of undesired pregnancy. These benefits include:

1. Reduction in risk of gonococcal associated pelvic inflammatory disease (Rubin et al., 1980)
2. A possible reduction in the risk of tubal infertility among low-dose oral contraceptive users (Cramer et al., 1987)
3. A reduction in the incidence of iron deficiency anemia
4. Arrest of progression of endometriosis

Risks of oral contraceptive use, including thromboembolism, hypertension, stroke, and mycocardial infarction, have been markedly reduced or eliminated (Porter et al., 1987). It is important to remember, especially when dealing with adolescents, that the risk for many of these events is extremely small and is categorically lower than for the same woman who is pregnant at term.

Choice of Oral Contraceptive   Many oral contraceptive preparations are available today. While different companies lay claim to different advantages offered by their pills as compared to the competition, suffice it to say that each preparation at comparable dosage levels and for clinical purposes is equivalent. Recently, generic oral contraceptives have become available. As with other medications, generic equivalents are not always equally bioavailable, and generic oral contraceptives should be used only if adequate clinical trial and quality control data are available.

In general, 35 μg of ethinyl estradiol should suffice as far as the estrogen component of the pill is concerned. Higher amounts of estrogen should only very rarely be considered and, even then, only with gynecological consultation.

The progestin component of the pill has been studied primarily because of its impact on lipid metabolism. While biochemical differences have been observed in patients exposed to different progestin preparations, the clinical significance of these relatively small differences remains unclear. Because the newer triphasic oral contraceptive pills offer the lowest total hormonal dose, these are ideal for patients initiating oral contraceptive therapy.

The health care provider should also recognize that certain medications can affect the efficacy of oral contraceptives and vice versa. Antiepileptic, antiasthmatic, and antituberculous medication may all affect or be affected by oral contraceptive metabolism. Antibiotics have also been shown to affect oral contraceptive metabolism, and some antibiotics may actually potentiate the steroid hormone effects of oral contraceptives. Because adolescents not infrequently are concomitantly taking other medications with oral contraceptives, these potential drug interactions should be familiar to the health care provider and discussed with the patient.

Because adolescents have a tendency to discontinue taking pills at the first sign of a symptom, such as a headache or a small weight gain, the possibility of short-term side effects should be discussed in advance. We provide a backup method of condoms and foam to be used if the adolescent discontinues taking her pills but continues to have intercourse.

Finally, while a syndrome of postpill amenorrhea has been described, the adolescent with regular menstrual cycles should be reassured that oral contraceptive use is not associated with future infertility. Negative perceptions of birth control methods have been documented to be the primary reason for some adolescents' avoidance of family planning services (Zabin et al., 1991). Clinicians who are aware of these concerns can help adolescents express their fears—so common among women of all ages in the United States—and perhaps allay them.

Intrauterine Devices

Intrauterine devices (IUDs) have been the subject of considerable controversy since they were first introduced. Because of the possible associations of IUDs with pelvic inflammatory disease and tubal infertility (Westrom et al., 1976), especially among women with multiple partners, we feel that this method of contraception is not suitable for adolescents in developed countries. Here, IUDs are best used in the situation of a stable, monogamous relationship, where the woman's reproductive needs have already been fulfilled. In developing countries, where the maternal and infant mortality rates are unacceptably high, and where patient follow-up may be difficult, the risk to benefit ratio may be different; the IUD is an effective means of family planning for a wider range of multiparous women. However, in view of the risk of fertility problems related to infection, this method should be restricted to those multiparous women who do not want additional children but who do not desire or cannot obtain sterilization.

Barrier Contraception

Barrier contraception of one kind or another has been known to humankind since antiquity. In the 1980s, barrier contraception has undergone a renaissance. In part, the renewed interest in barrier contraception stems from the relative absence of side effects, safety (the lowest mortality is registered for barrier contraception with early termination of pregnancy for contraceptive failures), and the misconceptions about the safety of other methods of contraception, specifically oral contraceptives.

The most reliable barrier methods of contraception, in widespread use in the United States today, are the diaphragm and/or the condom. When used in conjunction with a contraceptive foam or cream containing nonoxynol-9, the method failure rates are less than 10%, with actual failure rates being less than 15%. Barrier contraception offers both advantages and disadvantages to the adolescent woman. The advantages include absence of any potentially steroid-associated side effects and some protection against sexually transmitted disease, pelvic inflammatory disease, and tubal infertility (Cramer et al., 1987). Disadvantages include inconvenience, a potential lack of cooperation by the woman's partner, and inability or unwillingness to achieve 100% method compliance.

In the 1980s and 90s, an additional reason has arisen for using barrier contraception, specifically condoms, and that is the recognition of heterosexual transmission of the Acquired Immune Deficiency syndrome (AIDS) or more specifically, transmission of the human immune deficiency virus (HIV). In a city such as Baltimore, where HIV prevalence has been estimated to be as high as 5%, precautions against acquiring HIV infection should be, and are, encouraged regardless of method of contraception. Latex condoms have been shown to prevent transmission of HIV virus particles, and nonoxynol-9, the most commonly used spermicide, has been shown in vitro to inactivate HIV. Therefore, the use of condoms and nonoxynol-9 in an adolescent, sexually active population, especially one with a known incidence of intravenous drug abuse, should be encouraged, even if alternative pregnancy prevention measures are already being taken. Ideally, especially when he will be responsible for the contraceptive method of choice, it is important to reach the male partner, but adolescents frequently have more than one sexual partner, and the clinician frequently has to counsel the young woman alone.

Summary

The purposes of adolescent health clinics are many. Screening for underlying medical conditions may be a more important function than had been previously realized.

Additionally, such clinics are frequently utilized for providing educational materials and counseling with regard to the adolescent's new found sexuality. As such, these clinics may best realize their potential by emphasizing education, counseling, and social support in addition to their health care provider role. In this way, misconceptions may be avoided, myth propagation reduced, and the broader goals of adolescent health care served.

While adolescents value their independence, freedom of choice, and personal autonomy, they also appreciate accurate, unbiased, nonjudgmental information and advice to assist them in their decision making. Given the problems of adolescent pregnancy and AIDS in this country, we owe it to the next generation of young adults to see that they are accurately informed in all areas of health.

21

Elective Abortion and the Pregnant Adolescent

Ronald T. Burkman

Approximately one million pregnancies in the United States occur among teenaged women each year. Almost one-half of these pregnancies are terminated through the use of induced abortion. This chapter reviews some of the characteristics of women in this age group seeking abortion care, highlights some of their demographic characteristics, and discusses the counseling, technical approaches, and issues involved in providing induced abortion services to young women. Much of the material and the recommendations presented are drawn from the experience of the Fertility Control Center of the Johns Hopkins Hospital, which was a separate unit established to provide abortion services between 1973 and 1986.

Demographic Considerations

Other sections of this book report extensively on a number of demographic features of pregnant women who are in the adolescent group. Considering the characteristics of young women seeking pregnancy termination, it should be understood that there is a considerable time lag between the occurrence of abortion-related events and their reporting in the literature. Most of the latest published information involves data collected in the early 1980s from the major abortion-monitoring programs of the Centers for Disease Control and The Alan Guttmacher Institute. Although some changes are likely to have occurred since then, the data still provide a reasonable overview of abortion services provided to teenagers in the United States.

Since 1980, using Alan Guttmacher Institute estimates, approximately 1.5 million legal, induced abortions are performed annually in the United States (Tietze and Henshaw, 1986). Of this number, 28.5% are carried out on women less than 20 years of age (Henshaw et al., 1985). Although the bulk of the procedures are carried out on women aged 18 or 19 years, a significant number involve younger adolescents. For example, among teenagers in the United States who underwent induced abortion in 1981, 3.5% were less than 15 years of age, 39.3% were 15 to 17 years of age, and 57.2% were 18 to 19 years old (Henshaw et al., 1985). Similarly, the abortion rates per 1,000 women in each of these age groups were 8.6, 30.1, and 60.1, respectively. The last of these rates was the highest for all age groups (up to 44 years) involved in the study. Our experience at the Fertility Control center in 1983 was somewhat similar to the national experience and similar to the findings from all Baltimore adolescents in that year (see Chapter 5). Among the 1,430 women presenting for abortion care, 521 or 36.4% were teenagers. Of the teenagers, 13.6% were less than 15 years, 48.8% were 15 to 17 years, and 37.6% were 18 or 19 years of age. The skewing of the distribution toward younger women probably represents the use of the facility as a referral center.

As noted elsewhere, the United States has the highest teenage pregnancy rate among developed nations of North America and Europe. For example, in 1981,

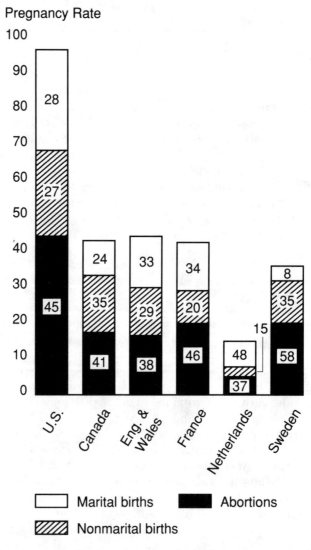

Figure 21-1 Percentage distribution of pregnancies and pregnancy rates, by outcome, for women aged 15 to 19, 1980 and 1981. (Reproduced with permission from Jones, EF, et al: Teenage pregnancy in developed countries: determinants and policy implications. *Fam Plann Perspect* 17(2):56, 1985.)

approximately 13% of women aged 15 to 19 years became pregnant (Henshaw et al., 1985). As shown in Figure 21-1, 45% of women aged 15 to 19 years, in 1980 and 1981, elected to terminate their pregnancies through induced, legal abortion. Although the proportion electing termination in the United States is not too dissimilar from other countries shown on the bar graph, the actual rate of induced abortion in this age group is roughly double that of most of the countries listed (Jones et al., 1985). Further, as is also quite apparent from the bar graph, the abortion rate alone in the United States is roughly equivalent to the overall pregnancy rates for teenagers in other westernized countries.

Among adolescents in the United States in this age group seeking pregnancy termination, approximately 95% are unmarried (Henshaw et al., 1985). The rates of abortion when compared between whites and nonwhites show substantial differences. In 1981, for women less than 15 years, the abortion rate per 1,000 was 5.1 for whites and 24.8 for nonwhites. Similarly, for women aged 15 to 19 years, the rates were 38.5 and 66.1, respectively (Henshaw et al., 1985). At the Fertility Control Center in 1983, among the teenaged women seeking care, 21.3% were white, 75.4% were black, and 3.3% were of other races.

When one relates duration of gestation at the time of abortion to the patient's age, it is quite apparent that teenagers in the United States undergo a higher proportion of terminations at later gestations than women in other age groups. As shown in Figure 21-2, in 1981, among women aged 14 years or less, almost 30% of abortions performed in the states surveyed were in the second trimester (Tietze and Henshaw, 1986). Similarly, among women aged 15 to 17 years and women aged 18 or 19 years, the percentages of pregnancies terminated in the second trimester were 18% and 15%, respectively.

At the Fertility Control Center in 1983, the percentages of women presenting in the second trimester were 63%, 55.5%, and 54.6% for women less than 15 years, women 15 to 17 years, and women 18 or 19 years, respectively. This distribution reflects the use of the Center as a source of referral. The delay in presenting for this care results in increased risk to these women, as both morbidity and mortality of induced abortion are directly proportional to duration of gestation. Unfortunately, the factors that relate to such delay are complex. Such factors include late recognition of pregnancy, difficulty arriving at a decision, the influence of family and peer groups, and perceived or real barriers that exist within the health care system (Bracken and Kasl, 1975; Bracken and Swiger, 1972; Evans, 1980).

In summary, large numbers of teenaged women present for abortion care in the United States. Although most are at the latter end of the age range, a considerable number are 17-years-of-age or less. Furthermore, the younger the patient is, the more likely she is to present at an advanced gestation. Also, more nonwhite than white teenagers request these services.

Abortion Care

The experience of presenting for an abortion procedure can be a traumatic one for any patient. However, for the teenager, the experience may be particularly frightening because, in addition to possible conflicts involved in the decision, they are more likely to fear the necessary reproductive tract examinations and procedures. Therefore, for the health professional involved in such care, providing ser-

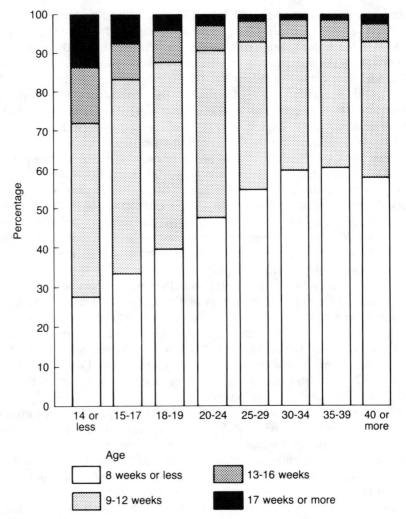

Figure 21-2 The percentage distribution of length of gestation at the time of induced abortion by age of patient (based on 1981 data). (Reproduced with permission from Tietze, C, and Henshaw, SK: *Induced Abortion: A World Review*, ed. 6. The Alan Guttmacher Institute, New York, 1986.)

vices to these young women requires patience, the ability to communicate, flexibility, a thorough understanding of the technical options available and their risks, as well as compassion. A number of authors have written extensively on the provision of abortion services (Castadot, 1986; Hern, 1984); this section highlights some of the important features, and comments on aspects of care of particular relevance to this young age group.

Initial Intake

Despite the difficulty obtaining an accurate history from a young adolescent, a thorough preoperative evaluation is important in order to assess duration of the pregnancy as well as to detect potential problems that might influence the outcome of the procedure. Included is a complete medical history, physical examination, including pelvic examination, and laboratory tests. The medical history allows one to detect possible serious conditions that could affect management of the patient. Of particular importance is the detection of symptoms that could indicate a complication with the current pregnancy. For example, a history of watery discharge might suggest ruptured membranes with resultant increased risk of infection; abdominal pain would require the exclusion of an ectopic pregnancy. The pelvic examination is of particular importance in assessing duration of pregnancy, because menstrual histories are frequently unreliable in this age group. In addition, it allows the examiner to elicit the cooperation of the patient and determine whether management during the abortion procedure will need to be modified. For example, if the patient is uncooperative and does not permit an adequate assessment of her pelvic structures, sonography will be needed to determine pregnancy duration, and increased sedation or even general anesthesia may be needed to complete the procedure. Minimal laboratory tests include a hematocrit or hemoglobin, Rh typing, complete urinalysis, Papanicolaou smear, and an endocervical gonorrhea culture. In young adolescents, especially those who appear unduly fearful or uncooperative during pelvic examination, the possibility that the pregnancy may be the result of sexual abuse should be considered.

Consideration should also be given to carrying out an endocervical culture for chlamydia because this age group has a high prevalence rate of infection with this organism. For example, in a recent study of women presenting for an elective abortion procedure at the Fertility Control Center, 29% of the women aged 19 years or less had a positive cervical culture for *Chlamydia trachomatis* (Barbacci et al., 1986). This finding is of some significance, as women in this same study who had a positive culture for chlamydia had a risk of postabortal endometritis approximately three times greater than women with negative endocervical cultures for this organism. Among pregnant adolescents below age 18 years in the Johns Hopkins Adolescent Program (HAC), 37% had positive cultures for *C. trachomatis* (Hardy et al., 1984).

Sonography

Sonography should be utilized relatively liberally in this age group. As noted above, menstrual history is often unreliable. In addition, duration of gestation is important in deciding on the need for certain approaches. For example, with a patient at 18 or 19 weeks gestation, the decision regarding use of a medical induction or dilatation and evacuation needs to be carefully weighed by the responsible physicians. Similarly, a very early gestation might allow completion of a suction curettage without use of laminaria tents.

Counseling

Counseling is a critical part of the preoperative evaluation. This process not only requires a detailed discussion and obtaining of informed consent but also some exploration of the patient's decision-making process, family dynamics, and ability to understand the ramifications of her decision. The patient must be advised of the risks, such as infection, hemorrhage, incomplete abortion or retained products of conception, and the potential need for major surgery, even hysterectomy. In most instances, it is advisable that the patient be accompanied by a parent or a responsible adult, particularly if she is in the early teenage years. Critical in the counseling process is the development of a supportive relationship between the health care team and the pregnant adolescent and her own support system. The counselor must try to allay anxiety and help the young patient sort out and cope with often conflicting feelings. Long-term goals of the process include helping the young adolescent better understand the reproductive process and helping her to exert control over the process in her future behavior, through her decisions about sexual contact and through her use of contraception. With family members involved, the counselor must also be able to identify sources of conflict and assist, if possible, with their resolution.

Finally, as part of the counseling process, it is important that the various statutory requirements dealing with funding or parental notification be understood by the patient. For example, if formal parental notification is required by law for adolescents in certain age groups, the patient will need to consider whether bringing her parents into the process earlier rather than having them notified by registered mail or telegram would be in her best interests. (Legal requirements are discussed in Chapter 10 and the sequelae of family consultation in Chapter 22.)

Staff Qualifications

As implied above, adolescents seeking abortion require special consideration if optimal outcome is to be achieved and further pregnancies prevented. An educational process, which takes into account the adolescent's lack of accurate information, her fear, and possibly her guilt about being pregnant, must be part of the overall procedure. Staff members must be supportive of the adolescent's decision, nonjudgmental, and understanding of her sexual behavior (even though they may not approve of it). They must be able to understand her level of development and the psychosocial circumstances in which she finds herself. In addition to a high degree of professional competence, flexibility, kindness, and honesty are essential.

First Trimester Procedures

The procedure of choice for terminating pregnancies in the first trimester is suction curettage. The operation is associated with low rates of morbidity and mortality, is readily performed on an outpatient basis, and can safely be carried out at free-standing clinics that are not directly adjacent to a hospital. However, despite the relative simplicity of the procedure, in order to reduce risks, practitioners must be thoroughly trained in the techniques involved as well as in the recognition and management of associated complications. For most women in this age group, the use of laminaria tents will substantially simplify the procedure as well as reduce the risk of cervical laceration. For example, in a review carried out by the United States' Centers for Disease Control between 1975 and 1978 of over 15,000 suction curettage abortions, the relative risk of cervical injury requiring sutures for women undergoing cervical dilatation by laminaria alone versus rigid dilators was about five times less (Schulz et al., 1983). Duration of gestation did not seem to be related to risk of injury. But, even when the data were controlled for use of laminaria tents as well as other risk factors, women aged 17 years or less still faced approximately a two-fold increase in risk of cervical laceration as compared with older women.

With appropriate counseling, most procedures even when they involve young teenagers can be carried out under paracervical block anesthesia with intravenous sedation. As noted by Peterson and co-workers (1981), the risk of death due to anesthesia-related or other causes is between two and four times higher for women undergoing the procedure under general anesthesia as opposed to local anesthesia. In carrying out the operation, the cervix is dilated to the minimal diameter needed to accomplish the procedure. After suction curettage has removed the bulk of the products of conception, the uterine cavity is checked for completion of the procedure utilizing a sharp curette. At the end of the operation, the products are checked for presence of fetal parts, placenta, and completeness.

The case fatality rate for first trimester terminations is less than 1/100,000 procedures, making this operation one of the safest available for women (Tietze and Henshaw, 1986). The major complications of suction curettage include hemorrhage, infection, cervical laceration, and uterine perforation. The overall frequency of these complications, including occurrence during the first few postoperative weeks, range from 1.2% to 5% (Castadot, 1986). Hemorrhage is most frequently secondary to retained placental tissue, a complication that is reduced by careful inspection of the tissue after completion of the operation. Infection is uncommon. The use of prophylactic antibiotics has been shown to reduce the risk significantly in most series (Grimes et al., 1984). Because many of the women who develop infections are found to have chlamydia on cervical culture, the use of tetracycline derivatives seems appropriate. This is particularly important as teenage women presenting to the Fertility Control Center were found to have a two-fold increased risk of postabortal endometritis compared with other women (Burkman et al., 1984). As noted previously, cervical laceration is more common in this age group; therefore, the use of laminaria tents is recommended to minimize this occurrence. Finally, the risk of perforation ranges between one to five times per 1,000 operations, a risk that should be reduced by careful adherence to the steps of the procedure listed above.

Second Trimester Procedures

In the early second trimester dilatation and evacuation (D and E), a modification of dilatation and curettage is the procedure of choice. Critical to the success of the operation is the use of laminaria tents in order to achieve enough cervical dilatation to extract the enlarged fetal parts. After 16 weeks duration of gestation, it appears that the use of either intraamniotic injection of urea with low-dose prostaglandin $F_{2\alpha}$ or the use of D and E results in similar rates of morbidity (Burkman and King, 1984). Regardless of the technique utilized, it is mandatory that practitioners be well-trained and experienced in carrying out the initial procedures as well as in the management of complications. It should be noted that an intraamniotic injection requires a facility that can manage such patients in labor as well as be able to complete a curettage promptly, if required for retained placental tissue.

The case fatality rate for second trimester procedures ranges from 1.2 to 7.1 deaths/100,000 operations (Tietze and Henshaw, 1986). Although reasonably low, the higher rate clearly supports the recommendation that the procedures should be carried out as early in gestation as possible and not delayed. The major complications of D and E are similar to those of first trimester suction curettage, with rates in most series being less than 1% when carried out in the early weeks of the second trimester (Tietze and Henshaw, 1986). The major complications of intraamniotic injections include hemorrhage, infection, cervical lacerations, and failed procedures. Hemorrhage, which can occur in up to 10% of procedures, is usually secondary to a retained placenta and is managed by curettage. Coagulopathy is a rare event that can be even further reduced by avoiding the use of hypertonic sodium chloride (Burkman et al., 1977). Infection is more frequently seen in association with prolonged injection-abortion intervals; therefore, careful monitoring and judicious use of adjunctive measures such as oxytocin or prostaglandin E_2 suppositories in the absence of labor can reduce the occurrence of this complication. Further, the use of prophylactic antibiotics was found to be particularly useful for this group of patients, as noted in a clinical trial completed in the Fertility Control Center (Spence et al., 1982). The use of laminaria tents has reduced the risk of cervical laceration to less than 1%. Finally, despite the use of ancillary measures, about 1% of patients will fail to abort. Therefore, in this event, practitioners need to be able to evacuate the products of conception through the use of D and E.

Long-Term Sequelae of Pregnancy Termination

A number of studies have examined the potential occurrence of late sequelae such as subsequent pregnancy complications (prematurity, spontaneous abortion, low birth weight, and ectopic pregnancy) and secondary infertility (Hogue et al., 1982). The vast majority of studies that have examined legalized abortion in the United States have failed to show substantial increased risk of adverse outcomes for most women. The only group that may be at increased risk of subsequent problems are those women who have undergone two or more prior termination procedures. (See Chapter 22 for further discussion of the consequences of abortion.)

Postprocedure Follow-Up

Follow-up after the procedure is utilized to detect any delayed complications and to provide additional counseling, particularly with regard to the prevention of future pregnancies. Although a detailed discussion of contraception in this age group is beyond the scope of this chapter, the utilization of oral contraceptives and barrier methods are most appropriate for these young women. However, more intensive initial counseling and follow-up is required in order to be sure that these young people understand appropriate use of the method selected, to detect and allay fears regarding side effects, as well as to detect the rare occurrence of more serious problems. It is important also to make sure that arrangements are made for continuing contraceptive services.

Summary

Adolescent teenage women represent a substantial segment of all women seeking elective abortion. Their care requires patience and understanding, as well as practitioners who are well-skilled in the application of abortion techniques. Overall, these young patients, despite presenting more frequently in the second trimester, have not shown higher rates of complications than other age groups (Tietze and Henshaw, 1986). The two complications that do occur more frequently in this age group are cervical laceration and postabortal endometritis. To date, long-term sequelae have not been shown to be a significant problem associated with elective abortion.

22

The Consequences of Elective Abortion

It has been clear for some years that abortion is a medically safe procedure for adolescents (Grimes and Cates, 1979). In the opinion of many, it is an appropriate procedure for girls to choose when they are too young to parent successfully, whose opportunity to become educationally, economically, and emotionally mature could be truncated by premature motherhood. Most Americans believe it should be available as an option to adolescents as it is to adult women. There are some, however, who have hypothesized that induced abortion may be dangerous to the mental health of the woman and that its consequences are not well understood. It has been proposed that large scale prospective studies are needed, enlisting young women in large numbers before they conceive, following them into the future when they may or may not conceive and may or may not elect to terminate their pregnancies (Koop, 1989). With approximately 42% of the teenage women who do conceive electing abortion rather than childbearing (Henshaw et al., 1989), it is important that its sequelae be thoroughly explored.

In the belief that a research design might address many of the problems identified in former studies and still make available its findings without an unmanageably large investment of time and funds, an investigation was undertaken to explore the consequences of pregnancy loss in seven major areas of interest. They included: education; economic status; household structure; health; growth; and sexual behavior, contraception, and fertility. In addition, psychological variables, specifically anxiety, locus of control, and self-esteem were examined. The subjects in this study were all inner city, black females, ≤ 17 years of age, who presented for pregnancy tests at one of two locations, the Johns Hopkins Children and Youth Program and Planned Parenthood of Maryland. The longitudinal study followed the young women for 2 years, incorporating a long baseline survey administered before they or their interviewers knew the results of their pregnancy tests. They were interviewed by telephone at 6 and 18 months, and in person at 1 and 2 years.

All three of the natural groups into which they fell were followed, providing a study sample and two control groups. The study population consisted of those whose index pregnancy tests were positive and who elected to terminate their pregnancies. The two control groups consisted of those whose index pregnancy tests were positive who elected to carry to term, and those whose index tests were negative.[1] The first control group was selected because, having discovered at the same time and place as the abortion group that they had conceived, they made the alternative decision, the decision to have a child. As one follows childbearers into the future, however, it becomes less and less possible to separate the consequences of the childbearing experience from the consequences of motherhood itself. In this respect, therefore, they differ from the abortion group. The second control group provides the opportunity to study young women who are unencumbered by a child from the index event when they are compared to the abortion group in future years, but who, by virtue of their suspicion of pregnancy, acknowledged that they were also engaged in sexual activity.

The emphasis of this research is on *change over time*. The extensive data collected from the respondents upon admission to the study make it possible to control for baseline characteristics when examining their condition subsequent to the index experience. Frequent contact, at 6-month intervals, makes it possible to focus a microscope upon many of the consequences of that experience for all three groups. Although the findings cannot be generalized to a larger population, they can give an accurate picture of the sequelae of abortion in an urban black population of adolescents.

Prior Literature

The consequences of childbearing among adolescents have been explored in many excellent studies, and the results of these investigations have been well summarized elsewhere (Hayes, 1987). However, the sequelae of abortion have not received such scrutiny and are rarely explored in youthful populations. When they have been examined, especially among grown women, the focus has generally been upon the effects of the abortion procedure on future fertility and upon its psychological effects. There is consensus that adverse psychological outcomes are rare, and that when such effects do appear, they are related to preexisting emotional character-istics and not necessarily to the procedure itself (Ashton, 1980; Belsey et al., 1977; Cherazi, 1979; Osofsky and Osofsky, 1972; Shusterman, 1976 and 1979). Not only are adverse outcomes rare (Adler, 1975; Blumberg et al., 1975; Brewer, 1977; Cvejic et al., 1977; Greer et al., 1976; Lazarus, 1985; Shusterman, 1976), but the decision to terminate an unwanted pregnancy may actually be associated with less psychological distress and therefore be more psychologically beneficial than car-rying to term (Brewer, 1977; Pare and Raven, 1970; Watters, 1980). In view of the fact that most adolescent pregnancies are not intended, and many clearly unwanted, one might hypothesize that the emotional advantages would therefore outweigh disadvantages among teenagers who terminate their pregnancies. Some researchers find that abortion is generally associated with a feeling of relief (Cates, 1980; Osofsky and Osofsky, 1972), and most find that any malaise that is identified following the procedure is short-lived. Among adolescents, it has been found that contraceptive use generally improves following abortion (Abrams, 1985; Cvejic et al., 1977; Evans et al., 1976; Gispert et al., 1984; Margolis et al., 1974), and that

---

[1]Because numbers in the group who miscarried were too small to analyze separately, they are not included in this report.

the risk of future unintended pregnancies to aborters is lower than the risk among childbearers.

Major flaws in prior studies have been well summarized by a panel of the American Psychological Association (1987). The panel identified the following recurrent problems: 1) a lack of controls; 2) control groups that differ on baseline characteristics; 3) difficulty in separating baseline characteristics from sequelae; 4) bias in observation when subjective measures of psychological response are utilized; 5) the confounding effects of intervening variables; and 6) the need for more than one follow-up observation, because some sequelae may be time-limited.

The present research attempted to address several of these issues. By restricting its compass to young women of similar age and similar economic background, it attempted to make the groups as comparable as possible. Therefore, while findings cannot be generalized to the entire population, they represent a closeup view of the 2 years following the index event among young people at high risk of unwanted conception. Because a substantial amount of retrospective data was collected at baseline, before the effects of a possible pregnancy could change the background information the young women gave us, it is possible to separate preexisting characteristics from sequelae in this largely prospective study. The only variables the suspected pregnancy could already have affected at the time of the baseline interview were those in the area of psychological function; as is seen below, by choosing an inventory that separates passing states from underlying traits, the problem of separating preexisting from pregnancy-induced characteristics was minimized. A total of 360 young women were admitted to the study; 2-year follow-up included approximately 90% of the baseline population. The methodology and results of this study have been described in detail elsewhere (Zabin, Hirsch, et al., 1989, 1990).

Characteristics at Baseline

Upon admission to the study, all three groups had a mean age of 16.1 years. Among those who terminated their pregnancies, almost three times as high a percentage was Roman Catholic as among the childbearing group, but in other respects the groups did not differ in religion. There were some differences among the women who were identified by the respondents as the female who "raised" them, but most of the differences were not significant. These women were no different in marital status and only slightly more likely to be working, to have graduated from high school, or to be older at the birth of their first children if their young daughters (or surrogate daughters) elected abortion than if they carried their pregnancies. (The majority, approximately 80%, of the respondents lived with their biological mothers, and if step and foster mothers are included, almost all the respondents had a mother in the home.) One significant difference in the homes of these young women was the fact that more of those who terminated their pregnancies reported that curfews were imposed on them on weekdays and weekends (72.3% versus 53.8% of childbearers and 66.0% of negatives). In various measures used to assess their economic well-being, the abortion group appeared to be insignificantly better off.

In fact, only educational variables discriminated significantly between the three groups. Almost all the subjects in all groups had been in school during the year preceding their presentation for a pregnancy test, but fewer of the childbearers were still in school when they entered the study. Expectations for future education were higher among the abortion group: fewer than 54% of the childbearing and negative test groups expected to continue their education after high school, compared with more than 71% of the abortion group. More of the latter group were in the appropriate grade for their ages when originally interviewed. However, grade point averages were similar: 79.5 for the abortion group, 79.6 for the childbearing group, and 79.3 for the negative test group. Almost all the respondents, in all three groups, expected to complete high school; only three young women in the entire sample did not expect to finish the 12th grade.

Several psychological measures were used. As suggested above, of primary concern to the researchers was the fact that baseline data, collected at a time of stress while awaiting the results of a pregnancy test, might not be representative of true baseline characteristics. Therefore, an inventory was sought that, when examining a characteristic as important as stress or anxiety, might separate temporary states of mind from underlying traits. The Spielberger State-Trait Anxiety Index (1983) was utilized for the purpose and apparently was able to make that separation. At baseline, the *state* measure was dramatically higher than the *trait* measure in all three groups, and those differences were highly significant ($p < .01$). However, differences between groups were small; the abortion group was insignificantly higher in the temporary state measure and lower in the trait measure than either of the other groups.

Two Years Later

In the tables that follow, both the 1- and the 2-year follow-up data are included, but the Ns refer to the numbers available for comparisons between the baseline and 2-year surveys. The samples at 1 year were slightly smaller, because some young women who were missed at the 1-year interview were reached the next year.

Educational Measures

Several educational variables were explored. Although there were only small differences between the three groups in the percentage attending school at the time of the first interview, the differences were large at 1 year and continued to increase at 2 years (Table 22-1). It is not surprising that most of the change occurred in the first year, because more and more of the respondents graduated over time, leaving smaller percentages available to drop out of school. It is noteworthy that, although the first year took the greatest toll among childbearers—as one would expect— the percentage of young mothers who graduated or were still in school continued to decline more quickly than it did for the other two groups in the second year. In another variable, the proportion behind in the appropriate grade for their ages, there were only small changes. Forty-eight percent of the childbearers were already behind in grade at baseline, as were almost 53% of the negative test group; only a few more fell behind in the next 2 years. Recall that grade point averages for the three groups were similar and that all groups had expected to complete high school. Thus, although their baseline characteristics suggested that the groups might attain different levels of education in the long run, they would not have predicted

Table 22-1 Educational Variables by Abortion, Childbearing, and Negative Test Groups, by percentages

	Abortion	Childbearing	Negative
N =	(120)	(86)	(92)
In school or graduated			
Baseline	99.2	90.7**	94.6
1 yr	92.5	74.7**	83.5
2 yr	90.0	68.6**	79.3*
	**	**	**
Behind grade for age			
Baseline	35.6	51.2	52.8*
1 yr	39.2	52.7	56.6*
2 yr	41.5	57.1*	57.3*
Negative educational change			
1 yr	13.5	31.6**	26.9*
2 yr	17.8	37.3**	37.4**

Asterisks (*) to the right of childbearers and negative subgroups refer to the significance of the difference between those groups and the abortion groups. Asterisks at the bottom of each column refer to the significance of the change between baseline and 2-year interviews. Ns refer to the size of the sample at baseline and at 2 years; a somewhat smaller number was reached at 1 year, but the data are included to suggest the direction of change over time.

$*p \le .05.$

$**p \le .01.$

that, in the absence of the index event, the childbearers and negative test groups would drop out of school before completing the 12th grade.

We use a summary variable, shown in Table 22-1 as "negative educational change," which indicates the percentage at each follow-up period who have dropped out of school without graduating, or if in school have not progressed the appropriate one or two grades. Two years after admission to the study, just under 18% of the abortion group, but over 37% of the childbearing and negative test groups, have suffered negative change in their educational trajectories. Table 22-2, however, suggests that it was not the abortion procedure itself that was responsible for the

Table 22-2 Educational Variables by Abortion, Childbearing, and Negative Test Groups and by Subsequent Pregnancy, by percentages

	Abortion			Childbearing		Negative	
	Subs. preg.		No subs. preg.	Subs. preg.	No subs. preg.	Subs. preg.	No subs. preg.
N =	(41)		(77)	(33)	(37)	(50)	(41)
Graduated or in school at 2 yr	78.0	**	97.4	60.6	69.4	78.0	80.5
Behind grade for age at 2 yr	58.5	**	30.7	57.6	58.8	53.2	61.0
Negative educational change	34.1	**	8.0	45.2	31.4	34.7	41.5

$**p \le .01.$

negative educational change experienced by a few members of the abortion group, but rather the experience of a subsequent pregnancy among those who conceived again. There are highly significant differences between the educational experience of those with a subsequent pregnancy and those without, differences that are not apparent in the two other groups. Among those with another conception, negative change paralleled the childbearers' experience, but among those without, the vast majority remained on course.

Because there were some baseline differences between the abortion group and the young women in the control groups, we asked whether it was possible that differences at 1 and 2 years could be attributed to baseline characteristics, rather than their experiences following the index pregnancy tests. A series of regression models tested that hypothesis and bore out the bivariate relationships reported above. Educational variables (grade for age, in school or graduated, educational expectations) were added singly and in several combinations, and in each case the importance of group status was confirmed, whether the abortion group was compared to childbearers or to those with negative tests. Similarly, when background variables from the baseline interview, such as self-esteem, anxiety trait, education of the female parent, and maintenance of a curfew, were included in another model, with negative educational change as the outcome variable, those in the abortion group remained in significantly better shape at 1 and 2 years following entry into the study. Background characteristics could not account for the observed differences.

Economic Measures

Regarding their economic well-being, the abortion group appears to have escaped the difficulties that were observed among the childbearers. We computed a summary measure of the economic well-being of the household by calculating the ratio of adults working to *all members* of the household, and, again, by computing the ratio of adults working to *all adults* in the household. Clearly, when a baby is added, as in the first calculation, one would expect the ratio to change; indeed, we observe such a change among the childbearers, whose households declined in this measure ($p < .01$) while the ratio improved in the two other groups (Table 22-3). The ratio improved slightly among childbearers in the second year. However, the improvement was greater among the abortion group, so that while differences between them and the other groups at baseline were not significant, they became highly significant at 1 year and 2 years following the index event.

The second ratio eliminates the effects of the baby, by including only adults in the household measure. Nonetheless, change was apparent: insignificant differences at baseline became significant 1 and 2 years later. It is not surprising that a subsequent pregnancy had an adverse effect on the job ratio as it did on educational achievement. When no pregnancy intervened, a higher proportion of girls in each group was working at the end of the observation period.

Closer analysis suggested that the adults in the childbearers' homes did not give up jobs they had at baseline in order to care for the respondent's child. Those who were working at baseline seemed to remain at work. Rather, the data suggest that it was the inability of the young woman herself to enter the job market that increased the differential between this group and those electing abortion. As those who terminated their pregnancies graduated from school, they entered the job

Table 22-3 Proportion of Adults Working by Abortion, Childbearing, and Negative Test Groups, by percentages

	Abortion	*Childbearing*	*Negative*
$N =$ (120)	(86)	(91)
Adults working/all in household			
Baseline	30.7	25.4	24.9*
1 yr	39.7	20.6**	28.6**
2 yr	46.1	26.4**	31.3**
	**		**
Adults working/adults in household			
Baseline	60.1	51.2	49.7
1 yr	62.3	48.6*	51.7*
2 yr	71.4	52.8**	54.0**
	**		
Negative job change			
1 yr	41.0	51.9	46.8
2 yr	30.8	44.2	46.6*

Asterisks (*) to the right of childbearers and negative subgroups refer to the significance of the difference between those groups and the abortion groups. Asterisks at the bottom of each column refer to the significance of the change between baseline and 2-year interviews.

$^*p \le .05.$

$^{**}p \le .01.$

market and increased the proportion of the family at work, a pattern that was much less common among those who had become mothers.

Once again, an attempt was made to control for baseline differences in a multivariate regression model. Whether the ratios of working adults were used in the model, or other baseline measures such as the family's receipt of food stamps or a social services check, membership in the abortion group remained significant. Once again, baseline characteristics did not account for the reported differences at 1 and 2 years.

Psychological Sequelae

Anxiety Index The Spielberger State-Trait Anxiety Index was used in an attempt to separate the transient state from the underlying trait; it would seem that it effectively did so (Table 22-4). At follow-up, these two measures were no longer significantly different, as they had been while the young women were under stress awaiting the results of their pregnancy tests. The state score, in each group, was dramatically lower at 1 year than it was at baseline, but the trait score had only decreased a little. This leads us to believe that the trait score is not unduly influenced by current stress and is therefore a useful measure. A national norm for high school females has been calculated by Spielberger (1983); at 1 and 2 years following admission to the study, the state and trait measures were closer to that norm among those who terminated their pregnancies than among either of the other groups. Although the abortion group seems to include somewhat less anxious individuals, the magnitude of *change* in the two years was not significantly different between the abortion and childbearing groups; it was small in both groups.

Table 22-4 Percentile Ranks of Scores on State-Trait Anxiety Inventory, and Self-Esteem and Locus of Controls Scores, by Abortion, Childbearing, and Negative Test Groups

	Abortion	*Childbearing*	*Negative*
N =	(116)	(83)	(84)
Anxiety-state			
Baseline	74.6	74.2	71.0
1 yr	45.6	50.6	52.1
2 yr	43.6	48.3	47.8
	**	**	**
Anxiety-trait			
Baseline	56.8	62.4	62.9
1 yr	48.3	51.2	59.5**
2 yr	45.7	52.0*	53.2*
	**	**	**
N =	(119)	(87)	(92)
Self-esteem			
Baseline	3.21	3.11	3.13
1 yr	3.31	3.20	3.23
2 yr	3.37	3.25	3.23**
	**	**	*
Locus of control			
Baseline	2.88	2.81	2.83
1 yr	3.00	2.87*	2.93
2 yr	3.00	2.88*	2.96
	**		**

Asterisks (*) to the right of childbearers and negative subgroups refer to the significance of the difference between those groups and the abortion groups. Asterisks at the bottom of each column refer to the significance of the change between baseline and 2-year interviews.

   *$p \le .05$.

   **$p \le .01$.

Self-Esteem and Locus of Control   Self-esteem was measured using the Rosenberg Self-Esteem Scale (1965). There were small but insignificant differences between the groups at baseline, with the abortion group slightly higher in this score (Table 22-4). All three groups experienced small but significant increases in their self-esteem between baseline and 1 year; the 2-year improvements in both the abortion and childbearing groups were significant at $p < .01$ and in the negative test group at $p < .05$.

A limited locus of control measure (Rotter, 1966) was used as well, and here, too, differences were insignificant at baseline. For all three groups, there was an increasing internalization of locus of control over the 2-year period, which is significant at $p < .01$ in the abortion and negative test groups. Thus, as time goes on, these groups apparently feel a greater measure of control over their environments, a change that does not take place to a significant degree among the young mothers.

A minimal decrease in a self-esteem score or increase in an anxiety score or a minimal externalization of locus of control may be of little substantive importance, even if the differences achieve statistical significance. In fact, the majority of young women improved in each of these measures. Therefore, we computed the percentage of each group who showed some adverse change, however small, in all three measures. During the first year, only 5.5% of the two control groups and 4.0% of the abortion group suffered such a change; this seems to indicate clearly that the young women who terminated their pregnancies were at no short-term psychological disadvantage. Once again, after 2 years, there was virtually no change in the abortion group. Only 4.5% experienced negative psychological change over the 2-year period. The childbearing group was similar to the abortion group in this respect. However, the negative test group showed a great deal more change, with almost 10% experiencing an adverse change in all three measures.

Multivariate models were employed as in the case of the educational and economic variables to test the role of group membership when baseline characteristics were controlled. Once again, they confirmed the bivariate findings: in this case, group membership did not make a difference. All the groups changed significantly over time, although the differences were substantively small. There was a high degree of correlation between change in one measure and change in another. But in no group was the amount of change in the scores significantly different from change in the other groups.

Outcome Decisions   Two areas relative to the psychological condition of these young women at the 1-year interview were explored. One related to the decisions the young women with positive tests made about their pregnancy outcomes and had to do with their satisfaction with their decisions; the other had to do with the manner in which the decision was made. There was no significant difference between the abortion group and the childbearers in their satisfaction with their decisions. Only 10% of the aborters and 13% of the childbearers expressed any dissatisfaction with these decisions 1 year later (Hirsch and Zabin, 1988). There were a few subgroups that seemed more likely to express dissatisfaction: they included the young women who, before the results of their tests were known, had reported that they leaned toward one pregnancy resolution but elected a different outcome in the end. It has been suggested that women who are pressured into a decision or have difficulty making decisions are at greater risk for negative feelings in the future; these findings would seem to support that hypothesis. Another subgroup who were somewhat more likely to be displeased with their decision was the group of young women who experienced another pregnancy subsequent to the index event. Finally, respondents who felt that their mothers did not care, or whose mothers did not support their decisions, were less satisfied than those whose mothers were positive and supportive. But whether they belonged to the abortion or childbearing group had no effect on their subsequent satisfaction.

Similarly, when the respondents reported that they spoke to their mothers and experienced their support, their risk of psychological change during the subsequent year was minimized (Hirsch and Zabin, 1988). However, those who did not seek the support of their parents were at no disadvantage. The only disadvantage accrued to those whose families were not supportive of the choice. One might ask whether the evidence suggests, then, that mothers should be involved in the abortion decision. It seems clear from the evidence presented here that these young girls were well able to determine the potential effect of involving their parents in the decision, because those who did not seek support and those who received support did equally well. Counselors in our programs have always suggested to their young clients that the participation of the family would be beneficial, and these results suggest that they are wise to continue doing so. However, the young women who decided not to involve their families appeared equally happy with their decisions and equally strong in the psychological measures we report as those who received family support; they were much better off than those who consulted their families and did not experience positive support. They needed the right to make that choice and apparently did so with discretion.

Subsequent Pregnancy

As suggested above, the occurrence of a pregnancy during the period between the initial outcome and follow-up played an important role in mediating many of the effects upon which we report. Clearly, those who bore their pregnancies following a positive index pregnancy test had less time in which to conceive than those who terminated their pregnancies, and much less time than those whose index tests were negative. In order to control for those differences in estimating the risk of conception, we controlled for the number of months following the original outcome. The longest period of exposure for which we could make that comparison was 18 months, because approximately 6 months out of the 24 months of follow-up had passed before most of the original childbearers had delivered. During equivalent 18-month periods, 58% of the negative test group, 47% of the childbearers, and 37% of the abortion group conceived. The vast majority of these conceptions were unintended, including 75% of those among the childbearers and 80% of those in the abortion group. Although more than half (58%) of the conceptions in the negative test group were also unintended, it is noteworthy that more of these young women reported that they actually wanted a child.

Contraceptive use was clearly related to the pregnancy rates experienced by these young women, with significant differences in use between those who did and those who did not conceive. Most striking was the difference in contraceptive use between the negative test group and those who terminated their pregnancies. Although the numbers available for analysis become small and great caution must be exercised in their interpretation, it seems that the abortion group was much more likely to contracept even when the desire to conceive or avoid conception is controlled. Among those who did not want to conceive, 84% of the abortion group used contraception all or most of the time, and among those who successfully avoided conception, that percentage rose to 94%. Although there were significant associations between the desire for a child and contraceptive use in the other groups as well, in none did that level of consistent use appear.

Conclusion

The results of this 2-year study make it clear that, relative to both control groups, the abortion group was doing well in the economic, educational, psychological, and contraceptive areas we explored. They suggest that the hypothesis that pregnancy termination is associated with adverse psychological effects, at least in the three areas studied here, must be rejected.

The favorable position in which these young women find themselves relative to the other two groups appears to be attributable to three factors: 1) They were slightly better off to begin with in their educational and economic prospects, although these differences were usually insignificant and did not account statistically for their later differences. 2) They had no reason to deteriorate in any of the economic or educational areas we examined, and, indeed, they appeared to stay on track, or better. 3) Because fewer of them conceived during the months following their index outcome, few suffered the additional burdens that such a pregnancy appears to have caused. The rare deficits experienced by young women in the abortion group appeared among the small subgroup that did conceive again; among the majority who did not, adverse outcomes were trivial in number. The importance of avoiding that subsequent conception is clear.

The need for counseling discussed throughout this book could not be made any more graphic than it is by the effects of pregnancy and childbearing reported here. The role of a subsequent pregnancy as a mediating variable when exploring the consequences of abortion, or the 2 years subsequent to a negative pregnancy test, emphasizes the necessity for counseling when the young woman presents for a pregnancy test. For those who will return for an abortion, it can be argued that there will be a better time for intervention; however, because it cannot be certain that the young woman will, indeed, return, the time of her test must be seen as an appropriate moment at which, at the very least, to establish a relationship of trust. For the young woman with a negative pregnancy test, it is the *only* occasion available. That so many of these young women, 58% of them, were pregnant within 18 months, suggests that the opportunity was missed.

All too often, the young people at greatest risk of conception are described as those who are most "hard to reach." In this case, we have identified a group that is not only easy to reach but has actually presented in an adolescent health facility. To allow the moment to pass, without a sufficiently intense period of guidance and education to help her avoid unwanted conception, is tragic, at best. What if she intends to conceive? Whether or not her desire is clearly formulated in her own mind, it is equally important to begin to unravel her reasons for that intention. Knowing the consequences of premature childbearing for her, for her child, and for her family, it should be clear that she is no less in need of help than the young woman who wishes to avoid a pregnancy and fails to do so.

Furthermore, recent analyses of these data suggest that the majority of those who had pregnancy tests were ambivalent about childbearing; very few were unequivocally desirous of having a child. But ambivalence was positively associated with childbearing as was a strong wish to conceive; only those who consistently report attitudes *not* conducive to parenthood were significantly less likely to bear a child during the study period (Zabin and Emerson, 1990).

If elective abortion is as medically safe a procedure as it is, and if it does not carry with it the negative consequences some had feared, clearly it should remain an option for these young women, as it is for women at older ages. The barriers, financial and other, that have been erected cannot be justified in view of these findings. Although counselors should continue to recommend consultation with families when any important decision is to be made by a minor, the rights of an adolescent as described in Chapter 10 must be supported. Fortunately, these findings suggest that the few young women who elected to make the decision without consulting their mothers appeared, on the basis of follow-up, to do so with good reason: they were no less happy with their outcomes, and in no worse psychological condition one year later, than those who had their families' support. They were much better off than those who had turned to their families and had not received support or had had their initial outcome decisions reversed.

But there are other barriers besides those that interfere with a minor's right to confidential treatment. There are barriers discussed in the introduction to Part IV, which derive from the differential between the counseling and support services received by those who carry and those who terminate their pregnancies. And there are the serious financial barriers that have made elective abortion least accessible to those who may need it most. Our data cannot tell us how many young women who wanted to terminate their pregnancies were unable to do so for financial reasons. They do tell us that one-third of the girls who became mothers felt, before hearing the results of their tests, that bearing a child would be a problem and having an abortion would not. Why, in the face of those beliefs, they bore children while children themselves cannot be determined here. What is clear on the basis of this study is that the consequences they would have suffered, had they chosen elective abortion, would have been neither as severe or as long-lasting as those consequent upon bearing a child. Not only in relative terms, but on each of our absolute measures, those who terminated their unwanted pregnancies were doing well.

Part V

The Johns Hopkins Pregnancy Prevention Program (Self Center)

From the service programs that are described in Part III, we gathered valuable experience and knowledge about how to work with teenagers. So had other caring providers all over the country. But nowhere in the country had there been a rigorously evaluated intervention that could document a reduction in adolescent conceptions. It was clearly time, in 1980 and 1981, to develop and test a preventive strategy based not only on the experience of those who worked with adolescents, but also on the evidence from research that described teenage sexual and contraceptive behavior as a basis for defining their service needs. Much of that research had taken place at Johns Hopkins.

In the first chapter, we outline some findings that help explain an apparent paradox in the adolescent statistics of the 1970s: the widespread use of a growing network of contraceptive services for teens with little visible impact on the pregnancy rate. Zelnik and Kantner (1980) had shown rapid increases in teenage sexual activity between 1971 and 1976, with continuing increases among young white females between 1976 and 1979, while the rate among young black women leveled off. In fact, it was high rates of sexual activity that had led to the establishment of services for these age groups, and without these preventive services, pregnancy rates would have soared. Contraceptive use tripled between 1971 and 1976. Although this rate of improvement did not continue, the availability of contraceptive services averted many thousands of abortions and pregnancies.

Challenge of Early Exposure

Risk of Pregnancy Early in Exposure

New findings helped us understand why the impact of available services had not been greater. In a study published in 1979, based on Kantner and Zelnik's 1976 data, we reported the high risk of conception to adolescents in their early months of exposure; Table V-1 shows that 35% of all young women who experienced coitus

Table V-1 Cumulative Percent of Women of 18 to 19 years of age Becoming Pregnant, and Cumulative Percent of First Premarital Pregnancies Occurring in the First 2 Years following First Intercourse

Months after first intercourse	% of women who become pregnant	% of first premarital conceptions
N =	(526)	(212)
1	7.5	21.9
6	17.4	49.6
12	22.2	61.2
24	34.8	84.3

From Zabin, LS, Kantner, JF, and Zelnik M. The risk of adolescent pregnancy in the first months of intercourse. *Fam Plann Perspect* 11:215–222, 1979.

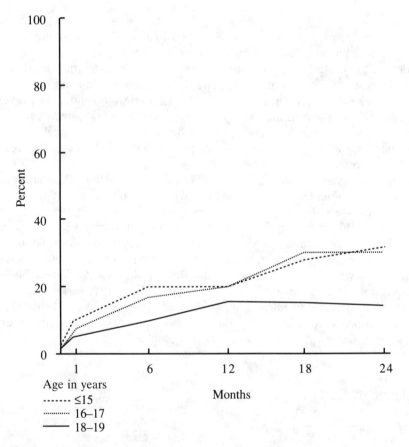

Figure V-1 Cumulative probability of first premarital pregnancy for sexually active girls 18 to 19 years of age at interview in months following first intercourse by age of first intercourse.

in their teens conceived within 2 years of sexual onset, half of them (17.4%) within the first 6 months. If all first premarital conceptions to teens are examined by the same life table technique, almost 50% occurred in the first 6-month period, 22% in the first month alone (Zabin et al., 1979). This finding should not have been surprising; most women, if fertile, conceive early in exposure. There had been some assumption, however, that irregular and anovulatory cycles might cause different patterns among the young and might reduce early risk. These data proved that the subfecundity of youth is a poor contraceptive, indeed. Those who initiated intercourse at 15 years of age and below had the highest rates of conception in the early months of their exposure (Fig. V-1). Among those who postponed first coitus to 18 or 19 years of age, fewer conceived in each period (Zabin et al., 1979). This differential by age of sexual onset was clearly attributable to differences in contraceptive use. Those whose onset was early were unlikely to use reliable methods; most of them used no method at all. Those who delayed coitus until 16 or 17 years of age were more likely to use a method, and young women whose first premarital coitus took place at 18 or 19 demonstrated contraceptive use patterns that compared favorably with those observed among older married women.

The evidence from this study made clear the importance of early intervention and focused attention on the need for alternatives to traditional free-standing or hospital-based contraceptive clinics. These had long been the first point of contact between adolescents and preventive care (in fact, reproductive health care is not infrequently the point of entry for adult women into the health care system, but it reaches only a small proportion of adolescents). The notion that schools must be involved, that reproductive education and services could not await the onset of coital activity, gained increasing acceptance.

The need for more information about the early weeks and months of sexual contact was evident from the data on early risk. It led to a study of young women attending 32 contraceptive facilities in eight major cities in the United States to learn more about the interval from first coitus to first clinic attendance (Zabin and Clark, 1981). The average duration of that interval among those attending a clinic for the first time was 16.4 months. The median delay was close to a year, or 9 months if those who came before first coitus were included.

This study confirmed the fact that coital activity in the early months of exposure was often sporadic, even rare, but it produced the startling information that 36% of the young women came to a clinic for the first time because they already suspected they were pregnant. Forty-two percent came for contraception after three or more months of coital exposure, sometimes after many years, and only 14% sought protection in anticipation of first intercourse. If unintended pregnancies were to be avoided, it was clearly imperative to reach all young people, both males and females, prior to the onset of sexual activity.

Shape of Intervention

What did we know about the behavior of adolescents and their reproductive health needs that would be of help in designing programs appropriate to their needs? Some of what we knew had come from our contact with adolescents over the years. Functionally, the problems of negotiating a health system, usually without the help of parents, were daunting. With limited funds for transportation, often without transportation at all, the prospects for successful appointment-making and appointment-keeping were dim. Unless clinics accept walk-in patients, the planning process they demand almost precludes attendance by young people, whose behavior is often impulsive. Costs, or even the presumption that costs might be involved, present insurmountable barriers to adolescents who often have no money. These difficulties, in combination with the embarrassment involved in an intimate examination and all of the problems suggested by the cognitive and emotional developmental status of the young discussed in Chapter 2, made the likelihood that a young adolescent would actually seek out services, and do so in time, appear remote.

The study of young women in 32 clinics amplified our understanding by showing that, while procrastination was the top reason for delay in attending contraceptive facilities, the fear of discovery by parents was a close second (Zabin and Clark, 1981). Confidential services were clearly of paramount importance. While almost four times as many blacks as whites (11.5% versus 3.0%) said a parent had suggested the visit, this was an infrequent reason for seeking care. Among young blacks, fear of parental discovery was considerably less acute than among whites; however, even among black girls, more than one out of four cited the need for confidentiality as a deterrent. Thus, while involving parents has continued to be a high priority among service personnel when it is deemed helpful, it was clear that confidential treatment for those who felt they needed it was an essential ingredient of effective service.

When the young women were asked what motivated their clinic selection, the fact that the clinic did not inform parents topped the list. It was followed closely by the patient's belief that the people of the clinic "really care about teens" (Zabin and Clark, 1983). The degree of support patients feel, the commitment of the staff to their young clients, has emerged over and over as a prime concern among adolescents in selecting a source of care.

Finally, our understanding of adolescent development suggested that prolonged contact was necessary if contraceptive continuation rates were to be improved. We knew from our work with young people that compliance is often difficult to achieve. Additional analysis of data from the original study of the risk of pregnancy to adolescents (Zabin et al., 1979) confirmed our observations. Using the life table methodology that had demonstrated an unusually high probability of pregnancy in the early months of exposure, a hypothetical case was created. We asked what could be achieved if *all* adolescents attended a contraceptive facility 1 month after first coitus and then experienced the pregnancy risks attributable to young women who use medical methods of contraception (Zabin, 1981). Our calculations showed that the overall risk of conception in a 2-year period would be reduced only about 40%. Approximately half the risk that remained would be attributable to the high probability of conception in the first month of coitus; the other half would be attributable to the risks teens experience even *after* adopting a medical method. Continuation and effective contraception require that frequent contact be maintained with the younger user. The school has been shown to be a location in which follow-up is a realistic expectation (Edwards et al., 1980).

From our experience in delivering services to teens, we had a few specific findings that helped us to visualize the shape preventive intervention should take. We were convinced that educational and medical services must be delivered in the same site at the same time; as important as counseling and guidance might be, young people might not value them enough to return once their medical needs were met, if they were only available at different times. We felt, however, that they should be delivered by different staff, because of the time that is required for adequate counseling, and because many of the skills that are needed are those of the social worker/educator/counselor. Even the most sympathetic, empathetic medical practitioner might not be the most appropriate person and would probably not have the unstructured time to play that role. Furthermore, the educator/counselor could reinforce and amplify the information imparted by the physician or nurse practitioner, and the team could function together in a case management model.

Finally, we believed that, although the school was the ideal locus of first contact, some bridge was needed between the didactic classroom setting and the nearby clinical services. A free-standing school-linked clinic would have the opportunity to deliver contraceptive and reproductive health services as few school-based facilities had been free to do. The challenge was to develop school-based components that would facilitate the flow from one site to the other and provide the symbiosis of education, guidance, and medical services that would serve our school populations best.

The Self Center

The program we describe in this section was conceived from the start as a self-limited experiment—a demonstration project with a strong evaluation component. Its design was based on all we had learned from clinical experience and research, and its staff were selected for their sensitivity to adolescents and adolescents' concerns.

The school-wide data on which the evaluation is based were collected by self-administered questionnaires in the junior and senior high schools in which the program would be placed, and in the control schools before the program began. Similar data were collected again at the end of each of the three program years at the experimental schools and at the end of the third year at the control schools. The nature of the program and the patterns in which students utilized its services are described in some detail in Chapter 23; the methods of education it employed are described in Chapter 24 by the Administrator of the Self Center, as the program came to be known. Results of its evaluation are summarized in Chapter 25. Details of the evaluation methodology have been published in book form elsewhere (Zabin and Hirsch, 1987). The survey instruments utilized in the study are reprinted in the appendix to that text, in order to make them available to other programs in which they may serve a similar useful purpose.

23

The Self Center
A School-Linked Pregnancy Prevention Program

In order to reach the population served by the Johns Hopkins Hospital with a primary pregnancy prevention program, the junior and senior high schools closest to the hospital were offered the opportunity to participate in a privately funded, 3-year experimental demonstration program. The schools, with enrollments of approximately 700 and 1,000 students, respectively, were located a few blocks apart; most of their students came from an inner city neighborhood characterized by public and low-cost housing. Because the senior high school was a magnet school, some of its students came from other locations in the city, but many others were from the same areas that fed the junior high. Although no accurate data were available on rates of pregnancy or sexually transmitted disease in these schools before the student bodies were surveyed, many young people from the area were served in the Johns Hopkins' clinics (particularly the Adolescent Pregnancy Program) and were known to be in need of reproductive health services. Furthermore, many of the students at a special school for pregnant girls had been referred out of these schools, documenting their need for early intervention.

Objectives

After receiving the support of the principals and approval of the concept from the Superintendent of Schools, the process of program development occupied an 8-month period. During that time, important preliminary objectives were met:

1. The principals and the Superintendent of Schools were thoroughly informed about the objectives and methods proposed for the model, both its service and research components, and they contributed to its final design.
2. Formalities required by the school system and its Health Council—a joint committee of the Health and Education Departments—were met, and necessary authorizations were put in place.
3. Each school family, including teachers and parents, was familiarized with the plan, and some parents and community members were enlisted into an Advisory Council.

4. Evaluation instruments, including surveys and service records, were designed and approved by the school authorities.
5. A store-front facility was refurbished as a clinic across the street from one school and a few blocks from the other.
6. Space in each of the schools' health suites was identified as the locus of the program in the schools.
7. Staff were employed and trained and oriented into the roles they would play both in the service program and in the collection of data for the evaluation component.

Thus, although a long period was consumed in preparation for the program, the time was well spent bolstering school and community support, which was reflected in the high level of acceptance the program enjoyed.

The program had several explicit objectives, some specifically related to the prevention of unintended pregnancy and others that addressed the developmental needs of the students. The prevention of conception was seen in the context of the whole person, of his or her physical, cognitive, and emotional development. Although the measurable goals were largely in the area of reproductive health, it was the overall purpose of the program to help the young people recognize the relationship between their sexual behavior and the aspirations they held for their own futures and to empower them to make responsible decisions. The quantifiable objectives of the program were to:

1. Increase the level of knowledge among all students in areas of physical maturation, human sexuality, contraception, and fertility, and the personal burdens and cost that can accrue from an unintended pregnancy.
2. Reinforce positive attitudes toward pregnancy prevention and instill realistic attitudes toward the role of premature conception and parenthood.
3. Postpone first intercourse among those not yet sexually active.
4. Increase the utilization of professional contraceptive services among those who were, or expected to be, sexually active.
5. Increase and improve the effectiveness of contraceptive use among those who were sexually active.
6. Reduce pregnancy rates in the schools, so that both the abortion *and* childbearing rates would decrease.

Many other less measurable objectives were realized by the staff as they addressed the educational and medical needs of the students.

The principal investigators believed that programs in these reproductive health areas were in need of evaluation to demonstrate whether they could or could not achieve these quantifiable goals. They were willing to commit time and resources to that assessment and found that foundations were appreciative of the financial demands of responsible evaluation. The evaluation was designed so that quantitative measurements could be made at several points in time to measure program effects.

Methods and Program Components

In the fall of 1981, all students were given a notification letter to take home to their parents telling them of a school-wide survey that was to be administered a few days later. Parents in the program schools were told that a program was to be introduced that would address problems of sexual behavior and pregnancy and that the questions, on the basis of which the program would be refined, would ask for personal information. They were told that participation in the survey was voluntary and anonymous. Any parent who did not want a child to participate could return a signed statement to that effect or call to request that he or she be excused. Several parents called to say how much they appreciated the fact that such a program would be offered; none of the parents in the program schools requested that their offspring be excused. Only two out of 2,000 in the control schools, who were told only of the survey, made that request.

Components of Service

Following the collection of baseline data (administration of the surveys is described in Chapter 25), services in the school could begin. In order to meet the young peoples' need for continuity of care, a team consisting of a social worker and a nurse midwife or pediatric nurse practitioner was assigned to each program school. The students became familiar with these two providers in several ways. They could become acquainted when staff, either together or individually, addressed each homeroom at least once in the course of each semester. They could meet them in their classrooms when teachers invited the staff to make special presentations as a part of one or another unit of instruction. Or the students could meet the staff individually or in small groups by coming to the health suite whenever they wished during the lunch period. That time slot is a long one in a large public school, covering several hours during which classes have staggered lunch breaks. Because the young people ate lunch during only a few minutes of their assigned lunch period, they were free to drop in for individual or small group meetings as they wished. They could also make appointments to see the staff individually at the clinic across the street.

In the afternoon, the two staff members from each school were in the clinic, called the Self Center,[1] which opened about 1:30 and remained open until all the young people were served, usually between 5 and 6 o'clock. The waiting room of the clinic was an attractive, bright, and cheerful place where students could come with or without appointments for discussions, educational films, and games. Individual consultation was available with the social worker and the medical staff, which was augmented by a nurse's aide and, on some days, by a gynecologist.[2] Contraceptive services were provided to females by the medical staff after examination and consultation with the social worker. Males could receive medical service if they wished; they could also receive condoms from the social worker after a private consultation without seeing the medical staff.

In order to describe the texture of the program, we focus our discussion on the day-to-day activities of the four staff members who provided the lion's share of the direct services to the students, the two social workers and the two nurses.

---

[1]"Make a life for yourself before you make another life" was its motto.

[2]Because Maryland permits the provision of reproductive health care without parental consent, including family planning and the diagnosis and management of sexually transmitted diseases, the clinic was able to provide confidential care.

The service program's principal investigator was seldom in contact with the students, and, although the Program Administrator frequently interacted with them in the clinic and was always available for special cases, her principal role was not that of a direct service provider. The principal investigator for the research effort and her team were rarely on site when the students were present.

The direct services rendered by the four key staff can be described in six categories, three of which took place in the school and three in the clinic. The school activities included classroom presentations, small group discussions, and individual counseling; the clinic activities can be summarized as group education, individual counseling, and medical services. Before examining the distribution of services among the students, it is important to get a feel for the quality of these staff/student contacts.

Classroom Presentations

The first contact between the students and the Self Center staff was often in the homeroom. The social worker, and at times the nurse, gave at least one full period presentation to every homeroom in her school every semester. The first class presentation each year acquainted students with the services that would be available to them. Often a film, "A Matter of Respect," in which Jesse Jackson focuses on adolescent pregnancy as a problem for males and females alike, was shown. Although these presentations were more structured than the small group sessions, they included interaction with the students, and the film was used as a catalyst for discussions related to values clarification, decision-making, and reproductive health. The most important goal of the session, however, was to establish a spirit of open communication between the students and the staff. Many of the students had never discussed personal subjects with adults before; it was essential that, from their first contact with the program, they should feel that it could, potentially, fill an important need in their lives.

Either the same semester or the following semester, a second classroom discussion took place, usually focused on sexual activity, pregnancy, decision-making, abstinence, contraceptives, and sexually transmitted diseases. More such meetings might take place, but two a year were mandated.

Group Discussion in School

When the program first began, both the social worker and the nurse were assigned to the schools during the morning of each day. After the first year, when it became clear that the social workers could respond to questions about students' contraceptive and health needs and that the students felt as free to ask these questions of them as to ask them of the nurses, the medical staff were sent to the schools only for specific programs. The social workers handled most of the school counseling program alone.

Relevant books, pamphlets, and games were available to the students in the schools' health suites. Spontaneous small group discussions often occurred there; they were either informal rap sessions or more focused discussions that were initiated by a group of students with a specific problem, or by the discussion leader who had identified a need among her young students. Questions about pubertal development, physical immaturity that may have led to teasing, suspected teenage prostitution or other abuse might be addressed. Or the social worker would pose questions about the student's future goals, peer pressure to use drugs and alcohol, sexually transmitted diseases (STDs), the consequences of teenage parenthood, male-female relationships, and the importance of decision-making skills. (Today, the prevention of AIDS—acquired immune deficiency syndrome—would be a major issue, but it was not when this program was initiated.) It was vital that professionals trained in group process be available to guide the informal sessions, because they were able to identify emotional needs that are difficult to elicit in more formal settings. Identifying these needs could lead to individual counseling by one of the program's staff, in the school or in the clinic, or could lead directly to referral to outside agencies. Of paramount importance to the program was the atmosphere created in the health suite: it was a hospitable environment to individuals and small groups and set the tone that encouraged many of them to make appointments to come to the nearby clinic.

School Counseling

The clinic was a more appropriate site for continuing counseling than the school; the academic schedule did not allow for prolonged consultation, and the clinic often provided a better sense of privacy and neutrality. Nonetheless, it was useful to have the social worker available for one-on-one guidance at school. The students would often seek out the Self Center staff to discuss such personal issues as relationships with the opposite sex, problems at home, the suspicion of pregnancy, and other matters that required confidential consultation. The social worker made a point of letting the young people know at what hours she would be available in the school for individual sessions. She utilized a group of students described as the "peer resource team," which is discussed below, to take care of drop-ins while she was engaged in private discussions of this nature.

Group Education in the Clinic

Almost all the young people who came to the clinic, whether or not they intended to see a provider for contraceptive services or guidance, were exposed to educational intervention. Some group discussions took place in the waiting room, where a film strip/audiotape cassette player was always available. A "rap room" was used for more organized sessions, often with an educator, and informal sessions with a few participants often coalesced around the educator, the Program Director, or a social worker in the waiting room. There were fewer time constraints on these discussions than there were in the school, where schedules were always tight. An after-school program tends to bring large numbers of students into the clinic at the same time and makes it important to find ways to utilize time that might otherwise be spent simply waiting for individual services. Some of the educational sessions in the clinic were organized around specific topics, whether proposed by the educator or the students. They were very similar to the discussions in the school health suite and placed similar emphasis on values clarification and personal decision making, although they also focused on didactic material in the area of reproductive education. The students were free to discuss personal experiences, physical growth, and body changes with puberty, menstruation, sexual behavior, male-female relationships, and so forth, but some of these discussions went further afield: nutrition, weight loss, personal grooming and makeup, and other issues that interested the young people sparked some special sessions.

Clinic Counseling

Students from the two schools could register as patients at the clinic for individual counseling with the social worker, a medical visit, or both. Most female enrollees had an initial interview that was essentially sociopsychological and elicited information on sexual experience, family relationships, school achievement, and the emotional status of the young woman. Following this interview, further individual counseling sessions were often arranged. The student could present for the first time because of a personal or family problem, a suspicion of pregnancy or sexually transmitted disease, a particular sexual relationship, or a school problem, but the majority gave their need for contraception as their presenting reason. The program's counseling mission was interpreted very broadly; the focus of the program on reproductive health did not imply that students were not free to bring a wide range of problems to the social and medical staff.

Because of a case management system in which the medical and social work staff cooperated to bring optimal service to the young people, the roles of the staff members were quite fluid. Much of the health education, for example, was provided during the individual counseling sessions. The social workers were empowered to dispense foam and condoms to male registrants and to female patients as well, and were equipped to counsel them in their use. They would talk to patients who had repeated bouts of sexually transmitted diseases, using these educational sessions to explore the reasons behind continued high-risk contact and exposure. As we will see below, the reasons that ostensibly brought the students to the clinic were often only a point of entry. Not infrequently, the initial psychosocial interview or subsequent counseling sessions turned up other, often more important, areas for the social worker and the patient to explore together.

Medical Visits

Although both males and females utilized the medical staff, the vast majority of medical visits were made by young women. Any female seeking contraception had a physical examination, and males with physical problems related to reproductive health were seen by the staff, as well. When young women presented for pregnancy tests they saw the medical staff, whom they could also consult for discussions of menstrual problems, for the treatment of sexually transmitted diseases, and for detailed discussions of their health needs. The medical staff did not interpret their mission as separate from the guidance role; when they identified emotional issues that interfered with compliance—with appointment-keeping, contraceptive continuation, early pregnancy testing, or follow-up visits—they became counselors as well as medical providers. Furthermore, although the clinic was identified as a reproductive health center, some serious conditions in other health areas were diagnosed, and appropriate referrals were made.

Texture of Program

The philosophy of the model is suggested by the range of services described above. It was predicated on an understanding of the young clients in the larger context of their developmental status, their family circumstances, their educational achievement and expectations, their future aspirations, and their social relationships. The program tried to help them recognize the role their behaviors played in relation to their ability to reach these goals and, in particular, the role their sexual decisions might play in limiting their horizons for the future. Because the students often held positive attitudes in these areas, the staff were able to focus on encouraging them to make their values and objectives explicit, and then on helping them to understand the implications of their actions. Thus they *empowered* them to make responsible decisions more often than they *changed* the value systems the students already held.

The students learned very quickly that the staff members of the Self Center were open to discussion of a wide range of personal issues. An unforeseen (and unmeasurable) bonus of the baseline survey process seemed to be the immediacy with which it communicated the scope of the program's interests, hence the kinds of questions that were legitimate to discuss with program staff. Nonetheless, considerable patience and skill sometimes were required to probe beneath the veneer, to uncover the problems that plagued the young people who came to the Self Center.

Case Histories

A few case histories will suggest the directions private consultations might take:

Anthony, 13 years old Although many seventh and eighth grade boys presented at the Self Center, one of the most memorable was Anthony; he was a 13-year-old seventh grader who had not yet begun his growth spurt. Like many other prepubertal youngsters, he strutted into the clinic requesting condoms. After a fairly lengthy private interview, Anthony was able to admit that he had only experimented with intercourse once. He did not foresee that he would be needing condoms in the very near future, and his real concern was that he was not as tall as the other boys in his grade.

To respond to his very acute worries about his growth and to assure him that both his growth and his lack of interest in girls were normal, he was given a chance to join a group of boys with similar concerns. The group's purpose was to teach the boys about development, to explore thoughts and feelings about growing up, and to allay anxiety about body size and, equally important, to show them that they were not alone. In addition to becoming a member of the group, Anthony was able to consult individually whenever he felt the need to talk. He was also weighed and measured every month.

As might have been expected, Anthony grew several inches and gained several pounds over the course of the year. He learned a lot about human sexuality, boy-girl relationships, birth control, and sexually transmitted diseases. Anthony made more than 30 voluntary clinic visits in the course of the next 12 months, and often brought his friends. Although many of his visits were unscheduled, he was always warmly received and encouraged to continue to drop in whenever he wished.

Sharita, 16 years old   Sharita had come to the clinic many times as a "visitor." Because almost all visitors were lured into the group education sessions, Sharita had often participated in these groups. However, because she claimed that she was not sexually active and had no need of medical services, she was not an enrolled patient. After several months of visits during which she declined invitations to make an appointment, Sharita requested a pregnancy test. The test was positive. Self Center policy mandated that youngsters with pregnancy tests be seen by a social worker. During her interview, pregnancy options were discussed. In addition, Sharita's obvious ambivalence about becoming pregnant was explored. The teenager was unable to make a decision about how she would handle the pregnancy and was encouraged to go home and talk to her mother, with whom she had a good relationship. The worker discussed with Sharita the feelings her mother might have about her daughter's pregnancy and helped the youngster to anticipate the emotions, possibly the anger and disappointment, her mother might express. The social worker made an appointment for Sharita to return the next afternoon to continue the counseling and told Sharita that she and her mother could come in together to talk if they so desired.

Sharita returned the next day after having spoken to her mother who was horrified by the news of her daughter's pregnancy. Because it was obvious to Sharita that her mother had many of the feelings she and the case worker had explored the day before, she was glad to have talked about them ahead of time. Both the young woman and her mother had agreed that Sharita should terminate the pregnancy. In their discussion, Sharita heard for the first time that her mother had been a teenager when she was born. Her mother did not want Sharita to struggle as she had and strongly encouraged the abortion.

Sharita's pregnancy was terminated. She became a successful family planning patient at the Self Center and graduated from high school without a repeat pregnancy.

Carol, 17 years old   Carol was a senior in high school and had been a patient in the Self Center for 6 months, during which time she had been treated twice for sexually transmitted diseases. Clinic policy mandated that teens who contracted STDs be referred to the social worker; this is because some STDs are reportable diseases entailing responsibility for notification of contacts and reporting to public health agencies, and also because the repeated contraction of disease may have behavioral as well as medical implications.

After much denial, Carol realized that contracting gonorrhea twice within 6 months could be indicative of a troubled relationship with her boyfriend. She felt she could handle the situation, however, and did not want any intervention from a social worker.

Two weeks later, Carol returned to the clinic to see the nurse. Her boyfriend had suggested that she be checked because he thought he might have given her gonorrhea again. The nurse talked with Carol about long-term health risks of repeated STDs, and the implications of her partner's behavior for the possibility of a happy future with him. After this episode, Carol was responsive to the suggestion that she and the social worker talk about her relationship with her boyfriend.

She accepted the referral and was able to explore the issue, although the relationship continued through two more bouts of STDs before Carol was able to terminate it permanently.

Not all of the students who utilized the services had interactions that probed so deeply, but even those whose contacts were less focused seemed to feel a sense of ownership of the program and a high level of comfort with the staff. This was due in large measure to their ability to utilize the facilities in so many different ways and to have free and informal access to the staff at both sites.

Peer Resource Team

The sense of ownership to which we refer could also have been bolstered by a group of students designated as a "peer resource team." Each year, several students—males and females in each school—received special training to function as outreach workers and assistants to the staff. Exercising great care to protect the privacy of the patients, the staff did not utilize the students as lay counselors or clinic helpers, but they were available in both sites to hand out materials and manage the equipment. More important, perhaps, was the visibility they gave the Self Center. They wore T-shirts or buttons saying "Ask me about the Self Center" and, theoretically at least, they encouraged students to acquaint themselves with its services. The staff invested a great deal of time in their education and support. Staff reports that the peer resource individuals were in constant contact with them are confirmed by the logs. The training of these 12 students seemed to contribute more to their own personal growth than it did to the program's referral network; few clients reported that they had attended the Self Center because of their contacts with the peer resource team.

Utilization of Program's Components

Sources of Data

Each individual student's contact with the clinic was well documented (See Zabin and Hirsch, 1987 for details). Sign-in sheets in the waiting room allowed a record to be kept of those individuals who visited the clinic and were exposed to educational interventions but were never formally enrolled for individual services. Registration forms were completed for every student seeking individual services, medical history forms for students who saw a nurse or physician, social records for those who saw the counselor, and a brief summary form, completed by the registrar, for visits that might not otherwise have been documented. Only one type of form was completed solely for research purposes; these were the logs, maintained daily by the four key staff, in which they recorded all contacts they had with the students in the school or in the clinic. While informal exchanges in the school corridors would not have been registered on the logs, any other individual or group contact was noted, making it possible to estimate the time invested in each component of service.

The school system provided the research staff with several "rolling rolls" each year, to permit them to establish a denominator that defined the student bodies of the two schools. This is not always an easy estimate to obtain, because students move in, out, and through schools and often do not appear in the school at which they are expected.[3] If everyone on any school roll is counted, many students will appear who may never have been exposed to the program at all. On the other hand, some chronic absentees do turn up in the school occasionally, and if the program is far-reaching and attractive enough to the students, even some of these chronic absentees may become participants.

Student-Staff Contacts

Table 23-1 suggests that 85% of the students were reached by at least one component of the program, with more males than females among those not utilizing its services (Zabin, Hirsch, Streett, et al., 1988). The figures in parentheses report the percent reached when the denominator for each subgroup is adjusted by the "chronic absentee" rate the school system estimates for that school/gender group. They suggest that a well received program may reach even some chronic absentees (although they also suggest that the absentee estimates for the junior high school students may be high.) (We cannot explain the large number of senior high males who did not attend classroom presentations, which should have reached all but chronic absentees; the school system reports a low, 11%, absentee rate in this group.)

Table 23-2 shows the large numbers of staff-student contacts that took place in the 30-month period of the demonstration (33,388) and illustrates the great popularity of the small group sessions that were carried out in the school health suites. More than 41% of all student contacts fell within that category, even more than took place in the classroom. Table 23-1 indicates that more than 50% of the students (or 67% if the denominator is adjusted to remove chronic absentees) took part in these small group discussions. A smaller percentage, about 35%, took part in group education in the clinic. This is particularly interesting because the discussions in the clinic were often related to the use of medical services and were required for those seeking contraception. On the other hand, the small group discussions that took place in the school were sought freely by the students, for their value in and of themselves. Among senior high school males, overall participation in the program approached the level of other groups only because of the school components; their utilization of the clinic was limited. In their case, as among all students, a larger *percentage of all students* was reached by classroom discussions, but the *number of contacts* in small groups was higher.

These numbers should be understood in relation to the actual months of exposure the students had to the program, especially its in-school components. Students who graduated from the junior or senior high during the first year of the program had only 5 months in which to utilize the clinic and 6½ months to be reached in the schools. Almost 37% of the students who seem not to have been reached by the program received only that abbreviated first-year exposure. Mean exposure of all students who had any contact with the program was 16 months, including summers and other vacations; of course, for many who were never really

---

[3]A more complete treatment of the methods used to obtain an accurate count of those eligible for service is available elsewhere (Zabin and Hirsch, 1987; Zabin, Hirsch, et al., 1986). Suggestions for summary estimates and more exhaustive measures which may be useful are outlined in both those references.

Table 23-1 Percentage of Students Using Program Services (and Percentage after Adjustment for Chronic Absentees), by Site and Type of Service, According to Gender and School Level

Site and type of service	All students (N = 3,944)	Female		Male	
		Jr. high (N = 1,001)	Sr. high (N = 1,163)	Jr. high (N = 1,132)	Sr. high (N = 581)
Total	84.9 (112.2)	87.1 (119.0)	87.0 (97.8)	82.2 (132.6)	80.7 (90.7)
School					
Class presentation	72.7 (96.1)	81.2 (111.2)	73.0 (83.9)	73.9 (119.1)	61.3 (68.9)
Group discussion	50.6 (66.9)	55.2 (75.6)	55.6 (63.8)	42.0 (67.7)	48.2 (54.2)
Indiv. counseling	15.2 (20.1)	15.3 (20.9)	29.8 (34.3)	4.3 (7.0)	8.8 (9.9)
Clinic					
Group education	26.7 (35.3)	24.2 (33.1)	42.1 (48.4)	21.0 (33.9)	12.4 (13.9)
Indiv. counseling	19.7 (26.0)	14.5 (19.8)	34.3 (39.4)	15.6 (25.2)	9.8 (11.0)
Medical visit	14.5 (19.2)	13.4 (18.3)	34.8 (40.0)	1.8 (2.8)	2.2 (2.5)

From *Family Planning Perspectives* (Zabin, Hirsch, Streett, et al., 1988).

Chronic absentee rates as reported by the schools were: junior high females, 27%; senior high females, 11%; junior high males, 38%; and senior high males, 11%.

in attendance, that could be a gross overestimate. The clinic did remain open in the summer, with substantially lower attendance; however, also on the basis of the rolls, the maximum time the *school* components were available to each student totalled an average of 250 days overall. The numbers of contacts reported on the logs suggest that, on each of the approximately 475 school mornings the staff spent in the schools, an average of 47 or 48 contacts were made. On an individual basis, in the course of their (250 day mean) exposure, students who interacted with the program experienced an average of ten, and a median of four, contacts. The most interactions were experienced by senior high females who averaged 16; the fewest by senior high males with 5.5. A median of three contacts were experienced by males in both schools and five by females. These averages, based on all students with contact with the program, include many students who experienced only the

Table 23-2 Number of Student Contacts with Program Staff, by Site and Type of Service, According to Gender and School Level, December 1981 to June 1984

Site and type of service	All students[a] (N = 3,944)	Female		Male	
		Jr. high (N = 1,001)	Sr. high (N = 1,163)	Jr. high (N = 1,132)	Sr. high (N = 581)
Total	33,388	9,175	16,095	5,475	2,565
School	22,633	7,211	8,655	4,445	2,254
Class presentation	7,188	2,354	1,875	2,260	683
Group discussion	13,742	4,503	5,614	2,114	1,460
Indiv. counseling	1,703	354	1,166	71	111
Clinic	10,755	1,964	7,440	1,030	311
Group education	5,377	1,007	3,600	594	166
Indiv. counseling	2,243	402	1,310	407	124
Medical visit	3,135	555	2,530	29	21

From *Family Planning Perspectives* (Zabin, Hirsch, Streett, et al., 1988).

[a]In this table and Table 25-1, 67 students are included who appeared on a school list or on staff logs but whose school or gender was unknown; column also includes 78 contacts with the program by these students.

classroom interactions. At the other extreme, some students were in constant contact with the staff, often over 100 and even over 200 times. The staff had the impression throughout the program that some of their most difficult cases—and neediest—monopolized much of their time. Their reports were borne out by this quantitative evidence.

Not only were females more likely to make numerous visits to the staff overall, but senior high school females were more likely than senior high school males to seek individual counseling at both sites and were much more likely to utilize the clinic. Clinic "enrollment" was required for those who used the services of the social worker or the staff at the clinic for individual services; this included some who needed continuing counseling and all who sought contraception or any medical service. Junior high school males, however, were as likely as females to see the social workers in the clinic. Although some students used the clinic only as an educational site, more of the students who attended the clinic came for individual services, as well. That is, they became clinic enrollees, either for medical or social work services, but usually for both. Using the base number of eligible students that controls for chronic absentees, 24.4% of all students enrolled; this includes a much higher percentage of those who were sexually active and therefore had a need for the clinical services. Overall, 85% of the female enrollees were sexually active (Hirsch et al., 1987), which is in accord with national estimates made in clinics serving teens in many parts of the country (Zabin and Clark, 1981). Approximately 48% of sexually active senior high school girls became enrollees. (Clearly, a large proportion of those who did not utilize the individual clinic services had established some source of contraception by the time this service was available to them. Others did so during the course of the demonstration. The staff encouraged their continued utilization of such alternative services because, especially if they were close to graduation, a source of continuing care was important to them.) In view of the 28-month period in which these clinic services were available to the two schools and in view of the gender and age mix in the target populations, attendance at the clinic facilities was extremely encouraging. Qualitatively and quantitatively, the services appeared to be a success.

Routes to the Clinic

We indicated above that the students could utilize the program in many ways; accordingly, their routes to the clinic differed, but for the vast majority, school contact came first. Most (75.6%) of the students who were reached by the program had their first contact with the Self Center staff in the classroom. Some moved on to the school health suite to see a staff member in a small group or individually, and a few had visited the health suite independently before hearing a lecture. Overall, 69% of the students who had some contact with the program had all their interactions with the staff in the school setting.

There were 31%, then, who visited the clinic at some time; among them, 22% came only for education, and 78% attended for both education and individual services. The vast majority of the latter group, referred to as enrollees, had some contact with the program in school before becoming enrolled in the clinic (Fig. 23-1). Only 14.3% of them did not interact with the staff at the school before their first clinic visit, and, even among that small group, some went on to use the school services between that visit and the day they actually enrolled. When the latter

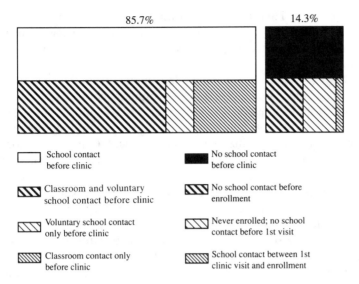

85.7%   14.3%

	School contact before clinic		No school contact before clinic
	Classroom and voluntary school contact before clinic		No school contact before enrollment
	Voluntary school contact only before clinic		Never enrolled; no school contact before 1st visit
	Classroom contact only before clinic		School contact between 1st clinic visit and enrollment

Figure 23-1 Percent distribution of all students attending clinic by route taken through program components.

group is included, only 12%, overall, did not have a school contact before becoming enrolled. Thus, the great majority, almost 88%, of those who used the individual clinic services had already become acquainted with and interacted with the staff at least once, often numerous times, in the school setting before the visit at which they enrolled for individual clinic consultation. The bridge between school and clinic, as originally postulated, proved to be important in facilitating clinic use.

Conclusion

As we will see in Chapter 25, the program achieved its goals beyond our most optimistic expectations. The data presented here demonstrate that the students utilized the program heavily and used it in the way the model was conceived. Although larger numbers of senior high school males would have been welcome in the clinic, overall utilization was high, and all subgroups of students appeared to find components that met their needs. Many of those who did not use the program appear to have been motivated to use other sources of care. The heavy utilization of the program by junior high males was one of its major successes and suggested the importance of contact with young boys during their pubertal years. This brief time period may provide a window of opportunity for reaching young males.

Another documented success was the utilization of educational, counseling, and medical components by the same individuals. The model linked these components because we believed young people needed that breadth of services. There had been clear evidence in the literature that education by itself did not reduce pregnancies. Nonetheless, the importance of education both for those who were sexually active and for those who did not yet require medical intervention was clear. Our understanding of the developmental status of the age groups we were serving made us see personal counseling as an essential ingredient in the calculus of behavioral change. Therefore, the fact that the modal group of medical visitors used all six categories of service was seen as a validation of the model: most students who used the medical staff received every kind of education and counseling the program offered.

Similarly, the progression of individual students from the school to the clinic described above, from class presentations to voluntary consultation, and from visits to the waiting room to individual service appeared to confirm our belief that any bridge we could provide between the classroom components and the medical components would facilitate the utilization of clinic services. Other conclusions reported elsewhere (Zabin, Hirsch, Streett, et al., 1988) include the following:

- The classroom exposure is an essential step that maximizes contact with a school population and serves many important purposes. This project demonstrated, however, that small groups were especially popular among these adolescents. The school was an excellent location for informal, small-group discussions; because the data suggest that relatively few students attended group sessions in the clinic unless they also came for some other clinic service, many students reached by the program could have been missed had not this school component been available. Furthermore, most of the clinic enrollees (more than 85% of the females) were sexually active; therefore, it may be that only in the school is there a real opportunity to delay the onset of coitus.
- Group education in the clinic was not used by as many *non*registrants as had been anticipated. There is evidence to indicate that some students used group education until they felt comfortable enough to ask for individual services; that is, they attended group sessions in the waiting room or the clinic's education suite before enrolling for medical and/or counseling services. However, the educational opportunities in the clinic were very popular and were heavily used by those who came for individual services. These patterns of use may show that the needs of nonregistrants were adequately met within the school, which is in keeping with the logic of the model.
- Individual counseling took place in the school and/or in the clinic; almost 40% of students who received personal guidance in one location received it in both. Counseling is often an ongoing and long-term process, which consumes a great deal of staff time.
- Senior high females require numerous reproductive health visits, especially for contraceptive services. Many more of them are sexually active than younger students are, and their visits represent a large proportion of the medical service load. Many who are engaging in coitus use oral contraceptives, a method that requires attendance at a medical facility not only for resupply but for support. Because there is frequently anxiety about the use of oral contraception, reinforcement and encouragement are important to keep this age group on a consistent regimen. Consequently, programs for senior high school girls must expect to deliver large numbers of clinic services.
- Mean numbers of staff encounters among male students are about one-half the numbers for females. Nonetheless, even senior high males sought out small group sessions in the school, although as a group they were least likely to use clinic services. A relatively large proportion of junior high school boys sought out the social workers in the clinic, both for information and counseling and as a source for condoms and foam. The fact that these staff members

were female and white did not seem to hinder their ability to serve as confidants, educators, and counselors to young males.

- The peer resource students were in frequent contact with the staff and drew heavily on their time. They profited on an individual basis from their involvement in the program, but their training and nurturing required time, energy, and financial resources. The intrinsic value of their services may have been worth the investment, but there is little objective evidence of their contribution. These data suggest that the development of a peer component should not be viewed as a means of saving staff time.

- A small number of clients can account for inordinate amounts of staff time. Although median rates of service usage appear reasonable in this program, they are considerably lower than the means, which are influenced by high extremes. In designing similar models one must ask whether the involvement of the staff in long-term, serious problem cases is a judicious use of their time. Given the particular staffing patterns of any similar model, decisions about when to continue and when to refer need to be made on a systematic basis.

- The concept of a school-linked clinic operation—or conversely, a clinic-linked educational and counseling project in a school—is one that appears to work. In terms of the flow from one setting to the other, and in terms of the use of a range of components, the model functioned as it was planned. Approximately one-quarter of the students encountered the staff in both settings. Some who attended discussions in the school health suite may not have wished to attend the clinic and might not have done so even if it were located in the school. For others, in-school contact served as a bridge to the clinic, where counseling and medical services could proceed without the limitations of school hours, calendars, and administrative controls.

- Formal efforts to involve parents, unfortunately, were rarely successful. Information is not available on the numbers of contacts with parents; they were often seen individually but rarely participated in group meetings about the program. Although students were encouraged to tell their parents that they utilized the program and although many did so, more time must be invested if parental involvement is to be achieved. Many of the parents were single mothers with other children. Most were poverty-stricken and faced frequent crises, such as eviction and lack of essential food and clothing. They may have had too many demands upon them to respond to casual invitations even when their children were involved. Greater faculty involvement would also have been appropriate but would have required time, as well; funding was not allocated in this program for that purpose. It is yet to be demonstrated that investing that time would increase participation in the clinical components of the program.

It should be noted that when this program was in operation, the AIDS epidemic had not become an issue. Today, the prevention of AIDS, as well as pregnancy, would be a major issue, and the promotion of abstinence and "safe sex" through the proper use of condoms as well as avoiding drugs would have to be stressed in all components. Although this program did emphasize both abstinence and condom use, both with success documented in Chapter 25, a program designed in the AIDS era would put different weight on its discussions of alternative protective methods.

Judging from the ways in which the students used the Self Center services, then, we would conclude that the program had a greater impact because it combined school and clinic components than it would have had if it had functioned in only one of those sites. It brought an encouraging proportion of the sexually active into the clinic, probably reached even some chronic absentees, and touched virtually all the students who were in regular attendance at the schools. It appeared to create an atmosphere in both locations where open communication was legitimized, even invited, and where sexual conduct, contraception, abstinence, and pregnancy could be discussed and responsible decisions could be made. Its impact is reported in Chapter 25, but even without the evidence it presents, the data discussed here suggest a high level of acceptance of the program among the students for whom it was designed. Clearly, their heavy utilization of the resources the program offered shows that the staff filled a real need for information and services, both among those who were already sexually active and those who were not. Their response to the staff and their patterns of utilization of the program's offerings suggest that both the school and the clinic components played a role in the program's success.

24

Sexuality and Health Education

Rosalie Streett

This chapter describes the central role that patient education played in the Self Center during its three-year history. Education, presented both in groups and individually, was the centerpiece of the pregnancy prevention effort and, along with much more extensive counseling than is usually found in clinics, contributed significantly to the success of the program.

The Self Center did not look, "feel," or function as a traditional family planning clinic. Perhaps this can be attributed to the somewhat unusual staffing pattern and design of the program. The administration, planning, and implementation of service delivery and daily supervision of the clinic were carried out by the Administrator who was an educator, rather than the usual physician or nurse. In addition, the core professional staff was comprised of two social workers, one of whom had an undergraduate degree in teaching, a pediatric nurse practitioner, and a certified nurse midwife. Other educators were available to conduct group sessions in their areas of expertise, as well.

Even the name of the clinic, the *Self Center*, reflected a different approach to adolescent pregnancy prevention. It connoted a need to take care of one's own body, while acknowledging and approving of the egocentricity of adolescents. The motto of the clinic, borrowed from a slogan used in a federal adolescent pregnancy prevention family planning campaign was, "Make a life for yourself before you make another life." This motto was printed on the stationery and frequently used in educational group discussions. The name and slogan set the theme for the program.

It is widely acknowledged that health care services, in order to be effectively utilized, must be *affordable*, *accessible*, and *appropriate*. The Self Center services were free. They were offered in the schools and in the clinic close by. Thus, they obviously met the first two criteria for successful programs. It is often the last criterion, that it be *appropriate*, that is lacking in programs for teens. Often, one finds that a clinic is, in name only, "for teens." The basic methods of service delivery, and the environment in which the services are delivered, remain the same as those in programs for adult populations. In the Self Center, the strong psycho-social and educational orientation of the staff was reflected throughout; they dominated the service design and its implementation. Acknowledgment of the special emotional and educational needs of young people formed the basis of an *appropriate* service design.

Informal Education in the Waiting Room

The clinic operated from a storefront building a few blocks away from the hospital. Because the adolescent pregnancy prevention program was the only one housed in that facility, we were able to create an environment that would appeal to and educate the teens who came there for services. As a result, the waiting area was bright and cheerful and the furniture arranged in ways that would allow for small conversational areas or individual seating, with a large table in the middle of the room for playing board games or doing homework. One section of the room was reserved for those who wanted to use the filmstrip/cassette machine that was always available and had an ever-changing selection of filmstrips from which to choose. These audiovisual materials covered such topics as: decision making, methods of birth control, how to say "No," anatomy and physiology, and relationships. The clinic users were taught how to operate the machine and encouraged to use it whenever they desired. In fact, it was used almost constantly.

The walls were decorated with posters with optimistic messages as well as a few of the more commonly seen "warnings to youth" about the consequences of adolescent sexuality. A large bulletin board informed youngsters of events in the community that might be of interest. Pamphlets on the reading and interest levels of the students were liberally spread around the clinic. Duplicate copies of some of the reading materials, particularly those on STDs and signs of pregnancy, were strategically placed in the bathroom and other more private locations in the clinic in order that a youngster might read them privately. (Confidentiality and privacy were strictly maintained, even to this degree.)

Information about local colleges and training programs was prominently displayed in the waiting room because we strongly believe that: 1) teens need to be oriented to the future; and 2) our expectations for their success had to be expressed consistently and often. Also in the waiting room were copies of articles on skin and hair care and other grooming and health interests of teens. In addition, there were many easy-to-read articles on relationships between boys and girls, teens and parents, and friends.

Among the games available were "Transformer," a game that requires the players to live through a 6 AM to 2 AM day as the parents of a baby, and "Human-opoly," a game that deals with issues of human sexuality. These games were popular and provided a novel method of educating youngsters about critical issues. As with the filmstrip/cassette machine and the written material, the games were available to our clinic visitors without adult help, permission, or supervision. Once again, we were acknowledging the teens' independence and expressing our trust in them. Interestingly, they did not betray that trust and were very careful in their use of the equipment and materials and virtually nothing disappeared.

The waiting area was also used as a site for informal educational groups. Clinic staff did not sit in their offices waiting for a youngster to appear but, instead, were often found sitting in the waiting room conversing with a small group of teens. The atmosphere was casual, welcoming, and friendly, and every effort was made to make the young people feel comfortable. The staff member in the waiting room skillfully entered into casual conversation with the participants, shifting the focus of the discussion toward relationships, decision making, and other topics that lend themselves to this informal setting and type of conversation. In many cases, these "talks" provided the social worker with the opportunity to invite a teen into her office to talk about an issue in more depth or to invite the entire group into the "Rap Room" to watch a film or have a longer discussion of a topic.

Formal Educational Groups in the Center

Everyone who came to the Self Center, whether visitor or patient, was asked to sign the roster and invited to participate in the group session planned for that clinic. The majority of visitors and all of the patients humored the staff and complied with this request. The staff felt it was important to engage as many of the youngsters as possible in this way, because we were aware that most of the visitors were potential patients who might need encouragement to enroll in the clinic. Thus, one frequently observed an empty waiting room and a busy "Rap Room" filled with students.

The Self Center held clinics each day after the close of school. One day a week was reserved for new patients who were being seen by the health care providers for the first time. On these days, a special group was held, congratulating the adolescents for being so responsible, welcoming them, describing all of the services, and teaching the basic methods of birth control, what they are, and how they work. In this group, the participants were shown the methods, handled the various devices, felt the foam, unrolled a condom, and were taught basic reproductive functioning, with the help of a teaching aid, the Magnell 77. When this group was over, patients began to be seen by the health care providers. The remaining teens stayed in the room and watched a film or continued their discussion; others were given initial interviews by the social workers. As a result, although the clinic was busy, only rarely did a youngster have to sit in the waiting room for an extended period of time.

On all days other than the one reserved for initial medical visits, a variety of topics were presented in the group sessions. The groups encouraged lively discussions and covered:

Anatomy and physiology
Birth control methods
Social, economic, and educational realities of teen parenting
Life options
Communication skills and personal relationships
Sexually transmitted diseases: detection, prevention, and treatment
Values clarification
Assertiveness
Support for nonsexually active teens
Media messages and how to "see through" them
Community resources
Decision making
Nutrition for teens on the go
Health issues

Techniques similar to the ones described in Chapter 18 were employed in these group sessions. Except in the school setting (see below), a lecture format was reserved for the method of last resort; on the whole, the groups permitted exchange of vital information, and the opinions of all of their members were valued. Two ground rules were presented at the onset and agreed to by the participants, ensuring that everything said in the groups would be confidential and that people would not laugh at each other's comments and opinions.

In these sessions, as in the waiting room, audiovisual materials were used. A library of films was developed, dealing with issues of teen fatherhood, handling difficult interpersonal situations, peer pressure, parent-teen relationships, abstinence, and the realities of teen parenting. Some of the teens were taught how to operate the film projector, thus freeing-up staff time.

Male Involvement

The Self Center was very fortunate to have a group of junior high school boys who visited the clinic on a regular basis. The boys, for the most part, fell into two categories:

1. Prepubertal boys who were concerned about their immature physical development, i.e., they had not started their growth spurt, and their sexual development was less advanced than that of some of their peers;
2. Youngsters who wanted condoms.

Each category, however, shared a common need—the need to discuss issues related to sexuality. Because many came from female-headed households that had begun with an adolescent parent, the boys often lacked important information about their bodies and feelings. They did, however, have fears related to their own normalcy, as well as an endless number of questions related to body functioning. Sometimes their mothers were too embarrassed to initiate conversations about sex; others did not know that such conversations were needed, and still others lacked the basic information. To meet the needs of the young boys, special afternoons were set aside for male groups. The junior high school provided an unparalleled opportunity to reach young males because of their anxiety about normal development; by senior high school, males were more reluctant to ask questions, and, unfortunately, many had dropped out.

In these sessions, we talked about violence and the role it played in their lives, the importance of fathers in the family, poverty and its role in teen pregnancy, the mechanics of human reproduction (male and female), and a host of other issues that interested the young men. The prepubertal boys, in addition to coming in for educational groups, came to the clinic for a monthly height and weight check, at which time we charted their growth with them and celebrated each new inch and pound. The sexually active young men were seen individually for the initial condom pick-up and were encouraged to drop by and talk to the social worker whenever they wanted.

Individual Education in the Center

Each new patient was seen by the social worker at the initial medical visit. At that time, a short interview was conducted and the teen and the social worker began to establish a relationship. As that relationship grew and as particular needs of the youngster became apparent, the social worker provided additional education and counseling to the patient. The individual educational sessions related to topics such as the use of contraception and how to gain access to community resources, or they were part of an ongoing counseling relationship. Patients were also seen on an individual basis by an educator or nurse. Usually, one-on-one education was either informal or resulted from referral by another staff member to address a particular educational need.

Education in the Schools

An important component of the Self Center was its close linkage to the two schools it served. As a school-linked clinic, the Self Center assigned each of the social workers to a particular school where she spent a few hours each day. Two of the days each week, the nurse was also present in the school. During their lunch periods, students were encouraged to visit the social worker to chat informally, play a board game, watch a film, or participate in a small group discussion. During these lunchtime "get-togethers," education and counseling were provided, and many appointments were made for the clinic.

Much of the education in the schools, however, was achieved through classroom presentations by the social workers and nurses. At the beginning of each semester, the Self Center staff gave a presentation to all the students in each homeroom. This was usually scheduled during English classes, because all students have the English requirement. This plan ensured that all students in regular attendance would be exposed to the clinic's services at least twice a year, and it provided the opportunity for the students to receive some education in sexuality to supplement the school's Family Life Education curriculum. The presentations were developed anew each school year, because many of the students would already have heard them during a previous year.

Additional education in the schools was left to the discretion of individual teachers. The Self Center staff spoke to the teachers early in the school year at a faculty meeting to explain the services provided both in the school and in the clinic. Teachers were invited to call upon the staff for presentations and to consider the social workers and nurses as resource people available to assist in the development and implementation of courses of study. There was great variation in the use of this resource. Some teachers asked the nurse midwife to coteach aspects of the curriculum dealing with childbirth or the reproductive system. The social workers were invited to discuss population issues, poverty, and human relationships. These invitations were wholly dependent upon the teachers' wishes, but did provide many additional opportunities for education in issues important to the prevention of premature sexual activity and its adverse consequences.

Summary

Health, sexuality, and family planning education, individual and in groups, was an integral part of a comprehensive approach to pregnancy prevention among high-risk, inner city adolescents, male and female. Delivered both in the schools and a nearby reproductive health clinic, this component formed a bridge facilitating the flow of students from the school to the clinic for further education and/or contraceptive service. It was a model that assisted the delivery of reproductive health services to adolescents who had little access to health care.

25

The Self Center
Program Evaluation

The school- and university-based program for the prevention of pregnancy among inner city adolescents described in Chapters 23 and 24 was conceived as a demonstration project from the outset; a strong evaluation component was therefore included in the model. Although there had been many expressions of concern about the problems of premature conception and unwanted childbearing, and although creative programs had sprung up in many parts of the country, at the time this project was designed there had been no strong evidence that pregnancy rates could be reduced, nor that any particular intervention deserved to be replicated. When our privately funded program was offered to two principals and the Superintendent of Schools, it was made clear that the grantors considered evaluation an important part of the project, which meant that permission to collect data adequate for rigorous assessment was a necessary condition to the implementation of the program. The Superintendent and the principals were not only willing to approve the necessary data collection but supplemented our efforts in many ways through the cooperation of their own statistical division. It was also necessary that the Superintendent designate two control schools and help in enlisting the cooperation of these sites, which did not have the advantage of the promised services to compensate them for their efforts. We attribute the cooperation of so many members of the school family to this project not only to the Superintendent's and the principals' concern for the well-being of their students, but also to the long months invested in laying the groundwork with them and with the community before the program began, as described in Chapter 23.

In this chapter we describe the sources of evaluation data and the methods by which they were collected. Results of the evaluation are described, followed by a brief discussion of the costs that were connected with the program's components. The cost study, and the detailed analysis of program utilization described in Chapter 23, were designed to help establish the contribution of each of the program's services. They have been described in detail elsewhere (Zabin, Hirsch, Smith, et al., 1988; Zabin, Hirsch, Streett, et al., 1988). To determine when a model should be replicated, we felt it was important not only to understand the value of the program as a whole but to identify the components that primarily were responsible for its overall success.

Evaluation Methodology

The primary objectives of the evaluation were to test the hypotheses that premature conception and childbearing among poor, urban adolescents could be prevented and that the school was an effective locus in which to reach adolescents for this purpose. Thus, as a basic premise guiding the evaluation, we made the decision that the study sample would be the school populations as a whole. It would not have been appropriate to restrict the study to the effects of the program on those students who availed themselves of the program's services. The most frequent argument put forward to promote the concept of school-linked initiatives is the notion that the availability of services will greatly increase the utilization of these services. If that concept has merit, as logically it should, a convenient and well designed program should have an impact on an entire school population, not merely on a self-selected subset that might have sought similar services elsewhere in the city. The evaluation of the Self Center project was, therefore, designed from the outset to assess changes in the knowledge, attitudes, and behaviors of the entire school populations and was based primarily on data from self-administered questionnaires in the program and control schools. In the program schools, the questionnaires were administered four times: before the program began and in the spring of the three program years. Those surveys are referred to below as Rounds I to IV, respectively. At the two control schools, also a junior and senior high school, surveys were administered at the beginning and end of the experimental period, making it possible to observe any secular changes that might have taken place while the program was in effect. The study sample consisted of students from the two program schools; 667 males and 1,033 females completed the voluntary, anonymous baseline questionnaire, representing 98% of the junior and senior high school students present on the day the survey was administered. Because there was lower attendance and lower enrollment when subsequent rounds were administered, smaller numbers completed those surveys. Refusal rates remained only about 2% to 3%. Round II included 498 males and 793 females; Round III, 450 males and 764 females; and Round IV, 506 and 695 students, respectively. The control sample utilized in this study was also drawn from two urban schools; although they contain racially mixed populations, only the black respondents are used in the comparisons that follow. Their socioeconomic status, measured by the percent qualifying for free lunch, is similar to that reported in Chapter 23 for the program schools, and according to the school authorities as well as the data we subsequently received, they appear to have been a good match. In the baseline survey, 944 males and 1,002 females are included, and at the end of the project period, 860 males and 889 females responded to the questionnaire. The great majority, over 95% in all four schools, produced satisfactory records whose completeness and internal consistency enabled them to qualify for inclusion in the analysis. Data from these questionnaires were coded and edited twice by different data handlers before the data were entered, verified, and cleaned.

Other sources of evaluation data made possible a process evaluation, a cost study, and a detailed understanding of utilization patterns. These sources included cost data from the Johns Hopkins University Financial Office, all clinic forms, including social work and medical records, registration forms, sign-in sheets, and even a "nonform form," to pick up any clinic visit by youngsters whose attendance on a particular day otherwise might not have been recorded. The records that contributed most to our understanding of the utilization of the staff were detailed logs maintained by the four key staff persons who were in regular contact with the students. The two social workers and two nurse practitioners maintained these daily logs purely for research purposes and noted each individual contact with a student in one of the six categories of service described in Chapter 23. In combination with the financial records, they made it possible for us to determine the approximate cost of each type of service and also to estimate the level of cost associated with students who utilized the program in different ways.

Problems in Evaluation

Because interest in school-linked initiatives has increased in recent years and because funders are becoming concerned about the effectiveness of the money that has supported these efforts, many of the methodological problems in evaluating programs in the school context are of considerable interest in their own right. Most of the problems we encountered can be generalized to other schools and other models; even when cities, school systems, and services differ, there are generic issues that complicate the evaluation process. They make the assessment of change particularly difficult as one seeks to measure program effects on a moving target; classes are changing their membership, and youngsters are growing up. Details of our methodology and a discussion of many of these problems can be found elsewhere (Zabin and Hirsch, 1987; Zabin, Hirsch, et al., 1986); here we will outline only those issues that must be understood to interpret the results.

There is a great deal of mobility into and out of individual schools, even those that serve designated communities. This is due, in large measure, to the normal pattern of graduation and promotion, but it is also affected by individual factors, such as changes in residence and transfers, and by institutional factors such as reapportionment and group reassignments. This fluidity, which is common to extensive school systems serving urban populations, makes it difficult to designate a denominator when analyzing the utilization of program services and complicates the description of exposure groups, as explained below.

Another challenge to evaluation is the fact that it is extremely difficult to find two schools, even within the same school system, that are truly comparable. Each school has its own character in curriculum and administration, even when following the same guidelines; they also vary in the economic and racial mix of students because of their geographical locations within the city. Sometimes even the proportions of males and females are different. Furthermore, special programs may be offered in some schools but not in others. Thus, it is extremely difficult to find control schools and may limit their usefulness once they are chosen; it is safer to use controls to establish the presence or absence of secular change, rather than to compare absolute numbers and/or rates at two sites at two points in time.

A few particular issues derived from these and other limitations are discussed briefly below.

1. Attendance varied considerably between fall and spring, even within the same school. Differences between the numbers cannot be assumed to be random. If there is a drop-off in attendance due to absenteeism and premature school termination, it will almost certainly select less motivated students, which can affect the characteristics of the school population at the two seasons. If data

are originally collected in the fall, before the initiation of the new program, follow-up surveys generally need to be administered in the spring, if one is not to lose all those students exposed to the program who will graduate or move on to other classes or locations. Due to the nature of school systems, it is unlikely that one would know of a new program a full year in advance, in order to be able to administer the baseline questionnaire in the spring and, even if that were possible, not all students would be reached. Therefore, minor differences in precise age distribution may exist, and, unless one controls for exact age, by month, these differences can affect the results. However, any differences of that kind that appear in the program schools would appear equally in the control schools, and thus do not affect comparisons between them. Furthermore, where cumulative measures are used and exact age may be important, the use of life tables corrects for these differences.

2. Program exposure cannot be predicted accurately by grade, because of the students' movement into and out of the schools. Although the comparison of survey Rounds gives the simplest picture of the student body as a whole in sequential years, it is not a reliable basis on which to estimate program effects because of these differentials in individual exposure.

3. Conversely, when exposure to the program is used to define subgroups for comparison, age distributions within each subgroup may vary: longer exposure, for example, is associated with older ages. Those who have just entered a junior or a senior high school in the fall are only available, by spring, for one-year exposure groups. The use of life table methods can, once again, help correct for age differences, exposure differences, and intervals following first intercourse, as will be clear below.

In the tables and figures that follow, exposure groups are compared. However, the results are reported by grade and sometimes even by school or school of origin. For some grades and exposures, there will be some cells with small Ns and some cells that are inapplicable. (For example, there are no seventh graders with exposure longer than 1 year or eighth graders with exposure longer than 2.) Zero exposure refers to the baseline information. One-year exposure is based on data from Round II of the survey but includes a subset of the students interviewed in Round III who entered the program schools in the second year of the program. Two-year exposure, similarly, includes all the remaining surveys in Round III, plus information from students who entered a program school in the second year and were interviewed in Round IV. Finally, 3-year exposure includes all the Round IV respondents who were exposed to the program throughout its 3 years of operation.[1]

Survey Administration

Before the surveys were administered, notices were sent home with all students in the program schools telling them that the school was planning to put in place a program, the objective of which was the prevention of school-age pregnancy. They were told that, in order to plan for that program, a very personal survey would be

---

[1]Problems in defining appropriate comparison groups, and the methodology used to address these problems, are described in detail elsewhere. See, in particular, the appendix to Zabin, Hirsch, et al., 1986 and Chapter 5 in Zabin and Hirsch, 1987.

administered to their offspring, which was to be answered anonymously. It was explained that, although the school's principal and the Johns Hopkins research team were anxious for all students' participation, the parent was free to call a given number at any time between 8 AM and 6 PM, the following several days, in order to ask that their child be excused. Only a few mothers called, generally to ask questions, but more often to thank the researchers for their interest in a problem that was of great concern to them as parents. The support of the students on the day of administration was equally heartening, with only an occasional individual declining to take part. Homeroom teachers, who had been briefed in advance, were given the questionnaires to distribute and some introductory material that they read to the students, once more offering them a chance to withdraw. Members of the research team were assigned to oversee no more than four or five classrooms each, so that they could circulate through them and respond to questions the students might not have wished to ask their homeroom teachers. At the control schools, a similar procedure was followed, although the notice to the parents could not promise a program soon to be offered to their youngsters. Nonetheless, cooperation was extremely high.

Baseline Data: Population Characteristics

High levels of sexual activity were reported in both the program and the nonprogram schools at baseline (Zabin et al., 1984). Almost 92% of the boys in the ninth grade in the junior high school reported being sexually active as did boys in the senior high; 54% of the junior high ninth grade girls, and 79% of the senior high school girls were sexually active, as well. In the seventh and eighth grades, more than 47% of the females had already experienced intercourse. Large proportions reported that they had used a family planning method at some time: approximately 71% of the junior high males and females and over 89% of the senior high students. However, far fewer had used any method at last coitus, a better measure of consistency of use; only 61% of the junior high females and 73% of those in the senior high had used a method of any kind at last coitus. Eleven percent of the sexually active girls in the seventh and eighth grades had already experienced a pregnancy, and in the senior high, over 22%. Even these figures were not unusual in similar populations; pregnancy rates in the junior high school at the program and control schools were very similar, and at the control senior high level, the baseline rates were even higher. On most of the characteristics we measured, there was no reason to believe that our students were not broadly representative of young people in an urban school system serving a preponderance of poor children.

Knowledge and Attitudes

Ten questions were asked of students between the 9th and 12th grades to determine their knowledge of the correct use of specific contraceptive methods and of pregnancy risks. Among females, scores on the 10 questions in the baseline data averaged 6.8. They increased with age from 5.4 among 9th graders to 7.4 among 12th graders (Fig. 25-1). Scores increased significantly overall during the program period; from 6.8 at baseline they increased to an average of 7.8 after 2 years or more. After 2 or more years of exposure, students in the 11th and 12th grades reached a high of 8.2; in the control schools, while they started at levels comparable to the program schools at baseline, they never exceeded 7.2. A significant increase was also observed among males in the program schools at each duration of program exposure. Changes in the control schools, among females and males alike, did not achieve significance.

One measure of knowledge frequently cited in the literature is response to a question identifying the fertile time of the month. Very low levels of information are frequently reported, even among young men and women who claimed to have had a sex education course. We prefer to consider responses correct if students reply that a woman's most fertile period is "2 weeks after her period begins" *or* "anytime during the month"; most good sex education courses teach young people that, with their often irregular cycles, the latter is the only protective assumption. When responses are coded in that manner, there is a highly significant increase in knowledge among program females, especially among younger girls (Fig. 25-2). The increase among males in the program schools is small and neither consistent nor significant. However, among control school males there is a decrease and among females only an insignificant increase during the same period of time. Unfortunately, even with the increases in knowledge brought about by the program, young women rarely exceed a 50% score on this variable. Nonetheless, we begin to see a pattern of change that becomes extremely important: younger students are beginning to achieve scores after program exposure that are higher than those achieved by older students prior to the onset of educational intervention. This earlier acquisition of knowledge can have a dramatic effect on behavior.

By the end of the program, significantly fewer of the program school students, male and female alike, rate withdrawal, rhythm, or douche as "good" or "very good" methods to protect against pregnancy (Fig. 25-3). This trend is already apparent, and already significant, among both males and females at the end of 1 year of exposure, and their knowledge continues to improve with longer exposure. No change in response pattern emerges among the students in the nonprogram schools. Thus, overall, there appears to be an increase in contraceptive and sexual knowledge, a difference that is generally significant in magnitude.

Attitudinal change is slight by any of our three measures. The first examined the proportions holding any positive attitudes toward teenage pregnancy; the second measured the percentage who cite a "best" or ideal age for childbearing below the age they cite as best for marriage. The third measured the percentage who believe that first sex is "okay" when the couple have "just met" or "date occasionally." We had found in a previous study that there was a significant relationship between holding a positive attitude toward adolescent childbearing and the ineffective use of contraception (Zabin, 1985). In the study population, as in our former study, few teenagers thought that having a child while of school age was a very good idea. Although there is a downward trend among females over exposures to the program, neither in this nor in our other attitudinal measures was there any marked or consistent change. Both males and females, in large numbers, cite an ideal age for childbearing (or fathering) younger than the ideal age for marriage; in many grades, over 50% shared this view. Fewer females hold this view after program exposure than before, and these differences are highly significant; however, among males the downward trend is weaker. In the control schools, however, there is no such trend; in fact, among females an increase is observed. Changes in the third measure are also inconsistent and insignificant.

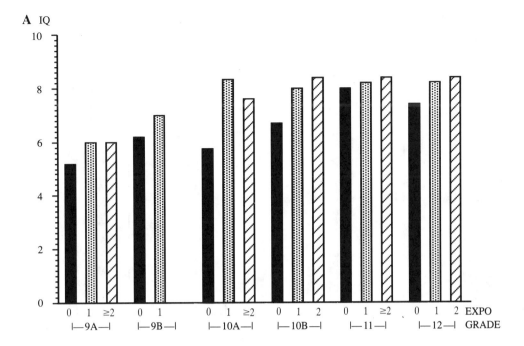

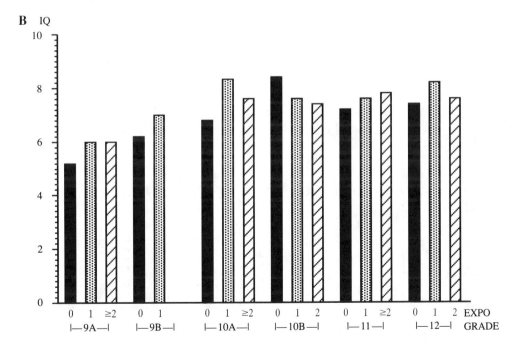

Figure 25-1 (**A**) Mean number of correct responses to questions on sex and contraception among junior and senior high school black females by years of exposure to a Pregnancy Prevention Program and by grade. (**B**) Mean number of correct responses to questions on sex and contraception among junior and senior high school black males by years of exposure to a Pregnancy Prevention Program and by grade. (See footnotes § and †† in Table 25-1 for description of A and B grade levels.)

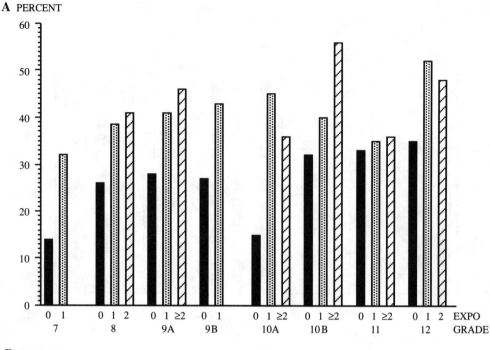

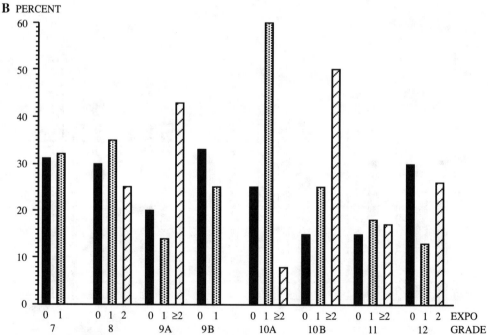

Figure 25-2 (**A**) Percent of junior and senior high school females identifying fertile period at correct time or any time of the month by years of exposure to a Pregnancy Prevention Program and by grade. (**B**) Percent of junior and senior high school black males identifying fertile period at correct time or any time of the month by years of exposure to a Pregnancy Prevention Program and by grade. (See footnotes § and †† in Table 25-1 for description of A and B grade levels.)

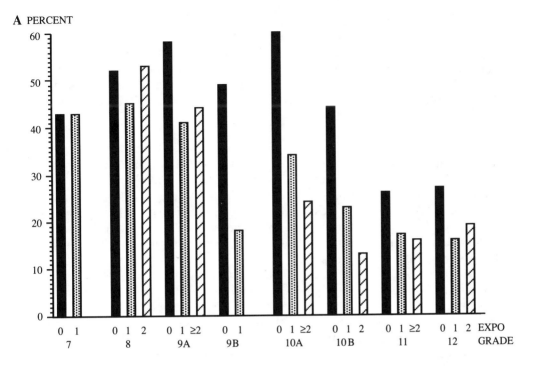

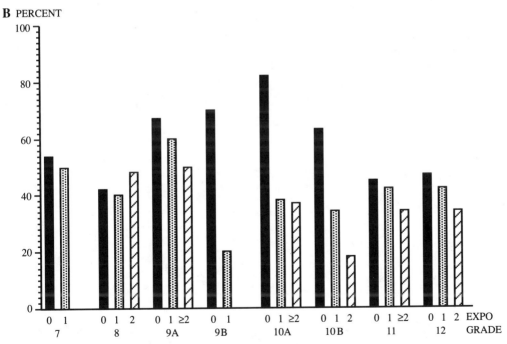

Figure 25-3 (A) Percent of junior and senior high school black females believing withdrawal, rhythm, or douche to be good or very good at preventing conception by years of exposure to a Pregnancy Prevention Program and by grade. (B) Percent of junior and senior high school black males believing withdrawal, rhythm, or douche to be good or very good at preventing conception by years of exposure to a Pregnancy Prevention Program and by grade. (See footnotes § and †† in Table 25-1 for description of A and B grade levels.)

The insignificant change in attitudinal variables reflects the fact that the majority of the students held rather positive attitudes toward contraception and rather negative attitudes toward adolescent childbearing before the program began. The opportunity for significant change was small, and although the trends appear to be in the direction for which one would hope, there was considerably less room for change in attitudes than in knowledge.

Behavior Changes

The most important effects that the program was designed to achieve were changes in pregnancy rates, both rates of childbearing and abortion. However, there were intervening behaviors that directly affect those rates. These include: 1) the age of coital onset, 2) the use of professional contraceptive facilities, 3) the effective use of contraception, and 4) the potential for reducing the frequency of coitus among those who were already sexually active, although at the outset we had not foreseen the possibility of change in this parameter.

There were, as we have indicated above, extremely high rates of sexual activity in the study populations, beginning at very early ages. This made it seem unlikely that a program that was in place for only 28 or 30 months could do much to change patterns of sexual initiation. It is only among the subset of the population not sexually active when first exposed to the program that one can look for such a delay. Figure 25-4 displays the cumulative percentage of female students 15 years of age and older, sexually active at each age, in the program in senior high school, comparing the histories of those exposed to the program for 3 years with those of students responding to the baseline survey. Using standard life table analysis, these curves indicate a median postponement of sexual initiation of approximately 7 months, from 15 years and 7 months before the program began to 16 years and 2 months after exposure to the entire program. Not surprisingly, among those exposed for only 1 or 2 years, the delays were smaller; some period of time is needed before

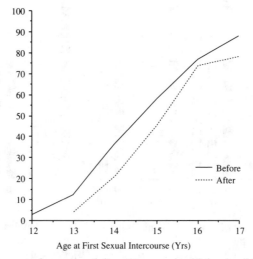

Figure 25-4 Age at onset of sexual activity among senior high school females within 3 years preceding surveys before and after Pregnancy Prevention Program. (From Zabin, Hirsch, et al. *Fam Plann Perspect* 18:119–126, 1986.)

the behavioral effects of intervention can be observed. Intervention needs to occur early in a population such as this and needs to continue for a prolonged period.

Although the before and after curves in Figure 25-4 are quite similar, and both show a rapid increase in sexual initiation between the ages of 13 and 16, it is noteworthy that there is a substantial difference in the proportions sexually active at ages 14 and 15. Approximately two-thirds more of the young girls had become sexually active by age 14 before the program began as compared with after 3 years of exposure. As we have noted in earlier chapters, it is in the early teens that sexual exposure is associated with the highest risk of unintended conception, so a delay such as this is of real importance.

Table 25-1 and Figure 25-5 illustrate birth control clinic attendance before and after program exposure. At every grade level, for male and female students alike, the proportion of sexually active students who attended a clinic (the program clinic or any other professional individual or facility for contraceptive services) increased substantially. There was no such consistent change in the control schools, indicating that these dramatic improvements were program related. Of particular importance to this program, which considered males as an equally important segment of the target population as females, is the fact that junior high school boys began to attend the clinic in percentages that parallel those reported in the baseline data by senior high school females. Literature on adolescents frequently bemoans the impossibility of reaching young males; these increases, and the increases among younger girls as well, are therefore, particularly heartening.

Even more encouraging is the timing of first clinic attendance relative to first coitus as shown in Figure 25-5. The graph includes females exposed to the program for 1 year and compares the timing of their clinic attendance to the probability of a similar subset using a clinic or physician for birth control services during the preprogram period. At the zero point on the horizontal axis is recorded the percentage of young women who attended such a facility in preparation for first coitus, while still virgins. Each month following first coitus is represented on the horizontal axis; increased percentages appear to have attended a clinic at every month. The steep rise in numbers attending between 0 and 3 months is particularly important for preventing conception, because of the high risk in early exposure. This table, as indicated, reflects only differences among those who experienced 1 year's exposure to the program; among those exposed as much as 3 years, 92% of female students age 15 and older attended some kind of professional service by the end of the observation period. That is a noteworthy achievement.

At baseline, we observed that there was an increase in use of the contraceptive pill with age, as one would expect. With exposure to the program, students at every grade level increased their usage significantly, in each time period. However, because increases were so much greater among the youngest than the oldest students, the differentials by age diminish over time. By the end of the program, some of the youngest grades report levels of effective contraceptive use higher than some of the older grades had reported before the program began. This is the pattern to which we referred above, a pattern that reduces the high risks of pregnancy experienced by the youngest girls by improving their levels of knowledge and, no doubt as a result of both knowledge and access, their contraceptive usage. In every school group except one subgroup of one grade, fewer than 20% of the sexually active female students were unprotected by a contraceptive method at their most recent coitus, once exposed to the program for 2 or more years. The fact that this is true

Table 25-1 Percentage of Sexually Active Female and Male Students Who Had Attended a Birth Control Clinic[a]; by Grade Level, According to Years of Exposure to the Program; Program and Nonprogram Schools[b]

Years of exposure to the program	Program schools, by grade										Nonprogram schools, by grade							
	Total[†]	Adjusted total[†‡]	7	8	9a	9b	10a§	10b§	11	12	Total[†]	Adjusted total[†‡]	7	8	9	10	11	12
Females																		
0	49.4	51.9	32.7	32.8	33.3	23.8	50.0	42.5	56.9	69.3	57.6	62.7	13.3	25.0	38.5	61.2	67.6	82.8
1	63.3	na	38.2	57.3	56.1	41.0	81.8	58.7	76.0	71.6	u	u	u	20.0	u	55.1	u	75.0
≥2	na	70.9	**	64.5	57.1	††	62.5	70.4	75.7	75.0	55.7	59.8	16.7	20.0	47.1	55.1	71.2	75.0
Males																		
0	15.6	16.3	12.4	23.8	16.3	12.5	5.6	10.3	19.7	14.5	10.4	11.6	5.6	19.0	6.3	10.5	13.8	9.4
1	27.5	na	37.1	33.7	25.9	16.7	20.0	17.4	25.8	26.8	u	u	u	10.5	u	15.2	u	u
≥2	na	47.6	**	61.9	44.7	††	63.6	33.3	34.3	63.6	10.8	12.1	5.6	10.5	8.3	15.2	15.7	10.1

From Zabin, LS, Hirsch, MB, Smith, EA, Streett, R, and Hardy, JB. Evaluation of a pregnancy prevention program for urban teenagers. *Fam Plann Perspect* 18:119–126, 1986.

[a]Female students were asked whether they had "ever been to a clinic or doctor to get birth control." Males were asked whether they had "ever been to a birth control clinic."

[b]Symbols are defined as:

[†]Standardized on the grade distribution of the program schools at the time of the baseline survey;

[‡]Omits grades exposed to the program for only 1 year;

[§]Grade 10a students came from the program junior high school; 10b, from junior high schools that had no program:

[**]These students could not have been exposed to the program for more than 1 year:

[††]Grade 9a is in the junior high. Grade 9b is the equivalent grade in the senior high school. Because no 9b students came from the program junior high school, they could not have been exposed to the program for more than 1 year;

u = unavailable.

Note: Years of exposure for nonprogram students refer to the interval since baseline survey. All differences between exposures zero and one and between zero and two or more in the program schools are statistically significant ($p < .001$ or $p < .01$). In the nonprogram schools, none of the changes are statistically significant. See the appendix of Zabin, Hirsch, et al. 1986 for a further discussion of these notes.

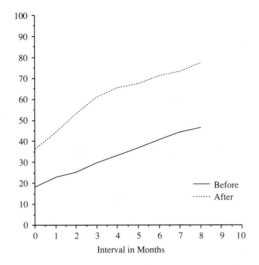

Figure 25-5 Contraceptive clinic attendance by interval from first coitus, before and after program (first coitus within one year of survey). (From Zabin, Hirsch, et al. *Fam Plann Perspect* 18:119–126, 1986.)

even of the youngest girls, those at the seventh and eighth grade levels, is in dramatic contrast to the poor contraceptive usage usually reported at those ages. Typical of the limited use of contraceptive protection generally reported among early sexual initiators is the experience of students in the nonprogram, control schools: there, between 44% and 49% of the students had used no method of birth control at last coitus. Only one grade in the control schools matched the level of protection found in virtually all grades in the program schools.

Impact on Pregnancy

Finally, we come to the crucial measure of program impact, changes in pregnancy rates in the program and nonprogram schools. Figure 25-6 illustrates these changes by picturing the cumulative percentage of sexually active students, grades 9 through 12, becoming pregnant during the 16-, 20-, or 28-month period prior to the survey of interest. Details of the increment-decrement life table methodology used to obtain these estimates are reported elsewhere (Zabin, Hirsch, et al., 1986; Zabin and Hirsch, 1987). Each set of bars compares pregnancy rates among girls available for a given period of sexual exposure during the program with pregnancy rates in a matched group of girls available for a similar period of exposure before the baseline interview. Included in these estimates are young women from the program and control schools who were transferred to a special school for pregnant girls. If these women had been part of a cohort exposed to the program in a school, they were attributed to that cohort even if they were no longer in the school when the survey took place. Because they represent some 10% to 20% of the pregnant students reported in each school year, and an even higher proportion of those who carry to term, the ability to include them in the estimate greatly improves the accuracy of this analysis.

As Figure 25-6 shows, a secular increase in pregnancy rates was occurring at the control schools, reflecting an increase in rates in Baltimore as a whole during

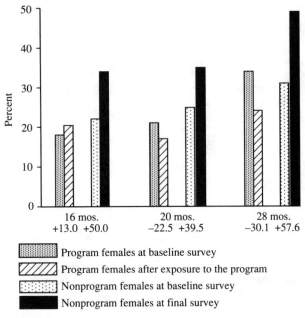

Figure 25-6 Cumulative percentage of sexually active females in grades 9 to 12 of the program and nonprogram schools who became pregnant during 16, 20, or 28 months prior to the baseline survey or subsequent survey, by duration of program exposure and percentage changes in these proportions. (From Zabin, Hirsch, et al. *Fam Plann Perspect* 18:119–126, 1986.)

the program period. During the 16-month exposure period, there was a 50% increase, which by 28 months had increased to almost 58%.[2] During the first 16-month exposure period in the program schools, however, the secular change had already slowed, and by 20 months' exposure, a reversal had begun, reflected in a decline of 22.5% in the pregnancy rate. That decline reached 30.1% for those exposed for the full 28 months the program was in place. Thus, although the two schools began with rather similar pregnancy rates, they ended up with a differential of almost 90 percentage points.

Of particular interest is the fact that both the abortion and the childbearing rates came down. As one might expect, it was the abortion rates that decreased first: they take less time to observe and, because they are all "unwanted" conceptions, they are most readily prevented by contraception. However, given time to measure fertility effects, childbearing decreased as well. The observed reduction in the pregnancy rate reflects the combined effects of these changes.

These analyses were performed examining different periods of exposure in different subgroups, and the changes appeared robust. The calculations are limited to students of 9th through 12th grades, because less information was collected on the exact timing of pregnancies among the seventh and eighth graders and because fewer of these younger girls become pregnant, making statistically valid compar-

---

[2]The reason the 20-month estimate is different, and the reason each baseline estimate differs, is because they cover different subsets of the population, drawn to match the periods of exposure against which they are compared. This methodology is essential if a true comparison is to be made; it is described in Zabin and Hirsch, 1987 and in the Appendix to Zabin, Hirsch, et al., 1986.

isons difficult. It appears that increases in pregnancy rates were even more rapid in the control junior high school during this period than among older girls; therefore, even though declines in the pregnancy rates among the younger program students were smaller than among the older girls, the differentials were still striking. Thus, the program also appeared to help these youngest girls to avoid the secular increases that were affecting their contemporaries in nonprogram settings.

One might well ask to what these changes in unintended pregnancy rates could be attributed. First of all, they must be attributed to the improved rates of contraception and the improved methods of contraception reported above. However, in addition to the improvements in contraceptive protection, the program appears to have been associated with reductions in the frequency of coitus in the program schools. In fact, mathematical models used to decompose changes in the pregnancy rate suggest that the reductions were due as much to reductions in coital frequency as they were to improved contraception (Zabin, Becker, et al., 1989). Furthermore, these models suggest that the changes in pregnancy rates reported by these young women are credible in terms of behavioral change they report. There has been some healthy skepticism about the validity of self-report in sensitive and personal areas; the correspondence between behavioral change and changes in conception lends considerable strength to the data utilized in this evaluation and suggests that evaluations can be based on the responses to appropriate and straightforward questions given by these young people when they are granted—and *believe* they are granted—complete anonymity.

Cost of Intervention

The changes reported here are dramatic, well beyond the magnitude predicted when we hypothesized that the program could have a measurable impact on pregnancy rates. Clearly, if one were to estimate the savings accrued to the community as a result of these reduced pregnancy rates, the costs averted would be substantial. Both in human and financial costs averted, the project was a major success.

Programs such as this one, however, carry costs of their own. This one had the financial advantages and disadvantages of being attached to a major university medical institution. Although this association no doubt added to some of its personnel costs, it probably reduced start-up costs and made possible the economical use of staff during vacation periods. This program also had the benefit of being rather luxuriously staffed. There is little doubt that similar services could, theoretically, be offered at lower costs; the nursing staff, for example, could probably have been shared between the two schools, and the peer resource group was of uncertain value. The figures calculated in connection with this program should, therefore, be seen as maximal. They are useful, however, not only because they allow us to see what these maximum costs might be, but also because they permit us to understand the relative costs of various components of service. Details have been published elsewhere (Zabin, Hirsch, Smith, et al., 1988; Zabin, Hirsch, Streett, et al., 1988).

Overall, school-based services accounted for 40% of the total budget and clinic services for 60%. The 3-year budget for the entire operation was $409,250, and the average cost per student served was $122, including those reached with every level of service utilization. The average cost per female was almost four times that spent on each male, and the average cost for each senior high school student was more than double the cost for each student in the junior high.

It is reported in Chapter 23 that the small group sessions conducted by social workers in the school attracted large numbers of students, many of whom would not have been reached had the services been offered only in an external off-campus clinic setting. An analysis of the costs associated with each type of service makes it clear that this small group activity was extremely cost-effective, as well. In fact, so many young people utilized the time the social workers had available for this type of consultation that the costs for each student contact were well below the per student costs of the classroom presentations. While classroom presentations each involved many more students, each required a full class period, and each required prior preparation. In contrast, the spontaneous, small group sessions often lasted only 15 minutes, and despite the small number of youngsters in each group, they were able to reach an astounding proportion of the student bodies.

Chapter 23 points out that the utilization of a wide range of services by those who sought medical consultation in the clinic was seen as a validation of the original model. Because the majority of enrollees had contact with the staff in the school and in the clinic, and because they availed themselves of group and individual counseling, the total cost for each of those who obtained contraceptive services was approximately $402 for the entire program period. For those who utilized these services for only 1 year, the costs averaged $188, with the average for females much greater than the average for males.

There has been growing interest nationwide in the use of high school students as outreach workers and even as counselors for their peers. Chapter 23 details the tasks for which a Peer Resource Team was utilized in the Self Center program. When analyzing the costs attributed to this group, the conclusions reported above are underlined; although the advantages reaped by these young people from their personal association with the program and its staff may have been great, their costs were high. If they are included, the cost per contraceptive patient increases from $402 to $432, because the peer resource students cost over $2,000 each when all their personal and training contacts are included. Although the decision to include such a team cannot be based on finances alone, to include such a component in an attempt to reduce overall staff costs does not appear useful.

The cost of individual counseling was high. Considerable time was devoted to each session, even more in the clinic than in the schools; hence the average cost per clinic counseling session was approximately $42, while those in the school cost a mean of $28. At first glance, it seemed surprising that the analysis demonstrated a lower per visit cost for medical consultation than individual counseling in the clinic. However, despite the higher pay attributed to medical personnel than to social workers, it was the duration of these social work sessions, which were often extensive, that increased the investment in this service.

The evidence from the cost analysis that the social work component was costly was no surprise; a decision was made to invest whatever was needed in this component of the program, which was considered from the outset to be one of its most important contributions. The fact that the costs *per visit* were higher than the per visit costs to the medical staff, however, was a surprise. They were higher because of the relative time invested in each encounter. Even when the price of contraceptives, medical supplies, physicians, and other medical support staff is included in the estimated cost of visits with the nurse practitioners or gynecologist, the per visit costs remained lower than those for individual counseling sessions with the social worker. This high cost of counseling necessarily raises a question as to whether unlimited consultation with the social work staff is a necessary component of a program such as this. The staff did, on occasion, attempt to refer individual students who required prolonged counseling to outside providers. They report that it was extremely difficult to convince the student to accept referral, because it was the personal trust that had been built up with the Self Center's staff that kept the students returning month after month. Parents, transportation, and costs of other providers may also have been deterrents. In fact, the students who required the most attention were not necessarily "successes." However, the entire program was predicated on the premise that these disadvantaged urban students required a personal investment of time and concern rarely available to them. In the absence of proof that similar results could be brought about with a lesser investment one would have to conclude that the time was well spent.

Summary

The findings of the extensive evaluation received nationwide attention when reported in 1986. At a time when all signs were that the problem of adolescent unintended conception was intransigent, the results demonstrated that abortion and pregnancy rates could be reduced and sexual onset postponed, by one and the same program. Critics of sex education and of contraceptive services for adolescents had claimed that discussion of intercourse and the responsibilities associated with it, and the provision of contraceptive services, would increase sexual activity. That hypothesis is rejected on the basis of these data; in fact, not only was sexual onset postponed among those not yet sexually active, but the frequency of coitus was reduced among those who had already initiated intercourse.

The intermediate behaviors that accounted for the reduction in pregnancy rates were those that the program could affect and reflected the high level of program acceptance and utilization reported in Chapter 23. Timely clinic attendance, especially among the young and among males, was dramatically increased, use of effective contraception improved, and unprotected coitus was reduced to levels rarely observed among these age groups.

The costs of these services, when compared to the cost of a single admission to a neonatal intensive care unit, were minimal, although they could, no doubt, be delivered for far less. The effectiveness of the small group sessions as a technique for reaching large numbers of students was amply demonstrated, and the low cost related to those services suggests their importance in future models. In combination with the presence of the staff in the schools, the nearby, free-standing clinic proved highly acceptable to the students. Because it was free to operate without the strictures of an on-campus facility, it combined proximity with the best in counseling and medical care that a major health and academic institution could offer. The program proved that when young men and women are provided with the supportive services they need, given a sense of their self-worth, and trusted to act with intel- . ligence and responsibility, they will respond. This model gave a cohort of students in two schools a chance to take control of their sexual lives, and the staff offered them a reason and the means to do so. It is a model that has proven itself and bears replication in other similar urban environments.

Part **VI**

Conclusion
Lessons from the Past and Directions for the Future

Adolescent childbearing is the end product of a series of behaviors that begin with the onset of sexual activity and continue through coitus, contraception, conception, pregnancy, and childbirth, and a series of decisions, conscious or unconscious, about those behaviors. Interventions are needed at every juncture. Regardless of whether we prefer one point of intervention to another, there are important decisions that must be made and vital services that must be available at every stage in the process. What are some of the recurrent lessons we have learned from the experiences reported here about the population that must be served in a poor urban setting, and about the possibility of creative intervention?

Lessons from the Urban Environment

Populations at Risk

We have described one urban population, the environment in which its children are acculturated, the characteristics of its teenage mothers, their partners, and their offspring. The picture is not an encouraging one. We saw in Part II that young mothers often represent a link in an intergenerational chain, perpetuating a cycle of deprivation and frequently of ignorance. The younger they are at the birth of their babies, the stronger is the relationship between childbearing and poverty and the less ready, developmentally, they are to provide the quality of parenting required to assure optimal development for their children. They often come from chaotic homes, have limited educational support, and are exposed to a range of risk behaviors. Their most serious problem, then, is one of poverty. The fact that in our particular urban setting they were predominantly, although by no means exclusively, black should not mask the fact that their underlying problem is one of deprivation, not of race; that distinction is important. In fact, in our city-wide data we describe a population of white adolescent mothers that appears to be more homogeneous in its poverty and to experience even less favorable outcomes after delivery than the black populations on which we report.

The fathers of these young adolescents' children, although often considerably older, are also poor, undereducated, and underemployed, and unlikely to provide the young mothers or their children with a bridge to a more favorable environment. If they are not married and do not live with the teenage mothers, most of them live with their own families; 22% of them have children by other women. Even if they stay in touch and provide human support—and many of them do—they rarely supply the young mothers with the wherewithal to break out of the intergenerational cycle in time to provide their children with a different environment during their formative years.

And what of the children? As we saw in Chapter 7, they are not only impoverished but biologically vulnerable. High-risk pregnancies common in their environment deliver them at double jeopardy, biological and social. Biologically, they are prone to the sequelae of low birth weight, which is a frequent consequence of high-risk pregnancy. They are prone to more accidents, more illness, and more hospitalizations in their first 18 months than children from more affluent settings. Social factors that result from their unplanned, unintended, and by their mothers' own report, often "unwanted" conception place them at risk of being raised by dysfunctional parents whose lack of information about child care and child development is compounded by their own immaturity. The infants' risks are also compounded by the dearth of services available to the young mothers: 16% of the mothers report that they have had to let their children go hungry and 18% report that they, themselves, have been refused medical care that they sought. Two percent of the children were removed from their families because of neglect and/or abuse within the first 18 months of life. It is the vulnerability we describe here that explains the findings of Furstenberg and others that even when the mothers do well, as some do against tremendous odds, their offspring often pay a heavy price.

These are the families we have attempted to serve. In recent years there has been a reaction against the notion that births to teenagers necessarily doom mothers, fathers, and children to a prescribed pattern of failure. Not only is that extreme and fatalistic expectation self-defeating; it is also untrue. Furthermore, it fails to address the question of causality, assuming as it does that it is the too-early birth that causes an adverse life history, rather than the history and the environment from which it came that encourage early, unintended parenthood. On the other hand, we must be extremely cautious when researchers describe adolescent parenthood as "appropriate" to the circumstances of the urban poor; however understandable a response it may seem to the pressures of the economic and social setting, if we don't want it for all our children we would do better to change that setting than to foster a self-limiting accommodation to it. In fact, it is a choice few girls would willingly make. Whatever the direction of causality, whatever the percentage of young women who would have succumbed to disadvantage even in the absence of a birth, and whatever the proportion who manage to overcome the economic, educational, and social stresses of early parenthood, for the vast majority of these young mothers the birth was unintended. For some it may have resulted from sexual abuse, for some, less overt exploitation, but rarely from an unambiguous commitment to childbearing. These factors alone suggest that these young women deserve whatever preventive options we can offer.

The Programs and Their Evaluation

As our review has suggested, the programs that have been developed in the teaching hospital environment of Johns Hopkins over the past two decades have, by and large, met their objectives. The original program for pregnant adolescents, the HAC program, has continued to provide high-quality, high-risk medical care, combined in a caring case management model with intensive health and parenting education and social support. When we compare pregnancy outcomes in that program with outcomes among similar groups of young women who received the same quality high-risk medical care, we begin to observe the positive effects of the counseling and guidance components. Not only social but medical outcomes are better because of supplementary services that are not primarily medical in nature. The same conclusions must be drawn when we compare the young women who remained in the program for teenage mothers and their children (the TAC component) with those who went through the HAC program and were subsequently referred to community facilities for follow-up after delivery. If anything, the young women who remained with the TAC program were a higher risk group, and yet their outcomes and those of their children were generally better than those who did not receive comprehensive care in a case work setting.

Both these programs were put to the ultimate test when their young clients were compared to mothers and children treated in an effective Children and Youth Program that offered follow-up care in specialized but traditional settings. The young women who experienced both the HAC and the TAC programs received medical care that was, in every respect, comparable to that received in the Children and Youth Program. However, they also received intensive social services and health and parenting education in the context of a case management system in which both the mother and the child were seen by an integrated staff in the same setting and usually at the same visit. The data reported in Chapter 19 appear to validate the comprehensive model.

Similarly, the pregnancy prevention program designed in cooperation with the Baltimore City School System, combining medical services with education and counseling, exceeded even our most optimistic expectations for success. That it reduced the pregnancy rate as dramatically as it did would have been proof enough of the value of this intervention; that it did so by reducing both the childbearing and the abortion rate, and that it did so while reducing the frequency of coitus and postponing the onset of sexual activity among students in the program schools should validate the program to those who look at prevention in very different ways. It should be clear that the conflict between policymakers who espouse abstinence and those who advocate giving young people the means to conduct their sexual lives responsibly is not helpful to those who most need help. The dichotomy between their strategies is political in nature and artificial in practice. The Self Center demonstrated very clearly that the two initiatives—i.e., the promotion of abstinence and the provision of contraception—can and should succeed side by side.

Finally, the programs we have discussed here achieved another objective; they demonstrated the importance of serious, academic evaluation. In the present fiscal straits that plague all human services, it is unfortunate that so large a proportion of funding goes into services that have never been proven effective. Conversely, there are probably excellent models that have achieved their goals that are not replicated because it has never been demonstrated that they did, indeed, succeed. With current pressures upon both public and private funding sources, it is realistic to demand that serious interventions include equally serious evaluation. It should be noted that to subject one's program to objective assessment is not an inconsiderable burden to place on a program staff. As we have suggested elsewhere (Zabin and Hirsch, 1987), "It takes courage to subject one's work to the scrutiny of outside researchers." Not every program director is prepared to find out whether program goals are met, and not every staff member is prepared to collect the data a thorough evaluation requires. Conversely, not every investigator is willing to make the commitment or the compromises that plague applied research in the service setting. However, the willingness of a program to state its objectives in measurable terms, to collect data relevant to those objectives, and to open itself to objective measurement is a requirement that those who support expensive and often controversial programs have a right to expect.

Directions for the Future

Whatever has been learned from this saga, the first principle that must inform public policy in matters of health care is the importance of primary prevention. Thus, policies that limit the availability of sexuality education which can encourage responsible behavior, or of contraceptives that can prevent pregnancy, are short-sighted. Policies that limit access to WIC to those on the margins of poverty until malnutrition is evident are self-defeating. The cost of extending the WIC program would be far less than the cost of medical intervention. Medicaid reimbursement for pregnancy and aftercare must be adjusted to cover the costs associated with psychosocial support, counseling, and health education and case management, if it is to assist these young women and their offspring in meaningful ways.

Cities cannot be left to do the job alone; our studies show that whereas births to teenagers at the national level represent 12.5% of all births, in a large city such as Baltimore they represent 22.0% of births within city limits and an even higher proportion in the areas served by an inner city hospital. Moreover, whereas nationwide 37.6% of the births to teens are births to adolescents ($\leq$17), in an urban setting a higher proportion, 45.1%, of teen births are to the younger, more vulnerable girls. Thus, on a nationwide basis fewer than 5% of all births are to adolescents under 18 at delivery, while in an urban setting the proportion may be twice as high (calculated from data for 1986 from the National Center for Health Statistics and the Baltimore City Health Department). It is the youth and vulnerability of these young mothers and their children that suggest the strategies and interventions we believe they require, but that should not imply that many similar strategies and interventions are not needed for disadvantaged women of all ages.

1. *There is an acute need for social support, health educational and medical services, all of which are optimized when they are closely coordinated.* A case management model in which an appropriately staffed team delivers a broad range of integrated services at the same site, whether in a hospital, a community or a school, appears to offer the best chance for success. Furthermore, the services must be readily accessible and free or at very low cost, because low income

adolescents have few if any financial resources. Medical services, particularly preventive services, are severely lacking for many who live at poverty levels; in some cases they are even scarcer for those living just above the cutoff point for subsidized care. Younger and older adolescents need far more than the crisis care that has traditionally been available to them. When delivering preventive services, especially those that involve the modification of behavior—contraceptive and parenting behaviors, for example—education, counseling, and medical interventions must go hand in hand. If health care is offered without an understanding of the young person's developmental level and social needs and without education and counseling, much of its potential will be lost. If counseling is offered without medical services (for example, sexuality education without family planning services), many young people will fail to make their way to the services they need.

2. *When pregnancy prevention programs make contraception readily available in the context of an educational and counseling program, those services* **do not** *promote sexual activity. In fact, our demonstration has suggested that they may actually postpone sexual onset.* What they *do* is to establish a basis for responsible behavior, create a climate for open and serious communication, and validate the notion that the sexual decisions a young person makes have direct implications for his or her future. When that message is explicit, young people can learn to behave responsibly; in the absence of any part of the education-counseling-contraception equation, they cannot make responsible decisions because they have not been offered the means by which to do so.

3. *Early pregnancy detection is essential and can optimize not only medical outcomes but the possibility of making an optimal choice.* Easily accessible and supportive centers for pregnancy testing may also turn out to be among the most important sites for pregnancy prevention. Based on our new findings reported in Chapter 22, there is the possibility that significant reductions in the childbearing rate and the abortion rate could be accomplished if subsequent conceptions to young girls with negative pregnancy tests could be avoided. We cannot quantify at this time the numbers of pregnant teenagers who have experienced at least one negative test before conceiving, but it appears to be a very large proportion; our small study suggests that it could be over 40%. Were strong programs to be directed to this high-risk group, the impact on overall rates of conception could be substantial. Generally, when public health research defines a high-risk population, it is usually and unfortunately a particularly difficult population to find. In this case, a high-risk group is identified for which we do not need to search in the larger community. These young women are in our clinics, waiting for laboratory results and, often, seeking our counsel. Many of them return repeatedly for tests; perhaps their visits are really cries for help. To let them leave without optimal support and preventive services only to see them again when they are, indeed, pregnant is unconscionable.

4. *The availability of low-cost or subsidized abortion services is critical for young women who desire but cannot afford the procedure; these services must be combined with counseling and follow-up contraceptive care to prevent subsequent*

conception. In our comparison of childbearers with young women who terminated their pregnancies, fewer than 4% of those who carried to term had wanted to conceive. Many of them, while awaiting the results of their pregnancy tests, thought childbearing, but not abortion, problematic. Knowing that abortion is not associated with adverse psychological consequences or the economic and educational sequelae that follow childbearing, it is tragic that so many adolescents, nonetheless, bear unintended and often unwanted children. Access to prompt, early intervention can be limited by the inability to pay or even by delays in locating the necessary funds. There is no way to estimate the extent to which outcome decisions were motivated by a lack of funding; certainly, many would have chosen to bear their pregnancies whatever the financial costs. But at the very least, they deserved a realistic choice. Nor do we know how many would choose abortion if it were offered more openly and without prejudice. Those who want to wait to bring a life into the world, who prefer to bring children into the two-parent families we hope they will have someday, deserve as much help and positive support as those who elect to become mothers as adolescents. And, as with all the services we recommend, these young women need counseling and ongoing support to avoid unintended conception in the future.

5. ***There is an urgent need for high-quality, high-risk obstetrical services for young women who carry their pregnancies in the early years post puberty.*** With intensive intervention, they do not experience negative outcomes with any more frequency than older mothers; in fact, their pregnancy outcomes may be more favorable. Without such intervention, even with adequate but routine prenatal care, their outcomes show them to be at higher risk. The comprehensive care necessary, once again, combines good medicine, good health and parenting education, and good social work support. In view of the far-reaching problems of pregnant and parenting adolescents and the broad range of their needs, practicing obstetricians or nurse practitioners cannot be expected to address all of their requirements, however dedicated they may be. General prenatal clinics are not equipped to offer the care these young women need, unless they are staffed with a professional mix appropriate to the multiple needs of their clients. In the long run, it is more cost-effective to offer the high-risk care and the personal education, guidance, and support these young teenagers require than to treat the medical consequences if their needs are ignored.

6. ***The need for health and parenting education for young mothers is clear.*** They are at high risk of conceiving again, further closing their options and those of their children. And they need help to overcome the potential effects of their youth on their vulnerable offspring. Parenting is almost entirely a learned skill; in our society, it is learned primarily by role modeling during a young person's formative years. An intergenerational pattern of adolescent childbearing guarantees that there will be few adequate role models; many will have been at risk of dysfunctional parenting during their own childhoods.

7. ***Following from the same principles that underlie services for young women, there is a need for services specifically directed to young men.*** The evidence seems clear that these services must reach them early, preferably before the seventh

grade, not only because they are more responsive to them during puberty but because so large a proportion of the boys at highest risk will be impossible to find once they have dropped out of school. Although city-wide data in Baltimore show that many of the fathers of babies born to teenage mothers are no longer teenagers themselves, their economically dependent state in their adult years, their patterns of repeated parenthood, and their lack of high school diplomas are evidence of the need to reach them while they are still in middle school. The message from our prevention program, however, is not a discouraging one: young boys, while experiencing puberty, were not only willing but anxious to participate in discussions, to seek guidance, ask questions, and to be a part of a program that explicitly addressed issues of concern to them. That should encourage others to offer them similar opportunities and should lay to rest the myth that these young men are beyond our reach.

8. *As a first line of defense, for males and females alike, there is the need for a broad range of programs directed at forestalling coital contact at early ages.* There is some evidence that youthful sexual onset can be postponed with early and intensive intervention. However, there is no evidence that a media blitz or exhortation alone can change behavior. New information must be processed and incorporated into one's knowledge base before it can be utilized. This process is facilitated by active participation that cannot occur under impersonal circumstances. However, there is evidence that young people can be helped to understand the irresponsible sexual messages they receive and can learn to hear them and take them apart and resist them. That implies more openness about sex; it requires that we acknowledge that by our silence we only confuse them. We leave them to decode negative messages from the media and from the streets with no responsible direction. With the explicit guidance of thoughtful and trained adults, with encouragement to communicate their concerns to parents, partners, and friends, and with the mentorship of role models who permit them to see beyond the images of their immediate environments, these interventions can have measurable success.

9. *It is essential that young people be given the information and services they need to make informed choices about matters that can profoundly affect their own lives and the lives of their partners and children. With the spread of HIV infection, the need for sexuality education has become more compelling than ever and the consequences of unsafe behaviors more dangerous.* The premature onset of sexual activity may be but one manifestation of a constellation of risk-taking behaviors common to inner city environments. Unprotected intercourse, often with multiple partners, in the same settings in which sexually transmitted diseases and intravenous drug use are prevalent may lead to problems more lethal than pregnancy. In several urban centers HIV infection has begun to appear in the teenage population, manifested by full-blown AIDS among young adults or even among older teens. HIV has been diagnosed in the HAC program population. Not only does that put the young mother at risk but her baby as well. AIDS babies and crack babies represent relatively new phenomena to those caring for pregnant adolescents, but they present a compelling reason for openness in discussion about safe sexual practices. If there was ever any doubt about the need for sexuality education or any lingering

hope that ignorance is protective, it should now be dissipated. We have not dealt here with the role of the schools whose responsibility for optimal sexuality education extends well beyond the prevention of disease. What is suggested here is the educational role of the categorical or medical program, an important role that pediatric staff can play with every patient from childhood on. Clinicians can prepare young patients from their early years to perceive the physician's office or clinic as a source of guidance and support if they: 1) establish direct, confidential relationships with young people rather than communicating only through parents; 2) open discussion at appropriate times about behaviors that can put health at risk; and 3) answer questions fully and honestly when, with the help of the clinician, the young person can put them forward.

10. ***We need to offer young people wider options, not just talk about them.*** While prep school children have the opportunity for after school enrichment, for study halls and dramatic clubs, for tutoring and remedial help, our inner city youth are pushed out onto the streets in the early afternoon. We have a rich physical resource in our schools, but they are closed to the communities that are most in need of them for hours every day and for months every year. Surely we could use these facilities better to enhance the lives of our young people and to help them maximize their potential. If they were given the enrichment their limited worlds deny them and given opportunities for job training and part-time employment as well, they would have the tools with which to create more meaningful futures, futures in which parenthood could play its appropriate role at an appropriate time.

11. ***We have learned the importance of the staff itself, of the individuals who will ultimately determine whether or not the service relationship helps to develop a young person's capacity to deal with the outside world.*** The term *self-esteem* has gained popularity in recent years. "Improving a young person's self-esteem" has become the avowed intention of many a program because it is believed that, whatever the influences upon young men and women, crucial decisions will depend upon how they perceive themselves and their futures. The importance of that objective is clear; what is less clear is how to accomplish it. Perhaps the term self-esteem focuses too much on the internal world of the adolescent, which may or may not be accessible to the service provider, and too little on the external environment and external relationships that help mold the young person's self-concept, relationships that are directly in the power of the provider to affect. No service provider can become an effective change agent in the life of a teenager without establishing a basis for trust; that which is offered must be real and deserving of trust. This involves a recognition that it is not the young person's attitude alone that needs to change; it is the external environment as well. In any program, the staff is a crucial part of that environment. If an intervention is to succeed, and certainly if it is to change a young person's image of him- or herself, it must first accord respect and engender trust. The ability to trust an adult, in turn, can have a profound effect on the young person's ability to trust him- or herself. The adolescents with whom we worked over the years had often been exposed to little in the outside world that gave them reason to believe in others or in

themselves. If the programs we present here had any measure of success, it was largely based on the dedication of the staff to building relationships of caring, confidence, and trust; only on that basis could they begin to build in the young people the ability to make rational decisions for their own futures, and when necessary, those of their children.

The "Immorality" of Adolescent Pregnancy

The young people with whom we have had contact in the course of this odyssey have told us over and over again, in many different and eloquent ways, that what they value most is "caring." They have communicated this face to face; they have shown it by their actions and told it to us in our research. "Why did you choose this clinic?" we asked young women in 32 clinics in eight cities. "Because they really care about teens" was the most frequent response.

A country that cares, one that respects all of its citizens equally, would open to adolescents a far brighter horizon than that facing the inner city youth with whom we have worked. Their housing, their schools, their streets, and their futures would look very different from the homes in which many of these young boys and girls are raised, the schools where they are warehoused more than they are taught, the streets that show them the worst the country has to offer, and the future that looks so bleak.

Because concerned citizens are scandalized by the discrepancy between what is and what might be, thousands of caring and creative individuals have organized hundreds of interventions, programs, and services to try to do what the nation should be doing for all its children. Private foundations search out the best for their funding; private institutions give them space, personnel, and support. In some cases public-private partnerships, cities and schools, hospitals and day care centers, and youth-serving agencies and clinics join hands to make a difference. It does not denigrate their efforts to recognize that the best their programs can do is provide bandaids to cover the deprivation many of these young people experience in their daily lives. That it costs so much in time, energy, and funding to intervene in limited ways does not take away from their efforts; rather it expresses the magnitude of the underlying wound. Anything we have suggested in these pages as an appropriate intervention, any models we proposed or methods we reported, cannot substitute for the basic changes that are needed to address the nation's malignant poverty.

If we lack the political will to face those underlying reforms, however, we will continue to need a growing investment in creative interventions to mitigate the effects of economic and social deprivation on the young. Sadly, in the area of intervention, the schizophrenia of the national psyche is evident: Whereas programs that serve young mothers and their babies can be funded and fielded with relative impunity, services to prevent conception among the sexually active or to prevent the initiation of unprotected coitus among young males and females at risk are subject to endless and often destructive debate. Symbolic of a schizophrenic attitude toward palliation versus prevention is the fact that, at Johns Hopkins, the programs we have described for pregnant and parenting teens became institutionalized, while the program to prevent first conception terminated when its categoric grant expired. It was replaced by school-based clinics that were not empowered to give contraception and that were unable to offer the substantial educational and counseling components that were documented to be the Self Center's most utilized and most cost-efficient services (Zabin, Hirsch, Streett, et al., 1988).

It remains sad but true that, however strong the program may be and however well-documented its positive accomplishments, in the absence of a crisis that has already occurred it is difficult to take action. It is easier to feed the hungry than to prevent hunger, easier to provide emergency shelter than to prevent homelessness. As hard as it is to field optimal and enduring services for young mothers and their children, it is even more difficult to reach those who have not yet conceived. It is hardly surprising that in the polarized climate of the last decade, spurious issues of morality have limited most efforts to prevent a first, unintended conception.

That is not the only form of schizophrenia that afflicts our society. Schizophrenia also besets American policy makers with respect to decisions about resource allocation as they choose between expensive, high technology, acute care and less costly preventive health initiatives. As the galleys for this volume are sent to the printers, a final note, an obituary perhaps, is in order.

Despite increasing numbers of 'children bearing children', comprehensive services for adolescents and their children in Baltimore are decreasing. The number of births, and the rate per 1000, among adolescents under 18 years of age continues to increase in Baltimore, in Maryland and in the nation (Maryland Governor's Council on Adolescent Pregnancy, 1990). However, as a result of the huge deficits in the national budget coupled with a recent deficit in the Maryland budget, resources for the health care of the poor are increasingly inadequate. The Hospital administration is under increasing pressure to contain costs. Funds to supplement services provided by Medicaid, i.e. for health and parenting education and psychosocial support for adolescent mothers and their children, made available through the state and city governments, have been markedly reduced. As a result, the comprehensive services provided in TAC have been eliminated. That clinic has reverted to a more traditional pattern of care, a system that, as we have shown in Chapter 19, is likely to be more costly in the long run.

A substantial reduction in the funds available for HAC in 1991 will, in all probability, have the same effect. Increases in the frequency of pregnancy complications and low birth weight are to be anticipated, with a concomitant increase in the cost of maternal care and neonatal intensive care, as well as long-term costs for handicapped children. An additional irony is that because of a cost-saving reduction in computer staff in the Department of Gynecology and Obstetrics, it will be more difficult for obstetricians to monitor the effect of these changes on pregnancy outcome, making service needs more difficult to document in timely fashion.

Lizbeth Schorr (1988) has shown that in most areas of educational, medical, and social intervention affecting adolescents, there are models that have worked. She finds, as we have found here, that the fact that a program does what needs to be done and does it well is no guarantee that it will be replicated. Indeed, it may not even guarantee its survival.

The Two Problems of Teenage Pregnancy

We spoke at the outset of "two problems of teenage pregnancy"; we allude to them as two "problems" rather than two aspects of a single problem because they differ not merely in their consequences but even in the circumstances that give rise to them and the nature of the phenomenon itself. We believe the implications of the monolithic term "teen pregnancy," so recurrent in the popular press, has been a barrier to intervention and has clouded the political debate surrounding an appropriate response. It has contributed to the polarization of those who see adolescent pregnancy primarily as an ethical issue and those who see it as an essentially social dilemma both in its genesis and in its effects.

The first problem, as described in Chapter 2, is that of unintended conception among young women, many of whom initiate intercourse in their older teenage years. It is a problem we see as essentially a product of changing mores among adults and youth; it is manifested by increasing sexual activity, premarital and extramarital coital contact, cohabitation, and, as an inevitable byproduct, exposure to sexually transmitted diseases, out-of-wedlock conception, elective abortion, and unintended childbearing. It is apparent in all parts of the western world and does not appear to be limited to any social, ethnic, educational, or economic class.

This report is focused on the second problem, that of pubertal, even prepubertal sexual initiation and often early postpubertal conception and childbearing. In our city-wide experience, when pregnancy occurred in young adolescents in middle-class families, there was usually recourse to abortion. Childbearing in the early and middle teen years is generally related to poverty and the underclass. The adolescents with whom our programs have interacted were almost always youngsters raised in impoverished settings. Of course, they, too, are exposed to the media that affect their older contemporaries; they, too, are touched by the sexual revolution. But because their underlying problem is one of poverty, it is important to understand that they need a great deal more than educational and reproductive health services; they need extensive support services as well.

Understanding these "two problems" entails an appreciation of the crucial differences between the sexual behaviors of older teenagers and the behaviors of true adolescents, between those who are able to choose their life styles and protect themselves from some of the consequences of their choices and those whose environments leave them little room for choice. It is important to make that distinction not simply as an academic exercise or even because of its implications for program design. It is important because our ability to address both problems has often been paralyzed by that confusion. It is our belief that the semantics of "teen child-bearing," suggesting that the population at risk, indeed that the problem itself, is homogeneous, has stood in the way of rational intervention. It has allowed conflicting views of sexual morality to overshadow what, for most young Americans, is a need for knowledge and services but for others is *also* an issue of economic deprivation.

For the vast majority of young Americans, the ground rules have changed. They are choosing to engage in premarital coitus. Legitimate questions can be raised about the safety and ethics of widespread nonmonogamous sexual activity at any age; the implications of our changing sexual mores are profound—implications for public health as well as for private values. But even those who want to undo the sexual revolution cannot change the moral climate by denying our young people the means to protect themselves. Whatever their age or behavior, they need to hear the unequivocal message that responsible sexual behavior means avoiding exploitation, disease, and casual conception. Young people are making choices all the time; they require the means to do so responsibly. Realistic education, an accessible, appropriate network of reproductive health services, and an opportunity to understand risks, explore value systems, and receive accurate answers to their questions offer the best hope that they will make rational—and perhaps even moral—choices.

The problem we have addressed throughout this book, however, is not one of sexual morality; it is a problem of economic and social environment. Arguments about the sexual revolution have no place here. More relevant issues are those concerned with poverty, vulnerability, and wasted potential. The conditions of these young people's lives cry out for social and economic intervention. They, too, need education and accessible reproductive health services with strong social support, but they also need jobs, counseling, and the right to make responsible decisions about a real and believable future. To imply that young people who are trapped in a cycle of deprivation have chosen to do what they do and to live as they live is the ultimate immorality. An environment that encourages a young girl to choose parenthood in her adolescent years has violated her childhood just as surely as if sexual contact had been forced upon her. The real immorality implicit in the sexual behaviors of the very young, in their stunted lives and those of their offspring, is the immorality of a society that cares little for them or is afraid to intervene.

Bibliography

Abrams, M. Birth control use by teenagers. *J Adolesc Health Care* 6:196–200, 1985.

Adler, NE. Emotional responses of women following therapeutic abortion. *Am J Orthospsychiatry* 45(3):446–456, 1975.

Agarwal, KN, Meenakshi, K, Shah, N, and Susheela, K. Placental morphological and biochemical studies in maternal anemia before and after treatment. *J Trop Pediatr* 27:162–165, 1981.

Alan Guttmacher Institute. *Eleven Million Teenagers–What Can Be Done About the Epidemic of Adolescent Pregnancies in the United States?* Planned Parenthood Federation of America, Inc., New York, 1976.

Alan Guttmacher Institute. *Teenage pregnancy: The Problem Which Has Not Gone Away.* Planned Parenthood Federation of America, Inc., New York, April 1981.

Allen, LH. Trace minerals and outcome of human pregnancy. *Clin Nutr* 5:72, 1986.

American Psychological Association, Public Interest Directorate. Psychological Sequelae of Abortion. Report to the Surgeon General, Washington, DC, 1987.

Ancona, RJ, Ferrieri, P, and Williams, PP. Maternal factors that enhance the acquisition of group B streptococci by newborn infants. *J Med Microbiol* 13:273–280, 1980.

Andrews, G, Tennant, C, Hewson, DM, and Vaillant, GE. Life event stress, social support, coping style, and risk of psychological impairment. *J Nerv Ment Dis* 166:307–316, 1978.

Antoniou, K, Vassilaki-Grimani, M, Lolis, D, et al. Concentrations of cobalt, rubidium, selenium and zinc in maternal and cord blood serum and amniotic fluid of women with normal and prolonged pregnancies. *J Radioanal Chem* 70:77, 1982.

Antonov, AN. Children born during the siege of Leningrad in 1942. *J Pediatr* 30:250–259, 1947.

Apgar, V. A proposal for a new method of evaluation of the newborn infant. *Curr Res Anesth Analg* 32:260–267, 1953.

Ashton, JR. The psychosocial outcome of induced abortion. *Br J Obstet Gynecol* 87:1115–1122, 1980.

Baldwin, W, and Cain, VS. The children of teenage parents. *Fam Plann Perspect* 12:34–43, 1980.

Baltes, PB, and Schaie, KW. *Life-span Developmental Psychology: Personality and Socialization.* Academic Press, New York, 1973.

Baltes, PB, and Willis, SL. Life-span developmental psychology, cognitive functioning and social policy. In Riley, MW (ed.), *Aging from Birth to Death: Interdisciplinary Perspectives.* Westview Press, Boulder, CO, 1979.

Baltimore City Preliminary Vital Statistics Report, Baltimore, MD, 1986.

Barbacci, M, Spence, MR, Kappus, E, Burkman, RT, et al. Postabortal endometritis and isolation of *Chlamydia trachomatis.* *Obstet Gynecol* 68:686–690, 1986.

Bauman, KE, and Udry, JR. Subjective expected utility and adolescent sexual behavior. *Adolescence* 16:527–535, 1981.

Beattie, AD, Moore, MR, Goldberg, A, et al. Role of chronic low level lead exposure in the aetiology of mental retardation. *Lancet* 1:589–592, 1975.

Belmont, L, Cohen, P, Dryfoos, J, et al. Maternal age and children's intelligence. In Scott, KG, Field, T, and Robertson, EG (eds.), *Teenage Parents and Their Offspring.* Grune & Stratton, New York, 1981.

Belsey, EM, Greer, HS, Lai, S, Lewis, SC, and Beard, RW. Predictive factors in emotional response to abortion: King's termination study IV. *Soc Sci Med* 11:71–82, 1977.

Benedek, T. Psychological aspects of mothering. *Am J Orthopsychiatry* 26:272–278, 1956.

Bettger, WJ, and O'dell, BL. A critical physiological role of zinc in the structure and function of biomembranes. *Life Sci* 28:1425–1438, 1981.

Bierman, BR, and Bierman, JS. Preoedipal fixation: its contribution to pregnancy in early adolescence. *Infant Ment Health J* 6(1):45–55, 1985.

Billy, JOG, Rodgers, JL, and Udry, JR. Adolescent sexual behavior and friendship choice. *Soc Forces* 62:653–678, 1984.

Billy, JOG, and Udry, JR. Patterns of adolescent friendships and effects on sexual behavior. *Soc Psychol Q* 48:27–31, 1985a.

Billy, JOG, and Udry, JR. The influence of male and female best friends on adolescent sexual behavior. *Adolescence* 20:21–31, 1985b.

Blumberg, BD, Golbus, MS, and Hanson, KH. The psychological sequelae of elective abortion. *Western J Med* 124:188–193, 1975.

Boyce, WT, Schaeffer, C, and Uitti, C. Permanence and change: psychosocial factors in the outcome of adolescent pregnancy. *Soc Sci Med* 21:1279–1287, 1985.

Boyer, KM, Gadzala, CA, Burd, LI, et al. Selective intrapartum chemoprophylaxis of neonatal group B streptococcal early-onset disease. I. Epidemiologic rationale. *J Infect Dis* 148:795–801, 1983a.

Boyer, KM, Gadzala, CA, Kelly, PD, et al. Selective intrapartum chemoprophylaxis of neonatal group B streptococcal early-onset disease. II. Predictive value of prenatal cultures. *J Infect Dis* 148:802–809, 1983b.

Boyer, KM, Gadzala, CA, Kelly, PD, and Gotoff, SP. Selective intrapartum chemoprophylaxis of neonatal group B streptococcal early-onset disease. III. Interruption of mother-to-infant transmission. *J Infect Dis* 148:810–816, 1983c.

Bracken, MB, and Kasl, SV. Psychosocial correlates of delayed decisions to abort. *Health Educ Monogr* 4:6–14, 1975.

Bracken, MB, and Swiger, ME. Factors associated with delay in seeking induced abortions. *Am J Obstet Gynecol* 113:301–309, 1972.

Brann, EA. A multivariate analysis of interstate variation in fertility of teenage girls. *Am J Public Health* 69(7): 661–666, 1979.

Braun, P, Lee, YH, Klein, JO, et al. Birth weight and genital mycoplasmas in pregnancy. *N Engl J Med* 284:167–171, 1971.

Brewer, C. Incidence of post-abortion psychosis: a prospective study. *Br Med J* 1:476–477, 1977.

Broman, SG. Long-term development of children born to teenagers. In Scott, KG, Field, T, and Robertson, EG (eds.), *Teenage Parents and Their Offspring*. Grune & Stratton, New York, 1981.

Broman, SH, Nichols, PL, and Kennedy, WA. *Preschool IQ: Prenatal and Early Developmental Correlates*. Erlbaum, Hillsdale, NJ, 1975.

Brooks-Gunn, J, and Furstenberg, FF, Jr. The Children of adolescent mothers: Physical, academic and psychological outcomes. *Dev Rev* 6:224–251, 1986.

Brown, H, Adams, RG, and Kellam, SG. A longitudinal study of teenage motherhood and symptoms of distress: The Woodlawn Community Epidemiological Project. *Res Commun Ment Health* 2:183–213, 1981.

Buchet, JP, Roels, H, Hubermont, G, and Lauwerys, R. Placental transfer of lead, mercury, cadmium, and carbon monoxide in women. II. Influence of some epidemiological factors on the frequency distributions of the biological indices in maternal and umbilical cord blood. *Environ Res* 15:494–503, 1978.

Bureau of the Census. *Statistical Abstracts of the United States, 1986*, ed. 106. National Data Book, Bureau of the Census, Washington, D.C., 1988.

Burkman, RT, Atienza, MF, and King, TM. Morbidity risk among young adolescents undergoing elective abortion. *Contraception* 30:99–105, 1984.

Burkman, RT, Bell, WR, Atienza, MF, and King, TM. Coagulopathy with midtrimester induced abortion: association with hyperosmolar urea administration. *Am J Obstet Gynecol* 127:533–538, 1977.

Burkman, RT, and King, TM. Second-trimester termination of pregnancy. In Symonds,

EM, and Zuspan, FP (eds.): *Clinical and Diagnostic Procedures in Obstetrics and Gynecology, Part B: Gynecology.* Marcel Dekker, New York, 1984.

Burt, MR. Estimates of Public Costs for Teenage Childbearing: A Review of Recent Studies and Estimates of 1985 Public Costs. A report prepared for Center for Population Options, Washington, DC 1986.

Burt, MR, and Levy, F. Estimates of public costs for teenage childbearing: a review of recent studies and estimates of 1985 public costs. In Hofferth, SL, and Hayes, CD (eds.): *Risking the Future: Adolescent Sexuality, Pregnancy and Childbearing*, Vol. II. National Academy Press, Washington, DC, 1987.

Butler, NR, and Alberman, ED. *Perinatal Problems. The Second Report of the 1958 British Perinatal Mortality Survey.* Livingstone, Edinburgh, 1969.

Campbell, DT, and Stanley, JC. *Experimental and Quasi-Experimental Designs for Research.* The American Educational Research Association, Rand McNally College Publishing Company, Chicago, 1963.

The Cancer and Steroid Hormone (C.A.S.H.) Study Group. Oral contraceptive use and the risk of breast cancer. *N Engl J Med* 315:405–411, 1986.

The Cancer and Steroid Hormone (C.A.S.H.) Study Group. Combination oral contraceptive use and the risk of endometrial cancer. *JAMA* 257:796–800, 1987a.

The Cancer and Steroid Hormone (C.A.S.H.) Study Group: The reduction of risk of ovarian cancer associated with oral contraceptive use. *N Engl J Med* 316:650–655, 1987b.

Card, JJ, and Wise, LL. Teenage mothers and teenage fathers: the impact of early childbearing on parents' personal and professional lives. *Fam Plann Perspect* 10:199–205, 1978.

Castadot, RG. Pregnancy termination: techniques, risks and complications and their management. *Fertil Steril* 45:5–17, 1986.

Cates, W, Jr. Adolescent abortion in the U.S. *J Adolesc Health Care* 1(1):18–25, 1980.

Cates, W, Schultz, KF, and Grimes, DA. The risks associated with teenage abortion. *N Engl J Med* 309:621–624, 1983.

Centers for Disease Control. *Family Planning Methods and Practice: Africa.* Centers for Disease Control, Atlanta, 1983.

Center for Population Options. *Teenage and Too Early Childbearing: Public Costs, Personal Consequences.* Washington, DC, 1989

Cherazi, S. Psychological reaction to abortion. *J Am Med Wom Assoc* 34:287–288, 1979.

Cherlin, AJ. The weakening link between marriage and the care of children. *Fam Plann Perspect* 20:302–306, 1989.

Chez, RA, Henkin, RI, and Fox, R. Amniotic fluid copper and zinc concentrations in human pregnancy. *Obstet Gynecol* 52:125–127, 1978.

Children's Defense Fund. *Adolescent and Young Adult Fathers: Problems and Solutions.* Children's Defense Fund, Washington, DC, May 1985.

Clausen, JA. The life course of individuals. In Riley, MW, Johnson, J, and Foner, A (eds.), *Aging and Society, III.* Russell Sage Foundation, New York, 1972.

Coopersmith, S. *The Antecedents of Self-Esteem.* Freeman, San Francisco, 1967.

Cramer, DW, Goldman, MB, Schiff, I, et al. The relationship of tubal infertility to barrier method and oral contraceptive use. *JAMA* 257:2446–2451, 1987.

Crnic, KA, Greenberg, MT, Ragozin, AS, et al. Effects of stress and social support on mothers and premature and full-term infants. *Child Dev* 54:209–217, 1983.

Crockenberg, SB. Infant irritability, mother responsiveness and social support influences on the security of infant-mother attachments. *Child Dev* 52:857–865, 1981.

Cunningham, FG, Morris, GB, and Mickal, A. Acute pyelonephritis of pregnancy: a clinical review. *Obstet Gynecol* 42:112–117, 1973.

Cvejic, H, Lipper, I, Kinch, RA, and Benjamin, PP. Follow-up of 50 adolescent girls two years after abortion. *Can Med Assoc J* 116:44–46, 1977.

Cvetkovich, G, and Grote, B. Psychological development and the social problem of teenage illegitimacy. In Chilman, C. (ed.): *Adolescent Pregnancy and Childbearing: Findings From Research.* Washington DC: U.S. Department of Health and Human Services, 1980.

David, HP. Unwanted children: a follow-up from Prague. *Fam Plann Perspect* 18:143–144, 1986.

DiMusto, JC, Bohjalian, O, and Millar, M. Mycoplasma hominis type I infection and pregnancy. *Obstet Gynecol* 41:33–37, 1973.

Dohrenwend, BS. Social status and stressful life events. *J Pers Soc Psychol* 28:225–235, 1973.

Dornbusch, SM, Carlsmith, JM, Bushwall, SJ, et al. Single parents, extended households and the control of adolescents. *Child Dev* 56:326–341, 1985.

Drillien, CM. *The Growth and Development of the Prematurely Born Infant.* Williams & Wilkins, Baltimore, 1964.

Duggan, AK, and Hardy, JB. City-Wide Assessment of Adolescent Pregnancy Programs: Impact on Mother and Child. Presented at the Annual Meeting of the American Health Association, Chicago, October 21, 1989.

Dura-Trave, T, daCunha Ferreira, RM, Monreal, I, et al. Zinc concentration of amniotic fluid in the course of pregnancy and its relationship to fetal weight and length. *Gynecol Obstet Invest* 18:152–155, 1984.

Dytrych, Z, Matejcek, Z, Schuller, V, David, HP, and Friedman, HP. Children born of women denied abortion. *Fam Plann Perspect* 7:165, 1975.

East, PA, and Felice, ME. Outcomes and parent-child relationships of former adolescent mothers and their 12-year-old children. *Dev Behav Pediatr* 11:175–183, 1990.

Eastman, NJ, and Jackson, E. Weight relationships in pregnancy. I. The bearing of maternal weight gain and pre-pregnancy weight on birth weight in full term pregnancies. *Obstet Gynecol Surv* 23:1003–1025, 1968.

Edelman, MW. *Families in Peril: An Agenda for Social Change.* Harvard University Press, Cambridge, MA, 1987.

Edwards, L, Steinman, M, Arnold K, and Hakanson, E. Adolescent pregnancy prevention services in high school clinics.*Fam Plann Perspect* 12:6–14, 1980.

Egbuonu, BS, and Starfield, B. Child health and social status. *Pediatrics* 69:550–557, 1982.

Elder, GH, Jr. Age differention and the life course. In Inkeles, A, Coleman, J, and Smelser, N (eds.), *Annual Review of Sociology.* Annual Reviews Inc., Palo Alto, Calif., 1975.

Elder, GH, Jr. Adolescence historical perspective. In Adelson, J (ed.), *Handbook of Adolescent Psychology.* John Wiley & Sons, New York, 1980.

Elkind, D. Egocentrism in adolescence. *Child Dev* 38 (4):1025–1034, 1967.

Elkind, D. Recent research on cognitive development in adolescence. In Dragastin, S, and Elder, G (eds.), *Adolescence in the Life Cycle.* John Wiley & Sons, New York, 1975.

Elkins, TE, McNeeley, SG, and Tabb, T. A new era in contraceptive counseling for early adolescents. *J Adolesc Health Care* 1:19–22, 1987.

Elkins, TE, Strong, C, and Dilts, PV, Jr. Teaching of bioethics within a residency program in obstetrics and gynecology. *Obstet Gynecol* 67:339–342, 1986.

Elster, AB, and Lamb, ME. Adolescent fathers: the understudied side of adolescent pregnancy. In Lancaster, JB, and Hamburg, BA (eds.), *School-age Pregnancy and Parenthood: Biosocial Dimensions.* Aldine De Gruyter, New York, 1986a.

Elster, AB, and Lamb, ME. *Adolescent Fatherhood.* Erlbaum, Hillsdale, N.J., 1986b.

Elster, AB, Lamb, ME, Peters, L, Jahn, J, and Travare. Judicial involvement and conduct problems of fathers of infants born to adolescent mothers. *Pediatr* 79:230–234, 1987.

Elster, AB, and Panzarine, S. Unwed teenage fathers: emotional and health educational needs. *J Adolesc Health Care* 1:116–120, 1980.

Elster, AB, and Panzarine, S. Teenage fathers: stresses during gestation and early parenthood. *Clin Pediatr* 22:700–703, 1983.

Emans, SJ, Grace, E, Woods, ER, et al. Adolescents' compliance with the use of oral contraceptives. *JAMA* 257:3377–3381, 1987.

Embree, JE, Krause, VW, Embil, JA, and MacDonald S. Placental infection with *Mycoplasma hominis* and *Ureaplasma urealyticum*: clinical correlation. *Obstet Gynecol* 56:475–481, 1980.

Erickson, JD, Oakley, GP, Jr, Flynt, JW, Sr, et al. Water fluoridation and congenital malformations: no association. *J Am Dent Assoc* 93:981–984, 1976.

Eriksen, EH. *Youth: Change and Challenge.* WW Norton and Company, New York, 1963.

Eriksen, EH. Identity versus Identity Diffusion, In Mussen, P., Conger, J.J. and Kagan, J. (eds.), *Readings in Child Development and Personality.* Harper & Row, New York, 1965.

Evans, AR. Patient Characteristics and Access to Abortion Services: Factors in Delay in Obtaining Abortion among Teenage Women. The Johns Hopkins School of Hygiene and Public Health, Doctoral Thesis, 1980.

Evans, GW, and Johnson, EC. Zinc absorption in rats fed a low protein diet and a low protein diet supplemented with tryptophan or picolinic acid. *J Nutr* 110:1076–1080, 1980.

Evans, JR, Selstad, G, and Welcher, WH. Teenagers: fertility control behavior and attitudes before and after abortion, childbearing or negative pregnancy test. *Fam Plann Perspect* 8:192–200, 1976.

Faden, RR, and Beauchamp, TL. *A History and Theory of Informed Consent*. Oxford University Press, New York, 1986.

Favier, M, Yacoub, M, Racient, C, et al. Metal ions in the amniotic fluid during the third trimester of pregnancy. Significant relationships between zinc level and fetal weight. *Rev Fr Gynecol Obstet* 67:704–714, 1972.

Fleischer, A, Schulman, H, Farmakides, G, et al. Umbilical artery velocity wave forms and intrauterine growth retardation. *Am J Obstet Gynecol* 151:502–505, 1985.

Forrest, JD. Proportion of U.S. Women Ever Pregnant before Age 20: A Research Note (unpublished paper). Alan Guttmacher Institute, New York, 1986.

Forssman, H, and Thuwe, I. One hundred and twenty children born after application for therapeutic abortion refused. *Acta Psychiatr Scand* 42:71–88, 1966.

Forth, W, and Rummel, W. Iron absorption. *Physiol Rev* 53:724–792, 1973.

Fost, N. *Ethical problems in pediatrics: current problems in pediatrics*. *Pediatrics* 6:2–31, 1976.

Foy, HM, Kenny, GE, Wentworth, BB, et al. Isolation of *Mycoplasma hominis*, T-strains, and cytomegalovirus from the cervix of pregnant women. *Am J Obstet Gynecol* 106:635–643, 1970.

Fraiberg, S, Adelson, E, and Shapiro, V. Ghosts in the nursery: a psychoanalytic approach to the problems of impaired infant-mother relationships. *J Child Psychiatry* 14(3):387–421, 1975.

Freud, A. Adolescence. *Psychoanal Study Child* 13:255–278, 1958.

Frommell, GT, Rothenberg, R, Wang, SP, and McIntosh, K. Chlamydial infection of mothers and their infants. *J Pediatr* 95:28–32, 1979.

Furstenberg, FF, Jr. *Unplanned Parenthood: The Social Consequences of Teenage Childbearing*. Macmillan, New York, 1976.

Furstenberg, FF, Jr, and Brooks-Gunn, J. The children of adolescent mothers: Physical, academic and psychological outcomes. *Dev Rev* 6:224–251, 1986.

Furstenberg, FF, Jr, and Brooks-Gunn, J. Adolescent mothers and their children in later life. *Fam Plann Perspect* 19:142–151, 1987.

Furstenberg, FF, Jr, Brooks-Gunn, J, and Morgan, SP. *Adolescent Mothers In Later Life*. Cambridge University Press, New York, 1987.

Furstenberg, FF, Jr, Winquist-Nord, C, Peterson, JL, and Zill, N. The life course of children of divorce: Marital disruption and parental contact. *Am Soc Rev* 48:656, 1983.

Gant, NF, Daley, GL, Chand, S, et al. A study of angiotensin II pressor response throughout primigravid pregnancy. *J Clin Invest* 52:2682–2689, 1973.

General Accounting Office. WIC Evaluations Provide Some Favorable but No Conclusive Evidence on the Effects Expected for the Special Supplemental Program for Women, Infants and Children. Report to the Committee on Agriculture, Nutrition and Forrestry, United States Senate. GAO/PEMD4, January 30, 1984.

Gispert, M, Brinich, P, Wheeler, K, and Krieger, L. Predictors of repeat pregnancies among low-income adolescents. *Hosp Commun Psychiatry* 35:719–723, 1984.

Glenn, FB, Glenn, WD, 3rd, and Duncan, RC. Fluoride tablet supplementation during pregnancy for caries immunity: a study of the offspring produced. *Am J Obstet Gynecol* 143: 560–564, 1982.

Gray, J, Cutler, C, Dean, J et al. Prediction and prevention of child abuse and neglect. *J Soc Issues* 35:127–139, 1979.

Greer, HS, Lai, S, Lewis, SC, Belsey, EM, and Beard, RW. Psychosocial consequences of therapeutic abortion: King's termination study III. *Br J Psychiatry* 128:74–79, 1976.

Grimes, DA, and Cates, W. Complications from legally induced abortion: a review. *Obstet Gynecol Surv* 34:177–191, 1979.

Grimes, DA, Schulz, KF, and Cates, W. Prophylactic antibiotics for curettage abortion. *Am J Obstet Gynecol* 150:689–694, 1984.

Grubb, G. Women's perceptions of the safety of the pill: a survey in eight developing countries. *J Biol Sci* 19:313–321, 1987.

Haggerty, RJ. The epidemiology of childhood disease. In Mechanic, D (ed.): *Handbook of Health, Health Care and the Health Professions.* The Free Press, New York, 1983.

Hambidgh, KM, and Baum, JD. Chromium nutrition in the mother and the growing child. In Mertz, W, and Cornatzer, W (eds.), *Newer Trace Elements in Nutrition.* Marcel Dekker, New York, 1970, pp 169–194.

Hamilton, DL, Bellamy, JE, Valberg, JD, and Valberg, LS. Zinc, cadmium, and iron interactions during intestinal absorption in iron deficient mice. *Can J Physiol Pharmacol* 56:384–389, 1978.

Hanson, SL, Morrison, DR, and Ginsberg, AL. The antecedents of teenage fatherhood. *Demography* 26:579–596, 1989.

Hanson, SL, Myers, DE, and Ginsberg, AL. The role of responsibility and knowledge in reducing teenage out-of-wedlock childbearing. *J Marriage Fam* 49:241–256, 1987.

Hardy, JB. *Factors Affecting the Growth and Development of Children.* The Johns Hopkins University Press, Baltimore, 1971.

Hardy, JB. Premature sexual activity, pregnancy and sexually transmitted diseases: the pediatrician's role as counselor. *Pediatr* 10:69–76, 1988.

Hardy, JB, Drage, JS, and Jackson, E. *The First Year of Life. The Collaborative Perinatal Study (NINCDS).* Johns Hopkins University Press, Baltimore, 1979.

Hardy, JB, and Duggan, AK. Pregnant and Parenting Adolescents: School Status During Pregnancy and Outcome for Mother and Child During First 15–18 Months after Delivery. Report to the A.S. Abell Foundation, December, 1988a.

Hardy, JB, and Duggan, AK: Teenage fathers and the fathers of infants of urban, teenage mothers. *Am J Public Health* 78:919–922, 1988b.

Hardy, JB, Duggan, AK, Masnyk, K, and Pearson, C. Fathers of children born to young urban mothers. *Fam Plann Perspect* 21(4):159–163, 1989.

Hardy, JB, and Flagle, CD. A preliminary evaluation of the Johns Hopkins Adolescent Pregnancy Program. Presented at a Symposium on Adolescent Pregnancy at the Johns Hopkins Institutions, Baltimore, Maryland, 1979.

Hardy, JB, Flagle, CD, and Duggan, AK. Resource Use by Pregnant and Parenting Adolescents. Final Report to the Office of Adolescent Pregnancy Programs on Grant No. APR 000906-03-0, June 1986.

Hardy, JB, King, TM, and Repke, J. The Johns Hopkins adolescent pregnancy program: an evaluation. *Obstet Gynecol* 69:300–306, 1987.

Hardy, JB, and Mellits, ED. Relationship of low birthweight to maternal characteristics of age, parity, education and body size. In Reed, DM and Stanley, FJ (eds.), *The Epidemiology of Prematurity.* Urban & Schwarzenberg, Baltimore, 1977, pp. 105–117.

Hardy, JB, and Streett, R. Family support and parenting education: an effective extension of clinic-based preventive health services for poor children. *J Pediatr* 115(6):927–931, 1989.

Hardy, JB, Welcher, DW, Stanley, J, and Dallas, JR. The long-range outcome of adolescent pregnancy. *Clin Obstet Gynecol* 21:4, 1978.

Hardy, PH, Jr, Hardy, JB, Nell, EE, et al. Prevalence of six sexually transmitted disease agents among pregnant inner-city adolescents and pregnancy outcome. *Lancet* 2:333–337, 1984.

Harris, RE, and Gilstrap, LC, 3rd. Prevention of recurrent pyleonephritis during pregnancy. *Obstet Gynecol* 44:637–641, 1974.

Harrison, HR, Alexander, ER, Weinstein, L, et al. Cervical *Chlamydia trachomatis* and mycoplasmal infections in pregnancy: epidemiology and outcomes. *JAMA* 250:1721–1727, 1983.

Harrison, RF, Hurley, R, and deLouvois, J. Genital mycoplasms and birth weight in offspring of primigravid women. *Am J Obstet Gynecol* 133:201–203, 1979.

Hayes, CD (ed.). *Risking the Future: Adolescent Sexuality, Pregnancy and Childbearing,* Vol. 1. National Academy Press, Washington, DC, 1987.

Heggie, AD, Lumicao, GG, Stuart, LA, and Gyves, ST. *Chlamydia trachomatis* infection in mothers and infants: a prospective study. *Am J Dis Child* 135:507–511, 1981.

Hendricks, L. Unwed adolescent fathers: problems they face and their sources of social support. *Adolescence* 15:861–869, 1980.

Hendricks, LE, Howard, CS, and Caesar, PP. Help seeking behavior among selected populations of black, unmarried adolescent fathers. *Am J Public Health* 71:733–735, 1981.

Hendricks, LE, and Montgomery, TA. Educational achievement and locus of control among black adolescent fathers. *J Negro Educ* 53:182–188, 1984.

Henshaw, SK, Binkin, NJ, Blaine, E, and Smith, JC. A portrait of American women who obtain abortions. *Fam Plann Perspect* 17:90–96, 1985.

Henshaw, SK, Kenney, Am, Somberg, D, Van Vort, J. *Teenage Pregnancy in the United States: The Scope of the Problem and State Responses.* The Alan Guttmacher Institute, New York, 1989.

Hern, WM. *Abortion Practice.* J.B. Lippincott, Philadelphia, 1984.

Higgins, AC. Nutritional status and the outcome of pregnancy. *J Can Diet Assoc* 37:17, 1976.

Hirsch, MB, and Zabin, LS. Effect of Pregnancy Outcome Decision Making Process on Satisfaction with Decision and Psychological Well-Being in Urban Black Female Teens. Presented at American Public Health Association Annual Meeting, Baltimore, November 1988.

Hirsch, MB, Zabin, LS, Streett, RF, and Hardy, JB. Users of reproductive health clinic services in a school pregnancy prevention program. *Public Health Rep* 102(3):307–316, 1987.

Hirst, BC. *A Textbook of Obstetrics*, ed. 5, p. 189. W.B. Saunders, Philadelphia, 1906.

Hobel, CJ, Hyvarinen, MA, Okada, DM, et al. Prenatal and intrapartum high risk screening: 1. Prediction of the high risk neonate. *Am J Obstet Gynecol* 117:1–9, 1973.

Hofferth, SL. Factors affecting initiation of sexual intercourse. In Hofferth, SL, and Hayes, CD (eds.), *Risking the Future*, Vol. II. National Academy Press, Washington, DC, 1987a.

Hofferth, SL. Influences on early sexual fertility behavior. In Hofferth, SL, and Hayes, CD (eds.), *Risking the Future: Adolescent Sexuality, Pregnancy and Childbearing*, Vol. II. National Academy Press, Washington, DC, 1987b.

Hofferth, SL, and Hayes, CD. *Risking the Future: Adolescent Sexuality, Pregnancy and Childbearing*, Vol. II. National Academy Press, Washington, DC, 1987.

Hofferth, SL, Kahn, JR, and Baldwin, W. Premarital sexual activity among U.S. teenage women over the past three decades. *Fam Plann Perspect* 19:46–53, 1987.

Hogan, DP, Astone, NM, and Kitagawa, EM. Social and environmental factors influencing contraceptive use among black adolescents. *Fam Plann Perspect* 17(4):165–169, 1985.

Hogan, DP, and Kitagawa, EM. The impact of social status, family structure and neighborhood on the fertility of black adolescents. *Am J Sociol* 90(4):825–855, 1985.

Hogue, CJR, Cates, W, and Tietze, C. The effects of induced abortion on subsequent reproduction. *Epidemiol Rev* 4:66–94, 1982.

Holder, AR. Minor's rights to consent to medical care. *JAMA* 257:3400–3402, 1987.

Horon, IL, Strobino, DM, and MacDonald, HM. Birth weights among infants born to adolescent and young adult women. *Am J Obstet Gynecol* 146:444–449, 1983.

Hurley, LS, and Baly, DL. The effects of zinc deficiency during pregnancy. *Curr Top Nutr Dis* 6:145–159, 1982.

Institute of Medicine. *Preventing Low Birthweight. Committee to Study the Prevention of Low Birthweight, Division of Health Promotion and Disease Prevention.* National Academy Press; Washington, DC, 1985.

Jessor, R, and Jessor, SL. *Problem Behavior and Psychosocial Development: A Longitudinal Study of Youth.* Academic Press, New York, 1977.

Johnson, TRB, Walker, MA, and Niebyl, JR. Pre-Natal Care. In Gabbe, SG, Neibyl, JR, and Simpson, JL (eds.), *Obstetrics: Normal and Problem Pregnancies*. Churchill-Livingstone, New York, 1986.

Jones E. Some problems of adolescence. *Papers on Psychoanalysis.* Bailliere, Tindall, London, 1950.

Jones, EF, Forrest, JD, Goldman, N, et al. *Teenage Pregnancy in Industrialized Countries.* Yale University Press, New Haven, CT, 1986.

Jones, EF, Forrest, JD, Goldman, N, Henshaw, SK, et al. Teenage pregnancy in developed countries: determinants and policy implications. *Fam Plann Perspect* 17:53–63, 1985.

Jonsen, AP, Siegler, M, and Winslade, WJ. *Clinical Ethics*, ed. 2. Macmillan, New York, 1985.

Jordan, EA, Duggan, AK, and Hardy, JB. Home safety education and injury risk in children of adolescent mothers. Submitted for publication.

Kellam, SG, Adams, RG, Brown, CH, et al. The long-term evolution of the family structure of teenage and older mothers. *J Marriage Fam* August: 539–554, 1982.

Kellam, SG, Ensminger, ME, and Turner, RJ. Family structure and the mental health of children. *Arch Gen Psychiatry* 34:1012–1022, 1977.

Keusch, G, Wilson, C, and Waksal, S. Nutrition, host defense, and the lymphoid system. In Gallin, JI, and Fauci, AS (eds.), *Advances in Host Defense Mechanisms*. Plenum Publishers, New York, 1983, pp. 275–359.

Kincaid-Smith, P, and Bullen, M. Bacteriuria in pregnancy. *Lancet* 1:395–399, 1965.

Klaus, M, and Kennell, J. Parent to infant bonding: setting the record straight. *J Pediatr* 102(4):575–576, 1983.

Klein, JO, Buckland, D, and Finland, M. Colonization of newborn infants by mycoplasmas. *N Engl J Med* 280:1025–1030, 1969.

Klerman, LV, and Jekel, J. *School-age Mothers: Problems, Programs and Policy*. Shoe String Press (Linnet), Hamden, CT, 1973.

Koenig, M, and Zelnik, M. Repeat pregnancies among metropolitan area teenagers: 1971–1979. *Fam Plann Perspect* 14:341–344, 1982.

Kohlberg, L. Stage and sequence: the cognitive developmental approach to socialization. In Goslin, DA (ed.), *Handbook of Socialization Theory and Research*. Rand McNally, Chicago, 1969.

Kols, A, et al. Oral contraceptives in the 1980s. *Popul Rep [A]* A6:A189–A222, May–June, 1982.

Koop, E. Health impact of abortion. *Congressional Record*, 135(33): E906, March 21, 1989.

Kynast, G, Saling, E, and Wagner, N. The relevance of zinc determination in amniotic fluid. Second Communication: zinc in cases of high fetal risk. *J Perinat Med* 7:69–77, 1979.

Lancaster, JB, and Hamburg, BA. *School-age Pregnancy and Parenthood: Biosocial Dimensions*. Adline De Gruyter, New York, 1986.

Lazarus, A. Psychiatric sequelae of legalized elective first trimester abortion. *J Psychosom Obstet Gynecol* 4:141–150, 1985.

Lerman, RI: Who are the Young Absent Fathers? (unpublished). Brandeis University, Waltham, Mass., 1985.

Lerman, RI. A national profile of young unwed fathers: who are they and how are they parenting? In appendix to Smollar, J, and Ooms, T (eds.), *Young Unwed Fathers: Research Review, Policy Dilemmas and Options*. A report from the Family Impact Seminar, Catholic University of America, Washington, DC, 1987.

Lieberman, E, Ryan, KJ, Monson, RR, and Schoenbaum, SC. Risk factors accounting for racial differences in the rate of premature birth. *N Engl J Med* 317:743–748, 1987.

Lind, T. Iron supplementation during pregnancy. In Campbell, DM and Gillmer, MDG (eds.): *Nutrition in Pregnancy*. London, Royal College of Obstetricians and Gynecologists, 1983.

Liskin, L. After contraception: dispelling rumors about later childbearing. *Popul Rep [J]* J28:J697–J731, Sept–Oct, 1984.

Little, RE, and Sing, CF. Association of father's drinking and infant's birth weight. (Letter to the Editor). *N Engl J Med* 314:1644, 1986.

Little, WJ. On the influence of abnormal parturition, difficult labour, premature birth and asphyxia neonatorum on the mental and physical condition of the child, especially in relation to deformities. *Trans Obstet Soc* 11:293, 1862.

Lovchik, JC. Chlamydial infections. *Md Med J* 36:54–57, 1987.

Madge, N. *Families at Risk*. Heinemann Educational Books, London, 1983.

Margolis, A, Rindfuss, R, Coghlan, P, and Rochat, R. Contraception after abortion. *Fam Plann Perspect* 6:56–60, 1974.

Marini, MM. Measuring the process of role change during the transition to adulthood. *Soc Sci Res* 16:1–38, 1984.

Marshall, WA, and Tanner, JM. Puberty. In *Scientific Foundations of Pediatrics*. In Davis and Dobbing (eds.), W.B. Saunders, Philadelphia, 1974.

Marsiglio, W. Teenage fatherhood: high school completion and educational attainment. In Elster, AB, and Lamb, ME (eds.), *Adolescent Fatherhood*. Erlbaum, Hillsdale, N.J. 1986.

Marsiglio, W. Adolescent fathers in the United States: their initial living arrangements, marital status and educational outcome. *Fam Plann Perspect* 19:245–251, 1987.

Martin, DH, Koutsky, L, Eschenbach, DA, et al. Prematurity and perinatal mortality in pregnancies complicated by maternal *Chlamydia trachomatis* infections. *JAMA* 247:1585–1588, 1982.

Maryland Governor's Council on Adolescent Pregnancy. *Fact Sheet*, January/February, 1989, March/April, 1989.

McAnarney, ER, and Hendee, WR. Adolescent pregnancy and its consequences. *JAMA* 262(1):74–77, 1989.

McAnarney, ER, Lawrence, RA, Ricciuti, HN, et al. Interactions of adolescent mothers and their 1-year-old children. *Pediatrics* 78:585–590, 1986.

McCormick, MC, Shapiro, S, and Starfield, BH. High risk young mothers: infant mortality and morbidity in four areas of the United States, 1973–1978. *Am J Public Health* 74:18–22, 1984.

McLanahan, SS. Family structure and stress: a longitudinal comparison of two-parent and female-headed families. *J Marr Fam* May:347–357, 1983.

McLanahan, SS. Family structure and the reproduction of poverty. *Am J Sociol* 90(4):873–901, 1985.

McPherson, K, et al. Early oral contraceptive use and breast cancer: results of another case-controlled study. *Br J Cancer* 56:653–660, 1987.

McQuillan, GM, Townsend, T, Johannes, CB, et al. Prevention of perinatal transmission of hepatitis B virus: the perinatal sensitivity, specificity and predictive value of the recommended screening questions to detect high risk women in obstetrical population. *Am J Epidemiol* 126(3):484–491, 1987.

Medical Letter, The. Prevention and treatment of the post-menopausal osteoporosis. *Med Lett* 29:75, 1987.

Merritt, TA, Lawrence, RA, and Naeye, RL. The infants of adolescent mothers. *Pediatr Ann* 9:100–110, 1980.

Meyer, RJ, and Haggerty, RJ. Streptococcal infections in families: factors altering individual susceptibility. *Pediatrics* 29:539–1962.

Miller, FJW, Court, SDM, Knox, EG, and Brandon, S. *The School Years in Newcastle-Upon-Tyne*. Oxford University Press, London, 1974.

Miller, FJW, Kolvin, I, and Fells, H. Becoming deprived: a cross-generations study based on the Newcastle-Upon-Tyne 1,000 family survey. In Nicol, AR (ed.): *Longitudinal Studies in Child Psychology and Psychiatry*. John Wiley & Sons, New York, 1985.

Mills, JL, Rhoads, GG, Simpson, JL, et al. The absence of a relation between the periconceptional use of vitamins and neural tube defects. *N Engl J Med* 321:430–435, 1989.

Montemayor, R. Boys as fathers: coping with the dilemmas of adolescence. In Elster, AB, and Lamb, ME (eds.), *Adolescent Fatherhood*. Erlbaum, Hillsdale, NJ, 1986.

Monzon, OT, Armstrong, D, Pion, RJ, et al. Bacteriuria during pregnancy. *Am J Obstet Gynecol* 85:511–518, 1963.

Moore, KA. Teenage childbirth and welfare dependency. *Fam Plann Perspect* 10:233–235, 1978.

Moore, KA, and Burt, MR. *Private Crisis, Public Cost*. The Urban Institute Press, Washington, DC, 1982.

Moore, KA, and Hofferth, SL. Factors affecting early formation: a path model. *Pop Environ* 3(1):73–98, 1980.

Moore, KA, Simms, MC, and Betsey, CL. *Choice and Circumstance*. Transaction Books, New Brunswick, N.J., 1986.

Moore, KA, Wertheimer, R, and Holden R. Teenage Childbearing: Public Costs. Third six-month report to the Center for Population Research, National Institutes of Health, Washington, DC, 1981.

Morgenthau, JE. Teenage pregnancies and abortion. *Mt Sinai J Med* 51:18–19, 1984.

Morris, NM, Mallin, K, and Udry, JR. Pubertal Development and Current Sexual Intercourse among Teens. Presented at American Public Health Association Meetings, Montreal, 1982.

Mott, FL. Early fertility behavior among American youth: evidence from the 1982 National Longitudinal Survey of Youth. Paper presented at the 1983 annual meeting of the American Public Health Association, 1983.

Mott, FL, and Marsiglio, W. Early Childbearing and Early School Leaving among Young American Women. Paper under contract with Employment and Training Administration, U.S. Department of Labor, 1985.

Mott, FL, and Maxwell, NL. School-age mothers: 1968 and 1979. *Fam Plann Perspect* 13:287–292, 1981.

Myrianthropoulos, NC, and French, KS. An application of the U.S. Bureau of the Census socio-economic index to a large, diversified patient population. *Soc Sci Med* 2:283–299, 1968.

Naeye, RL. Causes and consequences of placental growth retardation. *JAMA* 239:1145–1147, 1978.

Naeye, RL, Harkness, WL, and Utts, J. Abruptio placentae and perinatal death: a prospective study. *Am J Obstet Gynecol* 128:740–746, 1977.

Naeye, RL, and Peters, EC. Amniotic fluid infections with intact membranes leading to perinatal death: a prospective study. *Pediatrics* 61:171–177, 1978.

National Academy of Sciences. Nutrition services and perinatal care. Committee on the Nutrition of the Mother and Pre-school Child. Food and Nutrition Board, National Academy of Sciences, 2101 Constitution Avenue, N.W., Washington, DC, 20418, 1981.

National Academy Press. Preventing Low Birth Weight. A Report from the Committee on Low Birth Weight of the Institute of Medicine. Washington, DC, 1985.

National Center for Health Statistics. Report of Final Natality Statistics, 1986. Vol. 37, No. 3 Supplement, July 12, 1988.

National Center for Vital Statistics. Advance Report of Final Natality Statistics, 1985. National Center for Vital Statistics 36(4) Supplement, July 17, 1987.

National Longitudinal Survey of Youth. Labor Market Experience of Youth. Center for Human Resource Research, Worthington, Ohio, 1966.

National Research Council. *Risking the Future: Adolescent Sexuality, Pregnancy and Childbearing*, Vol. I. Hayes, CD (ed.), National Academy Press, Washington, DC, 1987.

Needleman, HL, Pueschel, SM, and Rothman, KJ. Fluoridation and the occurrence of Down's syndrome. *N Engl J Med* 291:821–823, 1974.

Needleman, HL, Rabinowitz, M, Leviton, A, et al. The relationship between prenatal exposure to lead and congenital anomalies. *JAMA* 251:2956–2959, 1984.

Neinstein, LS. *Adolescent Health Care*, ed. 2. Urban & Schwarzenberg, Baltimore-Munich, 1991.

Niebyl, JR, and Youngs, DD. The sexually active female adolescent. *Primary Care* 2:571–584, 1975.

Niswander, K, and Gordon, M: *The Women and Their Pregnancies: The Collaborative Perinatal Study of the National Institute of Neurological Diseases and Stroke*. W.B. Saunders, Philadelphia, 1972.

Niswander, KR, Singer, J, Westphal, M, Jr, et al. Weight gain during pregnancy and prepregnancy weight. Association with birth weight and term gestation. *Obstet Gynecol* 33:482–491, 1969.

Olds, DL, Henderson, CR, Jr, Chamberlin R, et al. Preventing child abuse and neglect: a randomized trial of nurse home visitation. *Pediatrics* 77:65–78, 1986.

Olds, DL, Henderson, CR, Jr, Tatelbaum, R, et al. Improving the delivery of prenatal care and outcomes of pregnancy: a randomized trail of nurse home visitation. *Pediatrics* 77:16–28, 1986.

Orlando, P, Perdelli, F, Casadio, M, et al. Presence of some trace elements in pregnant women of Genoa. *G Ig Med Prev* 19:62, 1978.

Ory, HW. Mortality associated with fertility and fertility control. *Fam Plann Perspect* 15:57–63, 1983.

Osofsky, JD, and Osofsky, HJ. The psychological reaction of patients to legalized abortion. *Am J Orthropsychiatry* 42:48–60, 1972.

Pare, CMB, and Raven H. Follow-up of patients referred for termination of pregnancy. *Lancet* 1:635–638, 1970.

Parke, RD, and Neville, B. Teenage fatherhood. In Hofferth, SL, and Hayes, CD (eds), *Risking the Future*, Vol. II. National Academy Press, Washington, DC, 1987.

Pascoe, JM, and Earp, JA. The effect of mothers' social support and life changes on the stimulation of their children in the home. *Am J Public Health* 74:358–360, 1984.

Paul, BW, and Schaap, P. Legal rights and responsibilities of pregnant teenagers and their children. In Stuart, IR, and Wells, CF (eds.), *Pregnancy in Adolescence Needs, Problems and Management*. Von Nostrand Reinhold Company, New York, 1981.

Perlman, SB, Kleman, LV, and Kinard, EM. The use of socioeconomic data to predict teenage birth rates. *Public Health Rep* 96(4):335–341, 1981.

Peterson, DR, Van Bellan, G, and Chinn, M. Sudden infant death syndrome and maternal age. *JAMA* 247:2250, 1982.

Peterson, HB, Grimes, DA, Gates, W, et al. Comparative risk of death from induced abortion at 12 weeks gestation performed with local versus general anesthesia. *Am J Obstet Gynecol* 141:763–768, 1981.

Piaget, J. Intellectual evolution from adolescence to adulthood. *Hum Dev* 15:1–12, 1972.

Pike, MC, Henderson, BE, Casagrande, JT, et al. Oral contraceptive use and early abortion as risk factors for cancer in young women. *Br J Cancer* 43:72–76, 1981.

Pitkin, RM. Calcium metabolism in pregnancy: A review. *Am J Obstet Gynecol* 121:724–737, 1975.

Pollack, S, George, JN, Reba, RC, et al. The absorption of nonferrous metals in iron deficiency. *J Clin Invest* 44:1470–1473, 1965.

Porter, JB, Jick, H, and Walker, AM. Mortality among oral contraceptive users. *Obstet Gynecol* 70:29–32, 1987.

Pratt, WF, Mosher, WD, Bachrach, CA, et al. Understanding U.S. fertility. Findings from the National Survey of Family Growth, Cycle III. *Popul Bull* 39:1–52, 1984.

The President's Panel on Mental Retardation. *A Proposed Program for National Action to Combat Mental Retardation*. Report to the President. U.S. Government Printing Office, Washington, DC, 1962.

Rapaport, I. Contribution a l'etude du mongolisme: role pathogenique du flour. *Bull Acad Natl Med (Paris)* 140:529–531, 1956.

Reiss, I. *The Social Context of Premarital Sexual Permissiveness*. Holt, Rinehart and Winston, New York, 1967.

Reiterman, C. *Abortion and the Unwanted Child*. Springer Publishing Company, New York, 1971.

Resnick, M. Adoption Decision Making Project. Research funded by the Office of Adolescent Pregnancy Programs, U.S.D.H.H.S., Washington, DC, 1984.

Riley, MW. Aging from birth to death: interdisciplinary perspectives. AAAS Selected Symposium #30. Westview Press, Boulder, CO, 1979.

Rivara, FP, Sweeney, PJ, and Henderson, BF. A study of low socioeconomic status, black teenage fathers and their non-father peers. *Pediatrics* 75:648–656, 1985.

Rosenberg, M. *Society and the Adolescent Self-image*. Princeton University Press, Princeton, N.J., 1965.

Rosick, U, Rosick, E, Bratter, P, and Kynast, G. Determination of zinc in amniotic fluid in normal and high risk pregnancies. *J Clin Chem Clin Biochem* 21:363–372, 1983.

Rossi, PH, Freeman, HE, and Wright, SR. *Evaluation: A Systematic Approach*. Sage Publications, Beverly Hills, CA 1979.

Rosso, P, and Lederman, SA. Nutrition in the pregnant adolescent. *Curr Concepts Nutr* 11:47–62, 1982.

Rothenberg, PB, and Varga, PE. The relationship between age of mother and child health and development. *Am J Public Health* 71(8):810–817, 1981.

Rotter, JB. The Rotter Internal-External Locus of Control. *Psychol Monogr* 609, 1966.

Rubin, GL, Ory, HW, and Layde, PM. Oral contraceptives and pelvic inflammatory disease. *Am J Obstet Gynecol* 144:630–635, 1980.

Sandstead, HH. The role of zinc in human health. In Hemphill, HH (ed.): *Trace Substances in Environmental Health*, Vol. XII. *Proceedings of University of Missouri's 12th Annual Conference on Trace Substances on Environmental Health*. University of Missouri Press, Columbia, MO, 1978, pp. 173–179.

Sarrel, P, and Klerman, L. The young unwed mother. *Am J Obstet Gynecol* 105:575–587, 1969.

Schlesselman, JJ, Stade, BV, Murray, P, and Lai, S. Breast cancer in relation to early use of oral contraceptives: no evidence of a latent effect. *JAMA* 259:1828–1833, 1988.

Scholl, TO, Miller, LK, Salmon, RW, et al. Prenatal care adequacy and the outcome of adolescent pregnancy: effects on weight gain, preterm delivery and birth weight. *Obstet Gynecol* 69:312–316, 1987.

Schorr, LB. *Within Our Reach: Breaking the Cycle of Disadvantage.* Anchor Press-Doubleday, New York, 1988.

Schulz, KF, Grimes, DA, and Cates, W. Measures to prevent cervical injury during suction curettage abortion. *Lancet* 1:1182–1184, 1983.

Schwartz, RM. What price prematurity? *Fam Plann Perspect* 21:170–174, 1989.

Scott, GD, and Carlo, MW. *On Becoming A Health Educator,* ed 2. William C. Brown Publishers, Dubuque, Iowa, 1980.

Shaw, RW. Adverse long-term effects of oral contraceptives: a review. *Br J Obstet Gynaecol* 94:724–730, 1987.

Short, RV. The evolution of human reproduction. *Proc R Soc Med* 195:3–24, 1976.

Shusterman, LR. The psychosocial factors of the abortion experience: a critical review. *Psychol Wom* 1(1):79–106, 1976.

Shusterman, LR. Predicting the psychological consequence of abortion. *Soc Sci Med* 13A:683–689, 1979.

Siegel, E, Bauman, KE, Schaefer, ES, et al. Hospital and home support during infancy: impact on maternal attachment, child abuse and neglect and health care utilization. *Pediatrics* 66:183–190, 1980.

Siegler, M, Rexler, AG, and Connell, AJ. Using simulated case studies to evaluate a clinical ethics course for junior students. *J Med Educ* 57:380–385, 1982.

Silber, J. Abortion in adolescence: the ethical dimension. *Adolescence* 15:461–474, 1980.

Silber, TJ. Ethical and legal issues in adolescent pregnancy. *Clin Perinatol* 14:265–270, 1987.

Silver, JJ. Ethical considerations concerning adolescents consulting for contraceptive services. *J Fam Pract* 15:909–911, 1982.

Simon, W, and Gagnon, JH. A sexual scripts approach. In Geer, JH, and O'Donahue, WT (eds.), *Theories of Human Sexuality.* Plenum, New York, 1987.

Simpson, JW, Lawless, RW, and Mitchell, AC. Responsibility of the obstetrician to the fetus. II. Influence of pre-pregnancy weight and pregnancy weight gain on birth weight. *Obstet Gynecol* 45:481–487, 1975.

Singer, JE, Westphal, M, and Niswander, K. Relationship of weight gain during pregnancy to birth weight and infant growth and development in the first year of life. A report from the Collaborative Study of Cerebral Palsy. *Obstet Gynecol* 31:417–423, 1968.

Singh, S. Adolescent pregnancy in the United States: an interstate analysis. *Fam Plann Perspect* 18(5):210–220, 1986.

Slome, C, Witherbee, H, Daly, M, et al. Effectiveness of CNMs. A prospective evaluation study. *Am J Obstet Gynecol* 124:177–182, 1976.

Smith, CA. Effects of maternal undernutrition upon the newborn infant in Holland. *J Pediatr* 30:229–243, 1947.

Smith, EA. A biosocial model of adolescent behavior. In Adams, GR (ed.): *Advances in Adolescent Development,* Vol. 1. Sage Publications, Beverly Hills, CA, 1988.

Smith, EA and Zabin, LS. *Young Teens, their Mothers, and Communication about Sex: Do Moms and Kids Agree?* Presented at American Public Health Association Annual Meeting, Washington, DC, November 1985.

Smithells, RW, Sheppard, S, Schorah, CJ, et al. Apparent prevention of neural tube defects by peri-conceptional vitamin supplementation. *Arch Dis Child* 56:911–918, 1981.

Smollar, J, and Ooms, T. Young Unwed Fathers: Research Review, Policy Dilemmas and Options. A report from the Family Impact Seminar, Catholic University of America, Washington, DC, 1987.

Solomons, NW, Helitzer-Allen, DL, and Villar, J. Zinc needs during pregnancy. *Clin Nutr* 5:63, 1986.

Solomons, NW, and Jacob, RA. Studies on the bioavailability of zinc in humans: effects of heme and noheme iron on the absorption of zinc. *Am J Clin Nutr* 34:475–482, 1981.

Solomons, NW, Pineda, O, Viteri, F, and Sandstead, HH. Studies on the bioavailability of zinc in humans: mechanism of the intestinal interaction of nonheme iron and zinc. *J Nutr* 113:337–349, 1983.

Sonenstein, FL. Risking paternity: sex and contraception among adolescent males. In Elster, AB, and Lamb, ME (eds.), *Adolescent Fatherhood.* Erlbaum, Hillsdale, N.J., 1986.

Spence, MR, King, TM, Burkman, RT, and Atienza, MF. Cephalothin prophylaxis for mid-trimester abortion. *Obstet Gynecol* 60:502–513, 1982.

Spielberger, CD. *State-Trait Anxiety Inventory*. Consulting Psychology Press, Palo Alto, CA, 1983.

SRI International. An Analysis of Government Expenditures Consequent on Teenage Childbirth. A paper prepared for the Population Resource Center, Washington, DC, 1979.

Stack, JM. Spontaneous abortion and grieving. *Am Fam Phys* 21:99–102, 1980.

Stamey, TA, Condy, M, and Milhara, G. Prophylactic efficacy of nitrofurantoin macrocrystals and trimethoprim-sulfamethoxazole in urinary infections. Biologic effects on the vaginal and rectal flora. *N Engl J Med* 296:780–783, 1977.

Standfast, SJ, Jereb, S, and Janerich, DT. The epidemiology of sudden infant death in upstate New York, II. Birth characteristics. *Am J Public Health* 70:1061–1067, 1980.

Stanford Research Institute. An Analysis of Government Expenditures Consequent Upon Teenage Childbirth. SRI International Health Services, for Population Resource Center, New York, 1979.

Starfield, B, Shapiro, S, McCormick, M, and Bross, D. Mortality and morbidity in infants with intra-uterine growth retardation. *J Pediatr* 101:978–986, 1982.

Stein, Z, Susser, M, and Rush, D. Prenatal nutrition and birth weight: experiments and quasi-experiments in the past decade. *J Reprod Med* 21:287–299, 1978.

Stein, Z, Susser, M, Saenger, G, and Marolla, F. *Famine and Human Development: The Dutch Hunger Winter of 1944–1945*. Oxford University Press, New York, 1975.

Steinberg, L. Single parents, step-parents and the susceptibility of adolescents to anti-social peer pressure. *Child Dev* 58:269–275, 1987.

Strobino, DM. The health and medical consequences of adolescent sexuality and pregnancy: A review of the literature. In Hofferth, SL, and Hayes, CD (eds.), *Adolescent Sexuality, Pregnancy and Childbearing*, Vol. II, *Risking The Future*. National Academy Press, Washington, DC, 1987.

Stubblefield, PG, Monson, RR, Schoenbaum, SC, et al. Fertility after induced abortion: a prospective follow-up study. *Obstet Gynecol* 62:186–193, 1984.

Suchman, EA. *Evaluative Research: Principles and Practice in Public Services and Social Action Programs*. Russell Sage Foundation, New York, 1973.

Tafari, N, Ross, S, Naeye, RL, et al. Mycoplasma T-strains and perinatal death. *Lancet* 1:108–109, 1976.

Tannahill, R. *Food in History*. Stein and Day, New York, 1973.

Taylor, B, Wadsworth, J, and Butler, NR. Teenage mothering, admission to hospital and accidents during first 5 years. *Arch Dis Child* 58:6–11, 1983.

Taylor, DJ, Mallen, C, McDougall, N, and Lind, T. Effect of iron supplementation on serum ferritin levels during and after pregnancy. *Br J Obstet Gynaecol* 89:1011–1017, 1982.

Teachman, JD, and Polonki, KA. Out of sequence: the timing of marriage following a premarital birth. *Soc Forces* 63:245–259, 1984.

Thompson, S, Lopez, B, Wong, KH, et al. A prospective study of chlamydia and mycoplasma infections during pregnancy: relation to pregnancy outcome and maternal morbidity. In Mardh, P-A, Holmes, KK, Oriel, JD, Piot, P, and Schachter, J (eds.), *Proceedings of the 5th International Symposium on Human Chlamydial Infections*. Elsevier Biomedical Press, Amsterdam, 1982.

Tietze, C. Teenage pregnancies: looking ahead to 1984. *Fam Plann Perspect* 10(4):205–207, 1978.

Tietze, C, and Bongaarts, J. Estimates for spontaneous miscarriages equal 20% of births plus 10% of abortions, developed for the Population Council. Cited in Henshaw, SK, Bonkin, EB, and Smith, JC, A portrait of American women who obtain abortions. *Fam Plann Perspect* 17:90–96, 1985.

Tietze, C, and Henshaw, SK. *Induced Abortion: A World Review 1986*, ed. 6. The Alan Guttmacher Institute, New York, 1986.

Udry, JR. Age at menarche, at first intercourse and at first pregnancy. *J Biosoc Sci* 11:433–441, 1979.

Udry, JR, Billy, JOG, Morris, NM, et al. Serum androgenic hormones motivate sexual behavior in adolescent boys. *Fertil Steril* 43:90–94, 1985.

Udry, JR, Talbert, LM, and Morris, NM. Biosocial foundations for adolescent female sexuality. *Demography* 23:217–230, 1986.

Villar, J, and Belizan, J. Calcium during pregnancy. *Clin Nutr* 5:55, 1986.

Villar, J, and Cossio, TG. Nutritional factors associated with low birth weight and short gestational age. *Clin Nutr* 5:78, 1987.

Villar, J, Repke, JT, and Belizan, JM. Calcium and blood pressure. *Clin Nutr* 5:153, 1986.

Villar, J, Repke, JT, Belizan, JM, and Pareja, G. Calcium supplementation reduces blood pressure during pregnancy: results of a randomized controlled clinical trial. *Obstet Gynecol* 70:317–322, 1987.

Vital Statistics. Baltimore, Maryland, 1985.

Wadsworth, J, Burnell, I, Taylor, B, and Butler, N. The influence of family type on children's behaviour and development at five years. *J Child Psychol Psychiatry* 26(2):245–254, 1985.

Wadsworth, J, Taylor, B, Osborn, A, and Butler, N. Teenage mothering: child development at five years. *J Child Psychol Psychiatry* 25:305–313, 1984.

Warkany, J, and Petering, HG. Congenital malformations of the central nervous system in rats produced by maternal zinc deficiency. *Teratology* 5:319–334, 1972.

Watters, WW. Mental health consequences of abortion and refused abortion. *Can J Psychiatry* 25:68–73, 1980.

Weiss, HB. Family support and education programs: working through ecological theories of human development. In Weiss, HB, and Jacobs, FH (eds.): *Evaluating Family Programs*. Aldine De Gruyter, New York, 1988.

Weiss, W, and Jackson, EC. Maternal factors affecting birth weight. In Perinatal Factors Affecting Human Development. Pan American Health Organization, Proceedings of the Special Session held during the Eighth Meeting of the PAHO Advisory Committee on Medical Research, June 10, 1969. Washington, DC, pp. 54–59.

Werner, EE. Stress and protective factors in children's lives. In Nicol, AR (ed.), *Longitudinal Studies in Child Psychology and Psychiatry*. John Wiley & Sons, New York, 1985.

Werner, EE. A longitudinal study of perinatal risk. In Farran, DC, and McKinney, JD (eds.), *Risk In Longitudinal Development*. Academic Press, New York, 1986.

Werner, EE, and Smith, RS. *Vulnerable but Invincible: A Longitudinal Study of Resilient Children and Youth*. McGraw-Hill, New York, 1982.

Westoff, CF, Calot, G, and Foster, AD. Teenage fertility in developed nations. *Fam Plann Perspect* 15:105, 1983.

Westrom, L, Bengsston, LP, and Mardh, PA. The risk of pelvic inflammatory disease in women using intrauterine contraceptive devices as compared to non-users. *Lancet* 2:221–224, 1976.

Whalley, P. Bacteriuria of pregnancy. *Am J Obstet Gynecol* 97:723–738, 1967.

Wibberley, DG, Khera, AK, Edwards, JH, and Rushton, DI. Lead levels in human placentae from normal and malformed births. *J Med Genet* 14:339–345, 1977.

Wilson, WJ. *The Truly Disadvantaged*. University of Chicago Press, Chicago, 1987.

Youngs, DD, Niebyl, JR, Blake, DA, et al. Experience with an adolescent pregnancy program. *Obstet Gynecol* 50:212, 1977.

Zabin, LS. The impact of early use of prescription contraceptives on reducing premarital teenage pregnancies. *Fam Plann Perspect* 13(2):72–74, 1981.

Zabin, LS. *Correlates of Effective Contraception Among Black Inner-City High School Students*. Final Report to NICHD, R01HD17183-02, 1985.

Zabin, LS, Becker, S, and Hirsch, MB. *Decomposing Pregnancy Rates in a School Population into Proximate Determinants*. Presented at the meeting of Population Association of America, 1989.

Zabin, LS, and Clark, SD. Why they delay: a study of teenage family planning clinic patients. *Fam Plann Perspect* 13(5):205–217, 1981.

Zabin, LS, and Clark, SD, Jr. Institutional factors affecting teenagers' choice and reasons for delay in attending a family planning clinc. *Fam Plann Perspect* 15(1):25–29, 1983.

Zabin, LS, and Emerson, MR. *Do Adolescents Want Babies? The Relationship Between Attitudes and Behavior*. Presented at the Annual Meeting of the American Public Health Association, New York, October, 1990.

Zabin, LS, Hardy, JB, Smith, EA, and Hirsch, MB: Substance use and its relation to sexual activity among inner-city adolescents. *J Adolesc Health Care* 7:320–331, 1986.

Zabin, LS, Hardy, JB, Streett, R, and King, TM. A school-, hospital-, and university-based adolescent pregnancy prevention program: a cooperative design for service and research *J Reprod Med* 29:421–426, 1984.

Zabin, LS, and Hirsch, MB. *Evaluation of Pregnancy Prevention Programs in the School Context.* D.C. Health and Company, Lexington, Mass., 1987.

Zabin, LS, Hirsch, MB, and Boscia, JA. Differential characteristics of adolescent pregnancy test patients: abortion, childbearing and negative-test groups. *J Adolesc Health Care,* 11:107–113, 1990.

Zabin, LS, Hirsch, MB, and Emerson, MR. When adolescents choose abortion: effects on education, psychological status and subsequent pregnancy. *Fam Plann Perspect* 21:248–255, 1989.

Zabin, LS, Hirsch, MB, Smith, EA, et al. The Baltimore pregnancy prevention program for urban teenagers: what did it cost? *Fam Plann Perspect* 20(4):188–192, 1988.

Zabin, LS, Hirsch, MB, Smith, EA, Streett, R, and Hardy, JB. Evaluation of a pregnancy prevention program for urban teenagers. *Fam Plann Perspect* 18:119–126, 1986.

Zabin, LS, Hirsch, MB, Streett, R, Emerson, MR, Smith M, Hardy JB and King TM. The Baltimore Pregnancy Prevention Program for Urban Teenagers. I. How Did it Work? *Fam Plann Perspect* 20(4):182–187, 1988.

Zabin, LS, Kantner, JF, and Zelnik, M. The risk of adolescent pregnancy in the first months after intercourse. *Fam Plann Perspect* 11:215–222, 1979.

Zabin, LS, Smith, EA, Hirsch, MB, and Hardy, JB. Ages of physical maturation and first intercourse in black teenage males and females. *Demography* 23:595–605, 1986.

Zabin, LS, Stark, HA, and Emerson, MR. Reasons for delay in contraceptive clinic utilization: Adolescent clinic and non-clinic populations compared. *J Adolesc Health Care,* in press, 1991.

Zelnik, M, and Kantner, JF. Sexual activity, contraceptive use and pregnancy among metropolitan-area teenagers: 1971–1979. *Fam Plann Perspect* 12:230–237, 1980.

Zelnik, M, Kantner, JF, and Ford, K. *Sex and Pregnancy in Adolescence.* Sage Library of Social Research, Beverly Hills, CA, 1981.

Zelnik, M, and Kim, YJ. Sex education and its association with sexual activity, pregnancy and contraceptive use. *Fam Plann Perspect* 14:117–126, 1982.

Zelnik, M, and Shah, FK. First intercourse among young Americans. *Fam Plann Perspect* 15:64–70, 1983.

Zuckerman, B, Alpert, JJ, Dooling, E, et al. Neonatal outcome: is adolescent pregnancy a risk factor? *Pediatrics* 71:438–439, 1984.

Zuckerman, B, Frank, DA, Hingson, R, et al. Effects of maternal marijuana and cocaine use on fetal growth. *N Engl J Med* 320:762–768, 1989.

Zuckerman, BS, Walker, DK, Frank, DA, et al. Adolescent pregnancy: biobehavioral determinants of outcome. *J Pediatr* 105(6):857–863, 1984.

Index